DEVELOPING READING EFFICIENCY

DEVELOPING READING EFFICIENCY

seek the ideas behind the words

Fourth Edition

LYLE L. MILLER

Emeritus Professor, Guidance and Counselor Education
and
Former Director, Uniwyo Reading Research Center
University of Wyoming

READING EFFICIENCY

Printed in the United States of America
Library of Congress Catalog Card Number 79-55778
ISBN 8087-3958-1

k l m n o p q r s t

RELATED PUBLICATIONS BY LYLE L. MILLER

Order from BURGESS PUBLISHING COMPANY, 7108 OHMS LANE, MINNEAPOLIS, MINN. 55435, (612) 831-1344

Developing Reading Efficiency, Fourth Edition **(GRADES 6-10)**

A basic developmental reading program primarily for students in grades seven through ten. Designed to improve reading efficiency with emphasis on rate, comprehension and vocabulary. Extensively used in junior and senior high school English and study skills classes with outstanding results. Also used in many special classes from mature fifth grade classes to community college classes. Included in each book are suggestions for teachers, scoring keys, rate tables and progress charts.

Personalizing Reading Efficiency **(GRADES 10-13)**

Designed primarily for older adolescents and young adults in upper high school and community college. Stresses to students that reading is an individual learning opportunity and an individual skill that gives personal satisfaction and helps them achieve personal and career goals. The material in this compact book develops flexibility in reading and expands the range of skills available for use by the student. Emphasizes self-motivation and self-control in reading activities.

Order from HOLT, RINEHART AND WINSTON, 383 MADISON AVENUE, NEW YORK CITY 10017, (212) 688-9100

Increasing Reading Efficiency, Fourth Edition **(COLLEGE & ADULT)**

This well-established workbook is a college level publication of reading exercises designed to improve competence in vocabulary, comprehension and reading efficiency. Appropriate for college English or study skills classes or for adult reading classes, and for individual study in the improvement of basic reading skills. Scoring keys, rate tables and progress charts are included.

Order from DEVELOPMENTAL READING DISTRIBUTORS, 1944 SHERIDAN AVENUE, LARAMIE, WYOMING 82070, (307) 745-9027

Maintaining Reading Efficiency, Fourth Edition **(RANGE OF MATERIALS FROM GRADE 7 TO ADULT)**

This workbook is an ideal supplement for any other classroom material focused on basic reading skills. It provides an opportunity to apply newly developed skills through concentrated reading practice for ten minutes or more on carefully standardized materials. The standardization and arrangement of materials provides a graduated increase in both length and difficulty for a wide range from junior high school through adult levels.

These materials have been used over a wide range of reading levels in secondary schools and adult classes for a period of over thirty years to develop self-motivation and concentration skills. The current edition reflects the best collection of content exercises derived from continued testing and screening throughout this period.

Reading Pacing Tape **(FOR USE WITH ANY OF BOOKS ABOVE)**

These tapes are designed to provide motivation and time control for the student who wants assistance in developing concentration skills and speed in completion of study or reading objectives. They can be used by individuals or in small groups to relieve a supervisor from individualized pacing or timing work. Tape includes an explanatory introduction, instructions for use, and a ten minute time sequence paced at five second intervals for individual measurement of time required for specific reading or study activity. One minute intervals are stressed also throughout the tape to provide check points for individuals who are working with "interval marked" standardized materials such as the exercises in *Maintaining Reading Efficiency.*

(1980 price: $6.00 per tape.)

Reading Efficiency Tests **(NORMATIVE DATA FOR GRADE 7 TO ADULT)**

This series of five different tests is designed for pre- and post-testing and for follow up studies. They provide five equally difficult sets of reading booklets and answer sheets, organized as a series of carefully standardized materials designed to provide comparable measures of reading rate, comprehension and efficiency. These tests are all comparable to text book reading materials. Each one includes basic information about some relatively little known country, with content dealing with history, geography, government, culture and people of that country.

Packaged in sets of 20, the test booklets sell for $7.50 and the answer sheets for $2.50 per package. Specimen Set of all five test booklets and answer sheets is $2.50 (1980 Prices).

Time Budget Sheet

These planning sheets have been used by students in high schools and colleges throughout the United States. A single sheet study aid for individual students who wish to improve study habits, these are ideal materials for orientation or study skills classes, and are available in packages of 100 or 500.

(1980 Price: $3.00 per 100 sheets, or $10.00 per 500 sheet package.)

Counseling Leads and Related Concepts

This short handbook for counselors or others provides a glossary of semantic terms used in the study of the counseling process. It explains and illustrates the dual aspects of "art" and "science" in the counseling interview, and provides a basis for a better understanding of the communication between counselor and counselee.

(1980 Price: $2.50 per copy.)

"Seek the ideas behind the words."

PREFACE

The Challenge of Time

An essay contest on the topic, "The Value of Time in Education", sponsored by the I.B.M. Corporation in 1938, challenged this author as a high school student to investigate the effective use of time. Much credit is due to an innovative and creative high school English teacher, Miss Greta Burns, who offered many suggestions and help and encouraged the writing of an essay which was selected as the State Winner in Montana! Little did anyone forsee that such an event in a small Montana high school would have long term implications of professional research activity on effective ways to organize time.

Throughout his years as a high school teacher, counselor and college student personnel worker, the author has been concerned about study skills and student success in school and college. His preparation in methods courses for teaching English has made him very conservative about the quality of teaching of basic language skills, however, and led to a high degree of skepticism when he first heard about speed reading programs.

When some students approached him in 1949 and asked specifically for help in learning to read faster, he underestimated the interesting and challenging project he was undertaking. Little did he dream that most of his professional reading and research activity for the next three decades would be devoted to the task of developing materials and methods to help people read faster and better.

The whole aspect of developing more effective ways of reading did renew his long term concerns for effective use of time, however, and he soon realized that efficient reading skills were probably the most challenging approach to the total problem of effective time usage. Reducing the time needed for essential reading activities was perhaps the significant key to achieving the time needed for other activities.

Certainly he did not claim to be a reading expert; if anything he was a real skeptic about speed reading programs. His concern at that time was with effective study skills in his capacity as a study skills instructor. In his role as a counselor, he was concerned with helping young people define and resolve their problems. These two perspectives made the question of speed reading a challenging one, both at the college and secondary school levels.

In seeking help at that time he found few, if any, experts, and only very limited source materials on any developmental reading programs beyond the sixth grade level. Today significantly more materials are available, but the supply is still limited of people who claim to be experts in the field.

So much of the reading process goes on in the eye and brain that no one can observe or study the real reading process to learn answers about it. All one can do is to observe behavior and record data in such a way that, bit by bit, he adds to knowledge and contributes to the improvement of methods and materials for the developmental reading program.

This author never expects to become an expert on reading, but he certainly has learned a great deal about the process and does know considerably more than he would have thought possible thirty years ago. More than any other thing, he has been impressed greatly by the observed behavior of many adolescents and adults who have discovered previously undreamed-of potential for learning through their experience in a developmental reading laboratory.

Needs and Purpose

In an age of space travel and color TV, we may take for granted some of our basic concepts of communication. Instantaneous communication of ideas, through radio, television, international Telstar relays, and constantly improving modern telephone services, literally has brought the world into our living rooms. There can be no doubt that we depend extensively on looking and listening to keep us informed today. In the midst of all of these modern developments, however, we find reports of increasing circulation of magazines, continuous publication of new books, expanding library facilities, and an ever-increasing volume of printed material being circulated through the mail. In our high-speed world of electronic and atomic wonders, we still find that reading is our most fundamental process of interpersonal communication.

Developing effective reading skills is perhaps one of the most significant objectives of ones' years in school, and is most meaningful in terms of future vocational and personal needs. With our rapid expansion of all kinds of knowledge, reading ability has become one of the most important factors of success in many fields today. This is true of the busy doctor or lawyer keeping up with recent developments through his professional journals, of the modern scientist analyzing the work of others through their research papers, of the businessman reading market reports and correspondence, and of the housewife seeking relaxation and relief from her daily problems through reading her favorite magazine. Reading is especially important to the conscientious student who is engaged in the search for understanding of the many new concepts in his chosen curriculum. All of these people need to read. More important, however, is the fact that all of them need more efficient reading habits to cover more in less time.

Many teachers in college, high school and junior high school are aware of the reading problems of adolescents and are attempting to deal with these problems. Remedial reading programs have been available for many years to help the student with specific reading difficulties or deficiencies. Developmental reading programs have developed rapidly in recent years, however, with a focus on the needs and problems of the "average" or "good" readers who need to read more in less time. *Reading Efficiency* programs are designed to increase one's ability to read more effectively.

Few readers can avoid the faster pace of living and learning and the parallel need to read more effectively. Efficient habits of reading are of value to any reader, and many college reading centers have engaged in extensive research on this problem. The first edition of *Increasing Reading Efficiency* (28)* was the product of such research in the Study Skills Center and the Reading Research Center at the University of Wyoming. Within a few years, Henry Holt and Co. arranged for the national distribution of this book, and it has become one of the most frequently used workbooks in college and adult reading programs. Now in its third edition, it is currently distributed by Holt, Rinehart and Winston, Inc., 383 Madison Avenue, New York NY 10017.

Developing Reading Efficiency was conceived a few years later to expand the concept of *reading efficiency* to meet the needs of younger adolescents in the secondary schools. Extensive use of these workbooks since then has confirmed the value of this approach to developmental reading, and stimulated further development of materials for secondary schools use.

Experimental work in many high school and junior high school classes has shown that few students read at speeds that even begin to approach their real reading capabilities. Although many teachers still place the stress on remedial reading, many instructors in study skills programs have come to feel that this emphasis is misleading, since it discourages many students from participating in reading training programs because they feel that they already have normal reading habits. Experience has shown, however, that *training in reading efficiency* can help any person who has a sincere desire for self-improvement. Therefore this manual has been developed as a basic series of exercises for group reading practice. Individuals who need specific remedial help usually can secure this assistance in addition to this group training. Those who are interested primarily in increasing reading efficiency may devote extra time to practice on longer reading exercises such as those provided in *Maintaining Reading Efficiency* (29).

Letters from many teachers and students who have used the *Reading Efficiency* books in many parts of the United States and abroad have convinced the author that this pattern of reading exercises has real practical value. Thousands of high schools and college students and adults seem to agree.

Developing Reading Efficiency (27) has the same basic pattern of organization as *Increasing Reading Efficiency,* but is focused on the reading needs of younger students. A streamlined version of the *Reading Efficiency* series for the upper high school was developed in 1976, and is published under the name *Personalizing Reading Efficiency* (31). These publications are now distributed by Burgess Publishing Company, Minneapolis, MN 55435.

Many additional materials such as standardized tests for reading efficiency, a *Reading Pacing Tape* and other teacher manuals and resources have been developed through the years and are distributed by Developmental Reading Distributors, Laramie, WY 82070. (307) 745-9027.

In attempting this revision of *Developing Reading Efficiency,* therefore, the author has been careful to preserve the basic format and exercise sequence of the earlier editions. Basic changes in this edition include restandardization and restructuring of all exercises in Series III, Phrase Reading, and a replacement of about 50 percent of the exercises in Series V through VIII in order to update materials and provide a better content balance. With these changes, this fourth edition of *Developing Reading Efficiency* should

*All reference numbers refer to the numbered selected references on page 27.

continue to provide outstanding service in developmental reading programs for many years to come.

Use of the Workbook

Although this workbook may be used for self-improvement practice by individual students, it was designed primarily for use with small groups of readers, where competition within the group may serve as a psychological motivation for increased proficiency in the drill exercises. With a planned supervision that emphasizes both self-improvement and competition with other readers, most members in a group will be pleasantly surprised by the improvement they can make in a series of reading classes. It is quite common for many students in a group to double or triple their reading efficiency if they make a sincere effort to do so.

Sources of Inspiration

In developing the series of reading efficiency books, the author is indebted to several sources for ideas and inspirations. In these reading workbooks he has attempted to incorporate some of the best of the ideas on developmental reading and of effective study. First of all, Dr. Francis P. Robinson (46) stimulated his interest in the field of study skills and reading needs of college students. Although many authors contributed to his understanding of the reading process, the author was most impressed by the concepts and basic reading drill sequences developed by Stroud and Ammons (51). The criticisms of hundreds of students in study skills classes and graduate students in methods classes and in research projects throughout the past three decades have contributed to the expansion and polishing of these ideas.

The inspiration of Oscar Causey and his work with a series of National Reading Conferences at Fort Worth, Texas (9, 10, 11), throughout the late 1950s was of tremendous significance. Answers were obtained to many questions about reading through the research efforts of a number of graduate students at the University of Wyoming throughout the years, as they selected some aspect of reading as a focus for their graduate theses. These included Jeanne Taylor, James Gordon Shaw, Kristen Solberg, Robert A.C. Jones, Dudley Sykes, Paul Koziey, Martin Faber, Ed Johnson, Linda Durham, Tom Marshall, Russell Washburn and many others.

Many authors and publishers have been extremely generous in granting permission to use their materials and to revise these materials slightly when necessary to develop them into standard reading exercises. Those whose materials appear in this published draft are acknowledged by the credit lines on the article, but many others had been just as gracious in granting permission to use their materials in developing reading exercises. Many of their exercises have been used extensively in the Reading Research classes at the Unversity of Wyoming.

The necessity for standard lengths of articles and balance and sequence of reading difficulty determined the final choice of exercises included in this book, but without the encouragement from *all* those who granted permission to use their materials in this way, this workbook would not have been possible.

Many suggestions and evaluative comments have come from teachers who have used the workbook in their classes. Recognition should be given to the exhaustive evaluative comments provided by critics William Moorhouse, Roy Morgan, La Verne Nelson and Charles Hadley, who were of great assistance in planning modifications for the earlier editions.

Special thanks should go to the following reviewers for their valuable critiques of the third edition and for their suggestions for improvements to be made in the new one: Mr. K. M. Ahrent, Oregon State University, Corvallis, Oregon; Mrs. Esther Argenbright, Nebraska State Department of Education, Lincoln, Nebraska; Mrs. Anne Cleaves, University School, Laramie, Wyoming; Mr. James E. Coomber, Concordia College, Moorhead, Minnesota; Mrs. Dorothy Gray, Ocean Junior High School, Ocean New Jersey; Mr. Wilton Greene, Fort Collins High School, Fort Collins, Colorado; Mrs. Barbara Mercer, Hudson's Bay High School, Vancouver, Washington; and Mrs. Donna Trujillo, University School, Laramie, Wyoming.

Special recognition should be given to staff members in the Reading Research Center at the University of Wyoming for their contributions in developing new materials. Especially deserving of credit are Cynthia Genoff, Nelda Hernandez, Carol Hult, Marcia Karras, Mary Ellen Latham, Jennifer Lundy, Betty Ramsey, Lorinda Redmund, Nancy Roberts, Stephanie T. Rispin, Sue Whiston, Bob White and Carrie Young.

The author's efforts on all of the *Reading Efficiency* materials would have been impossible without the encouragement and enthusiastic support of his family, all of whom were involved in many stages of development, experimentation and evaluation of the materials. Especially significant was the contribution and constant support of his wife, Grace M. Miller, who has done so much on the completion of this Fourth Edition of *Developing Reading Efficiency*.

L.L.M.

Laramie, Wyoming
January 1, 1980

CONTENTS

To the Teacher

Survival

With the publication of this fourth edition, *Developing Reading Efficiency* will have survived for more than twenty-five years in the academic marketplace. During this period, the *Reading Efficiency* books have had a profound impact on the lives and reading habits of many thousands of individuals. By increasing their reading efficiency, many people have been able to live much fuller lives and to engage in many more activities than would have been possible otherwise. Many of them have found a great deal more pleasure in reading and have come to recognize reading as one of the important keys to success in their lives. The strongest supporters of the continued use of this book are those individuals whose positive personal experiences have demonstrated how they could improve their own personal perception and retention of verbal symbols.

In that period of time, *Developing Reading Efficiency* has been used by several hundred teachers in secondary schools, colleges, and adult education programs. Many of these teachers have written back to the author to share student reactions and to make suggestions for improvement. With the benefit of those suggestions, each revision has reflected some improvements over the earlier editions.

Although this book originally was designed as a companion to *Increasing Reading Efficiency* for use at the secondary level and primarily as an instrument for Junior High School use with able readers, it has proved to be practical at many other levels and in many other types of group and individual situations. It has been a useful tool of many teachers with differing perspectives and purposes.

For those who have been behaviorally oriented, it has provided a carefully structured sequence of drill materials designed to bring about specific modifications of basic reading behavior. Such changes can be functionally defined and carefully measured to reflect the individual's attainment of his goals and expectations.

For those more interested in the affective aspects of learning, the materials have provided a basis for bringing about attitudinal change about reading, study skills, and personal responsibility. Many teachers comment on the value of the suggestions and the application of reading skills to practical needs. Changes in self-concept often seem to be significant outcomes of the development of flexibility in reading skills. Flexible reading habits lead to broader interests and make it more possible for students to become involved at greater depth in those things that are of real interest and challenge to them.

The practical use of this book seems to range from its use as *the* basic workbook in some groups or classes on reading improvement to simple personal application by a single student. In the first case, it seems to serve as the basic instrument for specific behavioral change in reading habits in a sixteen-to-twenty-hour structured program of carefully planned and supervised reading experiences. On the other end of the scale is its use by an individual student who purchases a single copy at the bookstore for his own program of self-structured self-improvement. By using the *Reading Pacing Tape* for stimulation and *Maintaining Reading Efficiency* (29)[1] for concentrated individual practice, such an individual could work out a fairly meaningful reading efficiency program for himself. Between these two extremes are many other variations of functional use in the classroom or reading resource center.

Within a wide range of experimentation and critical examination, the earlier editions of *Developing Reading Efficiency* seem to have proved the continuing value of this material sufficiently to justify further refinement and revision in this fourth edition.

Demands for Reading Efficiency

The constantly increasing explosion of knowledge and the resultant publication of increasing numbers of challenging and stimulating books and periodical articles have made good reading a key to a wide range of vicarious experiences. The success of so many highly advertised commercial reading programs seems to be ample evidence that many people want to read better and faster. It has been a concern of this author for many years that public schools and colleges have not been more responsive to these needs. Surely, our schools could offer all of the best characteristics of most of the commercial reading programs at a fraction of the costs being charged for these commercial programs.

A focal point of attention for this author for the past thirty years has been the development of appropriate instructional materials for developmental reading programs with the hope that these materials might at least provide a sound basis for personal development of reading skills in a variety of settings. This fourth edition of *Developing Reading Efficiency* is the latest of a long series of publications that have evolved from the reading research activities of the Uniwyo Reading Research Center.

A Family of Reading Efficiency Books

The popularity of *Increasing Reading Efficiency* (28), first published by Holt, Rinehart and Winston in 1956 and now in its fourth edition, has demonstrated the value of such materials for college students and adults. Subsequently, the first edition of this book, *Developing Reading Efficiency* (27), was published by Burgess Publishing Company and has been equally effective, primarily for younger students. *Increasing*

[1]All reference numbers refer to the numbered selected references on page 27.

Reading Efficiency and *Developing Reading Efficiency* are parallel in structure and may be used in the same class to meet the needs of students with varying degrees of reading capability.

More recently, a third workbook, *Personalizing Reading Efficiency* (31) has been published by Burgess Publishing Company in 1976. With structure comparable to the other two books, this one is designed specifically for the upper high school years. It is a condensed version with only half as many exercises as the other two and planned specifically for classroom use without the exercises for suggested outside practice.

A fourth workbook, *Maintaining Reading Efficiency* (29) was developed as a supplement to the basic workbooks and can be used as an extension of any of the three basic books mentioned above. *Maintaining Reading Efficiency* is especially appropriate to help students develop self motivation, control and concentration for longer periods of time in intensive content reading. When used with a pacing tape to help motivate individuals to achieve personal goals, it is very helpful in reinforcing the use of skills built up by work in the basic workbooks.

This book and other tests, pacing tapes, and related study skills materials are available from Developmental Reading Distributors, 1944 Sheridan, Laramie, Wyoming 82070. (307) 745-9027.

Resources for Teachers

One reaction of teachers using the earlier editions of the Reading Efficiency books was that materials for teachers should be included *in the workbook itself,* rather than in a separate teacher's manual. They also suggested that the teacher's section should be expanded to cover several basic points of concern to the teacher. In response to those suggestions, this brief section for teachers has been developed, and sets of answer keys arranged on perforated pages for easy removal have been included at the back of the workbook. These have been separated into two sections so that teachers may remove the even set for control of classroom exercises if they desire, while leaving the keys for odd numbered exercises in the books for outside practice.

Teachers who desire more specific suggestions on methods and materials for teaching developmental reading are encouraged to secure the more comprehensive manual for teachers, *Teaching Efficient Reading Skills* (33).

Purpose of the Workbook

Increasing Reading Efficiency originally was designed to promote the mutual development of reading speed and comprehension through carefully controlled group activity. Although the author has received abundant evidence of effective and highly gratifying use of the workbook by individuals and in individualized settings in reading clinics, he still emphasizes that the materials were intended primarily for use in groups, where competition with oneself and with others in the group tends to provide parallel patterns for psychological motivation. The author is firmly convinced that this dual competitive pattern, supported by a teacher who can provide a system of both group and individual motivation, provides a stimulus more appropriate than any specific pattern of mechancial or machine-oriented motivation.

With a primary goal of increasing rate along with maintenance or improvement of comprehension skill, other aspects such as vocabulary improvement and critical reading skills are of secondary importance in the overall structure of the book. with full recognition of the basic importance of higher level study skills, analytical reading, critical reading, and vocabulary development, one must recognize that any attempt to expand this book to include comprehensive coverage of all these points would result in an extremely bulky and expensive volume and would represent a sacrifice of some currently established and meaningful sequence of exercises. Teachers seeking these other types of emphasis are encouraged to consider other appropriate materials on the market. Many of the materials listed in the Selected References on page 27 are appropriate for such use.

In summary, then, this material was designed primarily for use in groups under the supervision of an able teacher who can motivate people to reach beyond their current grasp. It was designed also for use with younger adolescents who have mastered the basic development of language skills. Older high school students might find greater value in the more newly created *Personalizing Reading Efficiency* (31). The original publication of the series, *Increasing Reading Efficiency* (28) is still the most appropriate one for college students and adults.

The Concept of Reading Efficiency

Although both rate of reading and comprehension are recognized as important aspects of reading ability, neither one is stressed in itself. Instead, this author places the stress on a combination of the two factors that he calls *reading efficiency.* This measures what might be called a "rate of understanding." Reading efficiency is computed by multiplying the rate (in words per minute) by the comprehension score (percentage of correct answers on tested material). This yields a "words-per-minute" figure that serves as a measure of the amount of material understood during a minute of time. Although one recognizes that ideas cannot be measured accurately in "words per minute," this stress on efficiency does seem to overcome some of the concern over comprehension loss in the early stages of reading improvement.

Early experimentation in the University of Wyoming Study Skills Center revealed that students seemed to attain lower comprehension scores for a period of time immediately after having successfully increased their reading rate. Consequently, much thought has been given to the provision of training exercises designed to bring about increases in *both* rate and comprehension. After years of observation and comparison, however, research seems to show that most students can make very substantial increases in rate with no significant loss in comprehension.

During the years in which the *Reading Efficiency* workbooks have been used in the Study Skills Center, group evaluations have revealed an increase in both rate and comprehension on comparable standardized tests administered at the beginning and end of the ten-week training period. *Maintaining Reading Efficiency Tests* (30) are published by Developmental Reading Distributors, Laramie, Wyoming 82070. With five different forms, these tests can be used effectively for such pre- and post-comparisons.

Also available from the same source is the *Reading Pacing Tape,* which can be used for individual pacing, or can be used with the group to free the teacher for more careful observation of individual behavior during reading activities. Studies with adult classes in the Uniwyo Reading Research Center have demonstrated that individuals who use the *Reading Pacing Tapes* for outside individual practice between classes have shown an average rate of improvement in reading efficiency more than fifty percent higher than those who used stop watches or other watches for timing on such practice.

Simultaneous improvement of rate and comprehension results from a careful integration of speed reading skills and higher level study skills. This can be accomplished by introducing students to techniques of self-recitation, reading for ideas, and recognition of textbook clues. The materials in this workbook are organized in such a way that the effectiveness of this approach is easy to illustrate to the students.

Do Not Expect These Characteristics

No one book on developmental reading can be all things to all people. Therefore, one should consider some of the things that this book is *not!*

It is not a "speed-reading" workbook. The author believes that teachers should deal cautiously with the idea of "speed" in reading. The gullible public often is given the idea that all reading difficulties are essentially speed problems. The recent flood of commercial materials and programs implies that improvement in reading rate will evolve miracles. At its very best, such claims oversimplify what may be a serious problem. A slow reading rate may very easily be a symptom of other reading difficulties, such as weaknesses in basic word recognition, interpretation skills, study skills, or even more serious physiological problems; or it may be a problem of attitude toward school and learning. The author already has indicated his concern for a balanced approach and for supervision by a teacher who can be observant of, and sensitive to, symptoms of other problems.

It is not a remedial workbook. The materials are designed for adolescents and adults who have already mastered basic language skills. Many other good materials are available on the market that emphasize basic language skills and remedial techniques.

It is not primarily a vocabulary builder. Vocabulary training is assumed as an essential supplementary activity. Exercises in this book allow for the basic identification of some potential vocabulary problems, but practice on vocabulary improvement is a matter of individual emphasis. The author would recommend a supplemental practice book such as *Basic Vocabulary Skills* by Davis (12) or *Developing Vocabulary Skills* by Joffe (19).

It is not a book for reading improvement through concentrated applied practice. This book involves much basic drill material. For those who prefer direct practice in reading content-oriented materials, the author would recommend *Maintaining Reading Efficiency* (29).

Basic Concepts of Reading

One of the confusing points to students and teachers alike is the absence of a universal definition of the term *reading.* Consequently, many people are writing and talking about *reading* and not meaning the same thing. Let us first explore the much quoted statement that no one can possibly read at a rate of more than 800 words per minute. This statement evidently is based on the following steps of logic:

1. Readers identify and recognize visual material only during eye pauses or fixations.
2. Research indicates that the average adult reader can recognize clearly only 1.1 words during such a fixation and that the most able readers seldom recognize over 2.7 words per fixation or stop.
3. Efficient readers require at least a one-fifth second duration to recognize any symbols during any stop.
4. Efficient readers, therefore, cannot hope to make more than five stops per second.
5. Therefore, it can be mathematically calculated that the very efficient reader who can see 2.7 words per fixation and who makes five stops per second will be able to read only 810 words per minute.

Thus the 800 words per minute maximum is established—based on a concept of *deliberate reading* that is defined as the act in which the reader *contacts all of the words visually and strives for complete comprehension.* Of course, this does not discount the fact that people can "skim" or "scan" at much more rapid rates, but to the "purist" this is *not* reading. For those with more practical interests, however, questions exist about all but the first step in the logic outlined above.

If the many demands for varied types of reading in modern society are considered, one can see why most teachers and students find acceptance of such an extreme definition impractical. But no other definition has been accepted universally. Therefore, each author should feel an obligation to make clear his own concept of the term.

As used in this book, the term *reading* means *that process of communication of ideas from one person to another through the medium of writing or printing.* More concisely, the purpose of reading is seen as *seeking the ideas behind the words.* Within this definition, skimming and scanning can be viewed as effective types of the total reading program, and the concept of reading rates beyond 800 words per minute is much more understandable and acceptable. Skimming and scanning are very effective ways to pick up ideas and to develop more effective eye span flexibility. Many students develop eye spans that can pick up several words, phrases and even full lines of type on a horizontal line. Recent experiments in vertical eye span reveal that many individuals can pick up key ideas from two or more lines of type at a time. Some readers feel that in skimming and scanning they can pick up large sections of a page at one glance and be sensitive to key ideas on content. Apparently the "2.7 words per fixation" idea does not have much meaning when one is reading for ideas instead of words alone.

Basic Points of Reference

Any development of materials is dependent on concepts developed for other purposes. Materials in this book are dependent for meaning on two basic concepts in addition to the "reading efficiency" concept previously described.

The basic vocabulary around which reading exercises in Series I, II, and III are built is the *Teacher's Word Book of 30,000 Words* (54) developed by E. L. Thorndike in 1944. All of the key words used in *Developing Reading Efficiency* have been checked also against the eighth grade level identified by Henry Rinsland in his publication *A Basic Vocabulary for Elementary School Children* (45) published in 1945. Considering the publication dates, one can see that many words of recent vintage are not included. The scope of these exercises is somewhat limited, therefore, by the basic word list. The author is unaware, however, of any more recent word list composed by a comparable authority.

The measurement of reading difficulty in all exercises in Series V through VII has been accomplished through the use of the Flesch formula (14). Although limited to only two basic factors, sentence length and syllable count per hundred words, this has been viewed for many years as one of the most efficient measures of reading difficulty for adult materials. Although it has been criticized widely by teachers of English, no one seems to have come forth with any better tool to serve the same purpose. So, with due recognition to its obvious limitations, this author has continued to use it for the family of Reading Efficiency books as the best available instrument for establishing some standardization of the relative difficulty of exercise material.

Development of the Reading Exercises

Of basic importance to the exercises in this manual is a provision for increasing eye span and for establishing rhythmic eye movements. Also basic is the need to increase rate of mental perception of what is read and so reduce the eye fixation time. These exercises were planned to provide training for all three of these purposes. In addition, the difficulty of the exercises has been carefully standardized to allow comparisons between similar exercises in sequences of gradually increasing difficulty. Such standardization involved length, readability level and type and number of test questions used.

All exercises in the introductory portion of this book and all of the exercises in Series V through VIII are labeled as to standard length and as to appropriate Readability Scores.

Standardization of the Materials

One of the major difficulties a few years ago in evaluating the results of a training program in developmental reading was the lack of standardized materials. The materials used in this book are now standardized as much as possible in order to make exercises comparable.

In Series I and II, answer frequency per column has been standardized, so that in each exercise the right answer will occur five times in each column.

In Series I and II, all key words occur in Rinsland's list of most commonly used words in eighth grade vocabulary lists (45). All words in the answer columns occur in Thorndike's list of 30,000 most frequently used words (54). Therefore, these exercises may serve also as vocabulary drills for secondary students.

In the phrase and sentence meaning drills, the key words have been checked against the same word lists. These exercises have been arranged in an order of gradually increasing length and difficulty.

The paragraph reading material in Series V, VI, and VII has all been reduced to standardized length so that rates may be obtained from tables. This material has been rated by the Flesch formula (12) and has been arranged in order of increasing difficulty—from fifth grade through the upper college level, with most of the material falling in the range of the junior and senior high school years.

Types of Exercises

The first exercises are designed primarily as speed exercises. In Series I, the major emphasis should be on the establishment of rhythmic eye movements and increased eye span. In Series II, understanding is emphasized, and most readers will slow down. Each error indicates a possible misunderstanding of three words that may serve as reading blocks. The key word obviously may be a problem as well as the one marked in error. But the correct answer that was overlooked also may be a clue to a vocabulary problem. Hence students should be encouraged to develop vocabulary lists, to study words missed to increase vocabulary and to practice using them frequently.

Series III continues this stress on understanding but deals with groups of words and emphasizes increased eye span and the grasping of ideas rather than words. In this sequence, stress is put on gradual increase of eye span in both a horizontal and vertical direction. Students should be encouraged to begin practice in comparing span for the two pairs of vertical phrases with the single phrase. As they become conscious of their ability to do this, they can shift to the columns of phrases in vertical arrangements to practice vertical rather than horizontal movement of the eyes. They should be encouraged to try to carry

over this skill to reading in newspapers and magazines.

Series IV concentrates on rapid scanning of basic ideas in a sentence. These exercises focus on initial interpretation of a key phrase and then quick recognition of similarities or differences between that idea and several subsequent ones. This prepares the reader to begin to recognize ideas in ways that will help him to use skimming and scanning skills more effectively.

Series V provides practice in high-speed reading for basic ideas. The tests on these materials consist of two questions relating only to basic thoughts or ideas in the material. Here both rapid reading and correct understanding are important. The questions are of the same type for each exercise. Questions are designed to pick up recurrent thoughts, basic themes, or overall purpose in the article. The primary purpose of this series, however, is to emphasize the development of high-speed reading with minimal emphasis on comprehension.

Series VI places stress on more accurate reading for short periods of time. Here again, the tests follow similar patterns for each exercise; but, in this case, they require more attention to detailed ideas and facts presented in the material. Errors should be used here as a means of helping students go back and look for key ideas and how they were presented, so that they will be better able to recognize important ideas in future reading. Usually a sixty percent comprehension score is a reasonable basis for continued practice in increasing rate. Scores consistently below sixty percent are clues of some more basic problems in study habits or retention skills.

Series VII demonstrates an application of the self-recitation technique and does much to give students definite evidence of the values of this study technique. It is designed to help them develop habits of *thinking* as they read. The exercises are matched with those in Series VI for readability, length, and type of questions asked; but here the reader is required to stop, think, and answer at intervals as he goes along.

Series VIII provides some initial practice in critical thinking and is designed to help develop an inquiring and critical mind. A series of short excerpts from undisclosed sources is presented with basic questions for consideration. Keys reveal the sources and purposes.

All of these series focus on particular aspects of building reading skills through short, concentrated practice exercises. Application of these skills in longer reading exercises is encouraged with supplementary materials such as the *Maintaining Reading Efficiency* (29) exercises which are designed for concentration skills and more long range retention of content materials.

Arrangement of Materials

Although these materials are arranged by groups in the sequence believed to be most advantageous, the groups are designed for some overlapping in class practice. For example, practice on "word meaning" exercises should be started when the class is only about 30 percent through the "word recognition" section. This overlapping in the four basic groups of exercises provides better continuity. The "idea reading," "exploratory reading," and "study reading" drills should be started at least by the second period of training and should be used regularly thereafter, using one of each to provide comparison scores.

If time is limited, the odd-numbered exercises may be used for individual practice and the even-numbered ones for group work. If time permits, however, all the exercises may be used for group practice.

The purpose and method of procedure for each set of exercises is given immediately preceding that set of exercises. These include "Suggestions" for students to think about. Students should be encouraged to read these before they start the series, and then to go back and review the suggestions again after having done one or two exercises in the series.

Progress Charts are provided on pages 297-305 for maintaining daily records of reading progress during the period of training. Keeping this daily progress chart is an important aspect of self-motivation. Teachers should clarify the use of these *progress charts* very early in the program and should check frequently to see if students understand and use these to set goals for self-improvement.

Teachers should encourage cross comparisons between the various columns of the Progress Charts, and urge frequent comparisons with the recorded test scores from the beginning test of the program.

Sequence of Exercises

This book can be used for reading improvement in many types of training groups. In general, the writer recommends a training period which extends over a minimum of nine to ten weeks. This will provide time for additional practice and application. A five-week training period has been demonstrated to be less satisfactory but still productive. Periods shorter than five weeks may have limited carry-over value. Outside practice between classes should be strongly encouraged. Many teachers use the odd numbered exercises for outside practice while the even numbered exercises are used in class.

As an illustration of a procedure for the overlapping of exercises—for college students or adults—one might consider the sequence used in the classes sponsored by the Uniwyo Reading Research Center. The pattern shown on page 333 is that used in a class that meets once weekly for one-and-a-half to two-hour sessions.

During the last half of the course, workbook practice should be supplemented by longer reading exercises from current materials or from standardized ten-minute reading exercises. The supplementary workbook *Maintaining Reading Efficiency* (29) provides a collection of standardized reading exercises appropriate for this purpose.

This schedule has evolved from the research and experience of several years in the Center. It seems to achieve a maximum integration of the values of the various types of exercises when used in an overlapping pattern. It also stresses the importance of taking time for group discussion on fundamental aspects of the course along with the skill building exercises.

The schedule also illustrates the use of standardized tests for the establishment of a baseline initial score on Reading Efficiency which can be used throughout the course for comparisons. The final test on a comparable standardized test provides the most objective basis for comparison with initial skills measured. Such pre- and post-tests are helpful for individual comparison and evaluation, but they are also helpful for making some mean comparisons for the total class to give the teacher some evaluation of the effectiveness of the class activities.

Motivation

Experience has shown that giving the exercises in overlapping sequence usually proves stimulating to the students. Although many teachers are concerned that verbal pacing or comments on ending times may be distracting, the general experience in the work at the Uniwyo Reading Research Center Laboratory classes has been that such vocal pacing and time calling not only seem to be effective, but that they help students develop concentration skills in handling verbal distractions.

All exercises should be clocked by a stopwatch, and the time, in seconds, should be called out for each student as he finishes. Frequently a "pacing" technique of calling out five-second or ten-second intervals helps to keep up the motivation, especially if the group exhibits signs of fatigue. The *Reading Pacing Tape* mentioned earlier provides a standard pattern of pacing at five-second intervals for ten-minute period with appropriate instructions. Many teachers find these tapes helpful for general classroom use with a reading class or for check-out to individuals who want to practice under some pressure outside the class.

The instructor must be alert constantly to provide encouragement and motivation, not only to the group as a whole, but to individual students as well. In addition to the pacing techniques mentioned before, one should suggest goals. For example, in Series I, one can suggest that most students should be able to finish in 30 seconds or less. In Series V, the instructor can suggest that all students should strive to complete these exercises in 60 seconds or less. Accuracy in setting realistic goals in different exercises depends upon the developmental pattern of any particular group as well as the teacher's experience with the materials. Observation and experience in a number of classes will provide the basis for projecting realistic goals which will challenge the best readers in each class.

Students always should be urged to improve their own scores. Students should be urged also to use the pacing interval marks in the center column of reading exercises to compare with verbal time pacing. By setting their own personal goals and marking these intervals, they can maintain a check as to how well they are achieving their own goals at one minute intervals or other intervals of their own choosing. Encouraging competition with other specific members of the group also is effective in many cases.

Watching the fastest reader and calling a finishing time a few seconds before he is through helps to keep him working at a maximum. Calling time intervals a few times after the slowest reader has finished may help him to avoid feeling that the whole class was waiting for him.

If a student seems to have fallen behind the class after an absence, the teacher should encourage him to do outside practice materials with the *Pacing Tape* or on a reading machine. If one or two slow readers hold up the whole class to the point that others are getting restless, however, something may need to be done to help both the individuals and the class. Rather than keep the whole group waiting, individual assignments can be made for slow readers. For example, one might ask them to complete only half an exercise.

Further outside practice should also be encouraged. Extremely slow readers who retard the whole group should be removed from the group if possible and given individual help.

Emphasis should be placed on keeping individual progress graphs up-to-date and encouraging students to compare results of the trends in their reading improvements. During the period between exercises, the staff member should circulate among the readers and provide individual encouragement.

If reading machines are available, a class demonstration with two or three class members may be an effective way of demonstrating to some skeptical individuals what their potential for eye movement really is. Thus, they may be stimulated to increase their self-motivation.

Scoring of Questions

Series I is self-scoring because identical words are to be selected. Keys for scoring the other exercises are presented on pages 317-332. In the completion questions, individual teachers should use their judgment in accepting "equivalent terms" for full or half credit. These perforated key pages may be left in the book for self-scoring or may be removed by the teacher to discourage advance study.

These keys are grouped according to odd and even numbers in case the teacher wishes to make one set available to students for their own scoring. Many teachers prefer to leave the keys for the odd-numbered exercises in the book and to remove the even-numbered keys for standardized testing in class.

Variations in Use

Many teachers have reported a wide range of application of *Increasing Reading Efficiency* and *Developing Reading Efficiency* in their classes. Innovative experimentation with different combinations or different sequences of exercises may produce better results. The author is always interested in hearing from teachers who have developed new and interesting ways to use these materials.

Length: 1700 words Readability Score: 54

To the Reader

Can you spare the time?

Do you have the time to do most of the activities which interest you? Do you want more time for things you really want to do? Is reading a threat for you, or does it help you keep pace with the fast-moving world?

Can you meet your expectations?

Every day thousands of students are facing the decision to drop out of school before graduating. On the college scene, only four out of every ten students who start ever attain their academic goals. In the daily routine, thousands of individuals lose their jobs because they can not do all that their employers expect. Often the problem is one of verbal communication. Frustration and failure lead many people into depression that may result in hospitalization or even suicide. How are you keeping up with all the conflicting expectations of family, friends, teachers, supervisors, employers, and community responsibilities?

Can you survive?

Survival is complicated by the rapid change that you encounter all around you. No previous generation faced the problems that confront you today. *The population explosion* has created many problems of competition for jobs, high unemployment, and increasing demands for flexibility in placement. *The knowledge explosion* overwhelms many by the mere quantitative aspects. The world body of knowledge now doubles every six or seven years. Last year over 1,000 books per day were published. *The technology explosion* has plunged our world into a super industrial revolution. Over 90 percent of all scientific inventions have been developed within the last twenty years, most of them since you were born! Within your lifetime there has been more technological progress than the world has seen in 50,000 years. Culture changes faster than individuals can adjust. Many fall by the wayside. How good are *your* survival skills?

Could you use a time-stretcher?

Do you reach the end of the day with unfinished tasks regretfully laid aside? Do you wish sometimes that you had just an extra hour or so in order to finish important tasks? Do you really have time to read the newspapers, magazines, and other recreational materials you would enjoy? Like many others, you may find that at least one third of your time is required for reading of some kind. At the same time, you probably recognize that your reading habits are not adequate to meet these demands, and you may become depressed when you can not keep the pace and complete the amount of reading you feel that you should.

No one has developed a "time-stretcher" to lengthen your days for you, but for years many educators have studied the problem of slow reading habits. Research since World War II, however, has led to many improvements in techniques and has encouraged new approaches to the problem of developmental reading. Reading centers today are using many techniques and group exercise materials that represent great advances over those used twenty years ago.

Developmental reading services are now available to many high school and college students and adults. Many participants in these classes have made astonishing improvements in reading rate without any serious loss in comprehension. Thus one is able to do, in five hours, the reading that once took ten hours. Many individuals have increased their reading efficiency much more than this. Saving these five hours for other activities can give you the "time-stretcher" of which you may have dreamed.

One reading authority once computed that the saving in time required to do all the reading in the nation, computed at only 50 cents per hour, would be more than five billion dollars if every Amercian over fifteen years of age were given reading training for at least a month (6)![1] Many industrial concerns have recognized this potential saving of manpower and have subsidized reading programs for their employees with very gratifying results. Many students have found free time for greater enjoyment of their school activities by registering for classes in efficient reading. What benefits could you obtain if you were to double your reading effiency? Would that help you to survive?

Are you ready to be exposed to a program to increase your reading speed? Some individuals who have become faster readers have not necessarily become better readers. If you have difficulty understanding what you read now, you will not be helped by learning to misunderstand faster. If you have a very inadequate vocabulary, you will not be helped to learn to skip any faster through unknown or vaguely defined words. In either case, you have the challenge of developing some basic skills and knowledge before you really can benefit from a developmental reading program. But first, let us explore a few attitudes you may have about reading.

[1] All reference numbers refer to the numbered selected references on p. 27, with the second number, if any, identifying the page number.

Exploding some myths

Before going further in your exploration of the reading process, you should consider some of the myths that students often use to rationalize their failure to improve their reading skills.

1. *No one can really read over 800 words per minute.* They can quote many authorities, especially those who have been critical of some of the commercial reading programs in recent decades. This statement is based on an analysis of typical eye movement patterns and typical eye fixations. If one accepts a definition of reading that involves an *actual eye contact with every word* in the material, then this limitation of 800 words is a fairly accurate statement. Most people use the term *reading* in a much broader sense, however. Reading is a communication skill used to *communicate ideas by means of the written or printed message.* In this sense, the upper limits of speed in communication have not been identified.
2. *Skimming and scanning are bad habits that I should avoid.* Again this is based on a misinterpretation of the critics of speed reading. Within the broader concept of reading, these skills are very valuable and essential aspects of efficient reading and effective study.
3. *My comprehension will drop if I read fast or skim.* There is no foundation in research to support this. Raygor and Schick (44, 29) made the following comment after an extensive review of research: "It is relatively easy for most people to make very significant increases in the rate at which they read without any loss in reading comprehension.
4. *Machines are necessary to improve my speed.* This idea is perpetuated by salemen for some media companies, but again Raygor and Schick (44, 29) report: ". . . experimental studies have shown no difference between the various methods and, in fact, have shown no advantage for any of the devices over the use of the book."
5. *My eyes won't let me read fast.* With the exception of a very few persons with severe physiological handicaps, research has shown that most people have the potential in the brain and the eyes to function at much higher levels of reading than they have ever tried. (33)
6. *It is wrong to skip passages in reading.* This is an old-fashioned idea still perpetuated by some teachers and guaranteed to make reading a deadly dull experience. All modern concepts of reading and study skills stress the importance of being selective and using judgment in deciding what to read and how much detail is needed.
7. *I must read every word to get meaning.* Many words are necessary to sentence structure or to an author's style, but are not essential in the communication of the basic ideas. Good readers learn to seek out those words that convey meaning and give minimal attention to many supporting words.

Set your own goals

You should realize, however, that your ability to increase your speed and comprehension significantly depends upon many variables—intelligence, physiological and psychological traits, general background of knowledge, motivation, previous reading, experience, diligence in doing recommended practice, and general attitude toward reading and toward the reading group with which you work. No one can predict how much you will improve from the pre-test to the post-test. People love to quote "averages" or outstanding achievements that seem dramatic, but there always are individuals all along the scale. Only you can determine your own achievement!

You must recognize also that there is no one speed of reading that you attain and maintain. There are many speeds that must vary with the nature of the reading activity and with your own familiarity with the materials. You should have a purpose in mind as you read. This purpose should help you understand more and remember better. The purpose is a determining factor in *how* you read. You may have many good and logical reasons for reading, but, at any one time, you should know *why* you are reading *that* particular material in *that* particular way.

Different people cannot and should not read at the same rate. You establish your own unique patterns of reading. You probably will be able to achieve a significant improvement by using these materials, but it takes a lot of self-discipline, hard work, and often monotonous practice to replace old reading habits with new, more effective ones.

When you finish this work, you should be able to identify substantial personal growth. Whatever your measured rate at that time, you should have achieved the flexibility of at least *four* rates. Your slower rate will be the one to use when you have to pay close attention to detail for later retention. You can have another (about twice that fast) when you read for relaxation.

When you skim for new ideas, you can go about four times as fast as your slower rate; and when you scan to locate specific material for specific purposes, your rate may be much higher.

Much more could be said about the reading process before you start your program, but perhaps a few suggestions and ideas thrown in along the way will be more helpful. At least some students who used this material before thought so! On the introductory pages for each new series of exercises, you will find "suggestion" sections. May I suggest that you read these again *after* you have done the first few exercises. In that way we can "keep in touch" as you read your way through the workbook.

Length: 5200 words — Readability Score: 51

I
How Do We Read?

Good reading is the key to your search for ideas. It opens the door to many opportunities to enrich your life. Your reading skills are essential aspects of self-preservation in a dynamic society. You probably place great importance on becoming a successful reader.

But what are the characteristics of successful readers? You might say that they are the ones who keep up with their fair share of the millions of words of printed material that is created in the world each day. This means that they are able to keep up with all of their personal and professional correspondence and to keep informed on signficant developments in their society from skimming newspapers and news magazines. They must find the time to deal with their daily mail and to keep up on developments in their business or professional field through many specialized professional publications. For a balanced life, they also find time for reading for pleasure in areas of their own personal interests.

For most students, success in reading those materials essential to all of their academic course work is merely a preparation for the challenge of the deluge of reading materials they will face when they leave the academic field and go out into the world of work.

Even if your plans do not include intense specialization for a professional field of work, you will still find that successful reading is an essential for coping with many daily problems in the modern world. Operating instructions for cars, boats, machines, appliances, and household equipment are a challenge to everyone. Unless you can read application forms, insurance policies, sales contracts, and employee memos effectively, you may miss many of the opportunities for personal improvement and protection open to you. You also may find yourself vulnerable to many unscrupulous salesmen or promoters. You have a real stake in your long-term effectiveness as a successful reader. You may find it very helpful to give some thought to how you became the kind of reader you now are, and to how you can move toward a higher level of success in your own reading.

Good reading involves not one skill, but many. Although some individuals can increase their rate of reading without specific training, few can improve—without such help—their comprehension, analytical skill, judgment, skimming and scanning skills, and the technique of adjusting their habits of reading to their purpose and the nature of the material. These skills require thorough understanding of the reading process and practice in a carefully planned program.

The first fact that must be recognized is that your present reading habits are the result of your early experiences in learning to read and your continuing experiences in reading over a period of years. These habits, practiced for many years, are hard to break. You may encounter many feelings of insecurity while you are in the process of substituting new habits for old. Therefore, you should give some attention to how you may have developed some of your present reading habits.

Development of Reading Habits

Many articles in popular periodicals have criticized public schools and current methods of teaching reading. You should be cautious in placing the blame for your habits on the schools you attended, however, and should consider several other factors that have affected your own particular reading habits. Consider the following factors and see which of them may have had an effect on your habits of reading:

1. Reading is not demonstrable as are speaking, walking, or problem solving. It is impossible to *show* someone how you *read.* It involves recognition of many symbols that have no meaning in themselves and that must be combined in innumerable combinations in order to convey meaning to others. The visible eye movements and fixations are only a small part of the total reading process involving a continuous invisible mental process.
2. The irregular supply of well-qualified developmental reading teachers in the last few decades has resulted in the assignment to reading classes of many teachers who possessed only limited interest, desire, or skill in the teaching of reading. Such teachers may have overlooked individual needs and problems in reading development. Unintentionally, they may have reinforced some negative self-concepts and created negative attitudes toward reading. Such teachers may have stressed reading every word, oral reading, vocalizing, and enunciating every syllable. Overemphasis on such factors may make some students feel guilty about any attempts to develop efficient silent reading skills. Under these circumstances, many young people continue to pass through our school systems without developing a sound pattern of basic reading skills.
3. Schools have been developing better methods of teaching. The children in elementary schools

today are getting better basic training in reading than their parents in the past. Many teachers now have greater understanding of the factors of reading and of the learning problems of the individual student. In all periods, however, some schools have developed programs that are more effective than those in other schools.

4. We have come through a period of conflicting philosophy about the basic approach to reading. Some teachers insisted that the "phonics" approach of sounding out syllables was the best method. Others were completely dedicated to the "sight reading" approach of recognizing words as units of meaning and developing a vocabulary by visual association. As a result, we had a great variation between different schools and even between teachers in the same school, with a resulting confusion on the part of the students. Fortunately, today most of our elementary teachers are recognizing that both "sight reading" and "phonics" have a place in developing reading skills. Unfortunately, they still are not in complete agreement on the best combination or sequence of application of these two ideas.
5. Our population has become increasingly mobile, and, as a consequence, many children do not follow the planned sequence of courses in a single school, but attend many schools during their elementary years. Thus they may miss a basic part of their reading instruction because it has not yet been reached in one school, but has already been covered in another school to which they transfer.
6. Overcrowded schools, in many instances contributed to poor reading because the problems of the individual student were overlooked and the teaching was directed toward the assumed average of the class. Better schools attempt to discover individual problems in reading through testing programs and observation, and try to provide special attention for slow readers by means of remedial reading classes.
7. Specific instruction in reading has placed emphasis on oral reading, and limited attention has been given to helping the student discover various techniques to be used in silent reading. Consequently, some people have carried oral reading habits into silent reading practice.
8. Instruction in reading skills often is terminated after the fourth or fifth grade. It was assumed by both teachers and parents that, having mastered the basic skills of reading, the student could make the adaptations of those skills to the different reading needs he would face later. Unfortunately, many individuals made few adaptations, and many adults today try to read adult-level materials, using reading skills appropriate for a fifth-grade level of reading.
9. Many students who feel that they are poor readers really are expressing an attitude rather than a limitation in skill. At some time, they may have had a very frustrating experience in a reading program, and they may still continue to carry bad feelings about reading that make them feel inadequate in facing current reading problems.
10. Many adolescents and adults avoid activities involving reading because they are self-conscious about some reading problems. As a consequence, lack of practice has made their existing habits even more ineffective.

The Process of Reading

A second important fact to recognize is that we do not read while our eyes are moving. Just as the motion picture is made up of many still pictures flashed before us rapidly, so our reading is a series of visual impressions carried to our brain in a rapid sequence. We stop for each glance and then move on for another glance at another word or phrase. Reading rate, then, is a combination of the amount we see at each glance, the length of time we hesitate for each eye fixation, and the speed with which the eye can move and focus on another unit of material.

The first of these factors is referred to as *eye span*—the quantity of reading material one can see at one glance. For some people this may be a single word; for others, one complete phrase; and for others, still larger units of thought. For the very rapid reader, this may be several lines or a paragraph.

The second factor is closely related to the thinking process. It is referred to as a *rate of perception.* How long does it take to register the impression of what you see and to transmit it to your brain, and how long does it take the brain to interpret what was seen? Unless one has had an injury resulting in damage to brain tissue, he probably is capable of a great deal of acceleration in this thinking process.

The third factor of rate is that of eye movement in shifting from one point of focus to another. This is primarily a physical factor requiring the acceleration of rhythmic habits of eye movement.

The average individual is not aware of this complex pattern of reading habits and, therefore, makes little effort to coordinate the factors affecting his reading efficiency. Recognition of various types of reading and adjustment of reading habits to the type and purpose of specific reading assignments are essential. Most individuals have developed a rather limited range of reading efficiency, however, and therefore have little leeway in adjusting to different types.

One of the greatest contributions of a reading program is that of increasing the ceiling on reading speed. As one increases this upper limit of reading speed, of course, he also increases his range of reading efficiency and develops greater flexibility in his reading habits. By focusing attention on reading habits and placing an individual in a position where he is stimulated to operate at his maximum, teachers find that most persons are capable of reading at least twice as fast as they had been doing. Thus the normal adult who may be reading at a rate of about 250 words per minute actually may be capable of reading 500 words per minute or more if properly stimulated. With practice and concentrated personal effort, this individual may learn to read at 750 to 900 words per minute. Many individuals have made even greater improvements; reading class records reflect many persons who have read 2,000 to 3,000 words per minute. Some reading centers have reported individuals who have achieved rates as high as 50,000 words per minute on certain types of material. The potential maximum reading speed of any individual is unknown. The possibilities for any normal adult seem to be limited only by his own interest and his determination to improve. Only *you* can determine just how fast you can read, but you can be assured that you should be able at least to double or triple your present reading rate and perhaps to achieve much more than that.

How Do We Read Faster?

Slow readers may possess any one or a combination of poor reading habits. Most of these habits can be changed by recognizing the factors involved in the habit. Glance over the list of poor reading habits below and see which ones may apply to you; then consider what you might do to change these habits.

Vocalizing. Sounding out each word as if you were reading aloud slows you down to a snail's pace. This may be only a mental pronunciation process, but frequently it is accompanied by the moving of the lips as you read. If you do this, try placing your finger tightly on your lips as you read until you have broken the habit of lip movement. Once the lip action is broken, you will find it easier to push yourself to faster rates where mental vocalization decreases considerably.

Word-by-word reading. Looking at one word at a time to be sure you understand it may obscure the overall meaning of the sentence or paragraph. Remember the old adage about the man who could not see the forest because of the trees. To break yourself of this habit, try reading for ideas instead of words. Try to grasp whole phrases in a glance and sense their meaning.

Word blocking. Stopping to worry about an unfamiliar word breaks the rhythm of your reading and makes you lose the trend of thought or miss some of the main ideas. If you do this often, you probably have a poor vocabulary and need to work intensively on building up a greater understanding of commonly used words. In many instances, you can find the meaning of a certain word in the context, however, if you will just keep reading with an emphasis on ideas instead of words. Later on, after you have finished reading, you can go back and check the dictionary for some of the words that troubled you. After looking them up, think about their meaning and try to use them several times in conversation or writing that same day. This will fix the meaning in your mind. But do not let new words upset you and make you feel self-conscious. Most people encounter new words in their reading and take them in stride, identifying their meaning from other words or phrases with which they are associated.

Number attraction. Some readers come to a complete stop every time they reach a number. They seem to want to study it carefully as if it were a completely different concept of communication. Unless you are studying thoroughly for detailed content, dates, and quantitative ideas, you should try to generalize the numerical idea into verbal symbols such as "many" or "few," "long ago," "recently," "next year," or similar clues that will help in getting general ideas from the material.

Word analysis. Stopping to analyze a strange word as to its origin, structure, prefixes, and suffixes may be a sound vocabulary building exercise, but it destroys the trend of thought in reading and may lead to many false impressions, as meanings of many words vary with the context in which they are used. We must look for the larger ideas. *Seek the ideas behind the words.*

Monotonous plodding. Keeping the same pace of reading in all materials, from light fiction to heavy study, is tiresome. You need flexibility in reading habits. Let yourself go on some reading materials and do not worry about comprehension. You are missing much of the enjoyment of recreational reading by applying to it the same type of reading used for study. Learn to adjust your rate to the type of material and the purpose for reading it. Good readers may read at a very slow rate if they want detailed understanding, but read at a rate of several thousand words per minute on fiction, light correspondence, and other materials they are reading for main ideas or for recreation.

Finger following. Following a line of print with a finger or with a guide of some kind always slows down the reading process because fingers can not move as fast as eyes. To break this habit, keep both hands in your lap if reading at a desk, or hold the book in both hands. Rely solely on your eyes to follow the printed page.

Head swinging. Moving the head from side to side as one reads is much more laborious than moving the eyes. In addition to slowing down reading, this increased muscular activity will hasten fatigue. If you have this habit, try holding your head firmly in place with your hands and force your eyes to do the moving until the habit is broken.

Clue blindness. Like the driver who is too busy watching the road to see the signposts that direct him to his destination, many readers become too involved in word reading to notice such things as headings, subtitles, styles of type, listings, illustrations, introductions, and summaries. These all are important clues put in by the author to help you understand his concept of what is important. Try looking through some materials, reading only the headings and the ideas set off by a different style of type or by listings, and see how much you can really get from these clues alone. Use the introductory paragraphs and lead sentences as clues to organization and the summary statement as a review of material read. Try to develop the ability to glance over some material and get an understanding of the author's style and the types of signposts he has erected for you.

Backtracking. Going back to reread words or phrases is an indication that you doubt your own ability to pick out the important material. It slows you down a great deal because you are constantly thinking back instead of looking ahead to spot new ideas. Consequently, you miss ideas until you have gone past them, and then you have to go back to pick them up. The more you backtrack, the more necessary backtracking becomes to you. Try to concentrate on reading everything *only once.* You will be surprised to find that you get an overall understanding of it without the mental underlining.

Rereading. Closely associated with backtracking is the habit of going back to read the whole assignment over again to be sure you understand it. Studies have shown that rereading is a fairly ineffective method of reviewing immediately after study (39). If you concentrate on doing a good job of reading in the first place, a few minutes of thinking about what you have read will be far more valuable than rereading. Try laying the reading material aside after you have finished it and thinking over what you have read. This not only will develop a better understanding of the material, but also will serve as an aid to remembering it later.

Daydreaming. Allowing your attention to wander to other things while you read leaves you with the feeling of having covered pages but having no knowledge of what you have read. To overcome this, you must develop the ability to concentrate on one thing at a time. This matter of concentration is complex and will be discussed in detail in Sections III and IV.

Programs for Improvement

Unless a person has a serious physical or mental handicap, none of the habits mentioned above is serious. All can be overcome with concentrated practice. Thousands of people have overcome them and established flexible reading habits that enable them to read several times more efficiently than they did before. Some individuals find that bifocal glasses limit their reading speed. Usually, this problem can be overcome by changing to reading glasses.

Colleges and businesses have come to realize the benefits that can be obtained by providing a training situation in which individuals can be motivated to achieve such changes of reading habits. Such reading programs try to force the individual to read faster by applying pressure of various kinds.

Some training centers rely heavily upon mechancial devices such as the reading films, tachistoscopic devices, flash cards, reading-rate controllers, and reading accelerators of various types. Some use these devices for group work; others provide them for individual practice. The reading center in your vicinity may have one or more of these types of training devices with which you can practice if you are interested in them.

Other centers rely largely upon group drill methods and the psychological pressure of competition within the group as a motivating device. In such situations, the instructor usually will use pacing techniques and a great deal of urging to get students to read faster.

Regardless of the program, much of the progress depends upon the motivation of the individual. Unless you really want to improve your reading and are willing to try out new ideas in an attempt to break old habits, you will gain but little from the experience. If you really want to improve and will try new approaches to reading, the possibilities seem unlimited for your improvement in reading rate.

How Do We Understand More of What We Read?

All of the techniques discussed above are designed primarily to increase rate of reading, but reading is a complex process, of which the rate is only one factor. In this workbook, emphasis is placed upon *reading efficiency,* which is a combination of factors. In order to understand this term, we should first define clearly what is meant in this book by certain other terms, such as rate and comprehension.

Rate of reading is a numerical expression of the amount of material covered in a unit of time. It is expressed in words per minute. Thus a normal adult reading rate of 250 means that a normal adult should be able to cover 250 words of the material he is reading each minute.

Just covering words or pages would mean little if you did not grasp some meaning from what you read.

Comprehension, therefore, is an essential factor in good reading. Let us stress, however, that perfect comprehension is not the ideal of good reading, for perfect comprehension would be almost synonymous with memorization of the material, and this is seldom essential. The degree of understanding is measured more commonly in terms of the understanding of the main ideas and basic facts expressed in the reading. In some reading, it is more important to get a fairly thorough knowledge of these facts than in others. Therefore, comprehension also should be flexible and should be adjusted to the type of material read and the purpose of reading. One hundred percent comprehension is seldom needed unless one is memorizing material. For most reading, a 60 to 80 percent comprehension is adequate. For light recreational reading, detailed comprehension is even less important. In studying, you should be concerned with more detailed comprehension, but should not depend on reading alone. Here you need to use a balanced study approach that will make use of other techniques of understanding and remembering material. These will be discussed in detail in Section IV.

One of the most important factors in improving comprehension is that of having a purpose for reading. This purpose must be personalized to be effective. Mere reading of material because an instructor assigns it is not sufficient. You, personally, must see some reason for reading the material and must be looking for something in the material read. There are several ways of developing this personal interest.

First of all, you should *think* before starting to read. Think about the subject matter covered in the material. What do you already know about it? What would you like to know about it? What do you know about the person who wrote the article? Is the author an authority? Is he or she well known for personal prejudice on this subject? Will the presentation be biased? Can you depend on statements being accurate and complete, or is the author likely to try to persuade you in certain ways by presenting only partial facts or distorting views of the problem? These are just some of the questions which you should ask yourself before starting to read, but thinking about them will help to establish a good mental attitude toward reading the article with interest and concentration.

After having spent a few seconds in thinking before starting to read, glance over the article quickly to look for clues. The headings and boldface print will tell you the direction that the article will take in presenting the ideas. This helps prepare you to recognize important points as they are presented.

A third point in helping improve concentration and retention of material is to concentrate on small units, one at a time. Intense concentration on the portion between two headings with a slight pause to rest your eyes and think about the material before going on to the next section will provide relaxation as well as help to organize your thinking.

Take a few seconds after each unit, and a longer time at the end of the reading period, to think over what you have read and to fix a mental impression. This will help you to retain that impression for a longer period of time. In short, an alternation of reading and thinking provides a greater comprehension of what is read.

In order to measure comprehension, you must be tested in some way to see how much you remember of what was read. Comprehension usually is expressed numerically as a percentage score. *The comprehension score is the percent of questions answered correctly in a test on the material read.* A good reader should be able to score at least 60 to 80 percent on such a test, depending on the number of questions asked and the amount of detail involved in the questions.

What Is Reading Efficiency?

Many students, in trying to increase their reading rate, become disturbed when their comprehension drops. Others trying hard to improve comprehension slow down in an attempt to get better understanding. Many reading teachers have found that the faster readers often secure better comprehension scores than the slower readers. Similarly, they find that, at the end of a reading training program, students often read at several times their original rate with comprehension as great as or greater than they did before starting training. Although most of them go through a period of decreased comprehension while they are working hard on increasing rate, they find that, as they become adjusted to reading at a faster rate, they are able to build up their comprehension again.

Neither rate nor comprehension really gives us the complete picture of reading skills. Reading at a rapid rate is of little value if you understand very little of what you have read. On the other hand, reading with a high degree of comprehension is of little value if you never have time to read all the material you are expected to cover. The most important factor is *neither* the speed at which you read *nor* the amount you can remember of what you read, but a combination of these: *the amount you can read and remember* per unit of time. In an attempt to express this factor and place an emphasis on the importance of this combination of skills, we use the term *reading efficiency* to represent the amount of material comprehended per minute of reading time. Efficiency is computed by taking the product of the *rate* of reading (expressed in words per minute) and the *comprehension* score (expressed as the percent of correct answers on a test over the material). *Efficiency,* then, is a numerical expression of rate of effective reading represented in words per minute. Let us compare the following sequence of scores to see how this works.

	1st test	2nd test	3rd test	4th test
Rate	150	200	400	600
Comprehension	80	70	60	70
Efficiency	120	140	240	420

If this individual were to consider only the decreasing comprehension scores during practice, he might become discouraged and stop pushing his rate improvement. By stressing the efficiency score instead of rate or comprehension, he gets a better picture of his real progress, however; and although his final comprehension score is still below his initial one, his efficiency score gives a better picture of the amount of material he can grasp in a unit of study time. This individual probably would find that he was accomplishing at least three times as much work in his periods of reading as was possible before, and the slight difference in comprehension could be offset by other techniques of remembering.

Throughout this book, stress will be placed upon the efficiency scores on reading exercises because efficiency seems the best expression of the effectiveness of reading habits.

Conditions for Improvement

In this chapter you have been urged to explore some new possibilities for reading improvement, recognizing some of the bad habits that may slow you down, some of the factors that influence these reading habits, and some of the terms used to describe the results of reading habits. We have presented the idea that anyone is capable of improving this reading efficiency unless prevented from doing so by physical or mental handicaps. The question remains: How can *you* improve your reading efficiency? Three conditions are needed to make satisfactory progress in the improvement of reading efficiency.

First of all, you must be convinced that you want to become a better reader. You must be willing to put in several hours of hard and sometimes monotonous work in reading practice. You must be willing to face the problems of being compared with others, of competing with others, and of working under pressure that may be irritating. You must be willing to cast aside established habits in order to try new ones. You need to be convinced that the time to be saved in the future, when more satisfactory reading habits have been established, is worth the sacrifice of several hours of your time now. If you can see the long-range value and are willing to work, your possibilities of improvement are practically unlimited.

Second, you will need to work with appropriate materials from which comparisons can be made to determine improvement. Unless the exercises you use are of comparable difficulty, misunderstanding and discouragement may follow. Unless all sets of questions are made up in comparable forms, your comprehension scores may vary because of the difficulty of the test rather than your degree of understanding. There will be a better chance of progress if you work from a workbook that has been standardized and that has comparable tests. The materials used in this workbook represent the results of many years of experimentation and revision in order to develop the best possible sequences of exercises. Note that all exercises are graded with a readability score. These scores are determined by the application of the Flesch formula (14) to the material. Exercises are arranged in a gradually ascending order of difficulty so that, as you learn to read faster, you also learn to read material of a little greater difficulty.

Finally, you must feel a sense of progress and satisfaction. Using your scores from one exercise to set goals for the next one will help sustain your motivation. You must compare results of today with those of yesterday and then set higher goals for tomorrow. The reading progress charts in this book help you to do that. They are organized in such a way that you can compare results on any particular exercise with others in that series, or with different types of exercises. Keeping your reading graphs up-to-date will help you to get an overall view of progress in increasing your reading efficiency. The extent of your growth in effective reading skills will depend upon your desire, your attitude, and your concentration.

A combination of motivation, concentration, and comprehension should lead you to a deeper level of understanding and to more effective retention of the materials you read.

Length: 1600 words

Readability Score: 50

II
Kinds of Reading

Recognize Types of Reading

If you want to evaluate your success as an effective reader, you might look at your ability to adjust your reading to the different types of materials and to your different purposes in reading. The greater the range of reading efficiency you have, the greater possibilities you have to judge what types of reading skills are most appropriate for what materials. Limited space in this workbook prevents the presentation of detailed analysis of the various types of reading and their application. However, a brief consideration of some of the major types of reading may help you to understand your present reading habits and your reactions to some of the work you will do in this book.

Purpose for Reading

Some authors see only two major classifications for your purpose for reading. Either you are reading for ideas or reading for facts. Either of these purposes has specific implications for you. These may be reviewed in considerable detail in two pairs of books; *Reading for Ideas* (40) and *Reading for Facts* (39) by Pauk and Wilson, or *Reading for the Main Idea* (42) and *Reading for Significant Facts* (43) by Alton Raygor.

In addition to these major classifications, one might add the purpose of "light" reading for entertainment and that of "heavy" reading for aesthetic appreciation of style, content, or philosophy. This type of reading involves a combination of intense concentration and uninterrupted contemplation that is not readily measured in terms of rate or comprehension.

Regardless of your basic purpose in reading, you constantly should use reading as a channel to improve vocabulary. Some good resources to help you improve your process of vocabulary development are *Basic Vocabulary Skills* by Davis (12), *Developing Vocabulary Skills* by Joffe (14) and *The Teacher's Word Book of 30,000 Words* by Thorndike (54).

Skimming and Scanning

These two terms are used interchangeably by many writers. They are denounced as inappropriate labels for reading by many critics of speed reading. Some writers refer to these activities as "semi-reading" skills. Many writers in the developmental reading field do recognize them as types of reading that have very significant meaning in the total reading process. They feel that these types are essential to the total development of flexible and efficient reading skills.

Both techniques involve reading by the "sign-posts"—the clues set up by the author. By using these you can learn to skip materials that are not of immediate interest to you and to locate more quickly those that you really wish to read in detail. Most textbooks are organized to make intelligent skimming possible. All devices such as chapter titles, sectional headings, ***boldface or italicized*** type, and underlining are clues to help you with this technique. Take time to think before you start to read, and get a good idea of just what you are looking for. Then clues can save a great deal of reading time by leading you right to the sections in which you are interested. This allows you to skip over the rest.

In recent years, some writers have attempted to establish a difference between the two terms. There is no general agreement on this distinction, however. Emphasis on scanning as a search for main ideas and on skimming as a search for specific facts or details is presented by both Norman (37) and Wood (56). They are presented in exactly the opposite pattern by Adams (1), Maxwell (25) and Thomas and Robinson (52). This latter position seems to be more widely accepted, however. It will be used in this publication. *Skimming* is that technique of rapid reading designed to identify the major ideas and relationships discussed in an article. *Scanning* is that technique used to locate and utilize specific facts or ideas related to a predetermined goal. Both skills require preplanning and intense concentration to be effective.

Skimming is the basic first step in the well-known SQ4R method of study discussed in Section IV. Skimming also can be very effective as a preliminary step to reading something more thoroughly. It gives an overview of what you can expect in the material.

Scanning is an essential aspect of any search for specific information. Use it in sources such as telephone books, encyclopedias, dictionaries, or general reference sources. It also is an essential aspect of the self-recitation study technique, which emphasizes reading to seek answers to predicted questions.

Idea Reading

Idea reading extends use of skimming techniques beyond the heading into the content paragraphs. It involves more comprehensive coverage of total word content, but in a highly selective fashion. It is essential in many types of business and professional reading as well as in much incidental and recreational reading. The basic meaning of many published articles could be condensed into a few simple statements.

This reading for the main ideas is a technique of rapid reading in which the eyes move rapidly. They catch large phrases at each glance and register with the brain only the most significant words or ideas in those phrases. Successful idea reading is perhaps one of the most difficult types of reading to master. It is also one of the most efficient. One can develop extremely rapid rates of reading with it. It means being familiar with the makeup of the English language as a means of communication. Rapid recognition of key sentences, illustrative words and phrases, and the skeletal structure of the sentence is essential to discovering the basic meaning. Idea reading means making quick decisions as to the relative importance of different sentences and paragraphs as you read. It means quick recognition of the author's clues and rapid association with ideas you already understand that relate to this material.

Exploratory Reading

Exploratory reading, or general content reading, involves more detail than the two types mentioned before. This type of approach is appropriate for longer articles in magazines, for descriptive literature, and for light fiction. It may be used for similar reading in which you wish to pick up a better understanding of some new ideas. You should use this technique on many outside references in which you wish to find background material, but in which you will not be tested for detail. Emphasis here should be placed on recognizing and understanding main ideas more thoroughly. You should relate them to other ideas in the article or to previous knowledge of the subject.

Study Reading

Study reading is a type in which you must get a maximum understanding of the main ideas and their relationships. This is the type you must apply to your textbooks. You may apply it to contracts, legal papers, technical manuals, instructions, and other similar materials. Here you frequently deal with materials that you must read and understand now and also remember for future use.

Clues are important. A preliminary scanning may be quite helpful. The actual reading process, however, needs to be an alternating activity between reading for ideas and thinking about those ideas. The actual reading process itself may be quite rapid, but greater skill must be developed in thinking and organizing the ideas for long-term retention. Many different study skills must be used to supplement the reading process. These are discussed in more detail in Section IV.

Critical Reading

Another type of reading that must sometimes be applied wisely is that of critical reading. You may find a certain article that tends to stir you to action. You may feel you should write to your congressman or rush downtown to buy some new and indispensable household appliance. Then you should stop and consider what you have read more carefully. Many periodical articles, books, and advertising materials are loaded with carefully worded propaganda devices. These are designed to sway your opinion or to sell you on some particular idea or product. Be careful that a rapid reading of the main ideas does not lead to false conclusions.

To apply techniques of critical reading, you should go back and consider carefully what you know about the source of the reading material. What are the possible biases or ulterior motives that its publisher or author may have? You also should consider what you know about the author's background experience and potential knowledge of the subject. You should watch the reading material for inconsistent logic or false analogies. Particularly important is an awareness of emotionally loaded words that appeal to basic emotions. With experience, you soon can learn to spot some of these types of appeals through quick scanning for the clues the author provides. Then you can beware of these techniques before beginning to read. In any reading, you should frequently ask yourself: "What is the author trying to make me believe and why?"

Analytical Reading

Certain sections of study materials require a much more thorough type of reading than those mentioned before. Mathematical theorems and problems, scientific formulas and certain definitive statements of key ideas require careful attention to each word and to its relative importance. You must approach such reading with a questioning mind, seeking complete clarification. You can learn to recognize such passages and to slow your reading pace to deal with such sections more adequately.

Identify and Adjust

By learning to recognize different types of reading and to judge what types of reading skills to apply to them, you may become more effective in your overall use of reading time. Streamline your reading activities to meet the needs of the time and the material to be read. Such judgment can be developed only from practice. This workbook will provide an opportunity to practice several types of reading, but you must apply the principles of efficient reading to the materials that you read every day if you hope to maintain really efficient reading habits.

Length: 1450 words — Readability Score: 48

III
Is Reading Enough?

Reading is what *you* make it. You can make your reading hard work, or you can make it an exciting adventure. It can be drudgery or relaxation. From the previous chapters you should have developed a better understanding of *how* you read and *why* you read that way. You understand *how* you can control further development in your reading skills to make them more effective for you. Your eyes and your brain have the potential to make reading skills work in any way you desire.

Only you can determine the ultimate effectiveness of your reading skills. But a word of caution is perhaps appropriate.

Overdependency on Reading

No one would question that reading is essential to personal development. Too many persons jump to the conclusion, however, that reading is the *only* respectable approach to learning. They tend to depend *entirely* on reading for gaining new ideas and for understanding them. They frequently consider audio-visual devices as mere recreational gadgets of momentary interest but of little lasting value. Such persons may completely ignore the possibilities of note making from speeches, conferences, seminars, and telephone conversations as an effective technique. They often consider note making in conjunction with reading as too much extra work.

Extreme dependency on reading may make you fearful of any techniques that might lower your reading comprehension even temporarily. This fear is the basis of much hesitancy in learning.

You may be afraid that if you develop faster rates of reading, you will lose some comprehension accuracy. Research shows that this is not a matter for concern (37). Most people are able to make very significant increases in their reading rates without any significant loss in comprehension. Many fast readers maintain comprehension levels much higher than the average for their age or grade.

But reading still has its limitations in comparison with some other means of communicating ideas. For most people, reading is one of the slower techniques of picking up ideas. A picture sometimes can convey as much information in one glance as several pages of descriptive literature could do. The oral statement often can be made to convey much more meaning than the same statement in print. The speaker can do this through the changes of tone or inflection and the verbal stress on certain words.

Identification With the Author

One way to get more understanding from the printed page is to seek a better understanding of authors as unique individuals. Find out more about who they are and what they have done. Use the title page or introductory comments to try to get a feel for their attitudes and enthusiasms. Try to visualize these authors as persons like yourself. They want to express themselves clearly to you, but they need your help to do it effectively. As you read, try to identify their attitudes, interests, and biases. Watch for their use of tone and inference. Study how they use words and figurative language to individualize their presentations. Seek evidence of their use of critical judgment. Watch for evidence of their distinction between fact, fiction, and personal opinion. Seek help if you need assistance in developing these skills of personal identification with the author. You can find many detailed suggestions in *Developing Reading Versatility* by Adams (1) or in *Reading for Ideas* by Pauk and Wilson (40).

Some Supplements to Reading

One reason some people feel so self-conscious about their reading may be that they are too dependent upon it. They may fail to associate it adequately with other means of communication. Think about some of the techniques that can be used to enrich its meaning.

Listening involves skills often overlooked and ignored. A speaker uses many "signposts" just as the writer does. He or she uses introductions and summaries during which you should be thinking. Relate what you hear to what you already understand. Changes of tone, pitch, and rate of speaking are used to emphasize certain points. Speakers use lead statements as headings to new topics. They frequently list or itemize points they think are important. The listener who is alert to these clues can learn a great deal during these concentrated periods of listening.

Thinking is the conscious process by which you try to control some of the activities of your brain. Thinking seems to be a very rapid, continuous process that may or may not be in tune with your reading or listening activities. Because thinking seems to go on at a speed so much greater than reading or listening, you must make a special effort to achieve some congruence in these activities.

Perhaps your thinking process can be focused on three phases of learning activity. First is the recognition of facts that are significant to you for some reason. Second is the fusing of your understanding of the purpose, function, and specific relationships of these facts with your existing knowledge. Third is the classification and filing away in the brain for future application and use.

Learning may be enhanced by a three-stage classification system. First, you identify the general topic of the author. What or who is he or she writing about? Next, what special area within that topic is the focus of this unit of reading? Finally, what attitudes is the author expressing about this special area of this topic? Such an approach may help you in seeing relationships and achieving long-term retention of significant information.

Note making is a very important technique for the busy students. By relying on brief notes, you can relieve the stress of detailed mental comprehension of many minute facts of temporary importance. Brief, well-organized notes taken on important reading assignments provide an excellent basis for review at a later time. An important aspect of good notes, however, is that they are *made* in the writer's own words rather than *taken* as a few random excerpts from the speaker's terminology (5).

Self-recitation of important points helps to keep them in mind. This process of predicting questions to which answers must be found requires occasional pauses to think over what is being read. The questions posed serve as a goal for reading. The pauses for thinking provide brief relaxation for the eyes.

Frequent review of important materials is an invaluable aid in remembering and will make later rereading unnecessary. Well-organized notes are a much more effective basis for review than reliance on rereading or on skimming again the material originally read on the subject.

Improving Comprehension

In the previous chapter, reference was made to several techniques that might be used to improve comprehension. These are all supplementary techniques not actually a part of the reading process itself but closely related to it. At this time, let us consider more carefully the actual steps involved in these activities.

Orienting Oneself to the Reading Assignment

Most efficient individuals operate on some sort of schedule. They plan a certain time of day for reading. By having regular times for certain types of reading work, they get into habits of thinking about these things at regular periods. This helps to establish a "mood" for reading. This can be intensified by taking a few minutes to survey the reading to be done, to arrange it according to importance, and to anticipate the questions that must be answered in the reading.

Getting the Overall View

In the consideration of any particular item of reading, rapid skimming of pages looking for key ideas will set up general idea goals to be attained. This will make the task more meaningful.

Reading to Find Answers to Questions

In the preview of the material, you will recognize several main topics. As you approach each topic, try to pose questions for yourself to give you a purpose for reading. You will find that looking for answers does much to focus your interest more sharply. This helps you attain faster rates of reading.

Visualizing and Making Associations

As you pause, at intervals, try to form a mental picture of the things about which you have been reading. Relate the ideas to something you already know and understand. Establishing associations with known facts will provide a more thorough understanding.

Making Notes from Materials Read

If you are reading to organize material for speech or a report or if you want some details for later use, take some notes *in your own words* during your pauses. Brief notes with personalized expression help you to organize verbal concepts more clearly. These notes should have more lasting meaning for you. If you have difficulty concentrating on important material, making notes forces you to think about it.

Reviewing

Use some time *regularly* to think over materials read during the previous few days and to pull together the important ideas from various sources. This is an invaluable supplement to the reading process. Ideas picked up from very rapid reading can be fixed more firmly in your mind for later use.

In Summary

These techniques will serve to strengthen your comprehension of what your read. They will make it easier for you to relax. They will allow you to read at a maximum rate without fear of losing comprehension. The time you save in rapid reading should provide an opportunity to use some of these techniques so important to remembering ideas and their relationships.

Length: 3100 words Readability Score: 62

IV

A Program for Effective Study

The ideas in the previous sections are basic to any sound program of study. You need to develop sound habits of study if you hope to live a balanced life and to survive in the competitive academic world today. You must provide time for both academic requirements and social opportunities. Many colleges are attempting to help students establish such habits by the provision of classes in "Study Skill Techniques." Such courses recognize reading as one aspect of study, but also point out that efficient reading *alone* is not enough to meet the competition of college classes today.

Let us look at some of the factors that are important in study. We might consider them by asking five questions about effective study:

What? Who? Where? When? How?

What Is Effective Study?

Many students, even some of those who receive good grades regularly, spend a great deal more time in study than is necessary. These students have developed study techniques that are laborious and time-consuming. Other students put in many hours in study, but seem to get little out of the time spent. They frequently complain about difficulties in certain courses, and the only remedy they can think of is to spend more time on that subject. In both circumstances the students probably are ignoring some basic principles about fatigue and span of interest. Instead of spending *more time* in study, they need to make *better use of the time* they do spend. You need to get the most possible good out of each hour spent on a course. This is what is meant by *effective study.* If you have effective study habits, you will spend *less* time on the same material and will understand it better than one who has not learned effective methods.

Whose Responsibility?

In high school, parents and teachers usually try to encourage study habits by providing certain times and places for study, and by trying to reduce possible interruptions. As you grow older, however, you find yourself more "on your own." Especially at college you will find that no one seems to exert much effort to *make* you study. By now you are supposed to be mature enough to realize that study is essential to success in school. One very important aspect of maturity is the personal assumption of responsibility for control of your time. Achieving freedom from control by others implies developing greater self-control and exercising self-discipline. Therefore, it is your responsibility to see that you provide adequate time for study. Other school activities will place many demands on you, and you will find it easy to devote to them time that should be given to study.

Some students realize too late that they have been neglecting their studies and try desperately to cram all their study and review into the last few days before examinations. When they fail the exams, they frequently rationalize and blame the instructor, their roommates, or someone else for their inability to keep up with the requirements of the course. With the keen competition present in college, poor study habits can undermine the entire enjoyment of a college program. An early recognition of this could save much unhappiness.

If you wish to improve your academic record, you must assume the responsibility *yourself* for keeping up-to-date in all your school work. The sooner you accept this responsibility seriously, the more likely you are to succeed in your school program. Specific suggestions to help you establish better study habits are given on the following pages.

Where to Study?

Some students are able to study almost anywhere. While walking or resting, they may be mentally organizing ideas. Many students, however, do not have this ability to concentrate in the midst of other activity. Even when seated at a study desk, you may find other ideas creeping into your mind to keep you from thinking about the school work waiting to be done. You may find it helpful to consider some of the factors that *you can* control to make that study desk a more effective place to work.

Auditory distractions usually can be controlled by selecting as quiet a place as possible. You can reduce, to some extent, distraction from outside noises. This may mean working out arrangements for study hours with your roommate and making an agreement not to have guests in the room during certain hours. If you find yourself unable to eliminate these distractions in your own room, then consider the scheduling of study hours in the library, where the atmosphere is kept as quiet as possible. Another possibility is the use of a vacant classroom for those free periods between classes.

Some students find that a radio or stereo set playing continuous music and set at a minimal volume creates a sound barrier sufficient to block out the variety of outside distracting noises. By careful selection of the station or of recordings, you can establish a stable sound background to which you can adjust and thus be protected from the uncontrolled sounds of your environment. In doing this, however, you need to keep your volume low enough to avoid creating sound distractions for others who work near you.

Visual distractions frequently are present without being recognized. The picture of a friend on your desk may take you off on a chain of pleasant memories every time you glance at it. The souvenir ash tray you picked up on your vacation trip last summer may recall many pleasant experiences. The colorful new sport jacket you wore to the last ball game may revive the excitement and competition you enjoyed then; the letter you got from home yesterday may start you worrying about the situation at home. The advertising on the desk blotter may stir thoughts of the good times you could have if you only followed the suggestions printed there. These and many other items frequently found on study desks may lead you to many minutes of daydreaming during the hours when you *think* you have been studying.

One of the first essentials in improving the place of study is to clear the desk of as many of these diverting influences as you can. If possible, the study desk should be cleared of everything except the textbook you are studying at the moment and the necessary papers and pencils for taking notes.

Next, consider what disturbing items lie in your range of vision as you sit at your desk. Any movement or activity within your range of vision may catch your eye and lead your thoughts astray. Consider carefully any objects that lie in the area of distraction. To do this, check the *angle of distraction* from your study desk. Any object falling within a 60-degree angle on either side of the forward view from your desk is likely to interfere with your concentration. Mirrors are especially disturbing as they expand the area of distraction to include a reflected area as well as the actual one. How many things in your room fall within this range? What do they make you think about? To improve your concentration you would be wise to move your desk so that the space included in this area of distraction is at a minimum and so that most of the wall surfaces included are blank. Ideally, then, a study desk should be placed in a corner, and the wall above it should be kept clear of distracting influences.

Lighting is also an important factor in concentration. Eye strain and general fatigue are the logical results of poor lighting. Do not depend on a single overhead light. You need a good desk lamp that will provide indirect lighting in your working area. Desk lamps that cause a glare on the books and papers should be avoided. In addition to a good study lamp on the desk, some other light in the room is needed to prevent sharp contrasts between a brightly lighted desk and a dark room. Extreme contrasts make the eyes tire more rapidly. A combination of a good, indirect desk lamp and an overhead light is considered ideal for effective study conditions.

Ventilation and temperature are important, too. There should be some provision for fresh air without a draft. If you cannot work with a window open, make a point of airing out the study room once a day. A warm room develops drowsiness and makes studying difficult. Usually, you can study best in a room that is slightly cooler than the normal living room temperature.

Avoid physical relaxation when trying to study. If you pick the easy chair or the bed as a place to study, do not expect to be able to concentrate very long. By relaxing physically, you invite mental relaxation as well. A good straight chair at a study desk is the ideal location for effective study.

Having one place for study *and study only* is important. If you study at the same place that you play games, do your nails, write your letters, or plan dance programs, you will find it more difficult to get to work. If, however, you use one desk exclusively for studying, you will find it natural to start concentrating when you sit there.

You can control the environment in which you try to study. Do not blame others for distractions. Take time to check out your study area, and do some reorganization to make it an atmosphere more conducive to effective study.

When to Study?

Your school program is one of your most important obligations and requires more time than you are likely to give to it without careful planning. The best protection against late assignments and the necessity for "cramming" is to budget your time as you go along and to plan a proper balance between work, study, and recreational activities. One of the best ways to do this is to use a *Time Budget Sheet*. A sample *Time Budget Sheet* is shown on pages 23 and 24. Copies of these usually can be obtained through your school bookstore. The success of such a time budget will depend on how carefully you plan it and use it. Several points should be considered. The suggestions on the back of the *Time Budget Sheet* are worthy of careful consideration. Read them thoughtfully; think about their meaning to you. Discuss them with your advisor or with a counselor if you need help in applying them to your own planning.

How to Study?

Probably no two students study in exactly the same way. You have learned certain techniques that seem easiest for you. If these techniques bring you understanding of the materials with a minimum expenditure of time, then you are probably satisfied with these study habits. If, however, you feel that you are not getting the desired results or that your methods are too time-consuming, then you should consider a change. If your present study habits are leading only to poor grades and discouragement, they should be discarded and replaced by a new set that may lead to more effective use of your time.

Many students fail to make effective use of new techniques of study because they are unwilling to give up the old techniques, even though these older ones have not produced the desired results. Often it is necessary to *unlearn* poor work habits before you can establish good ones. If you wish to develop a greater efficiency in your study, you must be willing to release some old habits in favor of some new ones.

Space in this book does not allow a detailed discussion of many of the techniques of study. You will find references on study skills in your library or your bookstore. For detailed suggestions on note making, you may read *Learning More by Effective Study* by Charles and Dorothy Bird (5). For specific suggestions on classroom and examination skills, you will find *Effective Study* by F. P. Robinson (46) very helpful. For detailed information on the preparation of reports and term papers, you can find assistance in *The Research Paper* by Hook and Gaver (18). *Tips to Improve Personal Study Skills,* prepared by the New York State Personnel and Guidance Association (35), is a concise pamphlet—an excellent reference to keep in your notebook. Other good books with detailed suggestions to improve study habits are *A Time to Learn* by Bandt, Meara, and Schmidt (4) and *Study Skills* by Carmen and Adams (7).

Three major techniques presented by Francis P. Robinson in his book *Effective Study* (46) have proved to be so helpful to many students that they merit a presentation here. These techniques can provide an excellent means of establishing important ideas in one's mind and retaining them. These may be identified as the three "S.R." techniques because these letters can be used as memory clues for all three techniques. All three require a high level of personal self-discipline and planning. Only you can make them work for you. In brief, these techniques may be applied as follows:

A. ***Self-Recitation.*** Ask questions of yourself as you study and as you review. Be alert at all times to the questions suggested about major ideas, and try to read for answers to them. In reviewing, ask yourself questions, and see if you can answer them; then check your answers against your notes. In studying for exams, try to predict the questions that the instructor may ask, and be prepared by these questions in the examination.

B. ***Spaced Review.*** Review briefly immediately after study; then review again within a week. Each week, schedule review periods where you can review all the material presented thus far in the course. These brief weekly reviews will reduce the necessity for any last-minute cramming before examinations.

C. ***The SQ3R Method,*** originated by Robinson (46), frequently has been referred to as the SQ4R Method for purposes of clarification. The following explanation of the six steps of this method has been presented by Miller and Seeman (34).

The SQ4R Method of Study

1. ***Survey.*** Glance over the headings in the chapter to see the few big points that will be developed. This survey should take only a few seconds and will show the several core ideas around which the discussion will be developed. This preview will prepare you for more effective study of the details in the following steps.
2. ***Question.*** Turn the first heading into a question. This should arouse your curiosity and thus aid comprehension. It will help to bring to mind information that you already know. In this way, your understanding of that section will be increased. The question will make the important points stand out.
3. ***Read.*** Read to answer the question. Make this an active search for the answer. You will find that your eyes tend to move more rapidly over the material, slighting the unimportant or explanatory details while noting the important points.
4. ***Recite.*** Try to recite the answer to your question without looking at the book. Use your own words, and think of an example. If you can do this, you know what is in the book; if you cannot, glance over the section again. If you jot down "cue" phrases in outline form as you do this, you will have an excellent basis for later review and study.
5. ***Repeat.*** Repeat steps 2, 3, and 4 on each succeeding section. Turn the next heading into a question, read to answer that question, and recite the answer by jotting down "cue" phrases in an outline. Read in this way until the lesson is completed.
6. ***Review.*** Look back over your notes to get a bird's-eye view of the points and their relationships. Check your memory as to the content by reciting on the major subpoints under each

heading. This checking of your memory can be done by covering up the notes and trying to recall the main points, then exposing each major point and trying to recall the subpoints listed under it. Save these notes for later use in *Spaced Review* activity.

SQ4R Applied to Problem Solving

A modification of the SQ4R Method to apply to mathematical-type reading that involves problem solving might be summarized as follows:

1. ***Survey.*** Look over the problems to see what types of logic they require and what basic formulas will ← 2700 be used. Try to make associations with practical situations in which similar problems might be encountered.
2. ***Question.*** Looking at the first problem, think through it to be sure you understand what is the unknown factor which you are to find and what are the known facts with which you can work.
3. ***Solve.*** Work through the problem to find the unknown factor.
4. ***Check.*** Substitute the answer you have found for the unknown in the original statement and see if it makes sense. Check through the basic formula to see it if balances with this value. ← 2800
5. ***Repeat.*** Apply steps 2, 3, and 4 to each successive problem in the assignment.
6. ***Review.*** Check over the whole assignment again to be sure you have completed all the assigned work and that your answers were reasonable. Be sure you understand the purpose of such exercises, and try to think of practical applications to principles involved in the problems.

Concentrate on End Results

The application of these three "S.R." techniques will free you from much of the tension associated with trying to get thorough comprehension from the reading alone. Frequently, students depend on one 2900 → reading of the material to grasp its entire content. The methods outlined above decrease the stress on detailed comprehension in initial reading. They provide other study techniques—skimming, questioning, reciting, and reviewing—to develop the understanding of material. This frees you to read as rapidly as possible with a major emphasis on *seeking the ideas behind the words.*

Improving comprehension requires a constant awareness of your own goals and a sensitivity to the ideas and organization of the author.

As you develop this technique of rapid reading, you usually will find that comprehension will improve 3000 → also. But more important than either is the efficiency of reading—that is, the amount you understand per unit of study time. By increasing the efficiency of the initial reading, you can find time for the other techniques, which will help build a more permanent comprehension of the whole body of material. More than that, a combination of efficient reading with effective study techniques should enable you to get more studying done in less time. So you should have more time to spend on other things you want to do. This is your ultimate reward for exercising self-control 3100 → of your own study habits and environment.

TIME BUDGET SHEET

SECONDARY SCHOOL FORM

S R STUDY PROGRAM — Spaced Review — Self Recitation — SQ4R Method

Prepared by
Lyle L. Miller
UNIVERSITY OF WYOMING

Name ____________________
(Study the suggestions on the back before making out budget)

SPACED REVIEW

	MON	TUES	WED	THUR	FRI	SAT	SUN	
12 - 2								
2 - 4								
4 - 6								
6 - 7								
7 - 8								
8 - 9								
Period 1								
Period 2								
Period 3								
Period 4								
Period 5								
Period 6								
Period 7								
4 - 5								
5 - 6								
6 - 7								
7 - 8								
8 - 9								
9 - 10								
10 - 12								TOTAL
TOTAL CLASS								
TOTAL STUDY								
				These three evening plans interchangeable				

SELF RECITATION

SURVEY **QUESTION** **READ** **RECITE** **REPEAT: QRR** **REVIEW**

SOME HINTS ON PLANNING A BETTER TIME SCHEDULE

Lyle L. Miller
Professor of Guidance and Counselor Education, University of Wyoming

The effectiveness of your time schedule will depend on the care with which **you** plan it. Careful consideration of these points will help you to make a schedule which **you** can control and which will **work for you.**

1. **Plan a schedule of balanced activities.** School life has many aspects which are very important to success. Some have fixed time requirements and some are flexible. Some of the most common which you must consider are:

FIXED:	eating	organizations	classes	church	work
FLEXIBLE:	sleeping	recreation	personal affairs	relaxation	study

2. **Plan enough time in studying to do justice to each subject.** Most classes are planned to require some homework. Most students should plan at least ten hours per week for such homework assignments. Of course, if you are a slow reader, or have other study deficiencies, you may need to plan more time in order to meet the competition of your class.
3. **Study at a regular time and in a regular place.** Establishing habits of study is extremely important. Knowing what you are going to study, and when, saves a lot of time making decisions and retracing your steps to get necessary materials, etc. Avoid generalizations in your schedule such as "STUDY." Commit yourself more definitely to "STUDY HISTORY" or "STUDY CHEMISTRY" at certain regular hours.
4. **Study as soon after your lecture class as possible.** One hour spent soon after class will do as much good in developing an understanding of materials as several hours a few days later. Check over lecture notes while they are still fresh in your mind. Start assignments while your memory of the assignment is still accurate.
5. **Utilize odd hours during the day for studying.** Make good use of your study hall periods and supervised study periods in class. These scattered free periods are easily wasted. Planning and establishing habits of using them for studying for the class just finished will result in free time for recreation or activities at other times in the week.
6. **Limit your blocks of study time to no more than 2 hours on any one course at one time.** After 1-1/2 to 2 hours of study you begin to tire rapidly and your ability to concentrate decreases rapidly. Taking a break and then switching to studying some other course will provide the change necessary to keep up your efficiency.
7. **Trade time—don't steal it.** When unexpected events arise that take up time you had planned to study, decide immediately where you can find the time to make up the study missed and adjust your schedule for that week. Note the three weekend evenings. Most students can afford no more than two of them for recreation, but may wish to use different evenings on different weeks. This "trading agreement" provides for committing one night to study, but rotating it as recreational possibilities vary.
8. **Provide for spaced review**—That is, a regular weekly period when you will review the work in each of your courses and be sure you are up to date. This review should be cumulative, covering briefly all the work done thus far in the quarter.
9. **Practice self-recitation as a device for increasing memory.** Organize your notes in a question and answer form and think in terms of questions and answers about the main ideas of the material as you review weekly. When preparing for exams, try to predict the questions the instructor may ask.
10. **Keep carefully organized notes on both lectures and assignments.** Good notes are one of the best bases for review. Watch for key ideas in lectures and try to express them in your own words in your notes. Watch for headings and bold face type in your reading to give you clues of main ideas for your notes. Take down careful notes as to exactly what assignments are made and when they are due.
11. **Always try to improve your study efficiency.** The SQ4R method of study is a very sound approach to improving comprehension. Details on this method can be found in the library in Chapter IV of "Increasing Reading Efficiency," published by Holt, Rinehart, and Winston, New York City 10017 or in Chapter IV of "Developing Reading Efficiency," published by Burgess Publishing Co., Minneapolis, Minnesota 55415.

Publisher:
DEVELOPMENTAL READING DISTRIBUTORS

1944 Sheridan Ave.
Laramie, Wyoming
82070

Length: 1000 words Readability Score: 53

V

Using This Workbook

The exercises in this workbook have been grouped according to types, each of which plays a distinct part in the development of more efficient reading habits.

Series I
Word Recognition Exercises

Word recognition exercises are designed to accelerate rate and to establish some rhythmic patterns of eye movement. As you proceed through these exercises, you will find yourself dealing with longer words. Here you will have an opportunity to break the habit of syllabication and to learn to pick up longer words at a single glance.

Series II
Word Meaning Exercises

Word meaning exercises, involve you in thinking processes as you are expected to identify synonyms at a rapid pace. The arrangement is the same as before, except that you now must think about word meanings. In addition to eye span and rhythmic eye movements, the factor of rate of perception has been added. Because all of the words used in these exercises have been taken from Thorndike's list (54) of the 30,000 most frequently used words in our vocabulary, these exercises also serve to point up potential weaknesses in your vocabulary list, which may need study. Any words missed here should be placed on a vocabulary list and studied carefully so that they will not remain as stumbling blocks to your reading.

Series III
Phrase Meaning Exercises

The third series introduces phrases and is designed primarily to increase eye span. At the same time, you continue to practice on rhythmic eye movements and perception of meaning under time pressure. These are exercises in which you should begin to sense an improvement in rate of reading as you learn to pick up several words at one glance. These exercises begin with short phrases and gradually build up in length until the last few exercises are composed of phrases of several words.

Series IV
Sentence Meaning Exercises

The fourth series consists of exercises in recognition of sentence meaning. Here increased eye span is further stressed, and, in addition, you are expected to recognize the key words that provide meaning for a sentence. This is basic training for the idea-type of reading, in which you strip the sentences of their verbal padding to pick up the basic ideas. This series provides basic training in quick recognition of key ideas, which is essential to developing your skills in skimming for new ideas or scanning to pick up specific content.

Series V
Idea Reading Exercises

Series V is made up of short articles from which you are to pick up the main ideas or basic themes as quickly as possible. On these you should apply your techniques of *idea reading* to attain maximum rates with only a general comprehension of the more basic ideas being presented. Primary emphasis in this series is on the extension of your upper limits in reading rate.

Series VI
Exploratory Reading Exercises

The sixth series is composed of readings of longer length and greater complexity. They provide practice in *exploratory reading*. In these exercises you develop skill in reading at a fairly rapid rate, while concentrating for greater detail in terms of general content and ideas, rather than specific facts.

Series VII
Study Reading Exercises

Here you must stop and *think* to answer questions at intervals in your reading. The basic purpose is to demonstrate how rapidly material can be covered even when you take time out for thinking and answering questions. Although not an exact duplication of the *study* reading, in which you develop idea outlines, these drills will provide an objective comparison of this type of reading. You can develop skills in reading shorter units more intensively and in interrupting your reading with short periods of thinking and note making. These exercises provide opportunities for application of alternating patterns of studying: think . . . read . . . think . . . write . . . think . . . read . . . think . . . write . . . and so forth.

Series VIII
Critical Thinking Exercises

Here you must think critically about all of the materials presented to you. Exercises are identified only by a number, and you have to try to detect the purpose and intent, author bias or propaganda, and attempt at emotional appeal. Emphasis here is not on rate, but on the quality of your thinking skill in dealing with unidentified material.

Computing Scores and Recording Progress

On each exercise throughout the book, you are to record time, rate, comprehension, and efficiency. Tables are provided for looking up your reading rates. Each exercise refers you to the table for rates for that exercise.

Keys for scoring exercises are located in the back of the workbook. After computing the comprehension and efficiency scores, you should compare these with scores on other exercises to determine your progress. Progress charts are provided on page 297 of this book to record your scores on each reading exercise. Keeping these progress charts up-to-date will help motivate you to try for continued improvement. Supplementary reading from longer exercises, such as those in *Maintaining Reading Efficiency* (30), will help you to establish more effective reading habits.

On the page preceding each series of exercises, you will find instructions and illustrations of the type of work to be done in that series and further suggestions about the purpose and use of that material.

Setting Personal Goals

As you move through each series, you can help motivate yourself by setting goals of consistent improvement. Before starting a new exercise, look back at the time on the previous one in that series, and try to cut your time a little bit.

You probably will find that your comprehension scores remain fairly constant as you increase your rate gradually. Errors in comprehension should be used to help expand your vocabulary. You *will not* automatically increase your comprehension by slowing down. Avoid the tendency to read more slowly whenever comprehension scores drop. Instead, go back and try to understand *why* you missed the specific items.

Effective use of these exercises should enable you to increase your reading speed at the same time that you are increasing your vocabulary and improving your skill in concentration.

VI
Selected References

1. Adams, W. Royce. *Developing Reading Versatility*, 2nd ed. New York: Holt, Rinehart and Winston, 1977.

2. Adams, W. Royce. *Increasing Reading Speed.* London: The Macmillan Company, 1969.

3. Adams, W. Royce. *Reading Beyond Words.* New York: Holt, Rinehart and Winston, 1978.

4. Bandt, Phillip L.; Naomi M. Meara; and Lyle D. Schmidt. *A Time to Learn.* New York: Holt, Rinehart and Winston, 1974.

5. Bird, Charles, and Dorothy M. Bird. *Learning More by Effective Study.* New York: Appleton-Century-Crofts, 1945.

6. Brown, James I. *Efficient Reading.* Boston: D. C. Heath and Company, 1952, 1965.

7. Carman, Robert A., and W. Royce Adams. *Study Skills.* New York: John Wiley & Sons, 1972.

8. Carothers, Robert L. *Strategy: An Academic Survival Kit.* Dubuque, Iowa: Kendall/Hunt Publishing Company, 1974, 1977.

9. Causey, Oscar S., ed. *Exploring the Levels of College Reading Programs.* Ft. Worth, Tex.: Texas Christian University Press, 1956.

10. Causey, Oscar S., ed. *Techniques and Procedures in College and Adult Reading Programs.* Ft. Worth, Tex.: Texas Christian University Press, 1957.

11. Causey, Oscar S. *The Reading Teacher's Reader.* New York: The Ronald Press Company, 1958.

12. Davis, Nancy B. *Basic Vocabulary Skills.* New York: McGraw-Hill Book Company, 1969.

13. Earle, Richard A. (editor). *Classroom Practice In Reading.* Newark, Delaware: International Reading Association, 1977.

14. Flesch, Rudolph. *The Art of Readable Writing.* New York: Harper & Row, Publishers, 1949.

15. Fry, Edward B. *Reading Drills for Speed and Comprehension.* Providence, R.I.: Jamestown Publishers, 1975.

16. Gerow, Joshua R., and R. Douglas Ling. *How to Succeed in College.* New York: Charles Scribner's Sons, 1975.

17. Hess, Karen M.; Robert E. Shafer; and Lanny E. Morreau. *Developing Reading Efficiency.* New York: John Wiley, & Sons, 1975.

18. Hook, Lucyle, and Mary Virginia Gaver. *The Research Paper,* 4th ed. Englewood Cliffs, N.J.: Prentice-Hall, 1952, 1969.

19. Joffe, Irwin L. *Developing Vocabulary Skills.* Belmont, Calif.: Wadsworth Publishing Company, 1971.

20. Joffe, Irwin L. *Finding Main Ideas.* Belmont. Calif.: Wadsworth Publishing Company, 1970.

21. Joffe, Irwin L. *Opportunity for Skillful Reading.* Belmont, Calif.: Wadsworth Publishing Company, 1970.

22. Klaeser, Barbara MacKnick. *Reading Improvement: A Complete Course for Increasing Speed and Comprehension.* Chicago, Ill.: Nelson-Hall, 1977.

23. Klein, Howard A. *The Quest for Competency in Teaching Reading.* Newark, Delaware: International Reading Association, 1972.

24. Locke, Edwin A. *A Guide to Effective Study.* New York: Springer Publishing Company, 1975.

25. Maxwell, Martha J. *Skimming and Scanning Improvement.* New York: McGraw-Hill Book Company, 1969.

26. Merritt, John E. (editor). *New Horizons In Reading.* Newark, Delaware: International Reading Association, 1976.

27. Miller, Lyle L. *Developing Reading Efficiency.* Rev. ed. Minneapolis: Burgess Publishing Company, 1967, 1972.

28. Miller, Lyle L. *Increasing Reading Efficiency.* New York: Holt, Rinehart and Winston, 1956, 1964, 1970, 1977.

29. Miller, Lyle L. *Maintaining Reading Efficiency.* Rev. ed. Laramie, Wyo.: Developmental Reading Distributors, 1962, 1967, 1973, 1978.

30. Miller, Lyle L. *Maintaining Reading Efficiency Tests.* Laramie, Wyo.: Developmental Reading Distributors, 1967, 1970.

31. Miller, Lyle L. *Personalizing Reading Efficiency.* Minneapolis: Burgess Publishing Company, 1976.

32. Miller, Lyle L. *Speed Reading in the Seventies.* Educational Leadership, Vol. 30, No. 7, 623-627.

33. Miller, Lyle L. *Teaching Efficient Reading Skills.* Minneapolis: Burgess Publishing Company, 1972 (A revision of *Accelerating Growth in Reading Efficiency).*

34. Miller, Lyle L., and Alice Z. Seeman. *Guidebook for Prospective Teachers.* Columbus, Ohio: The Ohio State University Press, 1948.

35. New York State Personnel and Guidance Association. *Tips to Improve Personal Study Skills.* Albany, N.Y.: Delmar Publishers, 1968.

36. Nielsen, Duane M., and Howard F. Hjelm. *Reading and Career Education.* Newark, Delaware: International Reading Association, 1975.

37. Norman, Maxwell H. *Successful Reading: Key to Our Dynamic Society,* 2nd ed. New York: Holt, Rinehart and Winston, 1975.

38. Panes, Paul B. *Reading the Textbook: Practice for Improvement in Subject Matter Areas.* New York: Thomas Y. Crowell Company, 1972.

39. Pauk, Walter, and Josephine Wilson. *Reading for Facts.* New York: David McKay Company, 1974.

40. Pauk, Walter, and Josephine Wilson. *Reading for Ideas.* New York: David McKay Company, 1974.

41. Piercey, Dorothy, *Reading Activities in Content Areas: An Idea Book for Middle and Secondary Schools.* Boston, Mass.: Allyn & Bacon Inc., 1976.

42. Raygor, Alton L. *Reading for the Main Idea.* New York: McGraw-Hill Book Company, 1969.

43. Raygor, Alton L. *Reading for Significant Facts.* New York: McGraw-Hill Book Company, 1970.

44. Raygor, Alton L., and George B. Schick. *Reading at Efficient Rates.* New York: McGraw-Hill Book Company, 1970.

45. Rinsland, Henry D. *A Basic Vocabulary for Elementary School Children.* New York: The MacMillian Company, 1945.

46. Robinson, Francis P. *Effective Study.* New York: Harper & Row, Publishers, 1946 1961, 1970.

47. Spargo, Edward. *Selections from the Black.* Providence, R.I.: Jamestown Publishers, 1970.

48. Spargo, Edward, *The Now Student.* Providence, R.I.: Jamestown Publishers, 1971.

49. Spargo, Edward. *Topics for the Restless.* Providence, R.I.: Jamestown Publishers, 1974.

50. Strang, Edward; James A. Giroux; and Livia J. Giroux. *Voices from the Bottom.* Providence, R.I.: Jamestown Publishers, 1972.

51. Stroud, James B., and Robert B. Ammons. *Improving Reading Ability.* New York: Appleton-Century-Crofts, 1949; 3rd ed. 1970.

52. Thomas, Ellen Lamar, and H. Alan Robinson. *Improving Reading in Every Class.* Boston: Allyn and Bacon, 1972, 1977.

53. Thorndike, Edward L. *The Teacher's Word Book.* New York: Bureau of Publications, Teacher's College, Columbia University, 1921.

54. Thorndike, Edward L., and Irving Lorge. *The Teacher's Word Book of 30,000 Words.* New York: Bureau of Publications, Teacher's College, Columbia University, 1944.

55. Walter, Tim and Al Siebert, *Student Success: How to Be A Better Student and Still Have Time for Your Friends.* New York: Holt, Rinehart and Winston, 1976.

56. Wood, Nancy V. *College Reading and Study Skills.* New York: Holt, Rinehart and Winston, 1978.

SERIES I
Word Recognition Exercises

Instructions

Series I exercises are designed to help you establish rhythmic habits of eye movement. The exercises are of equal difficulty, and you should be able to reduce the time necessary to complete them quite rapidly. Keep practicing on them until you are able to complete an exercise in 20 seconds or less.

In these exercises are two columns of words, one with a single word and the other with five words. The first column contains the key word. On each line this key word is repeated somewhere among the five words in the other columns. You are to locate this identical word as rapidly as possible and underline or check it. Then you proceed to the next line and so on till you have finished. As soon as you have finished, raise your hand, and the instructor will give you your time in seconds. Record this time. and look up your rate in the table on page 307. (Find your time in Column I, and then look in Column II for your rate.)

Next go back, and check your work to see if you have marked any words that were not identical with the key. Count your errors, and record them at the bottom of the exercise. Compute your comprehension by multiplying the number of correct answers by four (4). Compute your reading efficiency on this exercise by multiplying the rate you secured from the table by this comprehension score. Round off the efficiency score to the nearest whole number. Record both the rate and the efficiency on the Progress Chart for Word Recognition Exercises on page 297.

These exercises begin on page 31; rate tables are on page 307; progress charts are on page 297.

EXAMPLE

. . . .

22. six		six	hexagon	fix	kiss	sex
23. oxen		often	toxin	shown	oxen	boxes
24. rite	X	kite	ritual	right	rate	rite
25. were		ware	we're	were	wear	went

Time 32 Sec. RATE (from table on page 307): R. 281

No. Correct: 24 COMPREHENSION (4% for each correct answer): (4 × 24) C. 96

I-O EFFICIENCY (R × C): (281 × .96) = 269.76 E. 270

Suggestions

Although the primary purpose of this type of reading exercise is to break up old habits of rigid use of eye muscles and to develop rapid rhythmic eye movements, there is also an aspect of logical reasoning and sound study skill application that you may begin to apply.

The practice of speeded recognition of exact duplicates in words tends to reduce the thinking process requirements and to allow one to concentrate on eye movements.

You might want to consider this as a game in quick recognition of symbols, however, and begin to apply some logical thinking to the activity. Man lives in a world of symbols and must learn to identify quickly a wide variety of items by size, shape, color, or location in relationship to other symbols. Thus we can "read" a highway sign by its shape long before we actually can see the words on it. We often can tell what brand of gasoline a station sells by the shape of its signs long before we can make out the words on those signs. Symbols help us to select our food, clothing, and recreational activities. Words are only verbal symbols, and we learn to recognize and use many of them as such without question or without deep thought process.

If this were a game in which you had to find boxes of an appropriate shape to pack something in, you would apply many skills once developed to help you in early learning experiences. Size and shape would be most important to you in selection. Although you cannot read words while your eyes are moving, you can form some impressions of size and shape. If you have a particular size and shape in mind, a word will sometimes seem to stand out from a group for you. The secret is in knowing what you are looking for so you can recognize it when you find it!

Let us consider the word in the first column as a symbol that we need to pack in the right size box. If we study it carefully as to size, shape, and unique irregularities in form, then we have some idea of what we need to look for in our "box pile" in the other column. A quick scan eliminates several of our choices because they obviously are too large or too small. So we have only one or two that have possibilities and that we might look at more carefully. A quick glance is often enough to convince us that one will do or will not do, and we quickly narrow our choice to the specific one that will fit our key word exactly. When we find the box that fits it perfectly, we do not have to search further.

Even if we did not understand meaning of words, we could still play this matching game with verbal symbols. Let us consider the basic rules of the game:

(1) Concentrate first on the key symbol to be matched. Form a visual image of its appearance, its size, shape, and specific characteristics. Know what you are looking for!

(2) Scan the answer section quickly for possible matching materials. Sometimes the perfect match will stand out clearly and can be identified without detailed searching. If not, the scanning at least eliminates some choices that obviously do not fit.

(3) Look individually at those most likely prospects identified in the scanning. Mentally match each one to your key, and discard it quickly if it does not fit.

(4) Concentrate on your key symbol and matching it. Do not take time to study in detail all of the five choices. When you have found the match for the key symbol, *stop* your search. There is no point in looking at other empty boxes when you have already selected the right one for your key symbol.

Even simple exercises like these can be more than visual activity. Routine reading process is more than eye movement and word recognition. It can be a challenge to logical thinking as well. Time spent in thinking and establishing goals can pay off in quick identification and selection from the alternatives presented. Scanning as a rapid reading technique is effective only if you *think first* and have some idea you are seeking. You can use these exercises to help develop your goal-setting and scanning skills.

Reading can be fun if you think ahead and plan as you read.

Exercise I-1

1.	beets	beast	beach	beetle	write	beets	
2.	civil	meat	civilize	civil	evil	civic	
3.	desert	desire	desert	design	resist	shoe	
4.	fabric	facilities	facetious	ruin	fabric	fable	
5.	gun	sun	foil	gum	gun	gunny	
6.	supply	super	support	supplemented	minister	supply	
7.	miner	concern	miner	diner	mine	mineral	
8.	pebble	pebble	peddle	double	medal	dose	
9.	redder	fish	reddish	gladder	redder	reduce	
10.	shrub	grub	tangled	shrub	scrub	rub	
11.	valves	vacuum	valves	annoyed	unusually	falcon	
12.	unwise	awhile	untie	objects	sail	unwise	
13.	begone	forgot	beware	bigger	begone	friend	
14.	clasp	clasp	head	clap	chap	class	
15.	cheat	cheaper	photo	cheat	check	chess	
16.	deer	dear	beard	dare	ever	deer	
17.	hadn't	haven't	hadn't	habit	sign	aren't	
18.	need	need	rose	meet	seed	mean	
19.	minus	minute	plus	case	minus	minor	
20.	peg	leg	pug	peg	few	pig	
21.	refer	reference	confers	dealt	differ	refer	
22.	ranger	ranger	rancher	ransom	ranking	medal	
23.	tape	tap	tape	stun	taper	ape	
24.	six	six	kiss	text	sixth	sized	
25.	we're	ware	let's	we're	were	we've	

Time __________ Sec. RATE (from table on page 307): R. __________

No. Errors __________ COMPREHENSION (100 − 4% for each Error): C. __________

I-1 EFFICIENCY (R × C): E. __________

Record on Progress Chart on page 297

Exercise I-2

1.	adopt	adapt	adopt	arrange	goal	adoption
2.	bellow	bell	bowl	peal	bellow	belt
3.	blink	light	oblige	punch	blink	blind
4.	devout	devour	vault	devout	pout	about
5.	race	face	false	chase	ridge	race
6.	hammer	manner	stammer	hammer	midst	pound
7.	job	rough	job	bog	jig	sob
8.	he'd	held	she's	he	he'd	would
9.	per	per	perch	stir	pet	pert
10.	pillar	piling	pillow	pillar	pill	coarse
11.	smelt	felt	rode	smell	melt	smelt
12.	thine	time	thine	forest	thing	thin
13.	he'll	she	hell	held	he'll	we'll
14.	bent	bent	broad	scent	regard	tent
15.	closet	cabinet	closed	tabby	clothes	closet
16.	mud	muddy	dumb	mud	bud	muddle
17.	fatal	fatal	fertile	fated	frost	total
18.	hath	hop	joy	hole	haste	hath
19.	jolly	jelly	jolly	holly	haste	jam
20.	mitten	hidden	smith	mitten	often	more
21.	pirate	pistol	jersey	pilot	pirate	rate
22.	sneak	ratify	sneak	neat	snake	sneeze
23.	sinner	fully	almost	singer	awful	sinner
24.	teeth	beneath	teen	aback	teeth	teeter
25.	villain	villain	void	silly	tell	house

Time __________ Sec. RATE (from table on page 307): R. __________

No. Errors __________ COMPREHENSION (100 – 4% for each Error): C. __________

I-2 EFFICIENCY (R × C): E. __________

Record on Progress Chart on page 297

Exercise I-3

1.	abuse	bruise	cord	abuse	bus	about
2.	betray	betray	take	better	trace	rush
3.	germ	fish	stern	worm	germ	gem
4.	dictate	delta	dirt	dictate	rain	dish
5.	scrap	band	scrub	rap	scrap	scrape
6.	harbor	hardy	harbor	lot	harrow	marry
7.	jumped	mumble	defect	jungle	rumble	jumped
8.	studious	studious	study	extra	stub	studio
9.	attain	sustain	rock	attain	attend	attach
10.	cast	caste	fast	casting	true	cast
11.	cycle	bicycle	cycle	master	cylinder	cyclone
12.	gill	sill	girl	gift	gill	silk
13.	pulp	pulp	pulse	pup	pulley	town
14.	beyond	below	beyond	yonder	frost	bead
15.	cog	cog	fog	cob	many	got
16.	dirt	skirt	funny	ditty	direct	dirt
17.	fellow	simple	fell	long	fellow	felt
18.	haste	last	haste	mask	nasty	aster
19.	jury	hurry	junk	jury	junior	fix
20.	monkey	monkey	key	money	monarchy	skunk
21.	style	mess	study	stiffly	stylish	style
22.	remove	remote	remnant	remove	move	take
23.	wager	bet	wages	wag	wager	wagon
24.	ten	tend	ten	bend	pen	acre
25.	volume	rescue	voluntary	volley	loom	volume

Time __________ Sec. RATE (from table on page 307): R. __________

No. Errors __________ COMPREHENSION (100 – 4% for each Error): C. __________

I-3 EFFICIENCY (R × C): E. __________

Record on Progress Chart on page 297

Exercise I-4

1.	awe	stop	awe	aware	awake	await	
2.	bog	log	boggy	bog	affect	dog	
3.	blew	escort	drew	screw	topped	blew	
4.	ditch	ditty	ditch	witch	mansion	itch	
5.	flash	moral	flake	flash	lash	flask	
6.	herd	curd	heard	hero	herd	bird	
7.	masses	masses	stock	massive	mash	master	
8.	sullen	pouch	sulk	sulky	sultry	sullen	
9.	plane	true	pane	plane	lane	plain	
10.	babe	baboon	babble	mercy	babe	baby	
11.	sober	sobering	sober	bolder	cold	sob	
12.	fetch	fetch	civil	etc.	catching	catch	
13.	goody	good	scorch	goodly	goose	goody	
14.	bonnet	sonny	bonbons	bonnet	risk	bone	
15.	racer	racer	race	eraser	south	tracer	
16.	dizzy	disease	forth	divide	dizzy	fuzzy	
17.	fleece	meeting	fleece	flee	fleet	feet	
18.	sunny	summon	summary	verbal	sunken	sunny	
19.	lard	lard	land	lord	hard	roll	
20.	master	mustard	master	access	must	busted	
21.	wean	wear	bean	luxury	weak	wean	
22.	severely	severely	severe	message	very	review	
23.	solder	rescue	older	solder	soldier	sold	
24.	thump	thumb	under	hum	hump	thump	
25.	weekly	meekly	weak	week	weekly	read	

Time __________ Sec.	RATE (from table on page 307):	R. __________
No. Errors __________	COMPREHENSION (100 – 4% for each Error):	C. __________
I-4	EFFICIENCY (R × C):	E. __________

Record on Progress Chart on page 297

Exercise I-5

	Key word					
1.	anybody	anybody	mixing	anywhere	anyhow	nobody
2.	bumper	twist	bundle	bumper	bunches	bumblebee
3.	cottage	cotton	phrase	luggage	cottage	cot
4.	easily	eagerly	easily	easy	surgeon	ease
5.	freight	lowland	freighter	eight	free	freight
6.	harmful	harmful	saddles	healthful	hurt	hurry
7.	liver	living	livery	liver	live	candy
8.	notebook	cookbook	lockers	note	notebook	noted
9.	preamble	preach	precious	township	preamble	precede
10.	saber	saver	safer	sober	wing	saber
11.	stable	staff	vain	stable	stage	tag
12.	trespass	trellis	trespass	road	trestle	trespasser
13.	apple	apple	appeal	apparent	misery	appear
14.	burner	force	burn	bureau	burner	bunnies
15.	couple	coupled	reserve	coupon	coupe	couple
16.	edged	edition	edged	yank	edge	editor
17.	frighten	fright	hairpin	freighter	afraid	frighten
18.	iceberg	ice	iceman	iceberg	cooking	icebox
19.	lock	lock	locker	idle	loft	local
20.	novel	sucker	novel	noble	nourishing	novelty
21.	sailboat	iceman	macaroni	sailboat	sailor	soil
22.	staple	staple	mixture	stable	table	fable
23.	triumph	triumphant	triumph	mulberry	trial	triumphal
24.	worry	hurry	stock	worldly	scurry	worry
25.	preservation	presentation	prevention	journalistic	preservation	reservation

Time __________ Sec. RATE (from table on page 307): R. __________

No. Errors __________ COMPREHENSION (100 – 4% for each Error): C. __________

I-5 EFFICIENCY (R × C): E. __________

Record on Progress Chart on page 297

Exercise I-6

1.	action	fraction	action	fact	act	actor
2.	colt	coax	jolt	colt	cotton	mother
3.	discard	discuss	cord	discourage	discard	office
4.	feud	turn	feud	feudal	fuel	rude
5.	heard	heard	heap	hearse	fording	cheap
6.	kettle	settle	kernel	kettle	kitchen	morning
7.	scope	mop	hope	shop	rather	scope
8.	report	sent	report	repose	pine	reprove
9.	sled	led	slowed	lead	sled	moist
10.	theater	theater	thaw	heater	theatrical	fooling
11.	actress	mess	die	actress	adventuress	address
12.	blank	blast	lower	blink	last	blank
13.	disguise	disgust	nesting	dish	discuss	disguise
14.	fifteen	sixteen	purple	fifth	fifteen	teens
15.	heap	leap	heap	heart	heaven	chair
16.	kinder	kindness	counts	hindered	kind	kinder
17.	mosquito	moss	faintly	mosquito	quite	mosque
18.	picker	lost	picker	picnic	wicker	pick
19.	regret	regret	regular	regard	great	grindstone
20.	sling	slang	sing	sling	slant	force
21.	therein	therefore	in	fiddle	therein	wherein
22.	wander	warmer	warden	warm	course	wander
23.	comforter	comforter	blanket	fortune	comfort	fort
24.	philosophic	philosophy	microscopic	physiology	philosophic	earnestness
25.	birthright	birthright	daintiness	right	birthplace	birthday

Time ________ Sec.	RATE (from table on page 307):	R. ________
No. Errors ________	COMPREHENSION (100 − 4% for each Error):	C. ________
I-6	EFFICIENCY (R × C):	E. ________

Record on Progress Chart on page 297

Exercise I-7

1.	brand	brand	ran	branch	student	brandy
2.	doz.	mature	dozen	doz.	buzz	box
3.	foolish	cool	fracture	fooling	foot	foolish
4.	holder	hole	holder	letter	hold	older
5.	ledge	led	ledger	perform	ledge	edge
6.	necklace	necktie	neck	necklace	jailer	lace
7.	polite	polite	politic	light	polish	depart
8.	rite	ivory	rite	right	kite	might
9.	spade	valve	space	paid	span	spade
10.	alphabet	alfalfa	alphabet	faintness	allegiance	allay
11.	breath	breath	breathe	council	beneath	breast
12.	drawback	drawer	heading	back	draw	drawback
13.	fore	mat	four	ore	fore	forty
14.	honest	modest	hornet	honest	honey	punch
15.	leisure	leisure	pairing	leisurely	exposure	sure
16.	negative	drain	neigh	neglect	neither	negative
17.	pony	pond	pony	pooh	purely	smug
18.	robe	robes	oboe	toxin	rob	robe
19.	special	special	serial	perfect	judicial	specialize
20.	tonight	tight	verses	tonight	tone	night
21.	whoever	whatever	whom	twenty	whoever	who
22.	consume	horseback	museum	consume	consul	resume
23.	tolerable	trouble	tolerate	tolerable	review	total
24.	consolation	journalistic	consolation	consonant	consolidated	solon
25.	allowance	masterful	allows	allowance	lowly	alloy

Time __________ Sec. RATE (from table on page 307): R. __________

No. Errors __________ COMPREHENSION (100 – 4% for each Error): C. __________

I-7 EFFICIENCY (R × C): E. __________

Record on Progress Chart on page 297

Exercise I-8

1.	audience	science	authority	quadrant	audience	auditorium
2.	caught	cavern	caught	causing	fish	caution
3.	damn	damn	damsel	prince	dam	damp
4.	entrust	entrance	trust	entrust	jackass	enter
5.	glassy	glassy	grateful	locality	glass	glassware
6.	influence	inflame	gossip	audience	influence	influenza
7.	mare	care	mare	halter	hare	margin
8.	purity	purify	jurist	pure	destroy	purity
9.	suitable	suckle	suit	snatch	suitable	suites
10.	celery	celery	celebrity	celebrate	salary	plant
11.	daring	dare	punch	darning	darling	daring
12.	modern	modern	molder	moist	rating	mole
13.	glory	sorry	energy	glory	gloria	grate
14.	initial	initiate	initial	milestone	initiative	injury
15.	marrow	fact	maroon	tomorrow	marrow	marry
16.	oven	over	make	oxen	oval	oven
17.	quake	quack	fuse	quake	quick	wake
18.	seems	seemingly	seems	seer	muzzle	see
19.	universe	universe	union	occupancy	unit	universal
20.	warmth	warmly	warm	warn	destiny	warmth
21.	sufferer	suffrage	stuffed	sufficient	sufferer	contacting
22.	automobile	autumn	auto	automobile	suet	automatic
23.	unhappy	unharness	unhappy	originality	uphill	happy
24.	secondary	stand	secede	second	primary	secondary
25.	outline	outlaw	line	outline	moldboard	outlet

Time __________ Sec. RATE (from table on page 307): R. __________

No. Errors __________ COMPREHENSION (100 − 4% for each Error): C. __________

I-8 EFFICIENCY (R × C): E. __________

Record on Progress Chart on page 297

Exercise I-9

1.	angry	angry	finish	anger	angel	argue
2.	brownie	brow	brownie	bruise	brown	courage
3.	coo	cook	coax	clue	coo	sue
4.	duration	durable	horseman	duration	during	double
5.	fountain	fountain	foundation	neither	founder	fought
6.	howl	troll	fowl	record	you'll	howl
7.	lilac	lick	prime	like	lilac	lily
8.	nobility	section	nobility	nobody	mobility	noble
9.	pour	pout	pound	sphinx	pouch	pour
10.	ruby	ruby	rubber	ruddy	silk	rub
11.	spot	next	spoke	spot	spoil	spout
12.	annual	courage	annoy	announce	annual	annually
13.	bud	bed	bud	lion	budget	buddy
14.	core	corn	cork	core	corner	each
15.	swollen	swollen	next	swell	swing	swept
16.	linoleum	linseed	scorch	lingered	linen	linoleum
17.	noontide	noodle	midnight	noontide	fertile	noonday
18.	preacher	preacher	preamble	preaching	tombstone	reach
19.	stump	such	stumble	lump	stump	roam
20.	spun	revive	spun	sprung	spur	sun
21.	trash	rash	trash	track	paper	trace
22.	woke	wolf	walk	kink	wake	woke
23.	humankind	mankind	humankind	human	disgust	humane
24.	framework	housework	stronghold	frame	framework	franchise
25.	transformer	horseradish	transfer	torment	transmit	transformer

---

Time __________ Sec. | RATE (from table on page 307): | R. __________

No. Errors __________ | COMPREHENSION (100 – 4% for each Error): | C. __________

I-9 | EFFICIENCY (R × C): | E. __________

Record on Progress Chart on page 297

Exercise I-10

1.	ambition	ambulance	ambition	ambitious	hurrying	amber
2.	brighten	brighten	anchored	bright	bring	light
3.	drip	hook	drift	dripped	drip	trip
4.	forgave	forgive	drills	forage	gave	forgave
5.	hornet	horn	hornet	honest	figure	horse
6.	level	level	lever	shelve	levy	levee
7.	postal	port	hemp	post	postal	postage
8.	romp	romp	stump	purple	roam	jump
9.	sphere	horrible	sphere	spill	sphinx	here
10.	tortoise	tortillas	torpedo	tortoise	famous	torture
11.	trample	tramp	sample	future	trouble	trample
12.	broaden	board	secure	road	broaden	broad
13.	force	forged	riding	fore	forth	force
14.	hostile	occupant	hosteler	host	hostile	fierce
15.	lid	fly	lie	lied	did	lid
16.	nickel	nasty	nickel	pickle	sickle	nick
17.	postage	posture	comment	postal	age	postage
18.	rosette	rose	phrase	rosette	rosy	rosin
19.	spite	room	spit	pit	spite	spice
20.	trace	trace	train	track	race	trachea
21.	windy	kindly	windy	window	wind	winged
22.	drunkard	drunkard	goggles	drunk	drinking	sunken
23.	contraction	contract	subtraction	contraction	delight	contrast
24.	nevertheless	whenever	lettuce	nevertheless	unless	never
25.	contentment	contempt	tenement	contentment	content	hieroglyphic

---

Time ________ Sec.	RATE (from table on page 307):	R. ________
No. Errors ________	COMPREHENSION (100 − 4% for each Error):	C. ________
I-10	EFFICIENCY (R × C):	E. ________

Record on Progress Chart on page 297

Exercise I-11

1.	aisle	air	island	first	isle	aisle
2.	bosom	handsome	ran	boss	bosom	some
3.	domestic	enthusiastic	rolling	dome	domestic	artistic
4.	flop	flop	crop	flow	float	ruler
5.	hillside	beside	hilly	fatal	hill	hillside
6.	lava	lavatory	lava	have	slave	mason
7.	helpless	helpless	helpful	harmless	help	cutter
8.	plow	plod	slow	plow	plot	too
9.	riches	muse	ditches	rickety	riches	rice
10.	somewhat	eighteen	what	some	somewhere	somewhat
11.	timber	timber	eager	limber	time	climber
12.	alert	ale	alert	apart	alarm	mercy
13.	bouquet	shortly	bouquet	boast	croquet	book
14.	does	pretty	dose	does	lose	dust
15.	fluid	fluid	flush	lurid	remain	flute
16.	lea	leaf	lea	flea	blaze	leave
17.	active	horse	activity	active	native	detective
18.	sorry	sorrow	sorry	morrow	sore	today
19.	tip	in	lip	tip	top	tipped
20.	whenever	topple	whichever	whatever	whenever	ever
21.	rightful	headache	rifle	rightly	harmful	rightful
22.	pneumonia	pneumonia	riot	ammonia	pneumatic	monitor
23.	historian	historical	hitched	history	monarch	historian
24.	congressional	congress	confusion	professional	congressional	share
25.	confusion	confused	notion	confusion	confess	confessed

Time __________ Sec.	RATE (from table on page 307):	R. __________
No. Errors __________	COMPREHENSION (100 − 4% for each Error):	C. __________
I-11	EFFICIENCY (R × C):	E. __________

Record on Progress Chart on page 297

Exercise I-12

	Key word					
1.	button	button	butler	suit	buttons	butter
2.	cowpox	bulls	coward	slip	cowboy	cowpox
3.	fruitful	fruit	looking	frugal	fruitful	frightful
4.	illustrate	ill	pose	sill	illustrate	illness
5.	loom	school	loom	loon	look	loan
6.	oaken	oaken	type	oxen	oak	oarlocks
7.	prick	prickly	medal	price	pick	prick
8.	sample	noose	trample	sample	simple	maples
9.	starve	carves	stale	staff	starve	perch
10.	truant	truck	truant	ring	truss	true
11.	harbor	scare	labor	harbor	pardon	arbitration
12.	calm	calmly	almanac	gold	palm	calm
13.	crash	crash	rash	mash	crater	smash
14.	eldest	roost	elderly	oldest	eldest	elder
15.	lovable	trouble	force	lovable	lovely	able
16.	cure	niece	curly	curious	curb	cure
17.	printer	start	prince	pint	printer	princely
18.	sandy	sandal	sandy	sundial	task	sand
19.	stem	stem	stern	steak	steep	corral
20.	tube	tubing	ebb	tube	tuck	tub
21.	wring	mate	whether	wither	with	wring
22.	immediate	immediate	occupants	medical	intermediate	immediately
23.	fundamental	funding	fundamental	presence	mental	funnel
24.	efficient	posterity	efficient	profits	effective	efficiency
25.	appreciation	apprentice	painful	appreciation	depression	appreciate

---

Time __________ Sec. | RATE (from table on page 307): | R. __________

No. Errors __________ | COMPREHENSION (100 – 4% for each Error): | C. __________

I-12 | EFFICIENCY (R × C): | E. __________

Record on Progress Chart on page 297

Exercise I-13

1.	bawl	tour	bowl	bale	bald	bawl
2.	chord	chord	foot	chore	choice	chorus
3.	denies	dens	denies	dense	punctual	denote
4.	explode	explore	expect	monkeys	explode	express
5.	groove	groove	gross	grove	root	salad
6.	irrigate	irradiate	irritate	tragic	irrigate	gate
7.	mid	mild	invite	middle	mix	mid
8.	paster	paste	paster	pantry	pasture	cord
9.	shingle	shining	shingle	treaty	single	shingles
10.	swim	taxi	swam	skim	swim	twin
11.	varies	varies	varied	variety	various	skating
12.	beaten	sweater	leaden	beater	mice	beaten
13.	churn	church	more	churn	chum	curl
14.	deposit	despise	deposit	depot	withdraw	dispose
15.	extent	tent	extensive	content	extent	opposite
16.	itch	itch	rip	ache	scratch	fetch
17.	mild	supper	mold	mild	milk	mill
18.	pattern	lantern	potter	patter	cushion	pattern
19.	shore	fork	short	shore	shown	shute
20.	vein	vain	vein	feat	veined	prop
21.	wig	met	wag	wig	fig	fiber
22.	synopsis	synopsis	ringing	symphony	symbol	mental
23.	recognition	reception	recognized	reckless	recognition	sanitation
24.	guarantee	warrants	guarded	guardian	vicinity	guarantee
25.	recede	samples	capture	recede	recess	raced

Time __________ Sec. RATE (from table on page 307): R. __________

No. Errors __________ COMPREHENSION (100 – 4% for each Error): C. __________

I-13 EFFICIENCY (R × C): E. __________

Record on Progress Chart on page 297

Exercise I-14

1.	camera	camels	camera	trust	camel	came
2.	creed	creed	creek	cried	creep	erase
3.	elm	ton	elk	alms	emblem	elm
4.	gag	gait	horse	gag	gadget	fade
5.	lukewarm	lumber	lukewarm	luckily	warm	vacancy
6.	o'clock	since	ocean	occurs	ooze	o'clock
7.	product	product	vulgar	produce	producers	productive
8.	satchel	satin	satisfy	satchel	sash	impose
9.	stir	handle	stirrup	skin	stir	stare
10.	turnip	turnpike	skip	turn	urn	turnip
11.	artist	missing	artist	ignorant	arrow	artistic
12.	canned	canner	yacht	canned	cannon	canyon
13.	criminal	crime	crisis	trucking	criminal	crimson
14.	emerald	emerald	empire	herald	head	emerged
15.	galore	allows	galore	gallon	gallop	trussel
16.	official	officially	vicinity	offices	official	office
17.	savage	serve	saves	crouch	savage	save
18.	stork	full	stork	strew	store	tore
19.	twist	aspen	twice	rill	twine	twist
20.	yoke	bore	yolk	yoke	woke	you'd
21.	progressive	progressive	acceptance	program	aggressions	progress
22.	luxuries	screwing	luxury	sundown	luxurious	luxuries
23.	impossible	impose	finishing	impossible	improbable	probable
24.	impervious	impatiently	sticking	imperial	impervious	imperfect
25.	armistice	armistice	armchair	studiously	armory	arithmetic

Time __________ Sec. RATE (from table on page 307): R. __________

No. Errors __________ COMPREHENSION (100 – 4% for each Error): C. __________

I-14 EFFICIENCY (R × C): E. __________

Record on Progress Chart on page 297

Exercise I-15

1.	bargain	bargain	sacking	margin	barge	bargainer
2.	chest	quack	cheat	chest	chases	slit
3.	define	defend	dell	deny	mild	define
4.	execute	executive	execute	occupant	excite	example
5.	gravy	gravy	grow	gravity	grave	gravel
6.	mention	mental	mansion	attention	mention	element
7.	parch	parch	bib	porch	pouch	arch
8.	ratify	rattle	ratify	reduce	cart	railing
9.	utter	usher	bear	usual	utter	us
10.	bashful	bath	bashful	recount	baseball	basin
11.	chill	chili	still	hill	magnify	chill
12.	deliver	livery	silage	deliver	delirium	delay
13.	mess	mum	table	mass	mess	message
14.	readily	readiness	reading	salute	readily	ready
15.	sheer	afraid	teen	shine	sheep	sheer
16.	sweeper	sweeping	swim	sweeper	sweetly	treaties
17.	vagabond	vagabond	themes	valuable	vapor	vacuum
18.	whine	white	whittle	victim	whine	while
19.	intestine	phosphorus	interrupt	intestine	interval	intimate
20.	shaped	shamed	happened	quaint	shifted	shaped
21.	suspicious	roughness	suspect	suspicious	susceptible	suspicion
22.	exhibit	exhibit	exit	strolling	exhausted	exhibition
23.	greenish	tomahawk	greedy	greenhouse	reduced	greenish
24.	investment	inventor	investment	invention	invitation	vaccination
25.	partridge	partition	partridge	particular	yeoman	parted

Time ________ Sec.	RATE (from table on page 307):	R. ________
No. Errors ________	COMPREHENSION (100 – 4% for each Error):	C. ________
I-15	EFFICIENCY (R × C):	E. ________

Record on Progress Chart on page 297

Exercise I-16

1.	ashore	fruit	shore	ashes	aside	ashore
2.	capper	capes	near	capper	capital	capture
3.	cruel	cruel	crude	cruise	glowing	fuel
4.	employ	employer	employ	capable	empower	employee
5.	gas	gorge	gash	gasoline	gas	gasp
6.	made	madly	mademoiselle	exact	madam	made
7.	omen	omitted	men	amen	omen	exit
8.	scarlet	scarlet	scar	scanty	scarcely	purple
9.	ugly	win	fly	urge	glee	ugly
10.	assent	assent	ascend	consent	assist	accent
11.	carcass	direct	canteen	confess	carcass	canvas
12.	cube	cub	cubic	high	cube	tube
13.	gem	germ	gem	gee	gin	force
14.	string	strung	sting	coarse	string	ring
15.	virtue	vivid	virtue	eraser	vision	violins
16.	unceasing	uncertain	mechanical	increasing	cease	unceasing
17.	property	frijoles	property	proper	propose	propaganda
18.	inciting	incident	exciting	inciting	license	include
19.	scientific	scientist	scientific	filler	science	terrific
20.	magnify	sturdy	magnitude	magnificent	magnetic	magnify
21.	encounter	encounter	encyclopedia	counter	encourage	skylark
22.	prosperity	prospective	largest	prosperity	prosperous	property
23.	operation	operation	operator	observation	operate	industrial
24.	incurable	curable	indebted	incurable	touring	incubators
25.	strawberry	straw	blueberry	strawberry	raspberry	headlight

---

Time __________ Sec. RATE (from table on page 307): R. __________

No. Errors __________ COMPREHENSION (100 – 4% for each Error): C. __________

I-16 EFFICIENCY (R × C): E. __________

Record on Progress Chart on page 297

Exercise I-17

1.	afford	affair	carding	afford	affect	front
2.	certain	certain	risking	central	certainly	certificate
3.	daybreak	daylight	daytime	schedule	break	daybreak
4.	goddess	goddess	phrase	golden	gods	sadness
5.	inquiry	inquiries	inquiry	requires	wailing	injury
6.	overseer	oversee	overseer	critic	over	overshoe
7.	quicker	question	battery	quickly	quick	quicker
8.	reunion	review	fixing	reunite	union	reunion
9.	deadly	dealt	death	decayed	deadly	dearest
10.	matters	hatchery	mattress	butter	merry	matters
11.	conclude	include	conclusion	concise	conclude	yeast
12.	heroine	zero	dawn	heroine	heron	hero
13.	playground	barometer	playing	playhouse	ground	playground
14.	grave	gravy	grave	wanderer	gray	grate
15.	thrifty	thrifty	footprint	shiny	thrift	thrive
16.	murderous	vacuum	murmur	murder	murderous	hideous
17.	lamb	land	lame	lamb	undeveloped	lamed
18.	compress	compose	comrade	hen	compress	compromise
19.	unsettled	doubtfully	unselfish	settled	unseen	unsettled
20.	spectacular	spectacle	spectacular	entering	spectator	specter
21.	oxen	oxen	often	toxin	sown	box
22.	inspector	instance	spectator	touring	inspector	inspire
23.	chance	chant	change	chance	courtesy	changing
24.	unpleasant	unpack	unpleasant	pleasant	unruly	columnist
25.	sensation	sensation	sensitized	sentence	herald	intention

Time __________ Sec. RATE (from table on page 307): R. __________

No. Errors __________ COMPREHENSION (100 − 4% for each Error): C. __________

I-17 EFFICIENCY (R × C): E. __________

Record on Progress Chart on page 297

Exercise I-18

1.	carrying	carried	carrier	carriage	carrying	switch
2.	engrave	engrave	engine	engraving	ruling	engage
3.	sandman	mansion	sand	scarlet	sandman	man
4.	orchard	orchard	orchestra	orchid	ordeal	pencil
5.	prudent	prune	student	prowl	telephone	prudent
6.	feature	creature	feature	feat	federal	academies
7.	moisture	moist	mixture	moisture	peculiar	hoist
8.	underneath	underground	false	undertake	underneath	underline
9.	sixpence	expense	roofing	sixpence	sixteen	sixtieth
10.	enormous	enough	enormously	immense	courage	enormous
11.	tenement	tending	sentiment	parliament	tenement	extreme
12.	maniac	mandibles	manikin	recorder	manicure	maniac
13.	sculpture	scripture	sculpture	meaning	scurvy	scuffle
14.	permission	permission	perhaps	mission	persimmon	rolling
15.	skinny	shrimp	skirt	rescue	skinny	skin
16.	accordingly	accordingly	skate	across	cross	accord
17.	remainder	remain	remainder	extreme	reminder	schooling
18	persistence	persistence	pursue	persist	permit	backwoods
19.	undoubted	doubted	undo	undecided	undoubted	perfect
20.	originate	oriental	crowning	origin	original	originate
21.	excuses	exhaust	lovely	excuses	existence	executes
22.	major	harbor	maize	major	delicious	majesty
23.	indication	dictation	indication	snatching	indigestion	indirect
24.	curiosity	currency	curio	herder	curiously	curiosity
25.	astronomy	astronomer	astronomy	astonished	infested	astray

---

Time __________ Sec. RATE (from table on page 307): R. __________

No. Errors __________ COMPREHENSION (100 − 4% for each Error): C. __________

I-18 EFFICIENCY (R × C): E. __________

Record on Progress Chart on page 297

Exercise I-19

1.	abandon	band	abuse	abandon	banana	backward
2.	display	dispute	display	dispose	identify	displace
3.	mission	missing	permission	fashion	lute	mission
4.	silvery	silver	slavery	silvery	silvered	lonely
5.	taxicab	cab	taxicab	toxin	ability	tropical
6.	bluebonnet	blue	resting	bonnet	bluebonnet	blueberry
7.	firmly	firmly	firm	first	finely	card
8.	laborer	excuse	laboratory	bore	laborer	labor
9.	dictate	direct	detect	estate	fighter	dictate
10.	perfume	perfume	refuse	perhaps	fuming	perfect
11.	rejoice	quaint	rejoice	voice	join	resolve
12.	thorough	finish	thought	thorough	though	rough
13.	abdomen	tabernacle	abandoned	abdomen	fundamental	practically
14.	adverbial	adverbial	advise	folding	advisable	verb
15.	financial	jealously	final	financial	trial	finance
16.	watermelon	discuss	melon	waterfall	watermelon	water
17.	responsible	respective	manage	response	sponsor	responsible
18.	solution	solvent	resolution	monkey	resolved	solution
19.	companion	comparison	companion	commotion	necessary	pension
20.	regardless	retard	regardless	homeless	relative	nevertheless
21.	resistance	resist	level	resolute	assistance	resistance
22.	mountaineer	maintain	kindergarten	mountain	mountaineer	mount
23.	knighted	knighted	glossy	night	neighborhood	knight
24.	clergyman	clergyman	candlestick	salesman	minister	accountant
25.	commonwealth	common	commotion	kettle	commonwealth	wealth

Time __________ Sec. RATE (from table on page 307): R. __________

No. Errors __________ COMPREHENSION (100 − 4% for each Error): C. __________

I-19 EFFICIENCY (R × C): E. __________

Record on Progress Chart on page 297

Exercise I-20

1.	balance	balance	charge	balcony	balanced	lance	
2.	charity	chariot	cherish	charge	drift	charity	
3.	decisive	decision	decisive	exclude	detective	derived	
4.	gradual	radiant	graduate	grader	invest	gradual	
5.	meantime	heading	meaner	meanwhile	meantime	text	
6.	painter	painful	painter	headache	pointer	painted	
7.	raided	railway	soldier	raided	regiment	rainbow	
8.	janitor	janitor	jingle	jungle	offer	banister	
9.	verdict	convict	fugitive	predict	verdict	allow	
10.	bandage	occupant	band	banana	banded	bandage	
11.	faithful	faithful	handful	faithfully	convince	harmful	
12.	insurance	insurance	endurance	dressing	insure	insult	
13.	grandpa	grandma	grandpa	insist	grandfather	father	
14.	sermon	service	sermon	serum	serve	vomiting	
15.	pancake	pantry	sturdy	pan	pancreas	pancake	
16.	upright	upper	carve	upright	right	upkeep	
17.	surgeon	surplus	surf	highland	surface	surgeon	
18.	witchcraft	witches	support	craftsmen	witchcraft	craft	
19.	sidewalk	sideways	beside	sidewalk	eighteen	walk	
20.	consideration	sensation	consideration	relation	vegetation	syllable	
21.	interfere	interfere	refer	confer	reference	hydrophobia	
22.	destroyer	battleship	description	destine	destroyer	destroy	
23.	pardon	parents	paradise	leopard	pardon	schedule	
24.	examine	exactly	boasts	examine	exciting	example	
25.	everybody	everyone	circus	everybody	evergreen	anybody	

Time ________ Sec.	RATE (from table on page 307):	R. ________
No. Errors ________	COMPREHENSION (100 − 4% for each Error):	C. ________
I-20	EFFICIENCY (R × C):	E. ________

Record on Progress Chart on page 297

SERIES II
Word Meaning Exercises

Instructions

In these Series II exercises, the emphasis shifts to a rapid recognition of *meaning*. Here each key word is followed by five others, one of which means almost the same as the key word. This exercise is the first to give you practice in reading for meaning. Here you want to scan as rapidly as you can, looking for similar meanings.

The directions are the same as for the preceding exercise. Look at the key word in each line, and then find the one in the answers that has most nearly the same meaning. Underline or check that answer, and go on to each succeeding line as rapidly as possible. When you have finished, ask for your time, and look up your rate in the table on page 307. Use the keys on pages 317 and 325 to check your errors. Find your number of errors and compute your comprehension by multiplying the number of correct answers by four (4). Compute your efficiency to the nearest whole number, and record scores on the Progress Chart on page 297.

Because these words are all among the 30,000 most frequently used words, you can use these exercises also as a check on your vocabulary. List all key words missed, all correct answers not underlined, and all words underlined in error on the vocabulary page; and look up their meaning. Try to study and to use these words until you have added them to your vocabulary.

These exercises begin on page 53; rate tables are on page 307; keys are on pages 317 and 325; progress charts are on page 297; vocabulary lists are on page 293.

EXAMPLE

. . . .

22. prefer		refer	preface	confer	peace	choose
23. dent	X	spent	bend	dens	split	dines
24. night	X	might	dark	nigh	blight	evil
25. film		haze	craze	limb	kiln	finest

Time 63 Sec.	RATE (from table on page 307):	R. 143
No. Correct: 23	COMPREHENSION (4% for each correct answer): (4 × 24)	C. 92
(Key on page 317)	EFFICIENCY (R × C): (143 × .92) = 131.56	E. 132

II-O

Words to be added to vocabulary list:

dent	night
bend	dark
split	blight

Suggestions

These exercises are much like the ones in the first series, but the same game does not apply because you have to know the *meaning* of the symbols in greater detail. Now you must recognize that symbols have various meanings and that your skill in playing the game depends on previous experience and knowledge.

Thinking about what you are doing is essential to success in these exercises, but to improve reading skills you must learn to think fast and effectively.

Many students waste time by doing unnecessary thinking that has no direct bearing on the rules of the game. Some dash off mentally in search of an answer without knowing what they are really looking for. Some become disturbed over the meaning of *six* words when the instructions stress the importance of only *one* key word.

Again the logical thing to do is to concentrate on the *key* word before beginning the search for synonyms. Just studying its physical characteristics of size and shape is not appropriate this time though. You must add another dimension of meaning *to you*. If the key word has no meaning to you, there is no need to go on to the answer columns. You have found a word that you need to add to your vocabulary; and until you do, it has no value to you as a symbol or a tool. If the key word has no meaning to you, just check it as an error to add to your vocabulary list for further study, and move on quickly to the next line.

In most cases, the key word will have some meaning for you. It may have several meanings. You have to sort out the various meanings it might have and to project in your mind these various possibilities.

Armed with several possible synonyms, you are ready to scan the answer columns. You may recognize one of these synonyms immediately and be ready to go on to the next line. If you do not see any of them at once, you may need to go back to the key and think of other possible meanings. Again you may be faced with a new meaning for this word, which you will need to add to your vocabulary.

There is little reason for you to take each of the five choices in the answer column and think about each one intensively, however. In fact, you may never read some of these choices at all if you are able to identify quickly and confidently the match for the key word. If you know what you are looking for and then find it, you can stop and go on to the next line.

Do not be afraid of making errors. They are a natural part of the learning process. But each error can be a means of improving your understanding of the language and your reading skill. Look upon errors as a means of pinpointing ideas that need further study and application in your communicative skills.

Use your errors in this series as steps to learning. *Think* about the key words that bothered you, that you guessed at, and that you missed! All of these words in these exercises are common words in your native vocabulary. If you do not understand them, they may become barriers to effective communication.

This book is not intended as a workbook in vocabulary building, but there are many such publications available. Ask your teacher or your librarian to suggest good materials for vocabulary development. An analysis of errors made in these exercises might help to identify the kind of vocabulary help that you need most. Your directions suggest that for each word missed, you should add three words to your vocabulary check list.

The Key word, the word marked incorrectly, and the correct answer that you overlooked are all words which need more attention to improve your vocabulary.

But do not stop with just putting them on a list! Think about each one. Try to decide why you missed it. Review you earlier experiences with the word. Do you have any feelings about it? Have you avoided or resisted it for some reason? Do you really want to add it to your vocabulary?

Your vocabulary list can be a real help in specific vocabulary expansion, but it will require time and effort on your part to accomplish this. There are no magic tricks for sound vocabulary development, but these words will come up again in some unexpected time and place, and you will be more secure if you have mastered them.

Use your dictionary as a first step. Most of these words are in a standard college dictionary. If you do not have a copy of your own, you should get one, and you should use it regularly. If a word is not in your desk dictionary, go to the library and seek it out in the larger dictionary there.

Once you find it, look at all the possible meanings presented. You will probably find that your experience has exposed you to only a limited aspect of the total use of the word. Write down several of the synonyms of the word. Take notes on the basic definition and derivation of the word, and then consider the various extensions or modifications of the term.

Thinking about words is not enough. you need to use them in speech and writing to make them functional. Try using your newly found vocabulary in various ways.

Some people like to use study "cue cards" to help develop fluency with new words. Setting up the word on one side of a card and the definitions and synonyms on the back of the card provides a good practice card that can be carried in your pocket and used frequently until the word has become firmly set in your vocabulary.

Constructive thinking and planned vocabulary development can make reading more interesting and meaningful. Logical thinking on these exercises can help you set up goals in reading and become more selective in your skimming and scanning activities.

Developing skills in rapid recognition of similar ideas or recognition of new concepts will do much to help you become a more efficient reader and will save you many hours of time that you may now be spending on unnecessary reading.

Exercise II-1

1.	brow	sow	forehead	now	bow	cow
2.	bully	fully	pulley	gully	tulip	tease
3.	cot	bed	rot	tot	bought	sought
4.	ease	tranquility	knees	breeze	squeeze	sleep
5.	freeze	lizard	jar	ice	care	iris
6.	noise	choice	mount	notice	source	sound
7.	lively	lovely	brisk	liver	rabbit	tile
8.	notch	pouch	foam	gulch	dent	dotted
9.	noble	head	bobble	fine	foal	hobo
10.	rag	tatter	lag	tag	gag	bag
11.	staff	raft	stick	laugh	half	show
12.	borrow	sorrow	bend	use	drench	direction
13.	worn	born	sworn	mourn	tired	foreign
14.	woe	arm	grief	art	bale	man
15.	dad	bad	pad	father	lad	mad
16.	dart	dish	dash	dice	disk	cart
17.	errand	trip	head	ferry	wand	tan
18.	goal	mole	sole	soul	score	role
19.	inn	fin	gin	hotel	skin	hinge
20.	meal	feel	peal	peel	powder	seal
21.	pagan	sage	twig	patrol	hag	heathen
22.	raft	craft	draft	soft	rational	mast
23.	scant	can't	pant	rare	saint	banner
24.	catch	match	adapt	crack	cattle	trap
25.	tyrant	pirate	hydrant	sour	dictator	dysentery

Time ________ Sec. RATE (from table on page 307): R. ________

No. Correct ________ COMPREHENSION (4% for each correct answer): C. ________

(key on page 317)

II-1 EFFICIENCY (R × C): E. ________

Record on Progress Chart on page 297

Exercise II-2

1.	bed	fed	red	head	cot	bred	
2.	civil	devil	shrivel	idle	level	polite	
3.	arise	mount	size	maize	nice	barge	
4.	fable	legend	table	stable	staple	gable	
5.	sum	bum	total	crumb	dumb	hum	
6.	jam	dam	damn	lamb	predicament	ham	
7.	mind	find	rind	memory	hind	bind	
8.	camel	dromedary	cancel	sample	trample	woman	
9.	weigh	weird	well	measure	sleigh	mellow	
10.	hide	conceal	loud	crowd	bowed	proud	
11.	injured	impaired	faint	quaint	saint	paint	
12.	fresh	aunt	veranda	pant	new	handle	
13.	begin	sure	pure	cure	originate	burr	
14.	bribe	tribe	describe	price	five	live	
15.	cone	phone	lone	roan	bone	shell	
16.	opinion	hog	bog	cog	doctrine	fog	
17.	flutter	hit	dart	kit	slit	bit	
18.	lucky	duchy	nervous	much	fudge	fortunate	
19.	lease	please	grease	contract	tease	peace	
20.	neat	heat	tidy	peat	beat	seat	
21.	pace	taste	gait	case	haste	chase	
22.	reside	beside	aside	decide	tide	dwell	
23.	slap	cap	map	slot	straight	pat	
24.	occur	fur	happen	sir	stir	burden	
25.	wallet	pallet	mallet	pocketbook	pale	pal	

Time __________ Sec. RATE (from table on page 307): R. __________

No. Correct __________ COMPREHENSION (4% for each correct answer): C. __________

(key on page 325)

II-2 EFFICIENCY (R × C): E. __________

Record on Progress Chart on page 297

Exercise II-3

1.	airy	light	dairy	diary	fairy	liver
2.	back	lack	support	tack	sack	sad
3.	odor	blink	smell	think	wink	summer
4.	roam	wander	come	foam	home	comb
5.	turkey	turbine	mummies	slag	fowl	fur
6.	yield	furnish	wild	sealed	reel	field
7.	fame	honor	quarrel	sorrel	moral	haul
8.	naked	sake	sacked	bare	baked	raked
9.	plow	allow	plot	cut	how	slow
10.	rich	pitch	wealthy	ditch	bit	wick
11.	sack	back	ravage	lack	hack	rack
12.	slant	slope	mop	chant	hope	can't
13.	wait	fate	date	rate	stay	mate
14.	reduce	erase	lower	flower	reed	dash
15.	beckon	reckon	second	long	section	signal
16.	suspend	confer	refer	postpone	affair	peevish
17.	eager	beaver	meager	lever	agent	anxious
18.	fury	furry	jury	brewery	ear	anger
19.	pen	few	threw	sew	cage	session
20.	mad	bad	bade	crazy	sad	lad
21.	olden	golden	stolen	den	ancient	altar
22.	responsible	phone	drone	elf	liable	lone
23.	rub	cub	tub	polish	tug	sub
24.	paste	waste	waist	taste	cowardly	dough
25.	brilliant	dance	ant	glance	branch	dazzling

Time __________ Sec. RATE (from table on page 307): R. __________

No. Correct __________ COMPREHENSION (4% for each correct answer): C. __________
(key on page 317)

II-3 EFFICIENCY (R × C): E. __________

Record on Progress Chart on page 297

Exercise II-4

1.	glance	lance	man	glimpse	dance	glade
2.	quack	lack	rack	pretender	back	cub
3.	colony	call	loan	loon	solo	settlement
4.	paces	faces	file	aisle	steps	races
5.	restrain	confine	train	content	hue	better
6.	yell	yes	cry	bell	knock	yellow
7.	keen	seen	sharp	bean	dear	lean
8.	mope	pop	top	cop	pout	flop
9.	ban	condemn	turbine	banana	fat	ran
10.	rack	back	tack	jack	stand	repeat
11.	slayer	thrill	player	clay	killer	kitty
12.	thaw	melt	saw	jaw	law	raw
13.	wage	salary	age	tan	cage	sage
14.	peaceable	able	fry	ability	friendly	family
15.	baby	fade	child	bake	lady	dance
16.	brief	grief	belief	sheaf	fief	short
17.	dump	jump	drop	bump	chunk	dumb
18.	fought	sought	caught	struggled	fault	ought
19.	drill	fill	troll	bill	pill	practice
20.	lit	kindled	fit	bit	kit	itch
21.	horn	born	corn	mourn	morn	trumpet
22.	prefer	close	preamble	credit	confer	choose
23.	reply	resort	apply	answer	fort	aerial
24.	spent	rent	exhausted	bent	can	dent
25.	tight	light	fight	snug	sight	night

Time __________ Sec. RATE (from table on page 307): R. __________

No. Correct __________ COMPREHENSION (4% for each correct answer): C. __________
(key on page 325)

II-4 EFFICIENCY (R × C): E. __________

Record on Progress Chart on page 297

Exercise II-5

1.	torrid	parched	horrid	flower	more	porridge
2.	bad	wad	tadpole	had	sad	poor
3.	covering	hoof	hook	hood	hoop	howl
4.	wind	mind	bind	kind	twist	tender
5.	frugal	nominal	struggle	stubble	economical	froze
6.	ignore	floor	door	overlook	roar	age
7.	hinder	tender	kinder	convert	prevent	habit
8.	display	pageant	play	page	limp	gym
9.	prey	pray	victim	ray	day	voyage
10.	salve	save	have	smooth	halve	shelve
11.	hymn	hunch	song	oral	coral	sorrel
12.	color	faint	collar	tinge	rain	tin
13.	writer	fighter	author	gladden	lighter	stab
14.	bat	rat	mat	fat	sat	stick
15.	burn	learn	far	churn	scorch	share
16.	endure	cure	bear	sure	pure	dead
17.	gain	gaps	gander	gorge	get	gentle
18.	gown	frown	down	dress	about	round
19.	map	nap	chart	lap	cap	gap
20.	menace	dentist	fine	apprentice	tent	threat
21.	parade	pageant	raid	party	braid	chart
22.	rash	adventurous	rare	flash	crash	hash
23.	scrub	power	dower	tower	courage	clean
24.	strut	nut	put	stray	brutal	brace
25.	unclean	impure	lean	uncle	incline	nice

Time __________ Sec. RATE (from table on page 307): R. __________

No. Correct __________ COMPREHENSION (4% for each correct answer): C. __________
(key on page 317)

II-5 EFFICIENCY (R × C): E. __________

Record on Progress Chart on page 297

Exercise II-6

1.	baker	cook	writer	shooter	rook	took
2.	abode	sewed	rode	dodge	pod	house
3.	salmon	fish	lemon	salad	bat	fellow
4.	trough	rough	gutter	sought	soft	golf
5.	flare	dare	care	bare	mare	blaze
6.	herb	grass	barb	bard	bird	grab
7.	grade	fade	raid	cage	level	stayed
8.	insult	attack	cult	result	sting	base
9.	weave	plate	late	rate	place	braid
10.	meant	rent	intended	sent	dead	fed
11.	sob	weep	rob	cob	rod	bob
12.	thrifty	sift	cliff	sniff	shriek	saving
13.	weed	seed	ready	really	plant	lead
14.	appeal	seal	prayer	real	apple	peel
15.	bust	rust	chest	must	cuss	dust
16.	bay	say	lag	inform	inlet	pay
17.	correct	reveal	color	merit	rain	revise
18.	frown	down	scowl	town	sound	sown
19.	declaration	clear	worm	announcement	squirm	sensation
20.	luck	much	duck	suck	chance	cluck
21.	occupants	western	occurence	renters	occupied	sleep
22.	proceed	produce	recess	advance	resist	arrow
23.	role	roll	dole	troll	part	pole
24.	spell	hell	well	relieve	bell	sell
25.	torn	thorn	worn	ripped	born	rope

Time __________ Sec.　　RATE (from table on page 307):　　R. __________

No. Correct __________　　COMPREHENSION (4% for each correct answer):　　C. __________
(key on page 325)

II-6　　EFFICIENCY (R × C):　　E. __________

Record on Progress Chart on page 297

Exercise II-7

1.	bauble	bubble	stubble	trouble	gobble	trifle
2.	blur	pure	stir	out	stain	endure
3.	brand	canned	goat	vote	planned	mark
4.	haven	port	raven	leaven	sort	sport
5.	butler	servant	room	broom	serve	butter
6.	knelt	felt	belt	cent	knew	bent
7.	mice	rodents	rice	lice	three	ice
8.	outfit	fit	outside	cost	snow	costume
9.	recall	stall	remember	fall	ball	gall
10.	calf	staff	fin	call	leg	lesson
11.	sworn	cursed	worn	horn	corn	born
12.	vapor	taper	mist	part	maker	favor
13.	allay	alley	alloy	ally	relieve	lay
14.	boyish	fish	dish	about	youthful	toy
15.	consent	yield	die	dye	fry	cry
16.	pill	fill	ball	pal	rill	fall
17.	flank	rank	sank	thigh	tank	thank
18.	habit	bit	rabbit	costume	fit	hit
19.	splendor	lend	door	spend	stately	fate
20.	brooch	jewelry	mist	jersey	roof	broke
21.	plod	clog	clod	toil	pod	fog
22.	sorrowful	sow	mournful	pants	full	pour
23.	sinner	system	sister	criminal	dinner	kiss
24.	persuade	time	person	tempt	inspiration	nation
25.	volcano	canoe	eruption	avoid	came	lane

Time __________ Sec. RATE (from table on page 307): R. __________

No. Correct __________ COMPREHENSION (4% for each correct answer): C. __________

(key on page 317)

II-7 EFFICIENCY (R × C): E. __________

Record on Progress Chart on page 297

Exercise II-8

1.	shrill	kill	keep	still	mill	keen
2.	clergy	energy	clerk	urge	clear	ministers
3.	devour	eat	devout	devote	devoid	sour
4.	vacant	dummy	cant	empty	haunt	pant
5.	ham	pork	ram	dam	jam	lamb
6.	jingle	tinge	tinkle	simple	jungle	single
7.	mishap	shape	missed	error	chaps	missions
8.	drug	drum	dugout	medicine	lesson	rug
9.	regarding	retarding	guarding	loading	harboring	concerning
10.	silverware	fair	fare	locksmith	bare	cutlery
11.	taxation	operation	relation	levy	sensation	station
12.	unclean	dirty	clear	until	pile	guide
13.	ammonia	pneumonia	phone	bony	bone	gas
14.	broom	loom	brush	doom	boom	tomb
15.	conquer	her	stir	overcome	churn	burr
16.	dove	love	pigeon	done	rove	move
17.	folder	shoulder	holder	solder	bolder	boulder
18.	stake	stem	lock	strew	wager	age
19.	littler	smaller	dresser	sticker	tester	sucker
20.	net	bet	met	yet	trap	new
21.	port	sort	harbor	sport	wart	more
22.	rage	sage	fury	page	cage	tan
23.	sly	tricky	cry	high	rye	try
24.	thick	thicket	sick	chicken	dense	lichen
25.	waste	taste	washer	waist	excess	haste

Time __________ Sec. RATE (from table on page 307): R. __________

No. Correct __________ (key on page 325) COMPREHENSION (4% for each correct answer): C. __________

II-8 EFFICIENCY (R × C): E. __________

Record on Progress Chart on page 297

Exercise II-9

1.	alligator	agitator	fascinate	crocodile	medium	cliff
2.	brand	mark	sand	grand	hand	land
3.	dedicate	devote	secret	freight	locate	donate
4.	wage	stage	wager	salary	dot	aged
5.	fondness	soundless	bigness	affection	afoot	jolt
6.	hoist	foil	ghost	moist	lift	loiter
7.	lecturer	picture	fracture	elect	speaker	cry
8.	necessity	bigness	need	city	complexion	nationality
9.	policy	police	rule	dolly	ice	glossy
10.	risk	danger	content	brisk	wrist	disk
11.	spacious	vast	gracious	specimen	narcissus	vacation
12.	token	broken	spoken	army	stay	sign
13.	buzz	fist	his	sued	hum	hive
14.	assume	room	pretend	doom	broom	spoke
15.	rule	statue	flute	sample	law	stature
16.	crook	brook	book	shook	look	hook
17.	speak	permit	remit	submit	salve	voice
18.	decorate	decent	vanish	adorn	deck	decay
19.	ability	table	legal	power	write	pillow
20.	make	male	form	rake	break	fake
21.	oral	sorrel	flower	moral	coral	spoken
22.	prow	sow	now	how	row	bow
23.	rural	pastoral	fuel	full	gruel	purchase
24.	squirrel	quarrel	chipmunk	whirl	churn	square
25.	tremble	thimble	assemble	shake	trouble	resemblance

Time __________ Sec. RATE (from table on page 307): R. __________

No. Correct __________ COMPREHENSION (4% for each correct answer): C. __________
(key on page 317)

II-9 EFFICIENCY (R × C): E. __________

Record on Progress Chart on page 297

Exercise II-10

1.	ashamed	claimed	mortified	named	tamed	rash
2.	shape	cape	form	grape	tape	happy
3.	crow	row	low	boast	bow	dough
4.	empire	aspire	inquire	dominion	require	pie
5.	reject	deny	elect	lute	rest	male
6.	lack	sack	rake	enable	enchant	need
7.	craze	age	dampen	sadden	each	enrage
8.	stubborn	stung	firm	following	escape	ice
9.	property	proper	density	prosperity	possessions	prospect
10.	scarf	veil	mock	skin	harp	daze
11.	straw	draw	thaw	paw	stalks	ball
12.	sack	rudder	shudder	utter	buddy	bag
13.	luxuries	tropical	riches	topic	surgeon	book
14.	behold	fold	gold	see	sold	bold
15.	chisel	fry	cheat	rain	gizzard	look
16.	excursion	lemon	trim	venture	screen	problem
17.	quickly	hastily	extradition	condition	tradition	quiet
18.	grocer	dealer	poacher	roach	brooch	loafer
19.	idea	for	flee	opinion	sea	cease
20.	mince	since	tree	rinse	hash	hind
21.	peal	echo	deal	feel	loyal	real
22.	recover	delivery	covered	mockery	stubborn	heal
23.	image	pole	dance	pride	form	female
24.	cease	neuter	robber	cute	stop	create
25.	unnecessary	commit	crazy	student	ugh	useless

Time __________ Sec. RATE (from table on page 307): R. __________

No. Correct __________ COMPREHENSION (4% for each correct answer): C. __________
(key on page 325)

II-10 EFFICIENCY (R × C): E. __________

Record on Progress Chart on page 297

Exercise II-11

1.	hear	beard	trouble	word	stirrup	listen
2.	cattle	tatter	fetter	gossip	cow	wine
3.	lady	woman	wanting	same	fame	light
4.	fashion	style	file	fasten	false	rub
5.	glare	share	gaze	graze	destroy	raise
6.	inflammation	veneer	information	clever	fever	flyer
7.	marble	wonder	sing	limestone	tomb	robber
8.	trip	boating	doubting	insulted	excursion	clause
9.	purify	clear	purchase	hear	testify	defined
10.	withdraw	music	conclude	isolate	date	fate
11.	secret	suburb	years	hidden	bid	terrace
12.	unpleasant	dude	rude	abundant	hood	food
13.	acorn	nut	ache	adorn	hut	torn
14.	bin	came	sin	win	box	name
15.	clear	friendliness	close	cleverness	transparent	lesson
16.	develop	envelope	mature	gallop	manure	gait
17.	hunger	furnish	furnace	carve	family	starvation
18.	yell	shout	bald	look	small	too
19.	jug	tug	rug	pitcher	hit	richer
20.	modify	solidify	granary	change	resist	honor
21.	tolerate	commit	endure	penetrate	sure	awake
22.	relic	frolic	soon	clip	sing	ruin
23.	false	slam	room	tan	doom	pretense
24.	suspect	respect	suspicion	must	rust	trust
25.	useful	awful	deadly	cover	doubtful	helpful

Time __________ Sec. RATE (from table on page 307): R. __________

No. Correct __________ COMPREHENSION (4% for each correct answer): C. __________
(key on page 317)

II-11 EFFICIENCY (R × C): E. __________

Record on Progress Chart on page 297

Exercise II-12

1.	shame	sash	flash	crash	bustle	embarrass	
2.	certificate	testimony	allowance	antimony	delicate	three
3.	dawn	fun	fawn	sand	morn	lawn
4.	erupt	decay	tempted	burst	snake	rake
5.	gall	fall	stall	cemetery	prosperity	sore
6.	inquire	require	ask	task	fire	fin
7.	massive	woman	rare	test	dread	heavy
8.	distant	oversee	mourn	torn	foreign	tree
9.	journey	adventure	best	west	test	twist
10.	senior	elder	junior	juniper	fell	riddle
11.	sulphur	suffer	element	cement	sultry	couple
12.	pity	rare	conversation	path	sympathy	city
13.	admit	admire	deceive	receive	calendar	purple
14.	bled	fed	lead	read	injured	extinguish
15.	club	rub	study	staff	raft	sub
16.	dig	rig	fig	thrust	shelve	big
17.	fawn	yawn	crawl	pawn	single	ridge
18.	hardware	tools	swear	fool	tear	rare
19.	kennel	funnel	utter	mutter	house	flannel
20.	beam	seam	ray	day	deem	say
21.	phase	phone	rate	state	case	raze
22.	supervisor	section	reflector	nectar	factor	director
23.	shown	threw	shower	mew	guest	revealed
24.	swollen	pollen	expanded	spend	boll	strand
25.	overcome	conquer	oven	swish	company	question

Time __________ Sec. RATE (from table on page 307): R. __________

No. Correct __________ COMPREHENSION (4% for each correct answer): C. __________
(key on page 325)

II-12 EFFICIENCY (R × C): E. __________

Record on Progress Chart on page 297

Exercise II-13

1.	tear	bear	rip	rare	shear	care
2.	calculate	regulate	glove	rate	estimate	nominate
3.	deceive	decent	cease	paw	caw	cheat
4.	excuse	refuse	refuge	pardon	amuse	news
5.	grave	lack	behave	serious	anxiety	cave
6.	intoxicated	liberal	free	concentrated	waited	drunk
7.	mental	rent	dental	gentle	intelligent	lent
8.	parcel	mark	bundle	cell	park	seldom
9.	rate	date	hate	gate	estimate	fate
10.	sage	wage	rage	age	brown	wise
11.	suspicion	doubt	position	interjection	condition	resolution
12.	usher	rush	use	she	escort	bush
13.	ahead	dead	front	red	said	bed
14.	boost	roost	boot	lift	hoot	door
15.	commit	comment	entrust	comma	comet	come
16.	disobey	refuse	hay	hey	bay	say
17.	film	haze	craze	hermit	limb	kill
18.	heavily	heave	hear	heat	labored	villain
19.	lame	same	cripple	blame	came	fame
20.	municipal	principal	money	city	cipher	cider
21.	sorrowful	sorrel	captive	plane	cupful	melancholy
22.	sample	haste	dish	taste	trample	same
23.	furry	soft	sure	sill	cure	hurry
24.	tassel	ornament	rascal	vessel	pass	castle
25.	vigor	victors	sick	liquor	or	strength

Time __________ Sec. RATE (from table on page 307): R. __________

No. Correct __________ COMPREHENSION (4% for each correct answer): C. __________

(key on page 317)

II-13 EFFICIENCY (R × C): E. __________

Record on Progress Chart on page 297

Exercise II-14

1.	abundant	bun	plentiful	abuse	misuse	dance
2.	bet	met	best	stake	belt	get
3.	coach	car	teach	broke	roach	loaf
4.	active	industrious	weak	large	diet	lie
5.	feather	father	farther	gather	weather	plume
6.	hark	harp	listen	ark	dark	bark
7.	entertain	interest	loosely	enter	hostess	certain
8.	moisten	mock	wet	moss	choice	ten
9.	persecute	cute	respect	torment	persist	person
10.	trust	depend	deny	lye	relax	relay
11.	situation	site	sit	shorter	capital	carnation
12.	tender	tend	actress	soft	ten	attend
13.	resolved	late	vacancy	ventilate	violate	determined
14.	smear	rear	ran	smooth	rub	shear
15.	bride	bridge	ride	pride	wife	side
16.	consul	official	consult	council	console	contract
17.	dresser	dropped	bureau	dress	masses	woman
18.	expect	anticipate	fore	see	forehead	forest
19.	hopeless	hop	hostess	endless	useless	careless
20.	likely	lively	live	like	lightly	probable
21.	nag	tag	bag	keg	torment	gag
22.	pouch	couch	pout	pour	bag	big
23.	resign	design	sign	tired	recite	quit
24.	soak	sock	joke	broke	oak	drench
25.	threw	drew	fly	flung	flute	brew

Time __________ Sec. RATE (from table on page 307): R. __________

No. Correct __________ COMPREHENSION (4% for each correct answer): C. __________

(key on page 325)

II-14 EFFICIENCY (R × C): E. __________

Record on Progress Chart on page 297

Exercise II-15

1.	mix	sick	picks	sad	stir	tick
2.	bloom	strew	flower	stew	few	flew
3.	tomato	comma	to	vegetable	mate	place
4.	release	distribute	expanse	expense	tribute	defense
5.	mean	meat	seen	vicious	dear	monkey
6.	heavy	levee	massive	levy	weave	boy
7.	watch	leap	over	observe	patch	wall
8.	mound	hill	round	sound	around	hound
9.	rot	oil	pot	caught	sill	spoil
10.	resist	oppose	cease	sister	fist	pose
11.	smear	pulley	fear	beer	rear	wipe
12.	quiet	silent	quick	quit	tack	question
13.	waterfall	cascade	water	crater	fall	waterfowl
14.	modify	altar	change	alto	halter	mobility
15.	bulb	tub	bulk	bull	tower	bud
16.	break	interrupt	truck	rapture	vicious	connect
17.	earnest	furnace	ear	serious	sardine	nest
18.	freedom	dome	free	kingdom	liberty	work
19.	hurl	curl	throw	swift	twist	turkey
20.	lone	bone	solitary	stone	son	done
21.	nursery	celery	nurse	purse	incubator	ivory
22.	excuse	exit	execute	text	use	pretense
23.	rib	bib	crib	bit	time	bone
24.	chief	chest	ruler	rein	rain	check
25.	direction	fact	sensation	course	direct	lack

Time __________ Sec. RATE (from table on page 307): R. __________

No. Correct __________ COMPREHENSION (4% for each correct answer): C. __________
(key on page 317)

II-15 EFFICIENCY (R × C): E. __________

Record on Progress Chart on page 297

Exercise II-16

1.	astray	bay	tray	day	wrong	waste	
2.	carrier	bearer	terrier	ferry	content	bare	
3.	cure	poor	heal	pure	sure	hurdle	
4.	engineer	guide	sheer	fear	rear	gnaw	
5.	cloth	there	close	back	crepe	century	
6.	enraged	age	angry	pant	enter	enclose	
7.	grudge	spite	rug	grub	shallow	empire	
8.	orbit	describe	fit	hit	path	prayer	
9.	knowledge	prune	wisdom	fence	know	led	
10.	safe	secure	wave	mission	saber	statue	
11.	stuck	attached	luck	truck	rude	tune	
12.	beneath	been	route	below	bell	boar	
13.	absurd	work	foolish	heard	lurid	fabric	
14.	upset	debt	let	kept	confuse	session	
15.	circumference	conference	circus	tense	practical	perimeter	
16.	describe	date	rate	fate	relate	rescue	
17.	earn	burn	ear	learn	color	get	
18.	gulf	rough	separation	golf	charm	fluff	
19.	diamond	fire	raid	jewel	fade	tadpole	
20.	mishap	nap	tap	mist	aisle	accident	
21.	penned	spend	rent	confined	sent	cent	
22.	refusal	trial	file	denial	foul	dedicate	
23.	server	compose	lever	weaver	conceit	tray	
24.	wise	stray	show	shrewd	rank	shred	
25.	touched	happy	tie	flush	couch	affected	

Time ________ Sec. RATE (from table on page 307): R. ________

No. Correct ________ COMPREHENSION (4% for each correct answer): C. ________

(key on page 325)

II-16 EFFICIENCY (R × C): E. ________

Record on Progress Chart on page 297

Exercise II-17

1.	scare	terrify	light	run	alike	taffeta
2.	generous	mesa	variable	benevolent	can't	general
3.	decision	revise	temper	terror	cut	conclusion
4.	evermore	forever	swore	tore	severe	boar
5.	grief	arouse	table	mournful	men	mama
6.	murderer	killer	mud	shudder	death	sturdy
7.	retreat	turn	arrange	recede	come	defeat
8.	pains	hurts	arm	deadly	care	trick
9.	railway	rail	railroad	railing	doorway	highway
10.	slave	slay	servant	refuse	violent	lie
11.	overthrow	over	case	race	replace	throw
12.	unusual	hair	fair	rare	snare	air
13.	ignorant	ignore	finger	uneducated	sour	significant
14.	butcher	butter	cutter	robber	stopper	copper
15.	college	office	ledge	league	university	cell
16.	pupil	three	ripple	polar	scholar	cider
17.	fertile	special	pacific	tile	ferment	abundant
18.	explanation	cavity	relation	donation	sense	constitution
19.	mighty	night	digest	sight	powerful	haughty
20.	pastoral	moral	sorrel	flowers	music	rural
21.	district	revise	construct	stricken	disc	region
22.	lattice	trellis	lettuce	radish	cabbage	latter
23.	believe	deceive	trust	receive	suspect	relieve
24.	taffeta	solid	fete	staff	fact	fabric
25.	remote	sway	distant	stay	tray	spray

Time __________ Sec. RATE (from table on page 307): R. __________

No. Correct __________ COMPREHENSION (4% for each correct answer): C. __________
(key on page 317)

II-17 EFFICIENCY (R × C): E. __________

Record on Progress Chart on page 297

Exercise II-18

1.	doubtful	dislike	hurt	uncertain	pinch	omit
2.	unite	concise	conceal	assemble	conceit	sooner
3.	estimate	confer	consider	consent	plate	contempt
4.	maid	serve	servant	horse	vertical	homemade
5.	forfeit	fortune	forefather	feather	fine	pore
6.	nostril	still	troll	fill	nose	trail
7.	lettuce	vegetable	terrace	fruit	certain	date
8.	free	freeze	lake	rocky	immune	grey
9.	bear	quarterly	notable	relax	tolerate	tortoise
10.	romantic	gigantic	loving	frantic	you	save
11.	somebody	some	someday	pomegranate	person	dome
12.	respect	rest	help	inspect	act	admire
13.	efficiency	ability	freedom	regent	frog	cedar
14.	lookout	flour	watch	doubt	mount	woodland
15.	rule	statue	stature	law	match	latch
16.	cupboard	closet	board	cup	rubber	clad
17.	deceive	receive	cheat	detect	rod	because
18.	eventual	evenly	effect	fact	funnel	final
19.	account	count	indicate	statement	torment	state
20.	instructor	factor	adapt	teacher	toy	erect
21.	cast	outbreak	mast	last	duty	mold
22.	purchaser	pursue	purse	chase	burden	buyer
23.	compound	unite	ponder	pound	around	competition
24.	stately	grand	lately	greatly	slightly	quietly
25.	bewilder	wild	turbine	content	ran	confuse

Time __________ Sec. RATE (from table on page 307): R. __________

No. Correct __________ COMPREHENSION (4% for each correct answer): C. __________
(key on page 325)

II-18 EFFICIENCY (R × C): E. __________

Record on Progress Chart on page 297

Exercise II-19

1.	angrily	secretly	silly	bitterly	picturesque	fully
2.	anxious	odor	concerned	gracious	generous	canyon
3.	convince	apple	convert	fence	rinse	onward
4.	durable	currant	insure	lasting	fable	lunch
5.	hurricane	bean	furry	cyclone	sour	hurrying
6.	however	yet	flower	sour	never	youthful
7.	likewise	also	bait	dike	size	bill
8.	opinion	reproduce	idea	fudge	juice	breezy
9.	poultry	chickens	sultry	poster	mostly	try
10.	rubbish	publish	dish	litter	furious	lumber
11.	richness	lesson	senseless	poorest	splendor	sadness
12.	transfer	exchange	differ	confer	refer	gopher
13.	banquet	feast	croquet	shut	quit	fang
14.	backbone	tone	telephone	phone	sack	spine
15.	cascade	contract	waterfall	cast	fact	watch
16.	ceremony	testimony	crane	money	formal	ferment
17.	snare	sue	sure	pare	trap	taste
18.	abandon	band	ranch	discard	done	bank
19.	fudge	fugitive	candy	internal	sandy	hermit
20.	disease	cease	release	occasion	sash	diphtheria
21.	overlook	book	cook	rover	neglect	dove
22.	birthplace	birth	earth	place	death	origin
23.	content	continue	relate	nominate	gather	satisfaction
24.	finish	disc	disk	dish	stop	sister
25.	intelligent	tell	gentle	abdominal	beneficial	wise

Time __________ Sec.
No. Correct __________
(key on page 317)
II-19

RATE (from table on page 307): R. __________
COMPREHENSION (4% for each correct answer): C. __________
EFFICIENCY (R × C): E. __________

Record on Progress Chart on page 297

Exercise II-20

1.	desire	rouse	covet	liars	cutlass	iris
2.	peasant	rustic	pheasant	resent	sent	scant
3.	original	duty	mouse	credit	greed	native
4.	redbreast	quench	west	rest	robin	best
5.	linen	soldier	sardine	cloth	officer	cabin
6.	immerse	unpleasant	bachelor	absorb	testify	imaginable
7.	highness	elevation	richness	bigness	sickness	weakness
8.	thankful	healthful	grateful	uneventful	armful	harmful
9.	produce	process	reduce	pipe	manufacture	unit
10.	satisfaction	multiply	petrify	deny	content	gather
11.	confess	dress	fuss	acknowledge	rest	anywhere
12.	floor	cooing	base	hoeing	doing	varnish
13.	highway	day	high	say	road	hey
14.	misfortune	disaster	salad	belief	forcing	formerly
15.	chemistry	chemise	history	science	artistic	shelves
16.	creator	theater	crater	ponder	producer	preacher
17.	exchange	range	rim	trade	disturb	text
18.	region	district	slavery	multitude	food	trash
19.	interview	consultation	made	one	twinkle	toes
20.	just	imperial	jute	make	raking	fair
21.	sportsman	worst	hunter	herald	dart	horse
22.	rebuild	skilled	filled	troll	meat	mend
23.	sadness	gladness	confess	dress	daddy	depression
24.	maintain	resist	exist	consist	relief	orator
25.	malaria	mountainous	tree	fuss	obey	disease

Time __________ Sec.
No. Correct __________
(key on page 325)
II-20

RATE (from table on page 307): R. __________
COMPREHENSION (4% for each correct answer): C. __________
EFFICIENCY (R × C): E. __________

Record on Progress Chart on page 297

SERIES III
Phrase Meaning Exercises

Instructions

In these Series III exercises, the emphasis on meaning is extended from words to phrases. They also should help to increase your eye span as you are to try to grasp the meaning of each phrase at a single glance. Do not read them word for word; treat each group of words as a unit of meaning. Each of the phrases is set off by spaces to allow you to concentrate on group meaning with a single eye fixation.

Look at the key phrase, and think about its meaning. Concentrate on the ideas you associate with this phrase. Then glance at the phrases that follow until you find one that means approximately the same as the key phrase. Try to shift rhythmically from each phrase to the next until you find the right one. Mark this correct answer by underlining or checking it, and and go on to the next line. As soon as you have finished the last line, ask for your time and look up your rate in the table on page 309. Use the keys on page 318 or page 326 to check your errors. Compute comprehension and efficiency scores as indicated in the scoring directions, and record your rate and efficiency on the Progress Chart on page 297.

Here again the key words in a phrase are a measure of your vocabulary. Take the key words from any phrases you miss, and list them in your vocabulary list for further study.

These exercises begin on page 75; rate tables are on page 309; progress charts on page 297. Keys are on pages 318 and 326.

EXAMPLE

17. to acquit	to assemble	to set free	likely to	one part of	to stop doing
18. about dawn	fun to see	to account for	over and done	break of day	power to
19. with promptness	without delay	all included	too many of	larger task	in lieu of
20. mountain top X	pine forest	highest peak	highly active	vacation time	now ended

Time 70 Sec.
No. Correct: 19
(key on page 318)
III-O

RATE (from table on page 309): R. 257
COMPREHENSION (5% for each correct answer): (5 × 19) C. 95
EFFICIENCY (R × C): (257 × .95) = 244.15 E. 244

Suggestions

These exercises should provide you with the greatest challenge and the greatest satisfaction of any of those you have done thus far. Here the game of reading becomes more complex. Rate of eye movement, increased eye span, and mental processing of verbal symbols become interinvolved; and you should begin to see your first real indication of *seeking the ideas behind the words.*

Here you should try to free yourself from the compulsion of word-by-word reading and to see that many words are more meaningful in groups than they are alone. You need to focus on the *phrase* as the unit of meaning and to learn to recognize such blocks of words as meaningful blocks in vocabulary development. As you learn to think in phrases, you will find it much easier to increase your eye span as well.

The first phrase is still the key unit to think about and to be sure you understand. From it you must organize your ideas and goals so that you know what you are looking for as you move to the answer block of phrases.

One of the major features of this series is the emphasis on increasing your eye span. From beginning to end, the phrases become progressively longer. If you can increase your horizontal eye span enough to continue to read all phrases in a single eye fixation, you should achieve real carry-over value to your other reading activities.

Materials in the first eight exercises of this series are arranged with two pairs of vertical phrases and one single phrase in the answer columns. Experiment to see if you can perceive the vertical pair as quickly as you can the single phrase. This should increase your sensitivity to your potential use of vertical eye span as well as your horizontal eye span.

In the latter part of this series, all phrases are arranged in a vertical order. Here the ideas are more important than the specific words, and you should practice vertical movements of your eyes, focusing on the center of the line and trying to stretch your eye span enough to get meaning from the whole line at one glance. Such skills are very helpful in newspaper and news magazine reading for new ideas and current information.

Practice with the vertically organized materials shifts your emphasis on key materials from the left hand to the top position; and you can see how headlines, headings, and lead questions are designed to help focus your thinking on theme ideas in preparation for the materials that follow.

Vertical skimming and scanning techniques become more important as you consider this type of reading. Some individuals begin to develop a vertical eye span that enables them to perceive and transmit to the brain larger units of verbal symbols.

Flexible readers learn to use vertical eye span to pick up several lines of verbal symbols at a single fixation, seeking general content and main ideas rather than specific detail. Quick overviews of several lines at one glance, being sensitive to key words and phrases, are essential aspects of skimming and scanning techniques. Continued practice with concentrated vertical eye span activity may develop greater mental perception of greater detail as well. Many very fast readers seem pleasantly surprised at how much content they can retain when they develop personal skills in expanding both horizontal and vertical eye span.

This series of exercises offers you the opportunity to experiment with a variety of adjustments in your eye span. Feel free to try out various ways of looking at these exercises to find ways that are easiest and most effective for you. You may be surprised to find that your brain is much more efficient than you thought in being able to handle larger blocks of verbal symbols.

This series of exercises should also provide a real challenge to your reading and thinking skills. Here you should begin to see the first real evidence of significant increase in rate of reading, but at the same time you should begin to appreciate the depth of meaning behind various word combinations. Quick thinking and sensitivity to a breadth of meaning variations become essential aspects of good reading skills.

Taking time to think about key ideas and to anticipate possible answers will make your reading much more interesting and should enable you to get a great deal more done in less time than before.

Exercise III-1

No.	Key phrase					
1.	diamond ring	in these days short period		a precious stone	is apparent an average	
2.	spoken word		to say something against him	be used to		full extent will provide
3.	a passage way	little less perhaps this		to all	an opening for practical way	
4.	share equally		that reason with those men	almost here		have their divide evenly
5.	very joyous	is taken quite happy		other hand	may pay for never again	
6.	in the middle		judgment of plan to go	about medium		has assumed by such as
7.	a mature person	one fully grown to wait long		benefit all	away from is merely	
8.	an insult		another day does not require	so you can		a verbal wrong plan to go
9.	to precede	college life not in here		affect all	to believe to go ahead of	
10.	human speech		make adjustment distinct sound	too loud		not yet heard may record
11.	to inspect	same always tend to do		view carefully	it is also likely to	
12.	a scamp		a rascal can be expected to	looks ahead		always able to fine person
13.	not very full	to ignore decline to state		have said	rather meager of the group	
14.	to droop over		may sound near the top	are near here		to be seen by to lean down
15.	to play	which occur often to amuse		these words	rates low are used by	
16.	large plant		so that he under no conditions	a big tree		green grass might be
17.	nose of man	for smelling does not involve		can define as	you can make such terms as	
18.	a meek person		along with her may be ahead	had some kind		has mild temper wanted to go
19.	church song	to be given many more than		one can go	not wish to morning hymn	
20.	act of hunting		free time a search for game	to enjoy life		lead to never will go

Time __________ Sec. RATE (from table on page 309): R. __________

No. Correct __________ COMPREHENSION (5% for each correct answer): C. __________

(key on page 318)

III-1 EFFICIENCY (R × C): E. __________

Record on Progress Chart on page 297

Exercise III-2

1.	to remember	set it up might lead again	to recognize again	can be to enjoy life
2.	pure gold	is equal to has shown to be	living alone	precious metal worth more
3.	bright gloss	can read by a high polish	to play as	it may happen great care of
4.	drain off	to empty out in this sense	perhaps others do	what is this be considered
5.	an opinion	the use of good life	state support of	because of a belief held
6.	a short novel	to advance need for more	prose fiction	to put into of the new
7.	rather narrow	the result of too active	other means than this	of little width more than ever
8.	a member of	in time of to belong to	the story of	in every way to consume
9.	without limits	endless in size most of us	new order of	subject to his limited views
10.	act as host	best way let that do	for that	his school entertain another
11.	the ground	surface of earth blue sky	the four levels	all above can be seen
12.	to poke	about half of to increase some	on each day	method of to thrust something
13.	given freedom	to obtain all as with him	made independent of	be sure to as with
14.	end ill will	we profess their names	he said	to make peace it appears
15.	omit something	present time leave it out	is made	public life until later
16.	noble person	possessing dignity was immediately	was able to	his own the work of
17.	large monster	way of was absent	its cause	the facts an enormous animal
18.	hold court	last year be said	distribute justice	make wise come down from
19.	be careless	should be without loss of	lack of	omit essentials it also
20.	confident person	he argued one who knows	stand upon	to guide the needs of

---

Time __________ Sec. RATE (from table on page 309): R. __________

No. Correct __________ COMPREHENSION (5% for each correct answer): C. __________
(key on page 326)

III-2 EFFICIENCY (R × C): E. __________

Record on Progress Chart on page 297

Exercise III-3

No.	Key phrase			
1.	sign of force	physical vigor afraid of war	for those	he grows up to say so
2.	looks flat	can develop their jobs stop	very rarely	no one could even surface
3.	sign of famine	in the period near to home	short of food	they are fine school
4.	showed spite	was reached in an age	could be	exhibited envy low point of
5.	always near	high rent close at all times	has also been	rural area the future
6.	to expose	to reveal freely along the way	leave alone	return to to describe as
7.	is desperate	not knowing buying in	look for work	showing off in great need
8.	of good humor	design for take more	a cheerful person	at work can often be
9.	in reality	true to life method of work	in each class	of this type may assume
10.	a shy fellow	on the surface in conflict	to build	a modest person a new home
11.	without delay	to forget to hurry	other times	less than his after these
12.	act of haste	we learn be a factor in	a rapid action	four days the sense
13.	will float	miles away a real income	higher rates	lighter than water the point
14.	marked imperfectly	no ambition is incorrect	has become great	the rest cited as
15.	to be exposed	open to view for the aged	arise from	to increase due to this
16.	ruling over	for reasons can afford now	coming of age	upper limit act of dominating
17.	being partial	the ideal of as defined by	to prefer	more alike in which
18.	as a result of	in the future too soon after	believe in	brought about by to report
19.	to startle	as a sign to frighten suddenly	to do with	to search for for many days
20.	to free	to assemble one part of it	certain hint	likely to to set free

Time __________ Sec. RATE (from table on page 309): R. __________

No. Correct __________ COMPREHENSION (5% for each correct answer): C. __________

(key on page 318)

III-3 EFFICIENCY (R × C): E. __________

Record on Progress Chart on page 297

Exercise III-4

	Key phrase				
1.	proper place	be sold at an election day	correct position	one year because of	
2.	tame horse	gentle animal a few years	this age group	in a box to do better	
3.	a gentle slope	useful to instead of him	a hot day	a gradual decline sort of	
4.	to grow small	to control no one can	they give	led by you decrease in size	
5.	abundant food	began in abundant harvest	a long look	to do good few if any	
6.	to be confused	child's life must not be	be unclear	is well to to consider	
7.	standing erect	upright position first period	over the top	has called to walk to	
8.	very durable	they are for peace only	a large part	to be stable the source	
9.	being drowsy	as well as said that	part of this	term used rather sleepy	
10.	to be desolate	first day lonely condition	sort of damp	to return his life is	
11.	be delinquent	in spite of strong arm methods	neglect of duty	goes on which are	
12.	to groan	expression of pain the desire for	pay for all	any later form of	
13.	a fixed limit	the center of are some more	for less	marked boundary may lead	
14.	cease to exist	two weeks the behavior pattern	to a degree	so often to destroy	
15.	present time	number of this very instant	more usual	this is not at one place	
16.	trudge about	our purpose as a whole	ramble along	is easier to by himself	
17.	chief concern	most valuable part new plan of action	in some	are able to declare	
18.	without grace	under the value to us	made upon	being clumsy to serve fish	
19.	to break down	to secrete is evident	most fundamental	on the stage to go to pieces	
20.	make difficult	as fast as to complicate	the content of	calls for who can be	

Time __________ Sec. RATE (from table on page 309): R. __________

No. Correct __________ COMPREHENSION (5% for each correct answer): C. __________

(key on page 326)

III-4 EFFICIENCY (R × C): E. __________

Record on Progress Chart on page 297

Exercise III-5

	Key phrase				
1.	prompts an action	go beyond it in some form		some motive	possible to define more to be done
2.	a forward step	brought to light will be found here	the rank order		to move ahead seldom mention
3.	on being decisive	pride and joy man of decision		from the rest	give us the word in some cases
4.	a careless mistake	not using care number of men	to leave home		of this group when he comes
5.	a catastrophe	can set up a passing phase		to represent all	all afraid to a sudden disaster
6.	unable to recall	to indicate it is possible to	act of forgetting		of modern life the cause of
7.	beginning point	real danger here a little older		among this group	the entrance go to college
8.	of no value	of all sorts completely worthless	to earn part		may be presented will have less
9.	to understand	gain full meaning in social events		an expert in	for that reason to be desired
10.	no fixed value	which relates to have been listening	they can help		be alert to no set price
11.	great enjoyment	show satisfaction to talk about him		the time being	to come down to think so
12.	to prove the act	comes to mind an end result	of this nature		well known confirm the deed
13.	to alternate	we talk about perhaps in a sense		to take turns	complex part of experimental period
14.	rather peculiar	taken for granted on the party line	upon the foundation		something odd too high
15.	most likely	when they agree without a doubt		lags far behind	become more fixed at the end of
16.	making attack	on the offensive also appear to be	for some reason		final answer provide for
17.	drive with force	on this point better risk		less selective	by such action make a thrust
18.	of little importance	in this process study made by him	a common matter		in any event often possible
19.	being unlimited	almost half of can best be		he should help	have no boundary in contrast to
20.	pattern to go by	need to know serve as a guide	back them up		did not know about the third session

Time __________ Sec. RATE (from table on page 309): R. __________

No. Correct __________ COMPREHENSION (5% for each correct answer): C. __________

(key on page 318)

III-5 EFFICIENCY (R × C): E. __________

Record on Progress Chart on page 297

Exercise III-6

No.	Key phrase					
1.	rushing for help	be taken as	hurrying for aid	tends to change	in this area	has been paid
2.	almost as simple	keep in mind	rate as superior	high level of	force of others	nearly as easy
3.	more than enough	the next series	on the test	in their review	more than needed	he may not
4.	in minute amount	very small quantity	below average	to possess mainly	exist among	who rates low
5.	either of the two	may accept this	fortunate enough	one or the other	in a study	there are two
6.	a colossal mistake	as a starting point	a great error	later than	as a sort of	in the light
7.	it became evident	may be assumed	a state of health	in terms of	an example to follow	plain to see
8.	not concerned with	the most interested man	what things	to predict what	not interested in	the most effective
9.	shameful action	disgraceful conduct	in the session	less accurate	new to them	would not accept
10.	on the contrary	loss to himself	grain of salt	just the opposite	try to group	more and more
11.	from the origin	as an agency	at the beginning	the influence of	are held to	provides a chance
12.	a small portion	no matter how	to make sure	an excuse for	to feel superior	a minute part
13.	being transparent	whole new area	to be fewer	they may turn	evidently clear	a small number
14.	break of day	about dawn	by the same token	the power to	called to account	it is interesting
15.	guilty of crime	advantage of	is usually bound	he who is a criminal	it may appear	low nor high
16.	to strongly desire	can be aided	wishing something	may thus help	be more able	some new ones
17.	willing to serve	may be apparent	there is trouble	may observe	an effort to	offer your help
18.	keeping clear of	described as	what extent	just before the	to avoid something	not exactly
19.	true to history	being factually correct	do occur together	has failed to	does not deny	the progress of
20.	of a lazy nature	who are already	average age of	dislike to work	years earlier	in adding up

Time __________ Sec. RATE (from table on page 309): R. __________

No. Correct __________ COMPREHENSION (5% for each correct answer): C. __________

(key on page 326)

III-6 EFFICIENCY (R × C): E. __________

Record on Progress Chart on page 297

Exercise III-7

No.	Key phrase					
1.	place of union	to bring out	a broad interest	a common junction	for college life	a study of
2.	a parting wish	to bid farewell	he can learn	eager to protect	the advice is	within the law
3.	an endless time	no matter how	on the side	give everything	incessant existence	may only be
4.	to set free	for their money	to the contrary	has to talk	no one expects	to grant liberty
5.	respect confidence	in the night	keeping a secret	without him	a message from	little interest
6.	that which ceases	we are here	just as it was	comes to an end	in the capacity	would not hurt
7.	display of wit	an exhibit of humor	it is difficult	in any type	aid in general	to state this
8.	its proper place	in the office	what he knew	this is done	correct position	major cause of
9.	out of reach	not even if	the passing of	the form of	is not clear	that which is beyond
10.	full of activity	there may be	being very busy	has the best	the same was true	only a step
11.	hold spellbound	best interest of	point of view	to fascinate	much depends upon	all but one
12.	an angry dispute	likely a quarrel	another type of	were not used	one item of	sets of forms
13.	great quantity	who will fail	of the action	some phases of	considerable amount	the purpose of
14.	without delay	all are omitted	the larger task	all to many	there is much	be punctual
15.	general order	to build up	regular procedure	be extended to	first of all	from the office
16.	threatening air	the latter plan	does not require	a severe look	will secure	be given first
17.	unite in a body	join in a group	of the present day	tend to avoid	the reason why	a lag from
18.	state of silence	beneficial to all	for other forms	any other kind	absence of sound	does not mean
19.	being sincere	may be both	have claim to it	the fault of	learns most from	honesty of mind
20.	roughy sketched	a completion of	not completed	some part of	some are operated	no small part

Time __________ Sec. RATE (from table on page 309): R. __________

No. Correct __________ COMPREHENSION (5% for each correct answer): C. __________

(key on page 318)

III-7 EFFICIENCY (R × C): E. __________

Record on Progress Chart on page 297

Exercise III-8

No.	Key phrase			
1.	promoted in rank	but hardly more	may suggest	rising in power
		any given day		be wise to
2.	should be granted	working hard	barely escaped	to leave alor
		to describe		should be allowe
3.	concerning truth	in assuming	as most likely	is far from home
		according to facts		as late as
4.	to do away with	to be elected	to dispose of	died instantly
		held until notice		allowed to search
5.	achieve the summit	to reach the peak	able to go	not convenient
		to avoid going		must fall back
6.	as a result of	all has been	always able to	brought about by
		it may be true		trying to climb
7.	ready to proceed	is confronted	in this case	tend to do
		not the thing		prepared to go on
8.	all by oneself	are all evident	he is afraid	to participate in
		away from others		will refuse to
9.	rest from activity	they may be	not very busy	as is usual
		to do something well		how to play
10.	act of killing	death by violence	if he has	who reads poorly
		is final to		habit of refusing
11.	worthy of respect	what to expect	so far as	decent in character
		in some places		it may be
12.	without a spot	may differ from	high level	so much more
		the most part		free from blame
13.	hold in position	most evil man	has stopped	annoyed to find
		keep from falling		not in accord
14.	a loud uproar	may be made to	a great din	the effect of
		could be observed		a decided drop
15.	something essential	very necessary	the bottom of	the only comfort
		which was done		in low value
16.	overly fatigued	in the future	very fact of	completely exhausted
		not so clear		happens often
17.	mountain lodge	were less active	counter to	social dancing
		the other end of		place for vacations
18.	a prompt person	most important	in our culture	turn the dial
		one who is punctual		an area in which
19.	brave person	little relation to	a motive for	one who is courageous
		same classroom as		be helpful
20.	broken to bits	shattered to pieces	show as great	are found to
		does not support		in all events

Time __________ Sec. RATE (from table on page 309): R. __________

No. Correct __________ COMPREHENSION (5% for each correct answer): C. __________

(key on page 326)

III-8 EFFICIENCY (R × C): E. __________

Record on Progress Chart on page 297

Exercise III-9

DIRECTIONS: In these exercises, the key phrase is located on the top line with the answers placed in a vertical column below the key phrase. Read the key phrase thoughtfully and then drop your eyes quickly to each of the lines below, trying to grasp the meaning of each phrase by a single glance. Place a check mark beside the phrase most like the key phrase.

1. to confuse things
   - to conclude by saying
   - and opportunity for
   - pave the way to
   - invite your attention to
   - to mix up

2. mark of distinction
   - to be outstanding
   - some of these issued
   - remains to be done
   - need for a system
   - a major obstacle

3. a time of crisis
   - can be depended upon
   - a critical moment
   - awarded to each
   - cost of providing information
   - free to choose

4. an abundant supply
   - the lack of time
   - one school of thought
   - more than is needed
   - to combine methods
   - a large section

5. contrary to reason
   - an emergency situation
   - result of experience
   - will profit
   - thought to be absurd
   - the required ability

6. very appropriate
   - be allowed to participate
   - in order to learn
   - will not remain
   - in cooperation with
   - especially suitable

7. the extent of space
   - capacity of anything
   - a disturbing failure
   - covering all phases
   - gaining more
   - an efficient answer

8. grasp the meaning of
   - on a large scale
   - to understand
   - to approve
   - in relation to the city
   - able to speak clearly

9. an acquired habit
   - secret sign
   - the greater interest
   - usual way of doing something
   - to organize
   - return in the fall

10. place of residence
    - to be washed away
    - to remove from sight
    - which seemed to him
    - where one lives
    - the other

11. lowest in a rank
    - a word of caution
    - marked by failure
    - held responsible
    - process of defining
    - the last in the series

12. that which confines
    - boundary line
    - to gain power
    - no right to expect
    - for what he plans to do
    - in other instances

13. suggestion of grief
    - kinds of pressure
    - a sound like a moan
    - not too cunning
    - confer with the group
    - the first activity

14. picture of a landscape
    - cannot be interrupted
    - deserves mention
    - a scenic painting
    - the final word
    - standard practice

15. state of being apart
    - a joint responsibility
    - person being referred
    - a kind of service
    - not public in nature
    - usually small

16. to make a recess in
    - will want to know
    - a simple question
    - for his own needs
    - an explanation
    - to set back

17. living a lonely life
    - a solitary existence
    - a small group
    - at a beginning level
    - to destroy the purpose of
    - a type of program

18. furnish with a loan
    - achieve the goal
    - provide financial aid
    - tend to disappear
    - a nursery school
    - to express oneself

19. neat in appearance
    - an appropriate suggestion
    - center of it
    - a tidy person
    - a separate volume
    - examine the situation

20. display of kindness
    - the rapid growth of
    - a sense of balance
    - best way out
    - an act of good will
    - few special changes

Time ________ Sec. RATE (from table on page 309): R. ________

No. Correct ________ COMPREHENSION (5% for each correct answer): C. ________

(key on page 318)

III-9 EFFICIENCY (R × C): E. ________

Record on Progress Chart on page 297

Exercise III-10

DIRECTIONS: In these exercises, the key phrase is located on the top line with the answers placed in a vertical column below the key phrase. Read the key phrase thoughtfully and then drop your eyes quickly to each of the lines below, trying to grasp the meaning of each phrase by a single glance. Place a check mark beside the phrase most like the key phrase.

1. forced to pay a fine
   - punishment for an offense
   - remains to be done
   - to be praised
   - level of skill
   - the fundamental terms used

2. be granted admittance
   - avoid the difficulty
   - used for centuries
   - no one can doubt
   - a thing observed
   - an act of entering

3. a definite difference
   - really agreeing
   - sort of estimate
   - in only one situation
   - in complete contrast
   - method of improving

4. to pass sentence
   - an economic necessity
   - not a part of
   - to pronounce guilty
   - obtaining accurate information
   - to be strained

5. make more difficult
   - generally accepted
   - to complicate matters
   - an easy change
   - one point of view
   - relations that

6. an innocent person
   - free from blame
   - to be arranged
   - one of the essentials
   - very accurately described
   - to fill in a gap

7. to hurl into space
   - of special importance
   - of the plan
   - degree of freedom
   - some previous opinion
   - to throw with violence

8. from now on
   - the same problem
   - the legal use of
   - a number of ideas
   - from this time forward
   - with the real issue

9. looked upon as an enemy
   - are less expensive
   - should be made
   - a military foe
   - type of floor covering
   - an estimated plan

10. cease from being
    - the important compound
    - to come to an end
    - the rate of speed
    - after much searching
    - the principal reason

11. to shape by cutting
    - words of wisdom
    - after much searching
    - kind of a tree
    - taking over too much
    - the art of carving

12. a flat boat
    - the immediate circle
    - meet the test
    - a large river barge
    - certain satisfactions
    - to discover when

13. an object of dislike
    - beyond the bounds
    - to have an objection to
    - to get pleasure from
    - moved by love
    - be supported by

14. admittance to a hearing
    - to be part of an audience
    - with wear and tear
    - may be acute
    - a new example
    - contacts in business

15. belonging to antiquity
    - feeling of mutiny
    - a staff member
    - to help others
    - time before midnight
    - anything very old

16. gruff in appearance
    - a main factor
    - rough in countenance
    - to stop growing
    - be initiated at
    - varying need of pupils

17. a friendly greeting
    - an ancient landscape
    - the new building
    - father and son
    - pleasant hello
    - a losing battle

18. the angry canine
    - one mad dog
    - not to be seen
    - to go forward
    - a disgusted cat
    - misunderstood husband

19. move forward in haste
    - at one time
    - likely to wander
    - to rush someplace
    - superior to long periods
    - would be favorable

20. secure from danger
    - found to promote
    - particularly effective
    - to retard forgetting
    - to be in a safe place
    - forced to check

Time ________ Sec.	RATE (from table on page 309):	R. ________
No. Correct ________ (key on page 326)	COMPREHENSION (5% for each correct answer):	C. ________
III-10	EFFICIENCY (R × C):	E. ________

Record on Progress Chart on page 297

Exercise III-11

DIRECTIONS: In these exercises, the key phrase is located on the top line with the answers placed in a vertical column below the key phrase. Read the key phrase thoughtfully and then drop your eyes quickly to each of the lines below, trying to grasp the meaning of each phrase by a single glance. Place a check mark beside the phrase most like the key phrase.

1. a desire for water
   - field of endeavor
   - not willingly change
   - a feeling of thirst
   - not to be disturbed
   - must guard against

2. rather indefinite
   - regarding the other
   - to know something
   - ability to exist
   - not certain to occur
   - resolution of conflict

3. execute the commands
   - discuss the alternatives
   - a source book of
   - discouraged with it
   - dealing with students
   - to be obedient

4. something in the future
   - that which is to come
   - to take the rap
   - sense of ill will
   - a simple program
   - may come from

5. a roaring laugh
   - result may decrease
   - showing glee
   - excellent argument for
   - not easy to accept
   - have more control

6. exempt from work
   - some simple rules
   - from the office
   - an acquired holiday
   - a direct proceeding of
   - holder of human values

7. guilty of crime
   - a cross-section of society
   - a parallel effort of
   - to help answer
   - one who is a criminal
   - a chain of events

8. to vanish in thin air
   - by this time
   - born of a need
   - too many people
   - to be defensive against
   - pass quickly from sight

9. fitting and proper
   - to be in right accord
   - our greatest fault
   - apt to respond
   - the latter part of
   - on the way toward

10. on his own accord
    - might be applied to
    - of his own free will
    - was addressed to
    - more evident signs
    - our prepared investigation

11. making a selection
    - stating our strengths
    - in a rough way
    - choosing from several
    - opinions of others
    - much more to be said

12. causing to assemble
    - much to learn
    - because of long life
    - for what they are
    - to come together
    - as a young profession

13. plain in manner
    - beneath the surface
    - suffer a kind of
    - most other fields
    - from outside behavior
    - simple in style

14. not completed in detail
    - roughly sketched
    - with whom we deal
    - often accused of
    - will readily recognize
    - may be expressed

15. considerable strength
    - from time to time
    - state of being strong
    - one of the solutions
    - a couple of hours
    - the human factor

16. only a glimpse
    - a big benefit for
    - no particular merit
    - source of irritation
    - a short hurried view
    - give every indication

17. that which is unique
    - become less concerned
    - it is essential
    - only one of a kind
    - jammed with affairs
    - to appear at ease

18. different from usual
    - everything possible
    - of the group
    - reason why
    - the largest amount of
    - changed in appearance

19. cease from motion
    - to stand still
    - thoughtful interest in
    - act of coming to
    - in one common connection
    - we cannot assume

20. sigh of gratitude
    - for all that happens
    - to be thankful
    - never seem to feel
    - a thing of confusion
    - the charge of

Time __________ Sec.
No. Correct __________
(key on page 318)
III-11

RATE (from table on page 309): R. __________
COMPREHENSION (5% for each correct answer): C. __________
EFFICIENCY (R × C): E. __________

Record on Progress Chart on page 297

Exercise III-12

DIRECTIONS: In these exercises, the key phrase is located on the top line with the answers placed in a vertical column below the key phrase. Read the key phrase thoughtfully and then drop your eyes quickly to each of the lines below, trying to grasp the meaning of each phrase by a single glance. Place a check mark beside the phrase most like the key phrase.

1. entitled to awe
   - should be an aid
   - a key phrase
   - imagined form
   - confusion while thinking
   - dedicated as sacred

2. to commit treason
   - level of popularity
   - betray a trust
   - the same experiment
   - to leave school
   - be allowed to decide

3. a wrong statement
   - it should always be
   - in the environment
   - much of the work
   - not according to facts
   - content of a book

4. the lowest point
   - bottom of the scale
   - respect for
   - cannot be helpful
   - contribute to misunderstanding
   - given careful attention

5. an act of exercising
   - newly decorated
   - operation of effectiveness
   - training for an event
   - not a legal one
   - economical manner

6. in terms of largeness
   - more beautiful than
   - form of advertising
   - to make contacts
   - very good reason
   - that which is immense

7. to impart knowledge
   - lowered into the sea
   - an act of teaching
   - simply lay limp
   - love the out-of-doors
   - did not appear

8. act of making just
   - state of excitement
   - await the results
   - to get an education
   - prove to be right
   - the village school

9. set form of procedure
   - an orderly arrangement
   - in a distant city
   - across the fields
   - ask his advice
   - the day before

10. a division of the year
    - a closely knit group
    - corn in the fields
    - one of the seasons
    - a short period
    - under no obligation

11. article of furniture
    - a table in a room
    - time to study
    - in order to present
    - conscious effort to look
    - train of thought

12. state of being near
    - recreation is fun
    - a sense of humor
    - in a close-by vicinity
    - give the keynote address
    - it is apparent

13. an agreeable reply
    - concerning the role
    - to change human nature
    - inclined to limit
    - structure of society
    - to answer yes

14. be in opposition to
    - to raise the quality
    - to be against
    - searching for words
    - be frightened by
    - bit of conversation

15. a gallant person
    - assigned to work
    - during slow period
    - more natural light
    - one noble in spirit
    - easily identified

16. state of inattention
    - lack of attention
    - usually enough
    - type of position
    - something hard to believe
    - near the state line

17. the inside of anything
    - pleasant experience
    - in the home
    - that which is interior
    - a great honor
    - compelled to study

18. keep possession of
    - a brave life
    - born in slavery
    - good deal of expense
    - to live in a small town
    - retain ownership of

19. to make an offer
    - almost immediately
    - to present for acceptance
    - almost like a dwarf
    - a great name
    - to show skill

20. slow to answer
    - not at all pleased
    - soon to be at home
    - an immediate appeal
    - to pause undecidedly
    - type of occupation

Time ________ Sec.	RATE (from table on page 309):	R. ________
No. Correct ________ (key on page 326)	COMPREHENSION (5% for each correct answer):	C. ________
III-12	EFFICIENCY (R × C):	E. ________

Record on Progress Chart on page 297

Exercise III-13

1. related to the newspaper

   a thirst for great fame
   a working compromise
   associated with the press
   dependence upon authority
   impress upon scholarship

2. the general run of things

   to withdraw from life
   a method of study
   the force of the spoken word
   to be determined about
   usual course of events

3. quality to respond

   wrote for publication
   learned men of the past
   very reasonable activity
   capacity of receiving impressions
   the unlimited activity of

4. a very hearty person

   a comparison of translations
   an ideal preparation for
   to be greatly praised
   to study mathematics
   one who displays warmth

5. a person who is interested

   cultivation of the body
   the development of good citizens
   one who is really concerned
   a sense of danger
   material to be memorized

6. a state of fascination

   overcome by amazement
   soon to become a famous man
   as head of the school
   during the hot summer months
   quality of good speech

7. characterized by kindness

   a means of style
   simple method of study
   energetic and pushing
   cruel action
   a pleasing person

8. sufficient to satisfy

   the language of instruction
   a leader in public affairs
   service to the state
   an abundant amount of anything
   a model of best style

9. something which is distinct

   excellent skill to reason
   a liberal education
   to cover a large area
   one of the regular elements
   set apart from others

10. following a given course

    acquired fame as a teacher
    agreeing to a set plan
    a method of instruction
    due to organization of
    close personal relations

11. throughout the universe

    the aim of the school
    the most striking contrasts
    best for the purpose of
    all over everywhere
    a careful use of words

12. be concerned with the result

    to make a new demand
    of the many studies made
    to anticipate the finish
    a variety of accomplishments
    along new lines

13. increasing in difficulty

    becoming more complicated
    an occasional work of charity
    to vary widely in capacity
    conditions of the time
    in their prime condition

14. to be scattered abroad

    to discover the nature of
    the scientific method
    that which is spread
    rights of the individual
    in the same way as before

(continued on next page)

15. looked upon as important

to be equipped with pins
thought to be significant
on the part of others
training in manual skills
to delay the growth of

16. according to the facts

related to the truth
to lack of facilities
no provision is made by
it is encouraging to note
should be considered now

17. an official announcement

the administration of the plan
authorized by proclamation
an agreement of opinion
a successful program
a series of serious talks

18. to be denied an opportunity

the most unusual feature
the plan in operation
to prove very helpful
hold back a privilege
out of the picture

19. a violation of the law

on a less extensive scale
an act which is wrong
social opportunity for all
suggested by tradition
forcing a rule upon men

20. that which might be available

to be secured possibly
the proper thing to do
helps to limit cost
to fulfill their purpose
the best chance of success

Time ________ Sec. RATE (from table on page 309): R. ________

No. Correct ________ COMPREHENSION (5% for each correct answer): C. ________
(key on page 318)

III-13 EFFICIENCY (R × C): E. ________

Record on Progress Chart on page 297

Exercise III-14

1. at a marked disadvantage

possessed with a severe handicap
a chance to leave
an opportunity to learn
included in this report
unable to attend now

2. process of becoming essential

does not rank very high
soon to be needed
a genius for remembering
an active force
the better choice

3. as frequently as needed

to think through a problem
to gain a great deal from it
as often as necessary
a conflict in the soul
to sacrifice truth

4. occurring once each year

welcoming the newcomer
more than this number
not upon a class foundation
an annual event or happening
to be isolated from fear

5. matter added to a book

helpful in this regard
be adopted generally
appendix of a book
less important than the other
of similar friends

6. to apply oneself to a task

to engage with close attention
to work and play together
necessary for the future
is being done carefully
take the part of

7. approximate or nearly exact

in the attainment of
close to being correct
the sense of belonging to
sharing in a common cause
on the honor system

8. to hear and then decide

a varied social program
the most repeated problem
brief word of warning
to submit to arbitration
the poorest showing

9. body of men armed for war

by those who instruct
securing more cooperation
military organization
far more recent origin
about every two years

10. that which is rudely finished

truth of the argument
the average length of time
sufficiently completed reports
equip the new engine
something made without skill

11. a violent start or attack

to injure another person
an efficient worker
more suited to serve
a different view of the matter
open to criticism

12. act of taking for granted

found most effective
acceptance of an established idea
to use up excess energy
advantage in keeping open
in their own planning

13. conspicuously cruel or wicked

resented the authority
a building program
used for special occasions
occur in another year
quality of being bad

14. to attempt to do something

the central part of
a wholesome program
to balance the cost
to make trials or experiments
social event of the year

(continued on next page)

15. activities at an auction

cutting down the cost
a drain on the resources
the most annoying problem
a series of
sale of goods to highest offer

16. having an actual origin

to better existing conditions
that which is real
on a less extensive scale
voluntary pay into a fund
opportunity for all

17. to clothe with legal power

definite boundaries
a philosophy of life
in an assured manner
to establish by authority
more difficult to attain

18. manuscript of an author

widely adopted means
may not be included in it
that written in his own hand
three times each hour
to arrange a date

19. a desire to turn away

feeling of dislike toward something
fairly well integrated
the most powerful force
a successful plan
noted by many

20. strong belief of truth

an artificial separation
it is quite evident
one can learn to swim
all learning situations
a faith of some sort

Time ________ Sec.	RATE (from table on page 309):	R. ________
No. Correct ________ (key on page 326)	COMPREHENSION (5% for each correct answer):	C. ________
III-14	EFFICIENCY (R × C):	E. ________

Record on Progress Chart on page 297

Exercise III-15

1. a radiant brightness

considered to be brilliant
to respond to the question
a change in employees
over a period of years
to receive the benefits

2. to give a bruise to

a surface injury to flesh
a little more under control
to be derived from it
the extent to which
included in the survey

3. to confer or bestow upon

the value of democracy
principles of sound health
that which is awarded
in the given order
to decide a given policy

4. not adapted to its purpose

opposing points of view
belief in any matter
something awkward or inconvenient
those elected to office
learn by living

5. directed or turned backward

rights of others
in a contrary or reverse way
social changes take place
a type of behavior
must be so guided

6. a defeating situation

wholesome way of life
adapted to local conditions
a major purpose
an uncertain and disgusting experience
it becomes true

7. dormitories used by the army

to select wise leaders
the amount of power
complete control of
concerns itself with
buildings which lodge soldiers

8. tract of barren land

has general error
under this type of
may lack knowledge
be present at all times
not capable of producing vegetation

9. combat between two persons

a possible disadvantage
serve to remind us
a battle between two individuals
important details
able to vote

10. lives by asking alms

be reduced to a state of want
in terms of its needs
have power to advise
a well-rounded opinion
must be decided

11. even flow of language

a fair representation
rise and fall of the voice
may safely be regarded
a small role
in the drama of life

12. to strike or cross out

on the highest level of thought
cancel out the effects of
a tenth of the total
indicate the bases for
the most important

13. the seat of government

a fair official record
count on personal appeal
for the best interest of
the capital city of a state
to try for office

14. exercising or taking care

an equal chance to
the great majority of
in position to dominate
a state of being careful
one most capable of working

(continued on next page)

15. that which effects a result

can be considered good
by making such mistakes
will learn for the better
one can hardly say
the cause of an event

16. a numbering of the people

certain other problems
taking a count of the population
merit certain attention
its primary purpose
to hold public office

17. thoroughly established

in an unsatisfactory manner
with serious consequences
can solve the problem
to keep a diary about
that which is correct

18. to be challenged to a combat

involved in the process
is to be arranged at once
a summons to fight
better than doing nothing
for the most part

19. to gather into one body

suggested by the title
a legal philosophy
based on two divisions
to assemble or mass together
may be expressed enough

20. a contest between rivals

to meet in competition
under what conditions
types of development
two principal objects of the job
can be separated

Time ________ Sec.	RATE (from table on page 309):	R. ________
No. Correct ________ (key on page 318)	COMPREHENSION (5% for each correct answer):	C. ________
III-15	EFFICIENCY (R × C):	E. ________

Record on Progress Chart on page 297

Exercise III-16

1. to maintain possession of

learn to cooperate
one's own behavior may be good
product of his experience
be limited to
to have and to keep

2. causes acute suffering

result in desired learning
effort should be made
never takes place simply
that which tortures
planned by nature

3. without the least delay

in any given situation
that which is done instantly
must be borne in mind
to win high marks
means to desired ends

4. an embarrassing situation

some sort of an award
the joy of participating
started at the time
a chance to appreciate
a confusing predicament

5. to beware of something

be on your guard
by which it may be achieved
most important to everyone
covered by study last year
from time to time

6. that which is subtracted

cuts across all activities
a search for friends
the part that is taken away
represented to all
to be well aware of

7. to wander from direct course

a brief description of
the form of inquiry
to designate all meetings
a degree of direction
having gone astray

8. a main division in a book

to mold public opinion
a somewhat greater degree
to arrange into chapters
to learn by doing
keep in touch with

9. talk in an informal manner

promote greater interest
idle chat in a conversation
a result of many requests
to grant freedom
to try to stop it

10. the chief of the group

giving some trouble to
a definite course
to prevent for safety's sake
the leader of the organization
in a hurry to go

11. to make clear and pure

to correct the issue or report
an intelligent finish
an interested group
a difficult time existing
to make a necessity

12. that which is classified

a chance to learn
spent to good advantage
the end of the year
something grouped into classes
not in itself harmful

13. a device for measuring time

instrument such as a clock
made for the sake of
to be considerate and fair
to keep before them
a period for study

14. an orderly body of law

closely related to
the one just discussed
to find some way
the wrong attitude toward
any system of rules or principles

(continued on next page)

15. of the farther side of

a distinct advantage
that which is beyond
in the graduate school
problems which arise daily
on various issues today

16. land beside a border

help to the committee
evidently of little value
that which lies next to
duplicate the work
very easily accomplished

17. that which is borrowed

at a later period
to receive with intention of returning
a primary advantage
chosen for their ability
only in one sense

18. the lowest part of anything

that which is the bottom
a possible opportunity
to learn democracy
unable to practice
a higher standard of living

19. a device used for stopping

not very probable
among the most important
in a very sincere sense
to apply a brake to
highest total number

20. well organized person

to be circled
combine to control members
characterized by efficiency
change from previous form
true in many cases

Time ________ Sec. RATE (from table on page 309): R. ________

No. Correct ________ COMPREHENSION (5% for each correct answer): C. ________

(key on page 326)

III-16 EFFICIENCY (R × C): E. ________

Record on Progress Chart on page 297

Exercise III-17

1. a king who rules over a kingdom

   an act of binding up wounds
   extending to a great distance
   in the direction of the wind
   a group of related plants
   the monarch of a region

2. situated below the normal level

   all under one household
   to suffer extreme hunger
   that which is relatively low
   having intimate knowledge of
   may not be interfered with

3. to magnify or to increase

   quality of being impure
   not of any one style
   an act of moving force
   an addition that improves land
   to enlarge either in fact or appearance

4. anything suggestive of a map

   land used for crops
   conducted in a false manner
   a representation of the surface of the earth
   to affect the conscience
   printed for several issues

5. one who volunteered to suffer death

   an approaching obstacle
   with excellent qualities
   along the sandy shore
   being of a very quiet nature
   one who will die for the sake of principle

6. to recall what has been learned

   surrounded by fresh water
   using the faculty of remembering
   in some other place besides this
   act of the legal officer
   sharp indication of results

7. represented on a small scale

   closely resembling someone
   as frequently as needed
   not knowing what to do now
   responded to the loud noise
   reproduced on a miniature level

8. a time unit of one minute

   working in pleasant surroundings
   the sixtieth part of an hour
   commenting on the subject
   tend to produce sleep quickly
   allowed special privileges

9. to be considered as moderate

   marked by serious crimes
   a resting place at night
   short pause in reading fiction
   which is within reasonable limits
   a bell-shaped flower

10. that which presents moral lessons

    a joint at this point
    system of teaching standards
    open hearth of a furnace
    in place of military services
    pertaining to the forefathers

11. to be classified as a dull person

    no possible hope for the future
    a moderately feeble-minded person
    showing a liking for all
    desire to conceal something
    realizing the real danger

12. something difficult to explain

    planned according to details
    to go out and search for work
    qualified for some type of work
    a complicated situation or mystery
    at a severe disadvantage

13. have but a little margin

    to have very narrow limits
    method of storing up energy
    including most of the past
    forgiving that which was done
    anticipate an approaching event

14. not engaged on either side

    acquire a feeling of belonging
    part of the life at home
    being in the same situation
    quality or state of being neutral
    involved to such an extent

(continued on next page)

15. to name as a candidate for office

a state of being nominated
usually not returned too soon
serious and of sincere purpose
forced to leave school
to clear their own thinking

16. that which is counted normal

various phases of the project
go toward their new job
of some value to others
does not vary from the average
development in growth

17. an obstacle or delay to

that which stands in the way
to be of some service
having a large vocabulary
one of the better opportunities
act according to arrangements

18. a type or fashion out-of-date

necessary for successful learning
instead of the other
counted as old-fashioned in style
being careful in what one does
in the light of changed plans

19. to prove or show to be just

an object of special devotion
decorations for festivals
to support or qualify an act
active hero of a great drama
to provide basic education

20. a cruel exercise of authority

under the oppression of a tyrant
one who usually does his best
for those who understand
before the opening performance
the one who is never on time

Time ________ Sec. RATE (from table on page 309): R. ________

No. Correct ________ COMPREHENSION (5% for each correct answer): C. ________
(key on page 318)

III-17 EFFICIENCY (R × C): E. ________

Record on Progress Chart on page 297

Exercise III-18

1. the act or process of explaining

a hello or greeting
to combine in a group
a network of pipes
operated by gravity
to make plain by means of illustration

2. having an intimate knowledge of

a state of being darkened
a large citrus fruit
a tiny particle
closely acquainted or familiar with
to act or serve as a teacher

3. accepted custom in dress

for extinguishing a fire
the gloom or melancholy
that which is in fashion
goal made by a drop kick
to catch a glimpse of

4. that which is frail or limp

any plant of a family
that which is without strength or hardness
divided into two equal parts
often used in police work
that which gathers

5. something that floats on water

a kind of a sealed tight structure
a tale of adventures
the center of the earth
an entire range or series
an exchange involving risk

6. the terminal part of the leg

the foot of an animal or a person
an increase in profits
to silence by authority
the activities of a public office
to hit a foul ball

7. sufficient or existing at all times

a large amount of light
to be everlasting or endless in length
to receive and keep
any of the various weeds
an opening through anything

8. the event which takes place

to impose restraint upon
a score made by playing
that which happens or occurs
the person in possession of
the acts of one who stores

9. one who acts as a witness

a place of business
a tight hold or grasp
a narrative of events
a person who gives evidence as to what happened
a natural elevation of land

10. quality of being excellent

to receive payment of
varying from the common rule
in some future time or state
to form or put into a herd
extremely good of its kind

11. state of going beyond limits

extent to which sound may be heard
lack of courage
in a state of good health
operated by the hand
that which exceeds what is usual

12. suitable to the end in view

sudden stroke of success
to hit the right note
a cart pushed by hand
appropriate for the desired outcome
where prisoners are confined

13. contrary to natural habits

state of being important
intensity of the influence
something considered as exceptional
careful noting the action of
occupy the same position

14. living in a state of disguise

of the substance of mental concentration
living under false pretenses
to follow as a pattern
quality of being immense
not separated in time or space

(continued on next page)

15. following in regular order

sequence with no interval or break
manage with efficiency
the flower of the plant
pertaining to water power
regard for the interests of others

16. delightful to a high degree

in the nature of an enchantment
an uncertain state of mind
marked by a lack of food
turn in such a state or position
to be held as captive

17. devoted to a sacred and holy cause

found on old walls and roofs
dedicated to a noble purpose
become the head of a family
passing through the earth
the character of a person

18. the customary thing to do

the famous place of execution
considered as promising too mucl
the usual course of action
belonging to a large order
of some remote ancestor

19. of the nature of a cover up

a tank holding green liquid
in order of arrangement
avoid an embarrassing position
that which can deceive
an exclamation of surprise

20. near the beginning of a period

so that all are included
arising from bad character
a confined portion of space
plants of related classes
that which happens early

Time ________ Sec. RATE (from table on page 309): R. ________

No. Correct ________ COMPREHENSION (5% for each correct answer): C. ________
(key on page 326)

III-18 EFFICIENCY (R × C): E. ________

Record on Progress Chart on page 297

Exercise III-19

1. the planet which we inhabit

   the earth upon which we live
   is divided by two or four
   what might not be expected
   in about the same place
   the period from sunset to darkness

2. the act or process of educating

   the melting or freezing point
   to develop and cultivate the mental processes
   triumph over a discovery
   a motor fuel
   to present on the stage

3. excess love and thought of self

   practice of referring too much to oneself
   in recommendation of someone
   the science of moral duty
   a river current
   form an opinion of

4. to have a grudge toward another

   a literary composition
   to feel envy of the other person
   one who writes essays
   to gain complete control
   exceptionally perfect or complete

5. exactly the same in measure

   a type of behavior
   the fulfillment of the conditions
   to be equal in quantity or degree
   equivalent to a triangle
   with intent to deceive

6. belief in what is untrue

   an error in the way a person thinks
   state of being erected
   from some particular date
   an instant of time
   to complete the plan of the work

7. that which no longer exists

   due to external causes
   that which becomes extinct
   way of winning the peace
   belongs to the newly formed group
   preceding the owner's name

8. that which is very convincing

   case demanding action
   testing all possibilities
   to be supported by evidence based on facts
   for use as evidence
   to reveal by signs

9. to be in the nature of a formula

   a noticed effort
   that which is breathed out
   to be given off as a vapor
   to have a guided or set form
   to release from some debt

10. to throw into a state of alarm

    terror excited by sudden danger
    serving as a warning
    given in excess of actual loss
    a model or a pattern
    any person earning his living

11. holding all it can contain

    that which justifies a fault
    to be full or complete in quantity
    permission to practice
    an officer of the state
    extremely good of its kind

12. the act of gaining something

    a bill of exchange
    to go beyond the limits
    the gathering or increasing of profits
    a testing of knowledge
    know the truth of

13. motion intended to express an idea

    condition of being fit
    a sending forth
    making an excursion
    gesture used to enforce an opinion
    suitable for the end in view

14. the act of giving a present

    connected with an institution
    to evaporate moisture from
    sold under false pretenses
    that which is expected
    to give a gift to someone

(continued on next page)

15. to move gently and smoothly

a laying out of money
a particular study or work
to unfold the meaning of
one who has special knowledge
the act or action of gliding

16. the mark set to bound a race

that which is exported
by means of an inquiry
the goal to obtain in winning the race
to search for a discovery
the influences of climate

17. in the nature of an interview

that which demonstrates
a common expression
usually followed by one
a meeting face to face with an employer
a public exhibition or show

18. act or process of irrigating

pertaining to character
expected to do his duty
imitation of greatness
beyond the established limits
to supply water to the land by canals

19. tract of land surrounded by water

seized to secure payment
to understand the void of space
commence or enter upon
unable to speak quietly
that which is regarded as an island

20. the first month in the year

without a sense of fear
the feeling of joy
cast light on a surface
January, named after the Latin God, Janus
being in the first division

Time __________ Sec. RATE (from table on page 309): R. __________

No. Correct __________ COMPREHENSION (5% for each correct answer): C. __________
(key on page 318)

III-19 EFFICIENCY (R × C): E. __________

Record on Progress Chart on page 297

Exercise III-20

1. to grant or pay a pension to

an allowance to one retired from service
various points along the way
soon after the movie
seeking a helping hand
those often in distress

2. an involved state of affairs

shortly after the rain
absorbed in international affairs
believed to be of sound mind
that which is confused
going inside the house

3. related to the matter at hand

as far as that goes
directly to the present condition
in many ways the best
this is suggested for all
not interested in stirring up doubt

4. capable of being molded or modeled

to return to something
concerned with the truth
soft and yielding in nature such as clay or plaster
should be removed at once
in detailed reply

5. suitable to the public in general

quality or state of being popular
small decrease in enrollment
recent flow of workers
should not be tolerated
for an hour or more

6. one who carries luggage for hire

many still stand in line
a lack of responsible help
wired for a public address system
at the same time each day
the duties of a porter

7. the state of being possible

to make better personal adjustment
within the powers of performance
on the part of the college
within each building
one of long standing

8. an act of safety taken previously

a feeling of security
able to make the grade
spoken of in various ways
a precaution taken in advance
who has learned to help others

9. a question proposed for solution

the prime purpose of
in reaching this goal
an inquiry relative to a problem to be solved
a set of new conditions
satisfied with everyone

10. under the protection of providence

safeguarded by divine care and direction
an overall plan
seriously looking forward to
it was evident to everyone
his greatest power

11. to solve or discover quite clearly

a state of being frozen
combined with another element
to puzzle out a mystery
a railroad baggage car
a likely conclusion

12. a measure containing two pints

expressed in mathematic symbols
glimpse of the future
the first in time or in place
a measure in music
a vessel holding one quart

13. to go from place to place

a rubber ball to be kicked
to ramble or wander with no set goal
support for the feet
to waste precious time
one in charge of an office

14. the purpose of a reservoir

one who loads a ship
directed manner of behaving
a person who seeks a fight
a place where anything is kept in store
to make a defense

(continued on next page)

15. made in the likeness of a robe

to attempt to defeat
the plot of a dramatic poem
action which is decisive
that which is not expected
a long loose outer garment

16. a sample portion of the whole

sudden hostile movement
the pupil of the eye
one expert in penmanship
a part presented for inspection
to form a mental image of

17. to scatter or distribute widely

the orbit of the eye
to separate in different directions
a very poor person
vessel with a narrow stern
a thing to be regretted

18. preceding in the order of time

coming first in correct order
a contest for a reward
of standard quality
to translate or interpret
prompt in action or thought

19. not ready or prompt in moving

wreck due to a collision
a thickly populated street
to be slow or tardy in action
water held up behind a flood-gate
part of a railroad

20. to patrol a given territory

his first voyage to Europe
should arrive any day now
please come whenever possible
he never will do that again
the guard going the rounds

Time ________ Sec.	RATE (from table on page 309):	R. ________
No. Correct ________ (key on page 326)	COMPREHENSION (5% for each correct answer):	C. ________
III-20	EFFICIENCY (R × C):	E. ________

Record on Progress Chart on page 297

SERIES IV
Sentence Meaning Exercises

Instructions

You should now be ready to combine some skills and to deal with total meaning of sentence units. The Series IV exercises are designed to develop still further your eye span and ability to recognize similar ideas quickly. This ability is of great importance in being able to read for meaning or in reading to find the answer to questions. Quick recognition of basic meaning is essential to developing rapid reading through skimming and scanning techniques.

In these exercises you are given a key statement that expresses a certain idea as the basic part of that sentence. Read this statement carefully, and identify the key words that give meaning to the idea. Then think quickly and carefully about its meaning. Ten statements follow this key statement. With each of these ten, you are to scan quickly, looking for key words and ideas. Then decide whether the basic idea is quite similar to that of the key sentence or whether it is basically different. If the idea is the same, place the letter *S* in the space after the number. If the idea is different, place the letter *D* after the number of the sentence. As soon as you have completed the last sentence, call for your time, and look up your rate in the table on page 311. Then correct your answers by using the keys on pages 321 and 329, and compute comprehension and efficiency as indicated. Then record rate and efficiency on the Progress Chart.

These exercises begin on page 105; rate tables are on page 311; progress charts are on page 297. Keys are on pages 321 and 329.

EXAMPLE

....

It is difficult for a woman to be a great mother unless her children have serious problems and need her help.

7.	Unless problems occur in the family, a mother has little chance to demonstrate her true value.		7. S
8.	Few women have problem children.		8. D
9.	A woman may never have an opportunity to show her real greatness	X	9. D
10.	It is easier for a mother to gain recognition and appreciation in times of stress.		10. S

Time 54 Sec.	RATE (from table on page 311):	R. 200
No. Correct: 9	COMPREHENSION (10% for each correct answer): (10 × 9)	C. 90
(key on page 321)		
IV-O	EFFICIENCY (R × C): (200 × .90) = 180.00	E. 180

Suggestions

With this series, we move to the recognition of meaning in still larger blocks. This series is designed to help you become sensitive to clues and new content. Think first about the key sentence. Be sure you understand and relate it to your previous knowledge and experience with this topic. Then you can begin to sort out ideas relating to it.

With the large bulk of mass mailing, extensive reading assignments, and the maze of periodical literature, you must be discriminating in what you read. There is no need to read variations of the same basic idea over and over again, unless, of course, you are doing extensive research on that topic. In that case, a good reader will be screening carefully for new ideas or different interpretations. In either case, assessing *what* you know first will speed the process of identifying new material.

Reading materials for new ideas or new perspectives can be done fairly rapidly if you already have an understanding of your own starting point. Skimming techniques can be used to help you pick up new concepts quickly and to decide which materials deserve more careful attention for more detailed information to extend your knowledge and understanding of the topic.

This series provides good practice in the basic steps of good study practice. First emphasize the careful thought about the key ideas to be studied—relating them to personal orientation and previous experience.

This group of exercises should provide good vocabulary experience, good exercise in a variety of sentence structures, and good application of concentrative skills and should incorporate into your reading rate a high degree of perception and comprehension in grasping ideas.

Application of this type of reading to research papers or general reading can produce some real time saving and some much deeper understandings. By setting up a theme idea that you want to support or to challenge, you can provide a focus and a purpose for related reading. This then enables you to do much more effective scanning and skimming to select materials appropriate for more detailed study.

Reading in this sense is much more than looking at words in a passing parade across a page. Reading is thinking, comparing, setting goals, questioning, and weighing the relative values of new ideas as they are found. Reading rate and efficiency in this type of reading involve much more than the traditional word-by-word measurement of progress on a printed page.

Perhaps this type of reading is best characterized by the advice:

Think first . . . then read . . . then react!

Exercise IV-1

A well-organized person is characterized by efficiency.

1. Well-organized people are prepared for any emergency. 1. ________
2. Efficiency is a quality gained by skilled organization. 2. ________
3. Well-organized persons usually handle most situations effectively and get good results. 3. ________
4. To become efficient a person must have a well-rounded social program. 4. ________
5. The inexperienced person could learn a lesson from the well-organized person. 5. ________
6. Good organization pays in that people can accomplish more for themselves. 6. ________
7. Efficient people are often considered to be slightly ridiculous. 7. ________
8. The quality of efficient organization is found only in the business field. 8. ________
9. The person who knows what action to take in many situations is usually quite efficient. 9. ________
10. Good organization and use of all one's resources and skills make one efficient. 10. ________

Time __________ Sec. RATE (from table on page 311): R. ________

No. Correct __________ COMPREHENSION (10% for each correct answer): C. ________

(key on page 321)

IV-1 EFFICIENCY (R × C): E. ________

Record on Progress Chart on page 297

Exercise IV-2

There are no special tricks for concentrating and none are necessary.

1. One of the first things that a college student must learn is the skill necessary for concentrating. 1. ________
2. Concentration is an art which college students will find very necessary in their studying. 2. ________
3. Special tricks for concentrating are not especially needed. 3. ________
4. Concentration, although difficult, does not require the use of particular tricks. 4. ________
5. Necessary tricks for concentration are special ones and not easily learned. 5. ________
6. It is necessary to learn to concentrate quickly. 6. ________
7. There are tricks necessary in learning to concentrate well. 7. ________
8. There are tricks to all trades. 8. ________
9. Special tricks are not necessary in developing an ability to concentrate. 9. ________
10. Concentration is a result of a series of special studies by a student. 10. ________

Time __________ Sec. RATE (from table on page 311): R. ________

No. Correct __________ COMPREHENSION (10% for each correct answer): C. ________

(key on page 329)

IV-2 EFFICIENCY (R × C): E. ________

Record on Progress Chart on page 297

Exercise IV-3

Spaced reviewing develops better understanding of material.

1. Spaced reviewing is another name for repeated reviewing. 1. ______
2. The best way to understand a lesson is to read it and read it again frequently. 2. ______
3. Review is necessary in order to pass the course. 3. ______
4. Reviewing once each week or at regular intervals is a good way to improve one's knowledge of a subject. 4. ______
5. Reviewing at intervals brings about better understanding. 5. ______
6. Teachers use repeated learning as a principal method to help students understand material. 6. ______
7. Better understanding is developed by frequent reviewing at regular intervals. 7. ______
8. The time of the reviewing of material is an important factor. 8. ______
9. To better understand material, one should read it carefully at least twice. 9. ______
10. Better understanding is a goal of all good teachers. 10. ______

Time ______ Sec. RATE (from table on page 311): R. ______

No. Correct ______ COMPREHENSION (10% for each correct answer): C. ______

(key on page 321)

IV-3 EFFICIENCY (R × C): E. ______

Record on Progress Chart on page 297

Exercise IV-4

Power equipment is not essential to productive activity on a farm.

1. Modern farming methods require mechanical tools on the farm. 1. ______
2. A farm may be able to produce quite well without power machines. 2. ______
3. Productive activity on farms can be accomplished without the use of tractors or similar equipment. 3. ______
4. Power equipment is not essential for production on a farm. 4. ______
5. Horses were once used for farming purposes, but since the extensive use of electricity they have become old-fashioned. 5. ______
6. Border farms are those which have no power equipment. 6. ______
7. Farms may become productive without the use of power equipment. 7. ______
8. Most farms in the United States are not self-supporting. 8. ______
9. The high cost of modern farming machinery has kept many farmers from developing their farms into productive units. 9. ______
10. Good lighting is not necessary on a farm. 10. ______

Time ______ Sec. RATE (from table on page 311): R. ______

No. Correct ______ COMPREHENSION (10% for each correct answer): C. ______

(key on page 329)

IV-4 EFFICIENCY (R × C): E. ______

Record on Progress Chart on page 297

Exercise IV-5

Geographical factors have something to do with the method of living.

The way we live depends on where we live. 1. ________

There is no connection between geography and living habits. 2. ________

3. Man's living is modified by nature's influences. 3. ________
4. The geography of a country will tell a great deal about the people residing in that country. 4. ________
5. Influence of climate is quite apparent in weather maps. 5. ________
6. Geographical environment may affect society indirectly by changing the human physique. 6. ________
7. Geographical environment is one of the factors that determines one's standard of living. 7. ________
8. Religious faith is a result of geographical location. 8. ________
9. Human behavior varies according to the time of day. 9. ________
10. Civilization developments that affect one's way of living are often determined by the physical conditions in any given locality. 10. ________

Time ________ Sec. RATE (from table on page 311): R. ________

No. Correct ________ COMPREHENSION (10% for each correct answer): C. ________

(key on page 321)

IV-5 EFFICIENCY (R × C): E. ________

Record on Progress Chart on page 297

Exercise IV-6

Contrary to popular opinion, forgetting is not simply a wearing away of once known impressions.

1. Forgetting is a loss of memory. 1. ________
2. Many people seem to have the mistaken idea that forgetting is merely a gradual loss of impressions once held. 2. ________
3. The process of remembering is complicated. 3. ________
4. Forgetting is not as simple a process as many people think. 4. ________
5. Popular opinion is often the incorrect opinion. 5. ________
6. Psychology is a subject in which one studies many things. 6. ________
7. Impressions which are gained during life make up what we call memory. 7. ________
8. Popular opinion on a subject shapes our opinions on that same subject. 8. ________
9. Impressions of a thing are the same as opinions about the same thing. 9. ________
10. Forgetting consists of more than just losing impressions once held. 10. ________

Time ________ Sec. RATE (from table on page 311): R. ________

No. Correct ________ COMPREHENSION (10% for each correct answer): C. ________

(key on page 329)

IV-6 EFFICIENCY (R × C): E. ________

Record on Progress Chart on page 297

Exercise IV-7

The process of change is one in which the invention comes before we anticipate its social effects.

1. Social effects of the inventions that occur are relatively unimportant. 1. ______
2. Instead of creating stability, inventions force us to unexpected adjustments to the effects they create in our society. 2. ______
3. Scientific developments always precede the social processes of adjustment which they cause. 3. ______
4. A delay should be declared on invention and scientific discovery until the social institutions of man catch up. 4. ______
5. Inventions already in existence have revealed little influence on our social order. 5. ______
6. We seldom know what social effect will take place due to an invention. 6. ______
7. Before this process of change can be controlled, it must first be anticipated. 7. ______
8. Social effects are generally not only not anticipated, they are not recognized. 8. ______
9. The problem of the control of social change resolves itself largely into the problem of the control of the effects of the environment. 9. ______
10. Inventions come before the social effects which they are bound to cause. 10. ______

Time __________ Sec. RATE (from table on page 311): R. __________

No. Correct __________ COMPREHENSION (10% for each correct answer): C. __________
(key on page 321)

IV-7 EFFICIENCY (R × C): E. __________

Record on Progress Chart on page 297

Exercise IV-8

Man fortunately can adjust more than most other animals.

1. Man is capable of making organic adjustments to environment more readily than most animals. 1. ______
2. Man's adjustment is not forever endless. 2. ______
3. Famine is one of the adjustments that man finds very difficult to meet. 3. ______
4. For thousands of years man was adjusted to an environment which called for muscular activity in the open air. 4. ______
5. The cities are an originally different type of environment from the country. 5. ______
6. Few animals could become adjusted to a variety of living conditions as easily as man. 6. ______
7. Adjustment between man and his culture always will exist as a very serious problem. 7. ______
8. Humans are able to become better adjusted to factory machines than animals such as the saber-tooth tiger were able to adjust to changing conditions. 8. ______
9. Down through the ages it has been seen that the human animal can adapt more easily than most of the animal kingdom. 9. ______
10. It is fortunate that all animals have learned to adapt themselves quickly. 10. ______

Time __________ Sec. RATE (from table on page 311): R. __________

No. Correct __________ COMPREHENSION (10% for each correct answer): C. __________
(key on page 329)

IV-8 EFFICIENCY (R × C): E. __________

Record on Progress Chart on page 297

Exercise IV-9

The conservation of natural resources is essential to the enjoyment of our national parks.

1. Conservation is largely responsible for the beauty of the national parks we enjoy. 1. ________
2. Many people mar the natural beauty of forests by being "litter-bugs." 2. ________
3. Conservation is a term which means the saving of the soil only. 3. ________
4. Conservation is a simple and easy way to make our forests a more enjoyable place to visit. 4. ________
5. Conservation is necessary for the survival of national parks which thousands of tourists throng to see. 5. ________
6. Conservation is a process which can be carried on only during the spring and summer months. 6. ________
7. The conserving of wildlife as well as the land and water makes our national parks enjoyable to all. 7. ________
8. A heavy penalty may be imposed if people are caught using forest trees for their own purposes. 8. ________
9. The national law prevents the states from planting trees on capitol grounds. 9. ________
10. Conservation in our national parks is an important part of our national recreation program. 10. ________

Time ________ Sec. RATE (from table on page 311): R. ________

No. Correct ________ COMPREHENSION (10% for each correct answer): C. ________

(key on page 321)

IV-9 EFFICIENCY (R × C): E. ________

Record on Progress Chart on page 297

Exercise IV-10

Careful selection in the breeding of dairy stock will pay dividends in increased milk production.

1. To mate the good bulls and good cows will result in more milk from their calves. 1. ________
2. Farmers should be more careful in selecting their dairy breeding stock if they wish higher milk records. 2. ________
3. It is necessary to have good dairy livestock for breeding if one expects a good milk production record. 3. ________
4. Dairy farmers find it profitable to invest in high quality stock for breeding purposes. 4. ________
5. Increased milk production is the aim of every dairy owner. 5. ________
6. Suitable food is required for all breeds of dairy stock. 6. ________
7. Certain types of cattle are better for dairy stock than some other breeds. 7. ________
8. The breeding of dairy stock must be done carefully to increase milk production. 8. ________
9. It is no wonder that many farmers have low milk production from their dairy stock since the quality is so poor. 9. ________
10. Careful selection in breeding of all livestock will pay dividends in increased production. 10. ________

Time ________ Sec. RATE (from table on page 311): R. ________

No. Correct ________ COMPREHENSION (10% for each correct answer): C. ________

(key on page 329)

IV-10 EFFICIENCY (R × C): E. ________

Record on Progress Chart on page 297

Exercise IV-11

Someone who is not firm and strong is often considered to be soft or weak.

1. A person who is not strong may have some degree of weakness. 1. ________
2. A pessimistic person may be called a "wet blanket." 2. ________
3. An ill person sometimes seems to be frail and weak to his friends. 3. ________
4. To be firm and unyielding is similar to being helpless and strong. 4. ________
5. Someone who is yielding and soft usually does not have characteristics of strength and firmness. 5. ________
6. One who lacks strength or firmness often can be easily influenced by other people. 6. ________
7. Contrary to popular belief, many of the strong willed people may be merely products of their environment. 7. ________
8. A considerate and soft hearted individual may be considered by others not to have "backbone". 8. ________
9. Environment plays a large part in determining whether someone becomes strong or weak. 9. ________
10. A person who has great flexibility usually also has all the characteristics which provide the strength and firmness which one needs for assertive behavior. 10. ________

Time ________ Sec. RATE (from table on page 311): R. ________

No. Correct ________ COMPREHENSION (10% for each correct answer): C. ________
(key on page 321)

IV-11 EFFICIENCY (R × C): E. ________

Record on Progress Chart on page 297

Exercise IV-12

The blueprints for the new school house have defects in that they fail to provide for sufficient fire protection.

1. The new school building is a fire trap. 1. ________
2. Blueprints for buildings are difficult to read without training. 2. ________
3. In making the school plans, provision of the least possible safety facilities to be used in case of fire apparently was overlooked. 3. ________
4. Sufficient fire protection has not been provided for in the plans for the school. 4. ________
5. The architect did not provide suitable safety plans for the new school house. 5. ________
6. The blueprints for the new school house are not suitable. 6. ________
7. In general, good blueprints for buldings provide suitable fire protection. 7. ________
8. The blueprints as drawn by the architect for the new school are not suitable as they fail to provide for protection from fire in some cases. 8. ________
9. The city law states that all schools must be fireproof. 9. ________
10. Sufficient fire protection for the blueprints of the new school has been neglected. 10. ________

Time ________ Sec. RATE (from table on page 311): R. ________

No. Correct ________ COMPREHENSION (10% for each correct answer): C. ________
(key on page 329)

IV-12 EFFICIENCY (R × C): E. ________

Record on Progress Chart on page 297

Exercise IV-13

The resources of the business have increased thrice within the last decade.

1. Business has been unusually good in the last three years. 1. ________
2. By studying records of the business we find that its resources have grown three times greater in the last ten years. 2. ________
3. Successful businesses must have resources greater than their debts. 3. ________
4. In a boom, business does well but in a depression, business does poorly. 4. ________
5. Increases in resources over a span of years are indications that the business is succeeding. 5. ________
6. During the last decade the business has increased its resources 300%. 6. ________
7. The increase in the resource of a business is a good indication of how well the business is doing. 7. ________
8. Careful records must be kept for a business so that the owner can tell how much his resources have increased. 8. ________
9. A triple increase of resources of the business is shown in the last ten years. 9. ________
10. The balance sheet for the business shows that the resources have tripled within ten years. 10. ________

Time __________ Sec. RATE (from table on page 311): R. __________

No. Correct __________ COMPREHENSION (10% for each correct answer): C. __________

(key on page 321)

IV-13 EFFICIENCY (R × C): E. __________

Record on Progress Chart on page 297

Exercise IV-14

Horseback riding is beneficial to the physique in general, but may have harmful effects on the leg bones.

1. When we ride horseback, the horse buffets the rider severely. 1. ________
2. A number of horses make up a herd. 2. ________
3. Horseback riding is good for one in spite of the fact that one's legs may be poorly affected. 3. ________
4. We receive some benefits from horseback riding, but may become bowlegged. 4. ________
5. Riding horseback is healthful exercise, but has a chance to cause curved leg bones. 5. ________
6. Dancing requires a certain amount of work plus natural talent in poise and balance. 6. ________
7. Horseback riding is good exercise, but it may develop unpleasant changes in the leg bones. 7. ________
8. "A donkey can walk between his legs without its ears being touched" is frequently said of the people who ride horseback a great deal. 8. ________
9. When one approaches the horse, the rider is expecting to engage in an enjoyable exercise. 9. ________
10. Riding generally is unhealthy from the viewpoint of general physical condition. 10. ________

Time __________ Sec. RATE (from table on page 311): R. __________

No. Correct __________ COMPREHENSION (10% for each correct answer): C. __________

(key on page 329)

IV-14 EFFICIENCY (R × C): E. __________

Record on Progress Chart on page 297

Exercise IV-15

History has shown that it is difficult for a president to be a great man unless some crisis occurs in his administration.

1. Presidents usually do not become greatly acknowledged unless there has been a serious crisis during their administrations. 1. ________
2. Social and economic control is generally exercised by the president in time of crisis. 2. ________
3. The history of many a country shows a period of particularly great power which is usually associated with the administration of an outstanding president. 3. ________
4. We tend to rate too highly the original quality and even the ability of the president in times of distress. 4. ________
5. Presidents of the United States have often taken credit for prosperity when it was due to favorable rainfall or to the discovery of gold mines. 5. ________
6. It is natural that presidents are blamed for business depressions which they play little part in making. 6. ________
7. Unless a crisis occurs during his administration, a president seems to have little chance of becoming famous. 7. ________
8. The difficulty of becoming president prevents many great men from securing the office. 8. ________
9. A man may become president who is not designated for greatness during his term. 9. ________
10. It is easier for the man in office to be a great president in the time of crisis. 10. ________

Time ________ Sec. RATE (from table on page 311): R. ________

No. Correct ________ COMPREHENSION (10% for each correct answer): C. ________
(key on page 321)

IV-15 EFFICIENCY (R × C): E. ________

Record on Progress Chart on page 297

Exercise IV-16

It has been pointed out that it is sometimes necessary to adjust yourself to those who fail to adjust to you.

1. People often find it necessary to make adjustments in their lives in order to satisfy other people's peculiar habits. 1. ________
2. It is sometimes necessary to force all others to adjust to one's desires for certain periods of time. 2. ________
3. We have learned in various life situations that sometimes we must follow other people's ways since they can't seem to follow our ways. 3. ________
4. International strain could be lowered if each nation could learn to adjust itself to other nations. 4. ________
5. Adjustment is a constant problem to the spider. 5. ________
6. Imitation is one way of adjusting one's life to that of others with whom one wishes to live happily. 6. ________
7. Other people in order to get along well with a certain individual may have to learn to adjust to him. 7. ________
8. It has been pointed out that there are always two sides to every problem which must be considered. 8. ________
9. Instead of going our own way when someone does not agree with us, it may be necessary to learn to make adjustments to his wishes. 9. ________
10. It has been pointed out that people like to have their own way. 10. ________

Time ________ Sec. RATE (from table on page 311): R. ________

No. Correct ________ COMPREHENSION (10% for each correct answer): C. ________
(key on page 329)

IV-16 EFFICIENCY (R × C): E. ________

Record on Progress Chart on page 297

Exercise IV-17

Surveying the site for the new highway was very difficult because of the rugged terrain.

1. Preparing the blueprints for the new highway was difficult due to the rough surface. 1. ________
2. Surveying for the new highway took almost three months due to the moisture in the soil. 2. ________
3. George Washington when a young man went on a surveying party for the site of the new Cumberland Road over difficult and rugged terrain. 3. ________
4. The new highway would have changed location to go through a certain section of the country if the terrain had been smoother. 4. ________
5. Many severely worn gulleys and prominent outcroppings of rock provided extreme obstacles in the beginning work on the new highway. 5. ________
6. Final location of the new highway is always of important interest to the people through whose land it might go. 6. ________
7. Rugged terrain made difficulties in surveying the site for the new highway. 7. ________
8. Engineers had difficulty in surveying the land for the new highway because of the very rugged terrain over which they worked. 8. ________
9. Surveying is not a difficult thing to do if the land is smooth and the land owners are cooperative. 9. ________
10. Broken and irregular land features caused the engineers a great deal of trouble in surveying for the new highway. 10. ________

Time ________ Sec. RATE (from table on page 311): R. ________

No. Correct ________ COMPREHENSION (10% for each correct answer): C. ________
(key on page 321)

IV-17 EFFICIENCY (R × C): E. ________

Record on Progress Chart on page 297

Exercise IV-18

The home economics courses taught in our high schools can be of great use to the boys and girls who take them.

1. Boys and girls who take courses in home economics probably will find them useful. 1. ________
2. The home economics courses taught in high schools are too easy to be of real use. 2. ________
3. The boys and girls who take home economics in high school learn many things that will be of value to them. 3. ________
4. The equipment found in the high school for the home economics course is so different from what the students have at home that they gain no real value from using it. 4. ________
5. One of the most difficult courses offered in high school is economics. 5. ________
6. Since most girls marry, home economics should be taken by them. 6. ________
7. Students in high school will find that home economics can be a very useful subject. 7. ________
8. Throughout the years of high school life the students should take those subjects which will be of the most use to them after they graduate. 8. ________
9. The boys and girls will find that the things they learn in home economics can aid them greatly. 9. ________
10. Home economics as taught in present day schools is of little practical value to boys. 10. ________

Time ________ Sec. RATE (from table on page 311): R. ________

No. Correct ________ COMPREHENSION (10% for each correct answer): C. ________
(key on page 329)

IV-18 EFFICIENCY (R × C): E. ________

Record on Progress Chart on page 297

Exercise IV-19

One of the student's problems is to recognize what should be known and then to fix it in memory so that it will be there when wanted.

1. One student problem is knowing what facts are important and then being able to remember them. 1. _______
2. Success of an individual depends on how well he adjusts to the new school environment. 2. _______
3. Repeated learning is highly desirable for students so that they may have the facts needed always in mind. 3. _______
4. Learning the important things is a problem and remembering them in order to use them is a part of that problem. 4. _______
5. A good way to study is to read the lesson at least twice, and then listen closely to the instructor. 5. _______
6. To recognize key ideas and to establish systems for maintaining them are two important problems in learning how to study. 6. _______
7. Many students find that one difficulty in studying is to be able to recognize what is important and to apply procedures for remembering ideas. 7. _______
8. Students find that it is important to separate the important facts and keep them in mind for later use. 8. _______
9. Universities are good places to learn what is important. 9. _______
10. Explaining the problems is the best way to learn important facts. 10. _______

Time __________ Sec. RATE (from table on page 311): R. __________

No. Correct __________ COMPREHENSION (10% for each correct answer): C. __________
(key on page 321)

IV-19 EFFICIENCY (R × C): E. __________

Record on Progress Chart on page 297

Exercise IV-20

To look upon the faces of high school seniors, one would never guess that at least one out of twenty eventually will be in a hospital for the insane.

1. The chances of a child being placed in a mental hospital sometime during his life are about 1 in 20. 1. _______
2. Being insane is just another form of illness, no more subject to blame than physical disease. 2. _______
3. High school students are very inclined to become mentally ill. 3. _______
4. Sentiment seems to prevail that mental illness is increasing in our society. 4. _______
5. Every individual who shares group life with others develops a personality. 5. _______
6. By looking at the faces of the high school seniors one can tell at least one belongs in a hospital. 6. _______
7. Hospital space should be enlarged to meet the heavy demands being made on it. 7. _______
8. The tragic fact that five out of a hundred high school seniors will eventually find their way to a mental hospital is hard to realize. 8. _______
9. High school seniors should face the fact that of their group, half of them will become mentally ill. 9. _______
10. One can't tell by looking at high school seniors that a certain per cent of them will enter a hospital for the mentally disturbed. 10. _______

Time __________ Sec. RATE (from table on page 311): R. __________

No. Correct __________ COMPREHENSION (10% for each correct answer): C. __________
(key on page 329)

IV-20 EFFICIENCY (R × C): E. __________

Record on Progress Chart on page 297

SERIES V
Idea Reading Exercises

Instructions

Series V should help you to develop the upper potential of your reading rate.

These exercises are designed to help you to read for ideas in short selections of material. These articles are all standardized at 900 words in length and should be read as rapidly as possible—preferably in one minute or less. In reading, you should try to grasp the main ideas, the recurrent theme, and the purpose for which the author seems to have written the article. Remember that headings frequently provide clues to this.

At the beginning of each article you will find the length of the article and the readability scores as computed by the Flesch Formula (14). The higher this score is, the easier the material is to read. General levels of readability are as follows:

READABILTY SCORE	GRADE LEVEL OF READING DIFFICULTY
0-30	College Graduates
30-40	College Juniors and Seniors
40-50	College Freshmen and Sophomores
50-60	High School Students
60-70	Junior High Students

Exercises are arranged so that each successive exercise will be a little more difficult than the one preceding it. Therefore, you will be striving to increase both your reading speed and your reading level. Spaced at intervals down the center of the page are numbers indicating the number of words read to that point. As the instructor calls time intervals, you can glance quickly at these numbers and note your approximate speed.

Read each article as rapidly as possible, and ask for your time when you have finished. This time will be given in seconds, and you then can find your rate of reading by using the table on page 313, which will give you your *rate of reading in words per minute.*

Then answer the two questions that deal with the main ideas of the article. You should have no difficulty in answering these correctly. In the multiple choice (MC) questions, select the answer that seems most appropriate, and place a check on the line before that answer. On the true-false (T—F) questions, circle either the *T* or the *F* to indicate your understanding of the accuracy of the statement. If you answer both of the questions correctly according to the key, your comprehension will be 100 percent, and your *efficiency* score will be the same as your rate. Missing one question cuts your efficiency to one half of your rate; so you should concentrate on the main ideas you read.

When you have computed your efficiency, turn to page 299, and record this score on your progress chart. If you have missed a question, you should record both rate and efficiency to show the comparison. Keys are on pages 321 and 329.

Suggestions

This series provides experience in the type of high-speed reading or skimming that is most frequently used in our daily lives when we want a preliminary processing of masses of reading material for later use or immediate disposal. Personal mail, business correspondence, professional journals, news magazines, and other current newspapers or news digests can be processed in this fashion.

The general purpose of this series is to help you get a quick identification of general content, general ideas, and author viewpoints and to use this quick review as a basis for your own selective judgment as to subsequent use of the materials. Often reading for further detail is unnecessary or inappropriate.

Effective use of idea reading involves use of headings and context clues in searching out key ideas. Posing questions from titles or headings helps to provide goals for reading.

Thinking first about the topic and what you already know about it will provide a mental setting in which you can best evaluate the general content that follows.

In this workbook, this series is provided as an opportunity for you to free yourself from the compulsion for detailed comprehension. Comprehension scores are relatively unimportant here, and you should not be disturbed if you occasionally miss both questions. You should push yourself to improve reading rate as much as possible in this series. Try to eliminate all backtracking. Experiment with new and expanded ideas of eye span. Consider the bad habits discussed in "How Do We Read?" on page 9, and concentrate on trying to overcome them as you practice on these exercises.

Let yourself go! See how fast you can breeze through these exercises without any concern for retaining content for any future use. You may be pleasantly surprised at how much you do remember even then. In the process, you may discover flexibility of eye usage that you had not recognized or used before.

Length: 900 words | Readability Score: 77

Exercise V-1

Young Thoreau's Tree

By Tom Browne

WAIT FOR SIGNAL TO BEGIN READING

A Single Spot

Early on a Saturday, when the morning was fresh and sweet, the neighbor boy I call Young Thoreau trudged up the road to my place and inquired, "Have you any wire?"

Now, I knew if Thoreau needed wire, it was for a good reason. I leaned on my hoe, for I had been busy gardening. "Yes, I have."

Frugal of words, he always got to the pith. "I would like to have some."

"There's a roll of it in the shed; help yourself."

He shot me a grateful glance from his dark Indian eyes. He uncoiled many feet from the roll, fastened it neatly with a bit of string, slung it across his shoulder, and headed toward Still Creek, a slow stream that meanders through the bottomlands.

Of course, I was curious about the wire and, as I continued my gardening chores, wondered to what use he would put it. I had to content myself, however, in the knowledge that he would tell me in due time, if he chose to.

For several days I had been hearing the harsh whining of power saws from the bottomlands. I was beginning to doubt, with more than usual annoyance, that there was a single spot in the world left inviolate to man. As it turned out, there was a connection between this disturbing noise and the wire.

Young Thoreau loved a simple tree—but a splendid, thickly foliaged tree that grew on the lush brink of Still Creek. In its shady branches he whiled away many hours conversing with the birds that momentarily shared it with him. Beneath, the creek flowed deep and smooth, rippled only by the jumping of fish; dragonflies droned on the quiet air; and animals—all Young Thoreau's friends—passed under his lookout: foxes with their reddish blushes of coat and immense brushes of tail, muskrats breasting the placid water, and long, dark mink sliding silently through the tangles.

A Wire Sheath

Several days later I took a day off from my gardening to wander the bottomlands, where I came across Young Thoreau perched in his tree. Its trunk, I perceived, was girdled with tightly-woven wire—an effective sheath against the ravaging teeth of any saw.

With the agility of a squirrel, Young Thoreau scrambled down to greet me, face beaming. As we seated ourselves beside the creek in soft wild redolent grass, neither spoke, fearing to break the magic spell of the woods or to still the happy twittering of birds among thickly leafed branches.

But the silence was not for long, for men had come to depredate again, and the whine of their saws smote our ears. Young Thoreau looked at me in anguish. "See!" he cried. "They are coming soon to cut down my tree."

"Who are coming?"

"The tree-cutters. The wood is to make furniture."

"How do you know that?"

"I asked, and that is what they said."

"How are they getting the logs out?"

"By big, long trucks. They snake them out by 'cat, breaking all the brush."

"You know about 'cats?"

He nodded lugubriously. "Those kind I don't like."

His chin jutted, and hardness showed in his eyes. "I will fight them," he said defiantly.

"All by yourself?"

"I can do it! I will find a way."

"Perhaps it will be better if I were to assist?

A New Ally

He grasped my hand joyously. And as we solemnly shook on it, I was acutely aware of the softness of his boyish clasp, the frailness of his physique, yet he had bravely set himself a task of monumental proportions.

We tarried long beside the gently flowing stream, each with his own thoughts, savoring the fresh fragrance of the woods but growing more apprehensive of the whining saws, the crashing of trees, and the dissection of their limbs. Finally we departed, but not before I examined Young Thoreau's handiwork in girding his precious tree. It had been executed masterfully, the wire woven tight and strong with meticulous care, then stapled fast. He was studying me the while with dark, impassive gaze.

"Excellent! Superb!" I said. "That will stave them off—for the time being, at least." He smiled broadly, happy at my opinion of his work. 700

I had already formulated a plan of action. So next day I set out for the county seat and consummated an excellent deal of purchasing one good, sound, wire-girt tree standing beside Still Creek, its branches reaching out over the limpid water.

It was worth many times the amount I had paid just to observe Young Thoreau watching stealthily from his hideout in the thick branches as the cutters approached his beloved tree, examined it, felt the strength of its wire with their rough hands, shrugged, and, picking up their saws, marched away.

The wounded undergrowth of the bottomlands is 800 fast healing. But the beautiful, choicest trees are gone. Not forever, happily, for nature has her own mysterious way of regeneration. But the finest of all the trees—Young Thoreau's—is still standing in all its magnificence. Only yesterday he asked me if I thought it safe to remove the wire from its trunk, as it might be "hurting" the tree.

I assured him it was perfectly safe to do so, and I think, to me, it was the most satisfying advice I ever 900 gave anyone in all my life. And the most acceptable.

______ STOP___ASK FOR YOUR TIME ______

Record time immediately and answer questions on content.

Time __________ Sec.	RATE (from table on page 313):	R. __________
No. Correct __________ (key on page 321)	COMPREHENSION (50% for each correct answer):	C. __________
V-1	EFFICIENCY (R × C):	E. __________

Record on Progress Chart on page 299

ANSWER THESE QUESTIONS IMMEDIATELY

1. (T—F) Young Thoreau's friend helped him by buying the tree.

2. (M.C.) The tree-cutters were using the wood for:

   ______(1) houses.

   ______(2) furniture.

   ______(3) pole fences.

   ______(4) shipbuilding.

Length: 900 words

Exercise V-2

Readability Score: 75

Black South African!

WAIT FOR SIGNAL TO BEGIN READING

What is it like to be a black South African? What is it like to live in Soweto? These are some of the naive questions I've come to expect from patronizing white liberals and overseas visitors. There are officially sponsored guided tours of the black townships, during which white sight-seers are shown how much has been done for us by way of housing, recreational facilities, schools and hospitals. But I often wonder whether people are ever told that we cannot own our houses. When they see our schools, do they realize that thousands of kids are turned away because there is not room for them? And are they told that the grinning black teacher who greeted them so humbly and politely is paid less than half of what his white colleagues earn, even though he has to work a double shift? Probably not. So what can I say about our life?

Survival

Soweto is sheer hell most of the time, and you have to stay on your toes to survive. One of the things you must watch out for is a pass raid. The pass book is a brown document containing the holder's name and picture, his place of work, his employer's signature, an official stamp and other entries. If you don't keep it up to date, you're in trouble. The other day, I'm heading to the train station where I meet a group of guys. "*Ko bomvu* (the signal is red)," they whisper in Zulu. I take the hint; the police are staging a pass raid. I've fallen behind on my poll tax (a tax only by Africans, who never go to the polls) and walking slam-bang into a pass raid is not the surest way to get to work. Carefully, I work my way around the police-infested streets until I reach the next station down the line.

Bad as it is, Soweto is not the worst place in South Africa. The government insists that our real homes are located in the far-off rural areas: "temporary sojourners in the urban areas" is how we're described. When our usefulness as workers is finished, we will be jettisoned in these "homelands," which many of us have never seen. We are always at the mercy of the "influx laws," which govern the Africans who work in white areas. Say a man who was born in Johannesburg marries a lady from Natal. For the wife to stay with her husband in Johannesburg, she must have a permit to reside there. If she does not, she is "endorsed out" of Jo'burg and has to return to her place of birth. And her husband cannot follow her to Natal because he is restricted to the area of Johannesburg.

On the Run

Life is hard in Soweto, and the payday is a cause for celebration. But you have to be careful with your money. I always shove my pay right under the soles of my feet inside my socks, because the *tsotsis* (hoodlums) will be out robbing people. Their modus operandi is as simple as it is crude. Take the way they treated my buddy Casey when they jumped him one night on the street. "They subjected me to the indignity of an unrehearsed striptease act," he says. "There was nothing I could do, boy. The jungle blades were gleaming in the dark. They took all my clothes and money. I had to scamper home in my birthday suit." He was lucky. The *tsotsis* often kill their victims.

Tsotsis live by the jungle creed. "Look, man, what do you expect me to do?" a young thug asked me once. "They've endorsed my pass and say I must go back to Zululand, where I was born. I left those *Bundus* (rural areas) years ago when I was a toddler, and I don't want to know the damned place. They hound me with this rotten pass, and I have to keep on the run all the time. I must also live."

Weekend Fun

A weekend in Soweto is always something to look forward to, when we visit our favorite *shebeens* (illegal drinking joints) and let our kinky hair down. One lovely Sunday morning we decided to go to the "United Nations," a lounge run by Sis Lou.

I put in our order, "We'll make it a *hajaah* (a half bottle of booze) and six beers, Sis Lou." With the booze sipping in, the talk becomes animated and the company lively. Louis Armstrong is plaintively singing "Nobody Knows the Trouble I've Seen" on the smart gramophone in the corner. He's still growling about his sorrows when the police burst in. One cop with a nose for booze goes straight to a ramshackle shed in the backyard. He whips out a bunch of keys and tries one after the other until the 800 door opens. From the shed they take out enough to stock a small bottle store.

Disgust

While we brood in jail at night, our families raise money for our fines. I am released the following morning, and when I get to work my white boss is fuming. "Why did you do it? I know lounges are closed Sundays, but you can buy your stuff on Saturday and enjoy it at home." He throws up his arms in disgust. "I'll never be able to understand the mentality of you people."

900 I think he may be right. He'll never understand.

_______STOP—ASK FOR YOUR TIME_______

Record time immediately and answer the questions on content.

Time ________ Sec.	RATE (from table on page 313):	R. ________
No. Correct ________ (key on page 329)	COMPREHENSION (50% for each correct answer):	C. ________
V-2	EFFICIENCY (R × C):	E. ________

Record on Progress Chart on page 299

ANSWER THESE QUESTIONS IMMEDIATELY

1. (T—F) The author is proud of the homes and schools provided for the black workers.

2. (M.C.) *Tsotsis* are:

______(1) hoodlums running in the streets.

______(2) bar lounges open on weekends.

______(3) signals warning individuals to watch for the police.

______(4) laws regulating the immigration of blacks into the cities.

Length: 900 words

Exercise V-3

Readability Score: 72

First Department Store Santa

By Mary Sabedra

WAIT FOR SIGNAL TO BEGIN READING

Because of his love for children and because his childhood in Scotland was one of poverty, James Edgar gave freely to those in need. He never understood why "the great gentleman" lived at the North Pole; "He is so far away."

A Shower of Pennies

Roly-poly James Edgar of Brockton, Mass., was America's first department store Father Christmas.

A native of Scotland who came to the United States as a child, he was the man who made American youngsters more aware of Santa Claus than they had been before.

James Edgar (who died in 1910) was a tall, well-rounded person with a ruddy complexion and a loud and hearty laugh. He had a rich, warm voice and wore a snow-white beard.

The owner of turn-of-the-century Brockton's department store, he loved children. On Saturday mornings, he would stand on the roof of his store and shower pennies down on them.

Every year on the Fourth of July, he hired all the trolley cars available so he could take every youngster in town on a picnic in the neighboring community of Avon.

If he heard of a child who was seriously ill, the best medical care available was dispatched immediately to the youngster's home. If there was a youngster who needed extra money to help out at home, Edgar was quick to hire him, even if there was no real need for a new employee.

Never Had a Childhood

"My life in Scotland was a poor one," Edgar once told an associate. "When I came to this country, I had to scratch to get by. I never really had a childhood. I was always out working. I think that is why I enjoy children so much. I'm trying to make up for the childhood I never had."

Edgar opened The Boston Store in Brockton in 1878. He was a showman of sorts and loved to dress in costumes to delight his children at the annual Fourth of July picnics. One year, he came dressed up as Uncle Sam. Another time, he appeared as George Washington. He also appeared as an Army General, in an Indian costume and in a Scottish outfit complete with kilt.

One year, his appearance as a clown brought such great response that he decided to wear the costume in his store the following Christmas. Every day, he wandered through the store dressed as the clown and selected the girl with the prettiest ribbon in her hair; she received a Christmas doll.

This went on for three or four years. Then, in 1890, Edgar decided to try a new costume at Christmas. He had a Santa suit made and the following week wore it in the store. The rest is history.

"I can still remember seeing Santa Claus for the first time," declared Edward Pearson, who was there that first day. "As long as I live—and I've lived quite a few years—I'll never forget that."

Mr. Pearson, in his 90s when interviewed, still had vivid memories of James Edgar, and of the day his parents brought him to The Boston Store to shop for a gift.

A Dream Come True

"Nowadays, Santa Claus is everywhere," said Mr. Pearson. "Back in 1890, we saw drawings of him in the newspapers and magazines. But we never thought we'd ever have a chance to see him in person, unless we sat up all night on Christmas Eve.

"You just can't imagine what it was like. I remember walking down an aisle of the store and all of a sudden, right in front of me, I saw Santa Claus. I couldn't believe my eyes. And then Santa came up and talked to me. It was a dream come true."

The following day, the department store was crowded with children and their parents. A week after Santa made his debut, there were long lines outside the store every day.

Originally, Edgar planned to appear for only a couple of hours each day in the Santa costume. This was supposed to be during the late afternoon after school got out. But his idea proved so popular he had to order a second Santa outfit. This costume was worn by "Jim Grant, a big floorwalker."

Soon the children were arriving by train from Boston and other surrounding communities. Some came from Providence, R.I. A few sophisticated New York youngsters showed up. Just about every child who could persuade mom and dad to make the trip to Brockton visited The Boston Store that Christmas.

During the year that followed, word of Edgar's great success spread across the nation. Thus in 1891, Santa made his appearance at a number of major stores. By the turn of the century, he had a throne in department stores in just about every large city.

Today, there are elaborate parades heralding ← 800 Santa's arrival in important cities. In smaller communities, he arrives at shopping plazas in helicopters.

In 1890, when James Edgar first had his idea, only a few thousand children had an opportunity to shake Santa's hand. He once said: "I have never been able to understand why the great gentleman lives at the North Pole. He is so far away. He is only able to see the children one day a year. He should live closer to them."

Even so, 86 years later, millions and millions of eager young children will whisper their Christmas 900 → secret into Santa's ear.

______ STOP__ASK FOR YOUR TIME ______

Record time immediately and answer questions on content.

Time__________ Sec.	RATE (from table on page 313):	R.__________
No. Correct__________ (key on page 321)	COMPREHENSION (50% for each correct answer):	C.__________
V-3	EFFICIENCY (R × C):	E.__________

Record on Progress Chart on page 299

ANSWER THESE QUESTIONS IMMEDIATELY

1. (T—F) The Santa Claus outfit was only one of many costumes used at times by the owner of the department store.

2. (M.C.) The first department store Santa was really:

______(1) Scot Brockton.

______(2) Jim Grant.

______(3) James Edgar.

______(4) Edward Pearson.

Length: 900 words

Exercise V-4

Readability Score: 71

Farewell Address

By Stephen Kitsakos

(Reprinted by permission from *Congressional Record,* July 9, 1974.)

WAIT FOR SIGNAL TO BEGIN READING

Tradition

(Representative John M. Murphy of New York state presented this address by a senior in New Dorp High School as a fine example of commencement addresses.)

As I think of this commencement, our new beginning, I am reminded of the past. And relating past experiences to myself, I sit and dwell over the years, those short-lived years that are the fundamenal seeds of my life. And I remind myself of a visit into the city. It was at a time all of us, and especially I, were developing, becoming immensely aware of the world around us: our families, our friends, our ← 100 ambitions, our goals, our lives.

New York is a racy town, full of adventurous things, throbbing taxis, intense excitement, and the constant flicker of men and women and machines. Taking this all in, I began to realize its haunting loneliness. When I asked myself why I should get this barren feeling, I began to realize it was because the city was empty of sincere emotion.

Futile Utopia

We cannot live in a society, a world, a place where emotions are inconstant—in Platonic republics where lives are vacuums. We cannot adhere to coups and juntas and oligarchies where creativity is ← 200 suppressed. We cannot exist on a forbidden planet where movements are clocked and man exists for time. And yet, we cannot and should not pursue some elusive El Dorado—some futile Utopia of dreams. For life can be lived with dreams and with reality.

Rudyard Kipling expressed this idea so conscientiously:

"If you can dream—and not make dreams your master . . .

If you can fill the unforgiving minute with sixty seconds worth of distance run:

Yours is the earth and everything that's in it.

And what is more—you'll be a man, my son!"

The Crux

This is the crux of our lives; the crucial point ← 300 where we lean back and smile in satisfaction, and say to ourselves, "It's been four years, and I'm proud of myself." And we should be; we all should be proud of ourselves. This is an era of awareness. No one has to say to us, "The world out there is tough." We know it; we realize it a little more than other generations did. But we are obliged to live in it and change it . . . if we can. We are obliged to dream in it. We are not out to 400 → save the world as crusaders, but we are spiritually high with concern, with emotion, and with hopes of eventual response.

Change

This is an age of constant change which can lead very easily to hypocrisy. It's been proven in every aspect of our lives—politically and socially. If we are sincere in our goals, our ideals, our special emotions—then we can be safe and not naive to discontent and disillusion.

Dreams

Perhaps the most disillusioned characters I have read have been in Fitzgerald's *Gatsby.* Gatsby, like us, dreams, yet as he vainly pursues the future, time 500 → carries him inexorably back into the past. He is the irony of American history—while we are the symbols: symbols of unity, symbols of pride, symbols of a prosperous wealth. We are not a lost generation, but a discovered one—one of hope and one of rejoicing. Our lives cannot be altered by a newspaper headline. We cannot adhere to devastation or dramatic tragedies. True, we can be inspired by them, but we cannot let them rule our passions. Fitzgerald described his world as a change from a fresh, green breast to a grotesque wasteland, where only the morally 600 → irresponsible can hope to survive. I describe it as a wasteland . . . with hope. Valleys of ashes cannot be created unless we create them ourselves. We can be wealthy, wealthy in self determination, wealthy in love. But wealth in a materialistic way is futile. There is nothing but aimless drifting. What follows is false goals, self-delusion, and finally destruction.

Smile

Let's look around at each other and smile. This is a joyous occasion. The tradition of commencement is one that will live and prosper, for it brings to close something obvious, and opens portals to something unforeseen. We should all take great pride in our school. It has given us the foundation to develop ← 700 principles which we must foster and perpetuate.

Farewell

And now we are ready, with cautious anxiety, yet filled with unbounded eagerness. In a few minutes, this will be a true farewell as we leave with sincere hopes that we are ready to pursue the unknown. We find our whole lives passing before us. Dreams of yesterday have taken shape and are now reality; but they were practical ones. We have all dreamed of this moment in our lives and now we can all say, "Wow! I have achieved something in my life." And it's a good ← 800 feeling.

When we leave tonight, we'll probably see many teachers crying. We'll be shaking hands with guys we've hated for four years. We'll be congratulating girls who have brushed us aside throughout our high school career. We'll probably flutter around a bit, maybe go to dinner and have a good time. But when it's over, we'll wake up without the pair of crutches that was our beloved New Dorp. There will be no one to lean on any more. Let us stand straight; we've learned to walk by ourselves. We'll smile and say, 900 → "Look out world! Here we come!!"

______ STOP __ ASK FOR YOUR TIME ______

Record time immediately and answer questions on content.

Time __________ Sec.	RATE (from table on page 313):	R. __________
No. Correct __________ (key on page 329)	COMPREHENSION (50% for each correct answer):	C. __________
V-4	EFFICIENCY (R × C):	E. __________

Record on Progress Chart on page 299

ANSWER THESE QUESTIONS IMMEDIATELY

1. (T—F) The author stated that this is an age of constant change which must be faced with sincerity and enthusiasm.

2. (M.C.) The speaker gave considerable emphasis to:

   ______(1) dreams.

   ______(2) goals.

   ______(3) fears.

   ______(4) threats.

Length: 900 words

Exercise V-5

Readability Score: 67

Maple Sugaring

By Richard Wolkomir

WAIT FOR SIGNAL TO BEGIN READING

New England winters look like picture postcards, with vistas of snowy mountains and valleys, frosty hamlets clustered about a white steeple, lonely hillside farms with smoking chimneys. But, as any native will admit, winters in the Northeast are much longer and colder than seems necessary. By February, snow-weary Yankee farmers are fiddling with their sap buckets.

To the New Englander, maple sugaring means more than a few extra dollars—it is a festival, a rite of spring. Sugaring begins with the first March thaw, and since the income from sugaring comes in just at property tax time, New England's farmers claim the 100 reason they go through all the work is for "tax money."

Discovered by Indians

New Englanders learned their maple sugaring from the Indians, who slashed the tree trunk with a tomahawk, inserted a hollow reed, and collected the dripping sap in a bark trough. They boiled the sap down to syrup by dropping red-hot stones into the trough.

Legend has it that the Indians discovered syrup when a squaw boiled her brave's moosemeat in the sweet water dripping from a maple tree—the sap turned to syrup and the brave was ecstatic. The Indians also believed that when the world was new, 200 syrup flowed ready-made from the trees. But the Great Spirit decided something so sweet should not come easily, and maple sugaring has been hard work ever since.

Little Change in Process

Today's maple sugarer works much as his great-great-grandfather did. The process begins in early March, when the farmer straps on his snow shoes and climbs his maple mountain to drill new tap holes. A tree must be at least 40 years old, "a foot through," and 60 feet high before it is mature enough for tapping. Into each hole the farmer inserts a hollow metal spout, or tap, and from the tap he hangs a 300 bucket. A large, old tree may have three, four, or more buckets hanging from it.

When the weather is right—warm days and freezing nights—sap rises in the tree and some drips through the spout and into the bucket. Every day's run is collected in a large tank atop a wagon or sled, depending on the depth of the snow.

Each tankful, which looks and tastes like water, goes back to the sugar shack for boiling down. Inside the shack is a long furnace called the arch. Atop 400 the arch is a huge steel pan filled with super-hot sap that boils, steams, and bubbles. Raw sap flows into one end of the pan, works its way through a continuous maze of compartments, and pours out the "draw off" end as maple syrup.

Traditionally, sugaring has been a family job, with everyone pitching in. An uncle and some nephews may be in the woods with the collecting tank. In the sugarhouse, the farmer keeps an eye on the boiling sap, occasionally dropping some cream in with an eyedropper to slow it down, testing syrup 500 for proper density. His son may have the tough job of cutting hickory logs while perhaps a grandson collects the syrup in cans and seals them. Meanwhile, the women of the family prepare meals and snacks.

In the last few years, syrup producers have begun to modernize. Oil-fired furnaces are no longer rare, and some farmers are experimenting with plastic tubing, strung from tree to tree and ending at the sugarhouse, thus eliminating the collecting tank.

These innovations lack the poetry of the old sugaring methods, but they are necessary. It takes 40 gallons of sap to produce just one gallon of syrup. 600 And to create enough heat to produce that one gallon requires a log of wood as large as a man, which must be split, sawed and dried. The old ways are too costly, and must vanish. But they are going slowly. Despite the hard labor, many New Englanders cling to the traditional methods just because they enjoy them.

Pride in the Product

So ingrained is the sugaring habit that when spring comes, families in the larger towns and cities will tap the single maple in their front yard and produce a pint of syrup on the kitchen stove.

Maple Sugaring

New England farmers regard their syrup the way (700) French vintners regard wine—they claim they can taste the difference between their neighbor's syrup and their own. And they judge a sugar bush by whether it is cold or stony, or sloping just right towards the sun.

Maple syrup, naturally enough, is a common denominator for New England cooking, the universal ingredient that appears in everything from candy to baked ham. Indians ate maple syrup on sagamite—corn meal mush to which they added grasshoppers or crickets according to the season.

Yankees use this natural confection for glazing ham, carrots, sweet potatoes, and for sweetening cucumber pickles and baked beans. They like it on (800) raised doughnuts, hot baking powder biscuits, pancakes, waffles, and French toast.

Traditionally, the syrup season is over when the first frogs begin to sing in April. Then the buckets are put away and the door is closed on the sugarhouse for another year. But enough syrup has been stored to last until next spring. Besides pouring it over his pancakes in the morning, the farmer uses it in a hundred other ways, perhaps because it reminds him during the long winter of the spring celebration that (900) will come with the first March thaw.

________STOP—ASK FOR YOUR TIME________

Record time immediately and answer questions on content.

Time ________ Sec.	RATE (from table on page 313):	R. ________
No. Correct ________ (key on page 321)	COMPREHENSION (50% for each correct answer):	C. ________
V-5	EFFICIENCY (R × C):	E. ________

Record on Progress Chart on page 299

ANSWER THESE QUESTIONS IMMEDIATELY

1. (T—F) New Englanders discovered the "art" of maple sugaring.

2. (M.C.) Some modernization of sugaring methods has occurred because:

______(1) farmers no longer have time to utilize the old methods.

______(2) the old methods are much too hard.

______(3) too many people have to be involved in the old methods.

______(4) the old methods are too expensive.

Length: 900 words

Exercise V-6

Readability Score: 64

Ranch Vacations

By Bill Thomas

(Reprinted by permission from *Travel,* May 1970.)

WAIT FOR SIGNAL TO BEGIN READING

Diamond Ranch is a 75,000-acre site that sprawls over a section of Wyoming so broad that even the cowboys who have worked there for years have not seen all of it. It is one of several ranches that have begun a tourist program under the auspices of a nationally franchised camping chain. Not all of the ranches are working ones, but some of them are and it is the hope that more and more active ranches will be brought into the tourist picture. Thus more visitors from across the country, many who have never seen a cow or calf closeup before, can get an education in how a working ranch actually operates.

Emphasis Is on Everything

Each of the ranches has a campground—in fact, the emphasis at most of them is on camping. But at the Diamond Ranch Kamp, it's on everything—fishing, exploring, rock-hounding, horseback riding, swimming and hiking.

Visitors to the ranch frequently have a chance to see purebred Arabian horses, now being raised by the Diamond's owners. These magnificent animals are fascinating to behold, and watching their fillies and colts frolic spiritedly shows how the breed develops its inborn traits of speed, grace and keenness.

It's a very unusual ranch, the Diamond, 13 miles off busy Interstate 25 north of Cheyenne. Turning off onto a dusty, winding gravel road, the very mood of the countryside makes one feel a sudden sense of well-being, a subtle ease.

If your way has been weary, the greeting of the folks at the Diamond is something to lift your spirits. From the time they bid you a howdy until you've been bedded down under the starlit Wyoming skies, you know this is truly the West, not much different than it was in pioneer days. And you enjoy the rustic atmosphere of it all, the pristine beauty. If you listen carefully as the moon rises above the small groves of cottonwood and aspen, you'll hear the distant howl of coyotes as the first cowboys and settlers who came through this country heard them.

If you'll listen carefully, too, you may hear the distant bawling of cattle or the whinny of a horse—and somehow you feel a closeness to the basic things of life that you never felt before. It's a good feeling as you drift off to sleep on your first night at a ranch.

Dawn comes early in this part of Wyoming and the workday begins before it arrives—at least for those who run the campground. The campground is invaded soon after daybreak by the cowhands and if you can sleep through that, you'd very likely sleep through a thundering stampede of cattle.

That campground, incidentally, will provide for about 30 units, with room for another 30 at every likely spot closeby. Just make sure you don't get too far back into the hills, however, or if you do, be sure to take a compass. This is big country.

If you should not want to rough it while at the Diamond, you may obtain a neat room in a remodeled barn, or you might prefer renting one of several housekeeping cabins. If you don't care to fix your own meals, there are two restaurants on the ranch, one for breakfast and snacks, the other, comparable to the plush world of dining in New York, Paris or San Francisco, is for dinner.

Land of Real Cowboys

Although there are many side attractions, this is really cattle country. The rangeland is so vast, the horizons so distant, a man can feel overpowered by the silence. It's picturesque country, the kind of land where you might see a blazing campfire in the middle of nowhere and, if you stopped to listen, you might hear a cowboy strumming a guitar and singing a western ballad you'd heard somewhere before.

Around Chugwater and other parts of this section of southeastern Wyoming, you'll see a number of genuine cowboys who still roll their own smokes, chew tobacco and are bowlegged from spending too many hours in the saddle. Their faces will be tanned by the sun and the wind, their clothes impregnated with the smell of a horse and a leather saddle. Their hands will be calloused from hours of roping cattle and branding calves, building fences and riding ranges.

Feeling of Freedom

This is the kind of country where the wind blows free and, perhaps because of the infinity of it, because of the wide open blue skies, because of the rolling hills and sagebrush land that rolls on and on forever, you identify with it and you, too, feel free. Sometimes the wind blows strong here—seldom during the summer tourist season—more often in autumn and spring when storms rage across the land.

The real value of a camping vacation on a ranch cannot easily be measured. It is a feeling, an atmospheric condition, a dimension removed from the way of life most of us are accustomed to. It is the peacefulness of a soft breeze blowing up a canyon, the howl of a pack of coyotes under a full moon, the melodic splash of a big trout in the pool nearby. Long after you've left the ranch, long after the cowboy's yodels and the strum of a guitar have been silenced by bitter winter winds and heavy snows, you'll still be remembering experiences from that summer.

______STOP__ASK FOR YOUR TIME______

Record time immediately and answer questions on content.

Time ________ Sec. RATE (from table on page 313): R. ________

No. Correct ________ COMPREHENSION (50% for each correct answer): C. ________
(key on page 329)

V-6 EFFICIENCY (R × C): E. ________

Record on Progress Chart on page 299

ANSWER THESE QUESTIONS IMMEDIATELY

1. (T—F) The author tries to convey to the reader that while visiting the Diamond Ranch, one acquires an unforgettable closeness to nature.

2. (M.C.) Which of the following was not mentioned as an activity at the Diamond Ranch?

_____(1) Horseback riding.

_____(2) Fishing.

_____(3) Mountain climbing.

_____(4) Rock hounding.

Length: 900 words

Exercise V-7

Readability Score: 64

The Polar Bear

By Savva M. Uspenskij

WAIT FOR SIGNAL TO BEGIN READING

Hard to Study

The polar bear, at a maximum weight of one ton, the largest of all living land predators—is not easy to study. While polar bears are not very shy of man all of the obstacles the would-be observer encounters—the ice flow, the piling up of hummock ice, countless cracks and leads between ice fields, frost and snowstorms, and the polar night that lasts nearly half a year—make first-hand research difficult or impossible.

However, even the little that we do know identifies the polar bear as one of the most "perfect" representatives of the arctic fauna. With its enormous streamlined body, wide paws and long agile neck, the polar bear swims and dives superbly—it lives not only on the ice, but in the open sea as well. And because food is often difficult to find, the bear is constantly on the move.

Important Milestone

When it is two to three months old and weighs only about twenty pounds, the cub leaves the snow den with its mother and takes its first uncertain steps on the ice. This is the most important milestone in its life, for from that moment on its journeys will never end. Only the adult female has the prospect of spending the winter in a den on some plot of land once in every three years. But even the bear's endless migrations are no guarantee of a successful hunt, and the huge animal's ability to survive prolonged hunger is as amazing as its capacity, when successful, to consume unbelievable quantities of food and quickly grow fat.

Since the Arctic is relatively small (the area of the Arctic Ocean is smaller than the territory of Europe), the polar bear's total habitat is also relatively small. Indeed, the actual motherland of these animals is really quite tiny, comprising a ring of islands around the polar ice cap, extending only as far south as northern Canada, Alaska, Norway's Svalbard, Greenland and the Soviet Arctic. In the fall, year after year, she-bears gather on those islands to "den up" and give birth to cubs. Here, often in the unmelted layer of last year's snow, the female digs out a maternity den, which may initially be merely a shallow pit; the drifting of snow completes it. Usually, however, she digs deep into a snowdrift, carving an entrance several feet long and sloping upward to one or two "rooms," complete with alcoves and even a ventilation hole in the roof! An average den may be seven feet long, five feet wide and three feet high.

In a polar bear's den—assuming, of course, that it has been vacated by the animal—two or three people can situate themselves without difficulty, and even spend a comfotable night. Its ceiling, although sometimes several feet thick, allows the light to pass through, and during the day there is a pleasant bluish light inside. Without fail, the bear's den is impeccably clean.

In the middle of the winter, the cubs—usually two of them—are born. Covered with a sparse, whitish wool, helpless, blind and deaf, they are not much larger than newborn kittens. The family leaves the maternity den in March or April, heading in a straight line toward the sea, and pausing frequently to rest in shallow dens the mother scrapes in snow or earth. For at least two years the cubs follow their mother over the ice, learning to eat seals and vegetation but suckling all the while. Often cold, and sometimes frightened, the cubs curl up in the mother's fur for naps. Sometimes they even ride on her back.

Simple Life

Outwardly, the life of the polar bear is as simple as its barren arctic environment. Roaming over the ice and through the freezing sea, it makes a kill, eats its fill and sleeps soundly on the spot. Then it rises, hungry again, to hunt another seal. Perhaps the only relief to this solitary drama—and the bear feels a need for others of its kind only at mating season—is the pestering crew of arctic foxes, ravens and gulls that may be attracted to the bear's kill. Powerless to drive the small creatures away, the giant eventually accepts their presence. And since a polar bear may consume only the skin and blubber of a seal, its followers are rewarded handsomely for their persistence.

Only when a large supply of food appears—such as an 800-pound bearded seal, or the thrown-out carcass of a whale—will several polar bears come together. Often maintaining complete indifference to each other, they sleep and eat to their satisfaction, then wander off in various directions.

Patient and Cunning

On the hunt, the polar bear is patient and cunning. Lying motionless in the congested ice for hours, it may cover its telltale black nose with one ← 800 white paw. Let a seal only peek out of its breathing hole and the white mass springs, one clawed arm snatching its prey in a blur of movement. In the summer, the bear must sneak up to a seal basking lazily on top of the ice. Hiding behind ice hummocks, avoiding cracks, it edges closer and closer, until it can catch up to its meal in huge one-two leaps. Or it may approach craftily from the water, submerging deeply to come up close by, or swimming slowly, pushing a 900 → piece of ice before it as clever camouflage.

_______ STOP__ASK FOR YOUR TIME _______

Record time immediately and answer questions on content.

Time __________ Sec.	RATE (from table on page 313):	R. __________
No. Correct __________ (key on page 321)	COMPREHENSION (50% for each correct answer):	C. __________
V-7	EFFICIENCY (R × C):	E. __________

Record on Progress Chart on page 299

ANSWER THESE QUESTIONS IMMEDIATELY

1. (T—F) The polar bear is a typical representative of Arctic fauna.

2. (M.C.) The polar bear begins a pattern of lifelong migration:

______(1) in the spring a few months after its birth.

______(2) only after it has reached maturity.

______(3) only if food is unavailable, thus forcing it to travel in search of food.

______(4) after it is one year old and no longer suckling.

Length: 900 words

Exercise V-8

Readability Score: 61

Waterfowl Woodcarving

By Charles A. Wechsler

(Reprinted by permission from *Minnesota Volunteer,* November-December, 1976.)

WAIT FOR SIGNAL TO BEGIN READING

Talent and Time

Can life be created from non-living matter? One northern Minnesota scientist is getting amazingly close.

Grant Goltz is a soil scientist at Chippewa National Forest. But it is not during his regular work-day that he is striving to replicate the miracle of life. The 33-year-old Goltz is creating life-like forms in the basement of his Bemidji home—as a hobby—from blocks of wood.

Goltz's hobby combines sculpting, painting and knowledge of taxidermy in creating such startling replicas.

Goltz is a versatile artist of immeasurable talent who, with a handful of tools and brushes creates extraordinary life-size replicas of wildfowl. 100

When I first visited Goltz, I was amazed at the life-like beauty of his hand-carved decoys. I found myself holding a decoy nervously, almost expecting the bird to explode into flight.

To bring such true-to-life qualities to a wooden sculpture requires both talent and time. Before carving, Goltz researches the species he plans to create. He may pour through dozens of books and magazines, studying pictures and drawings for anatomical structure, and searching for the ideal pose. If still not satisfied, he may take his own photographs of live birds.

"I learned taxidermy at 15 and this has helped me 200 to better understand how birds are put together. This knowledge enables me to create a more life-like bird, especially a standing model," says Goltz.

A Meticulous Craftsmanship

The carving process begins with two blocks of basswood, which Goltz rough-cuts into a head and body. Once these forms have been sanded smooth, he uses an assortment of knives, gouges, and wood-burning tools to carve, etch, and burn in every feather. Head and neck feathers are simply etchings, but for the larger feathers, Goltz will meticulously create every tiny feather vane and barb.

The head and feet require even more precise 300 work. Goltz gouges out the twin nostrils at the top of the bill. At the base of the bill, his patient hand carves the rows of minute lamellae which ducks use to strain food from the water. He even carves the eyelids so they droop naturally over the glass eyes.

If the bird is a "stander," Goltz recreates the tiny scales which cover the feet of waterfowl and the paper-thin webbing between the toes.

Still, the decoy is not finished. Now, Goltz the meticulous craftsman must become a precision painter. Referring to a study skin or mounted 400 specimen, he uses oil-based paints to duplicate the irridescent hues and soft tones which vary from feather to feather over the bird's plumage.

The entire process, from researching his subject to the final application of several coats of paint, may take from 40 to 60 hours, depending on whether the model is a decoy or a stander.

Goltz's talent as a wood carver seems even more amazing when one considers that he completed his first carving just three years ago. "My wife Suzy asked me to carve an owl," he recalls. "It took several weeks 500 to complete and the final product looked terrible. I said to myself that I could do better than that."

For the next year, he carved miniature song birds. Then one day he read an advertisement for a book on carving life-size birds. He wrote for the book, and from its pages, a master woodcarver was born.

"With help from the book," Goltz remembers, "I managed to carve a full-size woodcock. It was a lot of fun. After that, the whole thing kinda snow-balled."

A Professional Hobby

Before long, Goltz had completed several waterfowl decoys for friends and area sportsmen. One 600 proud owner of a Goltz creation urged the artist to enter the 1975 International Decoy Contest at Davenport, Iowa. There, Goltz put several of his birds up against more than 300 decoys entered by carvers throughout the country.

Despite the odds, the young Bemidji artist made an impressive showing. One of his decoys captured the best of show trophy in the amateur decorative division. His other creations took two firsts, a second, and an honorable mention in various classes.

Since that first competition two years ago, Goltz has won top honors in several other decoy contests, including this year's International where, competing as a professional, he captured another cluster of first-place awards and narrowly missed another best of show trophy.

700 ←

And so, word of Goltz's skill as a woodcarver continues to spread. Accordingly, demand for his decoys also continues to increase (already he is six months behind on meeting his orders). Though he receives $300 for a waterfowl decoy and $500 or more for a stander, Goltz is reluctant to turn his hobby into a career.

"At this time, I find carving to be very relaxing and enjoyable," he explains. "I don't want it to get out of hand. If I feel too pressured, the quality of my work might suffer. I like to work at my own pace . . . to work on several birds at a time . . . to be able to set aside the whole thing and go hunting or fishing."

800 ←

This relaxed attitude toward his new-found avocation is helpful. It enables Goltz to painstakingly reproduce every minute body and feather detail, thus instilling a life-like quality in his decoys.

But there is something else, something less tangible, that makes his wooden birds so realistic. Possibly it is that Goltz, like other accomplished artists, puts his own heart and soul into the making of each creation.

900 →

______ STOP__ASK FOR YOUR TIME ______

Record time immediately and answer questions on content.

Time __________ Sec.	RATE (from table on page 313):	R. __________
No. Correct __________ (key on page 329)	COMPREHENSION (50% for each correct answer):	C. __________
V-8	EFFICIENCY (R × C):	E. __________

Record on Progress Chart on page 299

ANSWER THESE QUESTIONS IMMEDIATELY

1. (T—F) Goltz makes his living by selling the life-like decoys he has created.

2. (M.C.) Which of the following steps is not included in the decoy making process described in this article?

______(1) Etching.

______(2) Oil painting.

______(3) Wood burning.

______(4) Plaster casting.

Length: 900 words

Exercise V-9

Readability Score: 61

Spring Turkey

By Joe Nemick

(Reprinted by permission from *Wyoming Wildlife,* March 1970.)

WAIT FOR SIGNAL TO BEGIN READING

Wild Turkey Hunting

A new dimension in wild turkey hunting began in Wyoming at sunrise on April 5, 1969. This was the opening morning of the state's first spring gobbler season. The opening of this season posed many questions in the minds of the farmers, ranchers, and sportsmen.

Would hunting turkeys during the spring interrupt the breeding season?

Would a large number of hens be illegally killed?

Would the added disturbance cause the hens to desert their nests?

In order to answer these questions, Game and Fish Department biologists conducted many exhaustive investigations before the season was proposed. Results of these investigations indicated that the answer was NO! It was felt that the experiences of other states which already had spring seasons enabled us to make predictions on the probable outcome of our own season. A spring gobbler season was recommended feasible for Wyoming.

To begin with, the idea of hunting game animals during the season when they are mating is not unusual. Deer are traditionally hunted during their mating season throughout the world and so are many other mammals.

In most southern states, spring gobbler hunting has been in practice for many years. In neither case has any harm been done to the productivity of these species. In the case of the wild turkey, two facts are responsible: first, turkeys are a polygamous species, and second, only toms are hunted.

Turkeys Are Polygamous

Polygamy is the habit that the male of some species has of taking more than one mate. In most wild populations, young are born or hatched in about equal numbers of males and females. This means that in a polygamous species, such as the turkey, more males are produced than can mate, and in a sense, these extra males do not function in the productivity of the flock.

In Wyoming, about ninety percent of the male turkeys are excess in this respect. One gobbler can mate with at least ten hens. Since hens and toms are hatched in about equal numbers, there are nine extra toms for each hen. Each hen needs to be mated only once to take care of the fertility requirements for her entire clutch of ten to twelve eggs, and she remains fertile for several weeks. Consequently, it was apparent that the removal of these excess toms would not affect the breeding season.

To answer the questions concerning illegal hen kill and nest desertion, it was decided that those states already having a spring hunt would be the best source of information. Queries were sent out, reports were read and all information was carefully analyzed.

None of the states contacted reported the illegal killing of hens or nest desertion to be of any significance. Even eastern states with as many as 30,000 hunters reported that this was not a problem. To make sure this held true in Wyoming, surveys were conducted during and after the 1969 spring season. Results showed that the loss of hens and nests during the season were very insignificant. Summer brood count surveys showed that in 1969 more hens brought off broods and had slightly larger broods than they did in 1968, which was a good turkey year; this occurred in spite of the severe April and June snow storms which caused destruction of many nests and newly hatched young. With the results of these surveys, we now have first hand information that spring gobbler hunting does not impair production.

Hunter Success Low

Hunter success during the spring season is generally low. Turkeys at this time are wary and widely scattered, making hunting difficult. Toms are very nervous, cautious, and alert during the spring. They usually travel alone and at the slightest disturbance will disappear into brush and safety.

Spring gobbler hunting is the ultimate test of a hunter's ability, knowledge of the outdoors, understanding of the habits of toms, camouflage, and use of a turkey call. For these reasons, only about twenty percent of the hunters can expect to kill a turkey.

To insure success of the season, from both the turkey and the hunter point of view, the dates for the spring season are carefully selected with these objectives in mind:

1. To open the season on a date late enough in the 700 spring to insure that most of the hens have been mated the single essential time.
2. To permit the season to coincide with the time toms are gobbling well and can be harvested effectively.
3. To terminate the season before a significant portion of the hens begin incubation so they will not be unduly disturbed.

The First Year

A year after the opening of the first spring gobbler season, most of the fears have subsided and it can be safely assumed that spring hunting does not damage a turkey population, but in many cases 800 actually benefits a population. Therefore, the spring season is an invaluable management tool in obtaining a selective harvest on the tom population.

A Last Word

The spring season is ideally tailored for the sportsmen rather than "meat hunters"! It pays off with sporting dividends, challenges and memories rather than pounds of meat. Continuation of this season depends upon sportsmen; their ability to distinguish toms from hens; their attitude toward ranchers and farmers; and their respect of livestock and private lands. Mistakes and abuses can affect future programs and seasons. Hunters the first year 900 established a good trend. Let's keep it that way.

______STOP__ASK FOR YOUR TIME______

Record time immediately and answer questions on content.

Time __________ Sec. RATE (from table on page 313): R. __________

No. Correct __________ COMPREHENSION (50% for each correct answer): C. __________
(key on page 321)

V-9 EFFICIENCY (R × C): E. __________

Record on Progress Chart on page 299

ANSWER THESE QUESTIONS IMMEDIATELY

1. (T—F) During spring gobbler hunting, about fifty percent of the hunters can expect to kill a turkey.

2. (M.C.) Decisions on spring gobbler season were justified *primarily* because:

_____(1) each hen hides and guards its nest carefully.

_____(2) there are more males than females.

_____(3) hens and toms are hatched in about equal numbers.

_____(4) the male turkey takes more than one mate.

Length: 900 words

Exercise V-10

Readability Score: 60

Legend of Tragedy

By Joyce Myres

(Reprinted by permission from *Empire Magazine*, July 18, 1976.)

WAIT FOR SIGNAL TO BEGIN READING

The West's widest known and brightest little plant has its legend of tragedy. One legend about the Wyoming State Flower was told to me by an old Wyoming Indian.

White Buffalo

A powerful medicine man lived in a village beside the Powder River, my informant related. He was called White Buffalo. One day, a maiden of this village—Running Deer—came to him seeking help. She asked the medicine man to make a love charm for her. She had fallen deeply in love with the brave He-Who-Walks-Tall, she said, and he was unaware of her existence. White Buffalo gathered the flowers of the paintbrush, ground them up finely with a flat stone and placed them in a medicine bag. Over this powder, he sang his incantations. He told the maiden she must sprinkle the contents of the bag upon her loved one that night; then this lover would be hers forever.

When night came, the two shadowy figures crept to where He-Who-Walks-Tall slept. Running Deer, accompanied by the medicine man, sprinkled the paintbrush upon her chosen man.

Within a month several ponies stood at the lodge entrance of Running Deer's parents. They represented the dowry—the price of the bride. A few nights later the couple, with dreamy eyes, retired to their own lodge and their life began. They would have barely more than a year together.

That first summer White Buffalo watched a dreamy-eyed Running Deer follow her husband about the camp. His old black eyes twinkled knowingly. He-Who-Walks-Tall adored his young wife. The charm had been good medicine. By the time summer fled, Running Deer was carrying a child.

While the golden leaves still clung to the aspen, preparations began for winter. The encampment moved farther down the Powder River, closer to their food supply of buffalo, deer and elk. Running Deer and the other squaws went out each day after the hunters' kill to skin, butcher and cure the meat which was then placed in skin bags for winter.

Running Deer made a ceremonial robe, in appreciation, for White Buffalo. The inside was covered with drawings of battles in which he had fought as a very young man, surrounds of the buffalo during his early hunting days and other events of the tribe. Raised designs were made from many porcupine quills and color was obtained from the juice of berries, which was also used for war paint. The red color came from the paintbrush.

Grey Wolf

When the brown of winter slowly left the earth and the green of spring stole upon the land, the first child of Running Deer was born. It was a boy. Then, one hot August day, the men of the village decided to go on a raid to steal ponies from a tribe to the south. Every man who was able rode from the camp. A few guards were left to protect the very old, the women and children. He-Who-Walks-Tall told Running Deer and his young son, Grey Wolf, goodby, saying he would return within a few days.

Village Raid

On the eighth day, the tranquility of the village was shattered by the savage cries of a band of marauding Indians. Women and children ran from their tepees. Screams of terror filled the hot summer air as those who tried to flee, blocked at the river, were pursued and killed. The old men, some of them nearly blind, numb in their terror, were cut down. The evil band had stolen everything they could lay their hands on, then heaped what was left on the lodges and set fire to it all. That night the burning village lit up the western sky.

At noon the next day, He-Who-Walks-Tall and the others approached the village. Ahead of them, they drove a large band of stolen ponies. The ponies caught the smell of the smoldering village before the men did and skittered away on nervous hooves. When the men stopped at the top of the hill overlooking the village, their eyes scanned the terrible scene which lay below. The only sign of life was a howling camp dog. Nothing stirred. Bodies were strewn about like broken dolls.

Revenge

He-Who-Walks-Tall dug his heels deep into the side of his startled paint pony. They raced to the scene below. He could not find Running Deer. Perhaps, he thought, she and the baby had been carried off. Then his eye caught the broken grass which led up river. He followed the trail with fear in his heart. Later he found Running Deer huddled under a ledge. She moaned at his touch, then opened her eyes. She barely recognized him. Her eyes clouded and she died in his arms, but the child lived. Crazed with grief, the tearful father ← 800 raised his arm to the sky, swearing vengeance.

Much later he and the other men tracked the marauding band and killed them all. He-Who-Walks-Tall was mortally wounded in the battle. He and his beloved Running Deer were buried together. His father, the old chief, took the child to rear and he became a great chief.

The following spring, in the shadow of the ledge where their hands last met, the fire of the paintbrush glowed, preserving forever the love of an Indian 900 → couple in its fiery beauty.

______ STOP __ ASK FOR YOUR TIME ______

Record time immediately and answer questions on content.

Time ________ Sec.	RATE (from table on page 313):	R. ________
No. Correct ________ (key on page 329)	COMPREHENSION (50% for each correct answer):	C. ________
V-10	EFFICIENCY (R × C):	E. ________

Record on Progress Chart on page 299

ANSWER THESE QUESTIONS IMMEDIATELY

1. (T—F) White Buffalo made his medicine bag from the powdered roots of the Indian paintbrush.

2. (M.C.) This legend is a story of the brief love affair of an Indian couple named Running Deer and:

   ______(1) Grey Wolf.

   ______(2) He-Who-Walks-Slow.

   ______(3) White Buffalo.

   ______(4) He-Who-Walks-Tall.

Length: 900 words

Exercise V-11

Readability Score: 59

A Bug Beats a Football Team

By Roy Mumpton

(Reprinted from the 1970 National Collegiate Athletic Association Football Program Feature Series, by permission of the Asssistant Executive Director.)

WAIT FOR SIGNAL TO BEGIN READING

It was shortly after noon on Sunday, September 28, 1969, Coach Bill Whitton appeared in a stage of shock. His hair was mussed. His shirt collar was open and crumpled. His tie was askew.

A Mystery

He has just watched for the third time, the films of his first Holy Cross football team's 13-0 hiding by Harvard the afternoon before. It was a horror movie because the Crimson defenders swarmed all over his Crusaders. Harvard's aggressiveness, so sharp in contrast, made it appear they had no offense at all.

"I can't believe what I see," said Whitton, who had been lured from a top assistant's post at Princeton to revive Holy Cross' fallen football fortunes and had watched his team stumble badly in its first game.

"These are good kids; I'm sure of that. I just can't understand it," he mumbled repeatedly.

Only a few days later Bill Whitton did understand.

His players, who had worked so hard to learn the new unbalanced-line T-attack and had been mighty impressive in a full dress rehearsal earlier, had been so lethargic simply because they were ill. They had been bitten by the hepatitis bug—a slow destroyer of energy.

Whitton, of course, had no way of knowing this.

Sure, Bob Cooney, a junior defensive end, had been hospitalized several days before the Harvard opener with what was thought to be a severe case of influenza. Other HC players became ill during the next week. There was suspicion of a flu epidemic.

Contagious Infection

It wasn't until Thursday that Cooney's illness was diagnosed as infectious hepatitis. The next day, a few hours before the departure for Hanover, N. H., and the game with Dartmouth, the entire squad was given immunization shots. Four boys were so sick they were hurried from the line to the college infirmary.

Three others became violently ill at Hanover that night and were rushed back to Worcester. Several others faced Dartmouth but had to leave after a few plays. The Indians' strong Ivy Leaguers rolled up a 38-6 score against a HC team which started without 11 regulars.

Back home again, the entire HC squad took a hurried blood test on Sunday morning. All were found infected, to some degree, with hepatitis. Some 25 of them spent several weeks in isolation in the college infirmary. "It's a disaster," sighed Coach Whitton, who himself had been very sick, but had carried on during the week of preparations for Dartmouth.

Holy Cross, the next day, was forced to cancel the remaining eight games of its schedule. So far as can be learned, this had never happened to a college football team before. So Whitton had encountered more hard luck than any new head coach in history.

Costly Illness

The disaster cost Holy Cross at least $200,000 in revenue from football, which had supported many minor sports. There were all the usual expenses, but no gate receipts for eight games, including the finale with Boston College which had been HC's home game and always a sellout as early as September.

Alumni and friends rallied their sympathies and their dollars and made it clear that they wanted Holy Cross to stay in football.

Dartmouth, an almost annual rival of the Crusaders the last 33 seasons, sent a check to Holy Cross for $1,000 and suggested that other ECAC colleges also contribute to ease the emergency. Boston College, HC's dearest enemy, sent $2,000. Army and Navy each put $1,000 checks towards the continuance of Crusader football. Brigham Young University, a Mormon institution, sent $500 to the Catholic school. South Carolina, which had never played HC in any sport, was a contributor, too. So were others.

More than 500 alumni sent $15 checks for souvenir season tickets when there wasn't a single home game.

Sacramento State launched a campaign to help and dedicated its season to Holy Cross with the team wearing the Crusaders' jerseys in its final game.

Fans in all parts of the country sent checks of $1, $5, and $10 with their sympathies. The fund swelled. It is not nearly the $200,000 HC lost, but it helped.

Fountain of Lethargy

It was a water fountain on the hilltop practice field, half a mile above the campus, which led to the hepatitis epidemic. Neighborhood kids, a whole family of whom had been infected by hepatitis, had been at the fountain during the summer.

700 ←

Most of the HC players were infected on their very first day of practice. (None of the freshman squad, which reported ten days later, became ill.)

At least 10 HC varsity footballers were so sick that they missed a semester of academic work. The ECAC granted three seniors another year of eligibility, and will consider the cases of the afflicted underclassmen later.

Held Spring Practice

800 →

Holy Cross, for the first time in some 20 years, had spring practice. "It was an absolute necessity," explained Whitton. "Our squad has the equivalent of two sophomore classes so far as football experience is concerned. Our seniors have played only two games, or less, in two years."

The Crusaders may have been down, but they seemed to have everybody behind them. The road back would be steep, but they hoped to climb it. Holy Cross looked to the future and was ready to forget the nightmare of hepatitis with a conviction that

900 →

happier days would be just around the corner.

_____STOP—ASK FOR YOUR TIME_____

Record time immediately and answer questions on content.

Time ________ Sec.	RATE (from table on page 313):	R. ________
No. Correct ________ (key on page 321)	COMPREHENSION (50% for each correct answer):	C. ________
V-11	EFFICIENCY (R × C):	E. ________

Record on Progress Chart on page 299

ANSWER THESE QUESTIONS IMMEDIATELY

1. (T—F) It was estimated that the disaster cost Holy Cross approximately $20,000 in revenue.

2. (M.C.) The disease which struck the Holy Cross football team was:

_____(1) influenza.

_____(2) infectious hepatitis.

_____(3) whooping cough.

_____(4) German measles.

Length: 900 words

Exercise V-12

Readability Score: 57

Ghost of the Prairie

By Rex Corsi

(Reprinted by permission from *Wyoming Wildlife,* December, 1973.)

WAIT FOR SIGNAL TO BEGIN READING

An Antelope or Gazella?

The animal we now refer to as the pronghorn antelope is a climax to about 20 million years of evolutionary changes and has occurred in near present form for at least one million years. Coronado called these animals *goats* and such a term was common with William Clark, of the Lewis and Clark Expedition and with fur traders of the 1800's. The first technical name, *Antelope americana,* was imposed by George Ord in 1815; the second and still official name of *Antilocapra americana* was bestowed in 1818 by the same naturalist.

In 1804 Clark described this animal as follows: ← 100

"September 14—in my walk I killed a Buck Goat of this Countrey, about the hight of a Grown Deer. its body Shorter the Horns which is not very hard and forks 2/3 up one prong Short the other round and Sharp arched, and is immediately above its face white round its neck, its sides and its rump round its tail which is short and white: Verry actively made, has only a pair of hoofs to each foot. his brains on the back of his head, his norstrals large, his eyes like a Sheep he is more like the Antilope or Gazella of Africa ← 200 than any other species of Goat."

September 20—"R. Fields Killed 1 deer and 2 Goats, one of them a female. She differs from the mail as to size being smaller, with Small Horns, Streght with a small prong without any dark about the neck. None of these Goats has any beard, they are all keenly made, and is butifull."

Beautiful Animals

Yes, the pronghorn are beautiful animals with an interesting color combination of black, tan and white. They have been called "Ghosts of the Prairie" and certainly not without reason. One moment you see ← 300 them and the next they are gone. With a low, bright sun to your back you will see them for miles, but without such ideal conditions, chances are the untrained human eye will only observe a small percentage of those animals present within sight range. Their color seems to uncannily blend into landscapes. But on the other side of the coin, antelope seem to detect objects, especially moving ones, at such extreme distances that human sight, to be comparable, must be aided by a binocular. And to further assist seeing 400 → ability, their eyes protrude from the head in such a way as to give a very large field of vision. Yes, they almost have vision from the back of their head. Such eyesight played an important role in survival and helped the animal endure severe tests through millions of years of evolution.

Credentials

But certainly excellent vision alone would not be enough to guarantee life and reproduction. Just as important was a streamlined athletic body with slender legs designed for extreme mobility. Speeding along 50 miles an hour over sagebrush plains is not uncommon for an antelope. And to further frustrate an enemy, 500 → they whirl and reverse direction with what appears to be only a light pause in the fast stride. With such credentials it is obvious this animal literally ran away from most enemies.

To the further dismay of its enemies, antelope have their own warning systems. A snort is commonly emitted at the least indication of something unusual in their surroundings. This audible warning can be heard at considerable distance by human ears and I suspect antelope hearing ability greatly surpasses ours. They also warn each other by erecting the hairs of their white rump patch. When erected these white hairs 600 → become visible for many miles. When hearing a snort or seeing the rump flash of a companion, many antelope have scurried away to safety from unseen danger.

Antelope show other evolutionary adaptations which, with possibly less surface glitter, have also contributed to their survival. Along with a slender body for speed, it was necessary that digestive organs be small. The stomach and cecum are small compared to a sheep's and allow for more mobility. Because of a small stomach, they depended upon plants which remained highly nutritious even during winter months. Sagebrush is such a food and it appears antelope 700 → evolution was closely associated with areas supporting this plant. A large liver to store a reserve of energy in the form of glycogen, and large kidneys for conserving water have allowed the antelope to live in a habitat too harsh for many other animals.

Disease-Free Lives?

Reproductive capacity of antelope is quite high. A doe will commonly conceive annually and bear twins each year. Young at birth are relatively odor free, which helps their early survival in a world of meat-eating predators. And to further aid their survival, antelope have evolved as relatively disease-free animals. They even seem to be bothered less by insects than most other animals their size. ← 800

Nature has a way of weeding out the weak links and allowing the stronger ones to live. Evolving over millons of years, the antelope has withstood crucial tests and survived. It is today a truly magnificent specimen of animal life, but so specialized in form and habits that it no longer is too adaptable to extreme and rapid habitat changes. Man almost exterminated antelope, but he later recognized the species as valued life and fosters its abundance today. Hopefully, antelope will remain in man's favor and will thrive during the 900 → era to come.

______ STOP__ASK FOR YOUR TIME ______

Record time immediately and answer questions on content.

Time________ Sec.	RATE (from table on page 313):	R.________
No. Correct________ (key on page 329)	COMPREHENSION (50% for each correct answer):	C.________
V-12	EFFICIENCY (R × C):	E.________

Record on Progress Chart on page 299

ANSWER THESE QUESTIONS IMMEDIATELY

1. (T—F) Coronado and other early pioneers identified the antelope as a goat.

2. (M.C.) The terminology of "ghost" for the antelope relates to:

______(1) the white markings on the head, side and tail.

______(2) their high level of mobility.

______(3) their color blending so well into the landscape.

______(4) their classification as an endangered species.

Length: 900 words

Exercise V-13

Readability Score: 54

Stadiums and Civic Pride

By Lorinda L. Redmond

(Reprinted from an original article of the Uniwyo Reading Research Center by permission of the Director.)

WAIT FOR SIGNAL TO BEGIN READING

Sports Franchises

If a community votes funds for sports franchises this is an indication that the people must want to expand such entertainment businesses. Operating such an entertainment business, the owners of sports franchises must expect criticism from the public. Of course the taxpayers want to know where their tax money is going. Is this not their right as citizens? Do priorities lie with the building of a new stadium or does the community wish to spend its money on necessary upkeep for its people?

In this age of economic and energy crisis we are presented with a problem of how to sell ideas to the taxed public, that is, appealing to civic pride. This indicates a need to pep up local patriotism by getting the public behind the franchise owners. Operating at the public's expense creates the necessity of letting the public in on such matters where their money is being spent.

Public building operations must be able to accept criticisms and protests concerning the allocation of millions of dollars spent for sports while simultaneously they are neglecting the needs of the public, such as upkeep of neighborhoods. Here, we are presented with the issue of where the needs lie within the community. A new stadium does not allocate power to a team which has power limitations. The opening of a new stadium is a celebration of the future of a team and a city. Where does this lead the public? Problems created by this issue within the community may bring about an occasion for many arguments about the high price which has been spent for such hopes of the future. How much does the consumer really know about where the money is going? If there are public money squabbles between franchise owners and teams this may have a tendency to sour the fans. Irate customers may claim that their support and allegiance are items of the past. However, when a season opens in a new stadium and there is a substantial increase in attendance over the previous season, it is hard to see the presence of citizen unrest. Perhaps this is an indication that the rejecting fans prefer to express their displeasure at close range.

New Stadium Projects

The dreams, frustrating defeats, enthusiastic projections, and vague promises of better times ahead for teams and fans seems to indicate that new stadium projects are justified by the public. Eventually, other necessities are overlooked for the time being and the public, in general, takes pride in the new stadium.

But what about the future, and also the present, regarding considerations of the upkeep of dilapidated areas of the town or city in which the priorities have been given to the sports franchises? The community must face these problems, as such problems are inherent every day. The people living in areas which need repair may have a hard time understanding that taxpayer's money, theirs included, is supporting the entertainment business and overlooking the present problems in the community.

But these consumers may also be included within the part of the community which accepts the building of a new stadium. This indicates a sense of pride which they wish to show for their community. They are proud to think about people from other communities coming to the new stadium in their community. The final outcome shows them to be proud of what happens within their community due to the new stadium. This brings in people outside the community, which increases the business.

Costly Showplaces

The millions of dollars spent for building a new stadium goes toward many luxurious items, such as flashing lights and fancy lighted boards. These ultramodern, flashing non-scoreboards may show replays, cartoons, and advertisements. Such luxuries may give the people in the community a feeling of being a big time business. Of course signs of unrest may be evident among the natives, but at least a small portion of the public seems to want stadiums and teams. If this were not the case, there would be no support for building new stadiums. If the public wants stadiums and teams the franchise owners get the support and backing they need to build them. Thus, they are building on the civic pride of the public. Once a new stadium is built with the support of the public therein, it is going to be this public's responsibility to help the community grow. Not only this, but the public must stay behind the franchise owners in order for this particular entertainment business to maintain success in the community.

By showing pride in the community's entertainment business, the citizens are helping to lead the community toward a prosperous future. Of course there are still bound to be signs of citizen unrest because of the difficulty in pleasing everyone. There will always be people who are not interested in sports and could care less even if their community grows due to sports. A good deal of criticism about priorities of importance for the growth of the community is bound to come from such dissatisfied citizens. They would much prefer to see growth in some other way for the community.

However, a general look at the attitudes about new stadiums reveals that civic pride is behind the activities of the groups which support such buildings. The overall attitude is that sports franchises are supported by a large majority who believe that stadiums improve the community.

_______ STOP __ ASK FOR YOUR TIME _______

Record time immediately and answer questions on content.

Time __________ Sec.	RATE (from table on page 313):	R. __________
No. Correct __________ (key on page 321)	COMPREHENSION (50% for each correct answer):	C. __________
V-13	EFFICIENCY (R × C):	E. __________

Record on Progress Chart on page 299

ANSWER THESE QUESTIONS IMMEDIATELY

1. (T—F) Criticism of stadium funding seems to reflect views that tax money could be spent more effectively on improving community problems.

2. (M.C.) Construction of a new stadium is primarily based on a:

_____ (1) desire to provide more seating for fans who are unable to attend games now.

_____ (2) civic pride in the community and its potential future growth.

_____ (3) need to provide financial support to local sports franchises.

_____ (4) careful analysis of total community needs for recreation and social programs.

Length: 900 words

Exercise V-14

Readability Score: 53

See It Made In Japan

By Dorothy Loa McFadden

(Reprinted by permission from *Travel,* June, 1970.)

WAIT FOR SIGNAL TO BEGIN READING

A trip to Japan is an artistic experience. The Japanese are so sensitive to beauty of line and color that even the food they serve you will be arranged as a picture. The dishes used at a meal at a typical Japanese inn will be examples of fine porcelain, lacquer and pottery, and their shapes will be interesting ovals, triangles, squares and rectangles. Your room in such a *ryokan* will be decorated with a single Kakemono picture, under which there will be a flower arrangement lovingly created to go with the painting.

As you will be surrounded by so many products of Japanese artistry, you will find added pleasure in seeing some of these lovely things made. The Japan Travel Bureau in Tokyo will be happy to arrange visits for you to some of the fine craftsmen at work today. Just tell them what you are most interested in seeing. Perhaps you collect porcelain or ceramics. Or you are interested in painting and woodblock prints, or your passion is delicately wrought jewelry. There is something for everyone in the art studios of Japan.

Tokyo Tour

There is a fascinating package bus tour available in Tokyo which is called the Tokyo-Art-Around-Town Tour. One of the stops is at a studio where the artists are painting and embroidering kimonos and the obi sashes to go with them. These are handed down through generations and are very expensive. You can watch the outline being drawn on the cloth, then the color work filled in.

Another stop is at a school for doll-making. Every Japanese girl is taught to make traditional dolls, just as she is always taught flower arrangement. The students in this school do not merely dress the dolls in colorful ceremonial kimonos, but actually make the bodies and paint the exquisite faces. Then they glue on the hair and dress in an elaborate geisha fashion. The end product is a fine piece of workmanship, often placed on a music box stand which plays typical Japanese *samisen* tunes.

Also included in the tour is a visit to watch an artist do sandpainting. A black background is used—sometimes it is a tray—and on this a design is made by strewing and brushing fine white sand. This is then affixed by slightly melting the sand from the head of an iron held over it. Scenes of snow-covered Mt. Fuji are most effective in this technique, also rushing brooks and cascading waterfalls. This is a delicate and unusual art form, very interesting to watch. If you decide to buy one of the paintings, I must warn you to have it carefully packed so that no wrapping touches the sand, then carry it home by hand. Shipping by mail knocks off much of the sand!

The tour also includes visits to an elementary school art class, a fabulous garden of miniature *bonsai* trees, and the witnessing of a ceremonial dance in a temple. It is a well-planned trip to really artistic experiences.

Kyoto Artistry

In Kyoto the travel bureau or your personal guide will arrange visits to a number of studios where you can see things made. One is the place where artisans are carving woodblocks for making those lovely Japanese prints. Sometimes as many as 30 blocks are used to make one picture, adding or superimposing a new color each time. You will really appreciate the prints you buy in the shops and see in art galleries, after you have watched this painstaking process.

Another famous Kyoto workshop carries on the ancient art of lacquer ware. This work was inspired by the Chinese, and the lacquer trees had to be imported as well. You will see the basic fibre or wooden foundation of the boxes and bowls, then the painting on layer after layer of lacquer. Each is allowed to dry hard and is laboriously hand-polished before the next layer is put on. Finally the designs are hand-painted on, usually in gold. Some studios specialize in making lacquered masks for use by the actors in traditional plays.

One of the most interesting crafts which you may also see in Kyoto is the making of Damascene jewelry. This is a very old art brought to Japan from Damascus by way of China in about 700 A.D. The foundation of each piece of jewelry is steel, on which the design is chiseled, then inlaid with 24K gold or silver. The piece is then treated with several acids and boiled green tea. After this several layers of lacquer are baked on the entire surface. The design then appears again after lengthy polishings with charcoal.

If you like to watch artists painting flowers, birds, *Kabuki* actors' faces or other typically Japanese designs, try to find a studio where they are decorating paper fans, paper lanterns, or the big kites used at 800 ← special festivals. These are flown by boys especially around the New Year, in exciting competitions. The object is not only to fly the most beautiful kite as high as possible, but also to cut the strings of your opponents' kites by crossing yours over, each string having been coated with crushed glass for this purpose.

Whatever city you may visit in Japan you will certainly be able to visit some of the famous potters at work, or a porcelain factory where you can see a delicate vase develop from the original forming to the 900 → final decoration.

________STOP__ASK FOR YOUR TIME_______

Record time immediately and answer questions on content.

Time __________ Sec. RATE (from table on page 313): R. __________

No. Correct __________ COMPREHENSION (50% for each correct answer): C. __________

(key on page 329)

V-14 EFFICIENCY (R × C): E. __________

Record on Progress Chart on page 299

ANSWER THESE QUESTIONS IMMEDIATELY

1. (T—F) One of the stops on the Tokyo tour is at the factory where kimonos and obi sashes are hand-painted.

2. (M.C.) Which of the following is not mentioned as part of the Kyoto tour?

______(1) A jewelry factory.

______(2) A school for doll-making.

______(3) A place where artisans carve woodblocks for making Japanese prints.

______(4) A lacquer ware workshop.

Length: 900 words

Exercise V-15

Readability Score: 50

Scrap the 1872 Mining Law

By Stewart L. Udall

(Reprinted by permission from *National Wildlife,* June-July, 1970.)

WAIT FOR SIGNAL TO BEGIN READING

The White Clouds situation is by no means an isolated example of how an antiquated law allows miners to misuse our public lands. It is really a microcosm of what has been happening across America for decades.

In the past, the myth of endless resources blinded us to the horrible results of reckless mining practices on our public lands. But times have changed and we realize now that we dare not destroy the few White Clouds that remain. The scars are far too deep. Our mountains have been stripped and gouged by copper miners in Arizona and Montana, by iron ore miners in Minnesota, by jade miners in Wyoming and coal stripping in Appalachia . . . all in the name of "progress." Some of this mining was vital to national growth . . . but far too much of it was carried out under a strip-and-run philosophy, needlessly reducing the quality of everyone's environment.

Antique Law

The real bogeyman at White Clouds is not the mining companies, nor the United States Forest Service, nor the people trying to save these beautiful majestic peaks. What is really wrong is the antique mining law of 1872 . . . a frontier law that protects the exploiter and ignores the values of scenery, wildlife, watershed and recreation . . . . *The law no longer serves the public interest. We need new laws that will.*

Five days before leaving the office of the Secretary of the Interior in January 1969, I wrote in a letter to members of the Public Land Law Review Commission: "After eight years in this office, I have come to the conclusion that the most important piece of unfinished business on the nation's natural resources agenda is the complete replacement of the mining law of 1872.

"Put simply, this obsolete and outdated statute inhibits the best kind of multiple-use management and operates as an outright giveaway of vital natural resources," I concluded.

The problem began in 1849 with the cry of . . . "Gold!" This magic word, with its hypnotic effect, lured thousands to the mining fields of the West.

Conditions in the camps were chaotic at first, but crude, common sense rules were adopted and spread from mining district to mining district. They soon had the force of frontier law and eventually were adopted as the American common law governing western mining activity.

Under the mining law of 1872 the discoverer of a valuable deposit can establish a legal claim to it merely by marking the boundaries of the claim and, if state law requires it, recording the location in the county office. There is no provision for notifying the Federal government of the existence, position, or size of the claim or of the fact that minerals are being extracted. Having staked his claim, the miner may continue indefinitely to enjoy what amounts to almost total ownership of the property, mining it or not as he wishes. His only obligation is to make $100 worth of improvements on his location each year, or risk being dispossessed by another claimant.

No Limits

The mining law of 1872 places the miner in a unique position. He has all the rights but none of the responsibilities that being a landowner normally entails.

There is no limit to the number of claims a man can locate and hold. Some individuals and corporations have been involved in the location of more than a million acres of largely untested claims.

A situation similar to the White Clouds occurred in the Pike National Forest, Colorado, a couple of years ago. Mining dolomitic limestone by open pit methods has scarred the beauty of parts of the front range of the Rocky Mountains. A huge, unsightly scar can be seen from a wide area including the Garden of the Gods Park and it spoils the once picturesque view of Pikes Peak.

The world's worst examples of strip mining, of course, are found in the East. One can only be appalled by the devastation of whole sections of once-beautiful forest lands. No war, no holocaust, could wreak such havoc as that which the strip miners have left in the once-beautiful rolling green hills of Appalachia. These gigantic scars are a monument to man's total disregard for his environment.

Open Opposition

Due to pressures from the mining lobby, passage 700 ← of a good mining law will be difficult. Conservationists will watch with interest the recommendations of the Public Land Law Review Commission each year. Though many commission members are "user" oriented, they may propose sweeping revisions which will consider the nation's stake in uses of the public domain for the benefit of future generations.

Let us hope they recommend mining laws which will protect the land for wildlife, for food, for timber, for people . . . recreation, living space, and scenery. Where mining is practical and necessary, the laws should require the mining company to have a leasing 800 ← arrangement with the Federal government in which regulations can be used to protect public values and in which the people will share in the profits realized. And lastly, the law *must* require restoration of the top soil and revegetation.

Until the slow wheels of government enact such a law, however, the short term stop-gap at places like White Clouds can be to deny construction of access roads on public lands if mining operations threaten prime public values. The National Wildlife Federation believes laws to accomplish this are already on the books if they are properly interpreted and 900 → enforced.

________STOP__ASK FOR YOUR TIME________

Record time immediately and answer questions on content.

Time ________ Sec. RATE (from table on page 313): R. ________

No. Correct ________ COMPREHENSION (50% for each correct answer): C. ________
(key on page 321)

V-15 EFFICIENCY (R × C): E. ________

Record on Progress Chart on page 299

ANSWER THESE QUESTIONS IMMEDIATELY

1. (T—F) Mr. Udall expresses great concern for the miners who are severely handicapped by the out-of-date legislation.

2. (M.C.) Which of the following does the writer feel is the greatest need for replacing the 1872 Mining Law?

______(1) Outdated legal terminology.

______(2) Too much power to Forest Service.

______(3) Mechanized mining.

______(4) No limits, no responsibilities defined for mining claims.

Length: 900 words

Exercise V-16

Readability Score: 49

Little Swift Fox

By Duane Muchmore

(Reprinted by permission from *Wyoming Wildlife* magazine, July, 1975.)

WAIT FOR SIGNAL TO BEGIN READING

Some called him swift because he seemed like the fastest animal of the plains; others called him kit because he was so small, but all agreed he was a fox. Fortunately, scientists stepped in to stop all the confusion and christened him *Vulpes velox.* Translated the name means "swift fox" but that didn't bother the laymen because the little critter is still known by both common names. Evidently the scientists didn't do too much homework either because it is now known that illusion of speed is due mainly to small size since the swift fox is scarcely faster than any other species of fox.

Two Kinds

Now, in more ways than one, the swift fox is in the spotlight. Since December, 1973 each state has been required to submit management programs designed to protect and propagate species designated rare or endangered. One of the two subspecies of swift fox in North America has been listed as endangered in Canada and this northern subspecies (V.v.hebes) is slightly larger, paler and has more gray color than the other subspecies (V.v.velox).

So far only the one subspecies is found in Wyoming. Unless you had the two animals side by side it would be difficult to distinguish between the subspecies. This is a problem some states have had to wrestle with when attempting to inventory endangered species. Without killing or capturing the animals it would be difficult to determine whether a particular endangered subspecies was actually present—and the Rare and Endangered Species Act does single out subspecies for protection.

Because the swift fox stays near its burrow and tends to be nocturnal, sighting records are scarce. In his book on *Mammals of Wyoming,* Long lists only five reports of swift fox taken in Wyoming. Seton emphasizes the lack of detailed information about this diminutive species of fox when he states, "Nothing is known of its mating beyond the fact that the creature pairs . . . " Such knowledge would seem self-evident if the species continues to perpetuate itself, but Seton is actually pointing out that swift fox are monogamous and the male and female probably remain together for life.

Because it is not much larger than a house cat, the swift fox is hardly detrimental to agricultural interests but it has been an unintended victim of coyote eradication efforts. Several references indicate swift fox are the least cunning of foxes and readily take poisoned bait.

Few and Different

These reynards of the grasslands were evidently never very numerous before the West was settled. Their ancestral range was limited to a strip of short-grass plains in west-central North America that stretched from the prairie provinces of Canada to southern Colorado.

Identifying features of swift fox readily distinguish them from other species of canids, but you'll seldom be in a position to observe these conspicuous characteristics. The pair of emerald reflections which you may see in your spotlight beam fail to disclose a black spot on either side of the muzzle and a black tip on the tail that easily sets the swift fox apart from the larger red fox.

Although similar in color to gray fox, swift fox are much smaller. In fact, any small fox with a black-tipped tail seen in Wyoming is likely to be a swift fox for there is only one record of a gray fox occurrence in the state. In addition, the swift fox is preeminently an animal of open plains while the gray fox is closely associated with timbered or brushy habitat.

Since many people are not aware of the presence of swift fox in Wyoming these inoffensive animals have suffered for misdeeds more properly attributed to coyotes. Inadvertently mistaken at night for young coyotes, swift fox may remain incognito until the fur buyer identifies them to a hunter and indicates the pelt is least valuable of those from wild canids. Thus swift fox, although they are unprotected in Wyoming, are not particularly profitable to hunt or trap.

Swift fox appear to be increasing. Of five specimens known to Long, four were taken in Carbon County before the turn of the century. A fifth specimen was reported from Laramie County in 1958 and more recently they were sighted in Nebraska in 1972 and found to be present in Laramie County through a scent station survey conducted in 1972.

One swift fox was purchased by a furrier in Laramie and another was killed near Cheyenne during the winter of 1973-74. Several were observed northeast of Cheyenne during the spring of 1974 and a pair were sighted in Western Nebraska on June 18, 1974.

Now More Numerous

Although the Executive Order banning use of poisons for predator control on public lands may now be affecting swift fox populations, interest in predator populations created by the order and the Rare and Endangered Species Act are in part responsible for more recent sightings of swift fox. At two scent station routes in Laramie county in 1972 there were 13 visits by swift fox, 23 red fox visits and 41 coyote visitations. Since each route consisted of 50 scent stations spaced along a fifteen-mile line and routes were at least 20 miles apart, Laramie County either had one "dog-tired" swift fox when the five-day survey ended or these nocturnal animals were more numerous than most people realized. In this case it seems if you stay out of sight long enough people begin to wonder what happened to you.

800 ← 900 →

______ STOP __ ASK FOR YOUR TIME ______

Record time immediately and answer questions on content.

Time __________ Sec.   RATE (from table on page 313):   R. __________

No. Correct __________   COMPREHENSION (50% for each correct answer):   C. __________

(key on page 329)

V-16   EFFICIENCY (R × C):   E. __________

Record on Progress Chart on page 299

ANSWER THESE QUESTIONS IMMEDIATELY

1. (T—F) The swift fox in Wyoming are most frequently seen in high timbered areas.

2. (M.C.) The swift fox described in this article are readily distinguished from other species because:

   ______ (1) they are smaller and have black-tipped tails.

   ______ (2) they are much quicker in movement.

   ______ (3) they are considerably larger in size.

   ______ (4) of their golden-brown color and emerald eyes.

Length: 900 words

Exercise V-17

Readability Score: 46

Tribute to a Lady

By Nicholas Hobbs

(Reprinted by permission from *Hogg Foundation News,* Fall, 1976.)

WAIT FOR SIGNAL TO BEGIN READING

Strength of Spirit

A guiding light for the Hogg Foundation was dimmed in August of 1975 by the death of Miss Ima Hogg, one of the principal donors to the Foundation and its stimulus since the founding in 1940.

"Miss Ima," as she was affectionately known by Texans, possessed a keen awareness of needs of people, particularly children, and a drive to bring forces to bear upon problems of all persons. Her leadership stemmed from her own alert personality coupled with an august presence and a pioneerlike strength of spirit. Together these traits created a spark that beckoned countless others to follow and support her causes.

Mourning seemed an inappropriate commemoration for a lifespan of 93 active years. Rather, it appeared fitting to celebrate that this magnanimous lady had lived such a long, rich, and full life. It also seemed a time to review the many changes and advances that had come about because of the concern of Ima Hogg and others of her family—her father, Governor James Stephen Hogg, and her brothers Will, Tom, and Mike Hogg.

First Lady of Texas

More than 2,000 invitations to "A Celebration" were issued by The University of Texas at Austin and the Hogg Foundation. Guests were friends and associates of Miss Hogg and the two institutions. The site was the Lyndon Baines Johnson Library on the campus. The program included a reception and a day of presentations by Foundation officers and University administrators and faculty who had known Miss Hogg and shared common interests. *Ima Hogg: First Lady of Texas,* a book especially written for the occasion, was introduced.

The commemorative event opened on Sunday evening, May 2, 1976, with a reception given by the President of The University of Texas at Austin. More than 800 guests gathered in the Great Hall of the Library.

The following day, May 3, was a day for reflection on Hogg family benefactions. A near-capacity crowd spread over the 1,000-seat Lyndon Baines Johnson Auditorium. Each guest received a copy of *Ima Hogg: First Lady of Texas,* by Louise Kosches Iscoe. The morning began with a slide presentation featuring family and news photographs dating from the 1880s—the decade of Ima Hogg's birth—to the present.

Opening speakers for the day were Allan Shivers, former governor of Texas and chairman of the Board of Regents of The University of Texas System; Lorene L. Rogers, president of The University of Texas at Austin; and Jack Josey, former member of the Board of Regents.

Public Restoration

Associate Professor of Architecture and Planning Wayne Bell spoke of Miss Hogg's extensive work in historical preservation. He showed slides depicting the family homes and other sites which were restored under her guidance and later were given to the public.

Other University faculty and former faculty whose areas of work paralleled concerns of Ima Hogg recalled their experiences in association with her: James B. Ayres, associate professor of English; Robert C. Cotner, professor of history; Joe B. Frantz, professor of history; Llerena Friend, professor emeritus of history; Ira Iscoe, director, Counseling-Psychological Services Center; Chester V. Kielman, University archivist; Robert L. Sutherland, Hogg Foundation president emeritus; Lonn W. Taylor, director, Winedale Museum of Cultural History; and Dorman H. Winfrey, director, Texas State Library.

Music was another of Miss Hogg's great interests, and its presentation on the program was by concert pianist James Dick. The former protege of Miss Hogg played a medley of favorite classics.

After luncheon was served to some 900 persons, the afternoon program focused on the work of the Hogg Foundation which was described by President Wayne H. Holtzman and Executive Associates Bernice Milburn Moore and Bert Kruger Smith. Their presentation was in conjunction with a multimedia display.

A talk on "Mental Health of Children and Families: A Concern of Miss Hogg," was delivered by Nicholas Hobbs, director, Center for the Study of Families and Children, Vanderbilt University. A condensation of his talk has been prepared as a new Hogg Foundation pamphlet and will be distributed quite widely.

University of Texas System Chancellor Charles A. LeMaistre closed the day's proceedings with a message on future perspectives—what further realizations may come to pass because of the devoted efforts of persons who were given inspiration by Miss 700 ← Ima Hogg.

Always a Special Grace

. . . Miss Hogg touched the lives of many people, always with a special grace. No one so fortunate as to know her was ever quite the same again. An outlander who saw her only a few times, I allowed myself to think of us as friends, a presumption, perhaps, but one shared by thousands I am sure, and never without reason, for she cared about so many people, remembered their names and interests, assumed their good will and their readiness to join with her in 800 → common and worthy cause. And, of course, expecting the best of others, she helped them find the best in themselves. Nobility is contagious. I surmise that everyone here knows himself to be the nobler in work and spirit, because of her, and is grateful for her beneficence. In celebrating her life we brighten our own in warm remembrance.

Some of you will remember her for shared interests in music, others in Texas history, still others in American antiques, in the Winedale restoration, in the theater, in flowers, in travel. I remember her for our shared interest in mental heath and in families and 900 → children.

______ STOP__ASK FOR YOUR TIME ______

Record time immediately and answer questions on content.

Time __________ Sec.	RATE (from table on page 313):	R. __________
No. Correct __________ (key on page 321)	COMPREHENSION (50% for each correct answer):	C. __________
V-17	EFFICIENCY (R × C):	E. __________

Record on Progress Chart on page 299

ANSWER THESE QUESTIONS IMMEDIATELY

1. (T—F) Ima Hogg was called the "First Lady of Texas" because she was the wife of the governor.

2. (M.C.) Of her many special interests, which of the following was not mentioned in this article?

_____(1) Slum clearance.

_____(2) Mental health.

_____(3) Historical preservation.

_____(4) Music and theater.

Length: 900 words | Readability Score: 45

Exercise V-18

Deathzone

By Bob White

(Reprinted from an original article of the Uniwyo Reading Research Center by permission of the director.)

WAIT FOR SIGNAL TO BEGIN READING

The Himalayas

Deathzone, that point in the earth's atmosphere above which the human body ceases to regenerate itself, becomes a standing challenge for men who dare to enter.

What are the factors which cause an individual to make a goal of the impossible? Does the force that drives an individual arise from a need to conquer the unknown or simply to achieve the unachievable? Human nature is also a part of that which is unknown but examples of men attempting, and sometimes achieving, the impossible are plentiful. Individuals seek the deepest parts of the ocean and risk being crushed by seven miles of water—others climb the peaks of the Himalayas and risk falling from a height of five miles or of suffocation at an altitude where the only living creatures there live without breathing.

According to scientists men can adapt up to 23,000 feet by producing oxygen-carrying red blood cells at accelerated rates. Beyond that elevation, no amount of rest, food or liquid can rebuild the body.

Makalu

Ten men attempted to climb the 27,750 foot peak of Makalu during the International Makalu Himalaya Expedition in the fall of 1974. The team consisted of ten men from six countries, none extremely well-known, but all experienced climbers.

Two of them reached the height of 26,000 feet, 3,000 feet into the deathzone, but were forced to quit before reaching the summit because of impending winter, sickness and dissent among the expedition members. The team did not take any oxygen with them.

Korich, member and one of the organizers of the expedition, said the group is trying to set an example by not using oxygen. He feels that mountain climbing has become less than it was intended to be. He would like to keep the purist element to climbing. For these reasons, the expedition members refused to take along any breathing apparatus to make the near vertical climb of the face of Makalu.

Makalu has been climbed before but this was the first time this route was attempted and no oxygen was used. The expedition was led by Fritz Stammberger of Germany, who has a personal conviction to climb the mountain. He had made three reconnaissance trips in preparation for the climb. Twice he reached 20,000 feet climbing alone, having experienced the hardships of being lost in infamous rain forests, home of the fabled Abominable Snowman, having his porters abandon him in a three-day snowstorm, and later being buried alive in an avalanche. He made a vow to return with a strong team of climbers to conquer Makalu.

The Expedition

By the fall of 1974, he had organized the expedition team which set out from Kathmandu, with native Sherpa porters to help them carry the 9,000 pounds of equipment and food. They had with them 250 pounds of medicine that would have to be sufficient to take care of any eventuality for the duration of the expedition.

The team members included Stammberger, who, in 1964, made an oxygen-less ascent of Cho Oyu (26,800 ft.) in Tibet; Arnold Larcher, an ice climber who had previously led an Austrian team to the Greenland mountains; David Jones, a rock climber from British Columbia; Malezic, who had experience on Annapurna and was a member of a 1972 Yugoslavian attempt on the South face of Makalu; Korich, base camp manager; Dr. Charles Clark of Colorado, who took care of the medical needs; Andre Ulrych of Colorado in charge of food; Mario Quesada of Argentina; Jeff Long of Colorado; and Bruce Gordon, also of Colorado.

A Few Close Calls

They traveled through the monsoon rains and steaming, leech-infested jungle, fording swollen rivers and crossing high mountain passes—a journey of 200 miles—just to get to the point where they would begin their ascent of Makalu.

"From that point on," Korich said, "you realize that you're all alone. It's understood that you have to take care of yourself. The mountain isn't very forgiving if you make a mistake, and, if you can't climb down by yourself, you stay there."

Korich admitted that the team had been very lucky. None died and there were no permanent injuries. There were a few close calls, though.

At one point, one of the climbers (Andre Ulrych) ← 700 was given a drug (diodiquin) to help him sleep. At the high altitudes, the drug made him delirious for several days, making the descent especially hazardous.

Hallucinations, infections and other ailments were an almost constant problem. One by one, the strong climbers were struck with illness or exhaustion. Morale began to sink.

Finally, on October 31, forty days after they began their ascent, only two climbers (Stammberger and Malezic) remained on the mountain. Facing temperatures of −35 degrees and 70 m.p.h. winds, they gave up their bid for the mountain, having reached a height of 26,000 feet. They returned home, ← 800 discouraged and frustrated, but not defeated.

The group will make another attempt to climb Makalu's South face in a second expedition. The first expedition cost them $20,000 and was largely financed by private donations. The second will be similarly financed.

Korich said it will consist of most of the same people and doctors from the University of Colorado Medical School interested in doing research on individual human responses and adaptive capabilities at such high altitudes.

Korich's reasons for going back are most simply and directy stated in that classic mountain climber's 900 → response, "Because it's there."

______ STOP__ASK FOR YOUR TIME ______

Record time immediately and answer questions on content.

Time ________ Sec. RATE (from table on page 313): R. ________

No. Correct ________ COMPREHENSION (50% for each correct answer): C. ________
(key on page 329)

V-18 EFFICIENCY (R × C): E. ________

Record on Progress Chart on page 299

ANSWER THESE QUESTIONS IMMEDIATELY

1. (T—F) According to scientists, man can adapt up to 26,000 feet, but needs oxygen beyond that to prevent damage to body tissue.

2. (M.C.) Which of the following reasons was not mentioned as a reason for giving up the plan to reach the top?

______(1) Cold and high winds.

______(2) Hallucinations and infections.

______(3) Inadequate financial support.

______(4) Extreme illness and exhaustion.

Length: 900 words

Exercise V-19

Readability Score: 43

Boy Has Bout With Bat

By Joyce Calistri King

(Reprinted by permission from *Health,* January 1975.)

WAIT FOR SIGNAL TO BEGIN READING

The Attack

A Reading, Pa., teenager was the victim in a horror story which took place in his own front yard. Scott Schultz was standing on the lawn talking to his mother when a bat swooped down and attacked him.

"At first I thought it was a really big butterfly," said the 13-year old.

When Scott heard his mother scream, "It's a bat!" he tried to brush the creature off his shirt, but the bat clung to the fabric.

Finally, he grabbed the small, mouselike bat, threw it to the ground, and crushed it with his foot. The two-inch bat, with wing spread of eight inches, was delivered to Dr. Richard H. Detwiler, a Reading veterinarian, who immediately had it tested for rabies.

As frightening as the attack of the bat was to Scott, the lab results were even more terrifying to the former Little League baseball player. The dead mammal's brain contained microscopic objects called Negri bodies. The diagnosis of rabies was definite.

The lab report was carried to the Schultz family by Dr. Bruce E. Ilgen, Dr. Detwiler's associate. He described the rabies preventive treatment that Scott must undergo in order to save his life. Fortunately, he was able to assure the boy that the injections he must receive daily for a minimum of 14 days were not as painful as sometimes feared. He spoke from experience, for the young veterinarian had undergone the preventive therapy as a teenager following a skunk bite.

The Therapy

The Schultz family immediately called Albert P. Schartel, Jr., D.O., longtime family friend and physician. Although Dr. Schartel has been practicing in the Reading area for 20 years, he—like many doctors in the area—had never before been called upon to treat a patient for rabies exposure.

Rabies vaccine (USP) was obtained from the local hospital, and every day for two weeks Dr. Schartel injected vaccine just below the skin in the area of Scott's abdomen. Rabies vaccine (USP) is a sterile preparation of killed fixed virus of rabies, obtained from a duck embryo which has been infected with fixed rabies virus. One cubic centimeter of the vaccine is injected on alternate sides of the abdomen in a criss-cross pattern. Therapy ended just four days before Scott celebrated his fourteenth birthday.

Scott, an active boy who loved the out-of-doors, was always fond of animals. He had seen bats while hiking in the fields that adjoin his home. But they had never come near him, and he had never feared the strange-looking winged mammals.

Bats are not solitary creatures. They are considered very social beings and often live in large colonies. Most species of bats feed on insects though several species feed on fruit. A South American species of bat called the vampire bat is known to suck blood from cattle by attaching itself to the animal's back. Bats rarely attack humans, however.

Rabies is one of the oldest diseases known to afflict mankind and animals. An inscription from ancient Mesopotamia (now Iraq), dated about 2000 B.C., gave an accurate description of rabies, including its manner of infection.

Stray dogs are most commonly responsible for transmitting the rabies virus to humans, although cats, foxes, raccoons, skunks, and particulary domestic farm animals may do so.

Greater Risk

In the past few years, the number of rabies cases among wild animals has increased. This means that humans are at greater risk of exposure to the usually fatal disease. According to the Center for Disease Control in Atlanta, Ga., the number of positive diagnoses of rabies in animals was up 34 percent last year. Of 4,392 infected animals, nearly half were skunks, with foxes, bats, and raccoons following in that order, then dogs, cats, and cattle.

Although today rabies seldom results in human fatalities in the U.S., it remains a potentially dangerous public health problem. Each year, more than 30,000 Americans are exposed to rabies and must be vaccinated.

According to the American Veterinary Medical Association, everyone bitten by a domestic or wild animal need not undergo antirabies vaccination. However, a physician should be consulted immediately after the bite has occurred.

"Any person bitten by a wild animal or anyone who comes into contact with the saliva of a wild ←700 animal should contact his doctor immediately," urges Dr. Schartel. "If possible," he adds, "the animal should be killed and sent to a pathology laboratory."

Since his bout with the rabid bat two years ago, Scott Schultz has experienced no side effects. The worst part for him was a tender stomach where all those shots were injected. He considers himself lucky that he didn't need booster shots. A month after his last shot, a sample of Scott's blood was taken, quickly frozen, packed in dry ice, and sent by airmail to the Rabies Diagnostic Laboratory Center. The lab report ←800 sent to Dr. Schartel showed antibodies present in Scott's blood, which meant he did not need additional injections. The vaccine must be given until antibodies are detected.

Scott's encounter with the bat has not affected his fondness for wildlife; he plans to major in forestry. "I'm glad I'm not superstitious," quips the lucky teenager, "there was a full moon the night that bat landed on my chest."

For more information on rabies, write to the American Veterinary Medical Association, 600 S. Michigan Ave., Chicago 60605, and ask for the 900→ booklet "What You Should Know about Rabies."

______ STOP ___ ASK FOR YOUR TIME ______

Record time immediately and answer questions on content.

Time ________ Sec.	RATE (from table on page 313):	R. ________
No. Correct ________ (key on page 321)	COMPREHENSION (50% for each correct answer):	C. ________
V-19	EFFICIENCY (R × C):	E. ________

Record on Progress Chart on page 299

ANSWER THESE QUESTIONS IMMEDIATELY

1. (T—F) The daily injections for fourteen days were more frightening to Scott than the bat attack itself.

2. (M.C.) Anyone who is bitten by a wild animal should:

_____(1) schedule the fourteen day therapy program at once.

_____(2) stay away from further contacts with animals.

_____(3) consult a physician immediately.

_____(4) write to the American Veterinary Medical Association.

Length: 900 words

Exercise V-20

Readability Score: 31

Harrah's Automobile Collection

By Celia Scully

(Reprinted by permission from *Travel/Holiday,* November, 1977.)

WAIT FOR SIGNAL TO BEGIN READING

Show Stoppers

Many Reno visitors take a leisurely break from casino activities. They board a motorized 1908 San Francisco cable car for a fascinating side trip to see some old cars.

Though top entertainers star nightly at Harrah's two Northern Nevada, hotel-casinos, the real show stoppers—as far as auto enthusiasts go—are hundreds of antique cars sitting in a converted ice house just three miles (five km) from downtown Reno. Turn back the pages of automotive history and there you'll find many of the classic, vintage and one-of-a-kind cars now on display at Harrah's Automobile Collection, the largest in the world.

Cars in the collection include two Bugatti Royales, each costing over $40,000 in 1931; the 1892 steam-powered Philion, an unlikely starter for an industry that revolutionized society; and the popular 1907 Thomas Flyer, winner of the longest, most grueling auto race ever run between New York and Paris—170 days and 13,341 land miles (21,466 km) from the starting line in New York City's Times Square.

On display, too, are antique and classic-model cars, owned by Hollywood and television celebrities, among them Wayne Newton's 1930 Duesenberg and 1934 Bentley; Bill Cosby's 1935 Aston-Martin; Dick Smothers' 1932 Ford Deluxe Phaeton, and Sammy Davis, Jr.'s 1970 Honda Tri-Chopper, an exotic three-wheel motorcycle. And that's only the beginning.

Showrooms

There are antique motorcars, airplanes, fire engines, toy cars, motorcycles, period costumes and a full-scale steam locomotive. The ten-acre complex of thirteen buildings also houses three large showrooms, a priceless research library, restoration facilities employing 87 skilled craftsmen, a cafeteria and saloon plus a Pony Express Museum containing Western artifacts and antique slot machines.

The 1,100 polished chrome and silver, colorful, mint-condition cars on view draw thousands of visitors each year to Harrah's Automobile Collection. It is recognized by both the United Nations and International Council of Museums as being the world's outstanding auto museum.

In the Beginning

The collection got its start in 1948 when pioneer Nevada hotel-casino magnate William F. Harrah acquired a 1911 Maxwell and a 1911 Ford. Next came a 1906 Model "F" Ford, then a 1902 curved-dash Oldsmobile. Today the collection totals 1,500 cars and lacks only about 60 more to be complete. But it's feared many of these vehicles no longer exist.

In fact, with automotive relics rusting in junkyards everywhere, scholars agree that the museum offers a rare opportunity to observe the birth, heritage and evolution of the automobile—from horseless carriage to rotary engine and beyond.

Visitors enter the museum by way of spotless restoration shops where they can watch master craftsmen working on various stages of stripping down and rebuilding cars to their original condition. When finished, everything—from the smallest brass manufacturer's plate to the color and even stuffing in the upholstery—is just as it was the day the car rolled out of the factory.

But the world champion Thomas Flyer is an exception one of Harrah's most challenging restorations, it took 40 craftsmen six weeks to restore the vehicle to its condition at the end of the New York-to-Paris race. One of the most vexing problems was how to duplicate the dust, wear and grime of the race. The solution was to drive the car several times through Nevada's rugged desert.

With authenticity a byword at the museum, craftsmen work closely with researchers. It's not uncommon for work to be held up for months while archives are searched, missing parts located or duplicated. Even when complex hood ornaments or other decorative features must be copied, the new part contains the exact material used in the original—whether it was wood, leather or fabric.

Hub of the activity is the research library established in 1955. Considered the finest of its kind, the library has on file restoration manuals for most of the cars in the collection as well as technical data on the many thousands of cars produced throughout motoring history. Several of its journals, manuals and periodicals are now collectors's items, with some dating back as early as 1885.

In the News

Harrah's Automobile Collection has been the subject of television specials, including Walter Cronkite's CBS Evening News in one of Charles Kuralt's "On the Road" reports, as well as many ← 700 articles in general and special interest publications.

Recently, craftsmen at the collection provided technical expertise for Shell Oil Company to use in making its edition of answer books aimed at giving consumers useful car maintenance tips. This is the first time Harrah's has ever shared its maintenance and restoration knowledge with the general public.

Opened in 1962, the museum is now housed in temporary quarters with free parking and free admission for children under twelve. Convenient transportation is available without charge from downtown Reno on either a 1906 motorized San 800 → Francisco cable car or vintage Fifth Avenue double-decker bus. Eventually the famed auto collection will be the feature attraction of Harrah's autoworld, a major resort-complex west of Reno now in the planning stages.

Today's visitors can stroll leisurely down show-case rows of Fords, Duesenbergs, Stanley Steamers and Packards. They can take "side trips" into the history of the race car or motorcycle. Yet enjoying the glamor and glitter of vintage cars isn't limited to car buffs. Grandparents fondly recall Stutz Bearcats, roadsters and rumble-seat romances while wide-eyed youngsters find it hard to believe the time-honored "tin lizzies" were the workhorses of the scarf-and- 900 → goggles era.

STOP ASK FOR YOUR TIME

Record time immediately and answer questions on content.

Time	Sec.	RATE (from table on page 313):	R.
No. Correct (key on page 329)		COMPREHENSION (50% for each correct answer):	C.
V-20		EFFICIENCY (R × C):	E.

Record on Progress Chart on page 299

ANSWER THESE QUESTIONS IMMEDIATELY

1. (T—F) One of the most perplexing problems in the unique restoration of the Thomas Flyer was duplicating the rust.

2. (M.C.) Harrah's Automobile Collection includes all of the following features except:
   (1) auto museum showroom.
   (2) model car salesroom.
   (3) restoration shop.
   (4) research library.

SERIES VI
Exploratory Reading Exercises

Instructions

The Series VI exercises are designed to develop your ability to read continuously one long article and then to recite on the material at the end. This type of reading will be contrasted with that of the exercises in Series VII, where you read in smaller units and do a spaced recitation. Many students argue that they do not have time for the SQ4R method of study or for self-recitation. A comparison of your efficiency scores between these two types of exercises is one of the best objective answers to your own possible hesitancy to try these study techniques.

As in Series V exercises, you will find the length and the readability scores at the top of each article and you will find the numbers in the center margin that will help you to estimate your speed. Articles become progressively more difficult as you proceed through the series, and here again you are working toward increasing reading speed and reading level. In this case, however, you have more material and more ideas to retain, and you will be tested more thoroughly on the material read.

When given the signal to begin an article, you should read as rapidly as possible, concentrating on main ideas and watching for any clues to those ideas. When you finish reading, ask for your time immediately, and check your rate by using the table on page 315.

Then go on to the ten questions on the material, and answer them as accurately as possible. Answer the (MC) and the (T—F) questions as instructed before. In the Completion questions (C), you are to fill in the word or words that will best complete the meaning of the sentence. After these are scored according to the keys on pages 322 and 330, you compute your comprehension by multiplying your number of correct answers by ten. You may then compute your *efficiency* by multiplying the *rate* by the *comprehension*. Record the efficiency score on the Progress Chart on page 299.

Suggestions

These are referred to as Exploratory Reading Exercises because they are designed to help polish tools of reading for new ideas, greater detail, or further understanding of materials with which you are already familiar. These may be materials already sorted by the Idea Reading approach and identified for a little more thorough reading. Materials identified by this type of reading for specific study purposes or for significant long-range use normally will be marked and set aside for study reading or critical reading.

Normally, this reading procedure will not result in long-range retention of details unless the content is closely related to personal needs and unless reading is reinforced by additional study skills focused on long-term comprehension.

For general reading about new ideas or new interests, this type of reading utilizes high-speed reading skills tempered with selective judgment of materials appropriate for more careful study.

Your rate on these materials will depend on much more than the arrangement on paper, the content, or the instructor's motivation. You will determine your rate and efficiency by your personal motivation and attitude. What you already know about the topic, how you feel about the topic, and what previous associations you may have with the topic or the author will have a strong effect on your reading activity.

In this longer reading material, one criterion is especially important, however, and that is your ability to concentrate for an extended period of time without interruption. This will require effort on your part. You will have to avoid the tendencies to daydream or to let your attention be distracted by any audio or visual factors of passing interest. Perhaps you should review again the materials on pages 19-24 of this book regarding concentration and basic study skills.

Content of these articles will cover a fairly wide range of material, some of which may be of immediate interest to you and some of which may not. For the purpose of these exercises, you should try to develop an inquiring mind and try to seek new ideas. You can apply a fairly rapid reading rate to such materials. You may be surprised to find out how much content you can pick up even at relatively high-speed reading.

Thinking about the title, checking out your own knowledge of the topic, and posing questions to which you want to find answers will provide a mental setting in which you should achieve effective concentration and maximum reading efficiency.

Length: 1350 words

Exercise VI-1

Readability Score: 80

Boo

(Reprinted by permission from *Wyoming Wildlife,* January, 1957.)

WAIT FOR SIGNAL TO BEGIN READING

You don't see them but you know that they're around. You don't hear them when they fly nearby.

Spooks? No—not quite. What you don't hear and don't see is one of the most interesting forms of wildlife that exists today—OWLS.

Because of their rather spooky characteristics, owls have been associated with some pretty unsavory characters, mainly witches, goblins and hob-goblins. Probably no other form of wildlife has caused as much superstition among men.

Even back in the days of Julius Caesar owls had a poor reputation. The Romans thought that they were evil omens and messengers of death. If an owl lit on a housetop death was soon to follow, taking all that lived inside. Even an owl hooting nearby started them shivering in their togas.

Early Greeks had a different concept of hooters. They thought of them as an emblem of wisdom. An owl's eyes are set on the head much like that of man, giving him the appearance of an intellectual scholar.

American Indians included owls in many of their mystic rituals. They thought that owls made pretty potent medicine. Shakespeare included them in scenes with witches, which didn't help their reputation.

Useful Birds

But owls aren't as bad as these imaginative people would lead you to believe. In fact they're handy to have around.

There are 300 known kinds of owls found throughout the world from the polar regions to the continents and remote islands of the sea. Many migrate annually.

Owls vary in size from the tiny elf-owl, no larger than a sparrow, to the powerful horned owls that grow to two feet in length. There are two families of owls. One includes barn owls and the other takes in all other species.

Many people believe that hooters can turn their heads completely around. One story states that if you circle an owl enough it will soon wring its neck off watching you. An owl's eyes cannot move. To change his line of vision the bird must turn its head. This is done with quick snaps, so quick that it looks like it turns the full 360 degrees. Some of the smaller owls have round markings that look like eyes on the back of their head. Country people in South America think that they have four eyes and can see behind as well as in front.

Most owls sleep all day and hunt all night. Their eyes are especially well adapted for seeing in the dark and they can spot nearly every moving thing. Some, while having perfect vision at night, are almost blind during the day and a person can easily walk up to them.

Owls sleep and nest in caves, hollow logs or tangled leaves and will take advantage of an abandoned hawk's nest to set up housekeeping. Snowy owls will make their nests on the gound. Burrowing owls live in prairie dog burrows.

Most birds don't have much use for owls and attack them while they sleep during the day. Crows, more aggressive than others, will often drive off the largest owls. Crow hunters take advantage of this by tethering owls.

Soundless Flight

Owls fly without making a sound. Their wing feathers have soft margins. This feature makes them great hunters because they can hit their prey without alarming them. They will hunt birds as well as rodents, and also rabbits. Usually they take the animal alive, flying to their nests to eat. Owls, like hawks, tear their prey apart and swallow the pieces whole.

There are 13 different kinds of owls found in Wyoming. They include the great-horned owl, great gray owl, Rocky Mountain screech owl, snowy owl, American hawk owl, Rocky Mountain pygmy owl, Western burrowing owl, Northern barred owl, long-eared and short-eared owls, Richardson's owl, saw whet owl and barn owl. Some are fairly common while others are only occasional visitors.

The *great gray owl* is the largest bird found in the State. It will reach a length of 33 inches. This owl is fairly common in the northwestern part of the State. The great gray owl spends much of its time in the Arctic and will only migrate south if food is scarce. Most of their size is made up of feathers which are needed to keep them warm in the frigid north. Without the feathers they would look quite small when compared with the great horned owl.

The *great horned owl*, called the Montana horned owl in this area, is fairly common. They are about two feet long. The horned owl is the most fierce and powerful of all owls, taking on anything from a rabbit to a turkey to satisfy its hungers.

Another large owl found here is the *northern barred owl*. They look as big as the horned owl but like the gray owl most of their size is made of feathers. Barred owls, unlike most of the others, have large black eyes.

Long-eared and *short-eared owls* are both found here, the long eared being more common. Long-eared owls have a cat-like face with pronounced feathered tufts on the top of their heads. Their plumage blends well with the surroundings, making them hard to spot. Both species reach a size of about 13-1/2 inches.

The *snowy owl* is an occasional visitor here and like the gray owl migrates when food is scarce in the Arctic. As the name would indicate, the bird is almost pure white.

The *American hawk owl* is a rare visitor here, spending most of its time in the Arctic. The hawk owl can be more easily seen than other owls because of its habit of perching on tall dead stumps. Hawk owls can hunt day or night.

Unlike the hawk owl, the *burrowing owl* spends most of its time on the ground. They're small owls with long legs and large, round heads. Their average length is 10 inches. The Western burrowing owl is a common summer visitor and can be found in the open prairie. Grasshoppers form the main bulk of their diet. They also eat mice, rats and small snakes.

The *saw whet owl* gets its name from the sound it makes. Its rasping cry sounds like a saw being filed. The saw whet is a small owl averaging eight inches. This owl takes advantage of abandoned woodpecker holes to set up housekeeping. Saw whets are found in the wooded areas of the State.

Richardson's owls are very rare in this State. Most of them are found farther north. Some call it "the blind one," believing that they cannot see during the day. They are often caught by hand. Even in the far north they appear sluggish except after dark.

Pygmy owls also take advantage of woodpecker holes for setting up their homes. This little bird reaches an average length of seven inches. Pygmies will eat insects and small mammals. They are not too common in Wyoming.

The *screech owl* has been one of the main causes for superstitions about owls. This bird is found throughout the United States in various phases and is one of the best known owls. The Rocky Mountain screech owl is found in the eastern part of Wyoming. His name is misleading for its call sounds more like a wailing than screeching.

In the south superstitious folks call them the shivering owl, a name perhaps with double meaning, describing the quality of the owl's notes and also the effect on the listener. Many think the appearance of this owl is a sure sign of death.

Barn owls are rare in this state. Their average size is seventeen inches. Some call them "monkey-faced owls" because of the similarity in their faces. Barn owls will rest all day saving their energy for night hunting.

Owls have proven of benefit to man time and time again and most everyone, if they're not too superstitious, will agree that they are handy to have around. They are interesting birds and may be as wise as the Greeks would have us believe. What other form of wildlife has caused so much consternation to man through the centuries.

_______ STOP __ ASK FOR YOUR TIME _______

Record time immediately and answer questions on content.

Time ________ Sec. RATE (from table on page 315): R. ________

No. Correct ________ COMPREHENSION (10% for each correct answer): C. ________
(key on page 322)

VI-1 EFFICIENCY (R × C): E. ________

Record on Progress Chart on page 299

ANSWER THESE QUESTIONS IMMEDIATELY

1. (T—F) Owls have always had a good reputation as they were considered to be very wise.
2. (T—F) Owls were included in the Indians' mystic rituals, as they were thought to make pretty potent medicine.
3. (C.) The most aggressive enemy of the owl is the ________________.
4. (T—F) Owls can turn their heads completely around on their necks.
5. (M. C.) Owls fly:
   ______(1) without making a sound.
   ______(2) quite noisily.
   ______(3) very high in the air.
   ______(4) very low in the air.
6. (T—F) Owls which prey upon animals never prey upon birds.
7. (T—F) Most of the gray owl's size is made up of feathers.
8. (C.) The almost pure white snowy owl will migrate when food becomes scarce in the ________.
9. (M. C.) An owl that spends most of his time on the ground is the:
   ______(1) saw whet owl.
   ______(2) hawk owl.
   ______(3) snowy owl.
   ______(4) burrowing owl.
10. (T—F) One of the main causes for the superstitions concerning owls is the screech owl.

Length: 1350 words

Exercise VI-2

Readability Score: 73

When Judy Died

By Ruth LuSan

(Reprinted by permission from *MS. Magazine,* February, 1977.)

WAIT FOR SIGNAL TO BEGIN READING

I hate it when little kids die; little kids are not supposed to die; they're supposed to run around and scream and yell and cry and tell on each other.

My sister Judy died a year ago when I was almost nine. When it happened, all I did first was get really mad at the man who hit her with his truck and then at God. Everyone kept telling me "God wanted Judy with Him." But why would He want that? Judy never went to church or prayed. I don't think He even knew her.

Judy was only six and really smart—she could read my brother Frank's books. He's 12. My dad always gets mad at Frank because Frank wants to be a helicopter pilot and not a lawyer like my dad.

I went with my parents to the funeral place. Frank stayed home and cried a lot. I only cried a little bit. I heard my dad crying in his room. My sister Janet came home from college and cried too. She told me that it's good to cry because then you won't get ulcers. The only one of us that didn't cry was my mother. I think she was mostly mad, like I was.

I didn't like the funeral place. When we opened the door, all these bells started ringing and this man came out and said, "Can I be of service?", real polite and softly like someone was asleep. My mother said, "Yes, we'd like to arrange a funeral." He said, "Certainly," and showed us his office.

It was 1:30 when we got home so we all sat in the living room and talked about Judy. No one wanted to go to school or work because they were afraid they would start to cry. I was glad I didn't go because it was math day. Judy was real good at math and always helped me with division. She was only in the first grade but she could add, subtract, multiply, *and* divide. My mom taught us to read and write and do math when we were really little. I can read and write, but that's all.

My sister Janet kept talking about Judy getting born and how funny-looking she was. Frank started crying again, and I started coloring my map of Australia. I really want to go there and drink beer like my dad did during the war. He was a typist in Sydney. My mom is a chemist, and they met in Cleveland.

I was on the way to the kitchen when the phone started ringing—it was Jeannie P. Vincent.

"I heard your sister died," she said.

"Yeah, she got run over by a truck."

"Do you think Judy felt anything?"

"I don't know; they say she died pretty fast."

"Oh well, see you at school. Bye."

Jeannie P. Vincent is my very best friend.

I came back into the living room. Frank wasn't crying any more, he was playing with his key chain. Once in a while a tear would come out, but he wasn't making any crying noises. Suddenly Janet asked when we were going to bury Judy. My father started telling us all the plans. He said that there would be a small service at the funeral place and then we would go to the cemetery. He told us that he would like to have the funeral tomorrow, but it was going to take a while for all the relatives to get here, the funeral would be Friday instead.

We went out to dinner that night because no one felt like cooking. I had a hamburger and onion rings and everyone else had steak.

In the middle of the night, I got up to go to the bathroom, and I heard Frank crying again. I looked in his room but he wasn't there, he was in Judy's room.

"Hey, Frank, you okay?"

"No", he was sitting on the floor.

I opened the door wider and walked in. He was holding one of the model cars he and Judy built together.

"Come on, Frank, Grandma told me on the phone that Judy was in heaven," I said. He just cried harder. He was still in there when I went back to bed.

Next morning, my mom drove me to school. As I was getting out of the car, she asked me to go to Judy's class and get all of Judy's stuff, and she handed me my note for being absent the day before.

Judy's teacher, Mrs. Farley, got kind of shaky when she saw me. All the little kids didn't know what was going on, so they asked me where Judy was. I told them she died, and they said "Oh" and went back to their desks.

Mrs. Farley handed me some papers and books and Judy's orange sweater and told me that she was sorry about Judy and walked me to the door.

When I got to my class, my teacher, Mr. Stoker, was all by himself correcting papers—everyone else was in the library.

"Hi, Mr. Stoker, sorry I'm late; my aunt came over and . . ."

"Do you have a note?"

"Yes, here it is."

He took it and read it two or three times. Then he looked at me over his glasses and said, "It is important to carry on—join the class at the library."

If your sister ever dies, don't go to school. People ← 900 act weird.

All day people got embarrassed and said dumb things. All the relatives were there when I got home. People were crying and hugging and I thought I was going to be swallowed up.

During breakfast the next day, all the relatives started crying and hugging again. Luckily, a limousine came and took us to the funeral place. Lots of people from our neighborhood were there waiting for us.

Everyone went in and sat down while two of the funeral people wheeled Judy's casket down the aisle. It was really small. ← 1000

My cousin, who lives about a block from us and who is a minister, did the service. He told everyone that Judy was really nice and never did anything wrong. I guess he doesn't remember the time she put toothpaste in Frank's ear.

After he finished, everyone went outside. They put the coffin and a lot of flowers in a big black car called a hearse. Then everyone got in their own cars and followed the hearse out to the cemetery.

It took us about a half hour to get to the cemetery. There were 29 cars in the line—I counted ← 1100 them when we were on a big wide curve in the road. The cemetery was real quiet, and there were lots of trees. They dug Judy's grave under an oak tree, just like the one we fell out of. The grave scared me. Everyone told me that it wasn't really Judy going under the ground, and that the real Judy would stay alive in our minds. The idea still scared me.

Uncle Paul and Aunt Joyce read out of the Bible while the rest of my uncles carried the coffin up the 1200 → hill. Arthur, my minister cousin, said some prayers and then everyone sang Judy's favorite song, the "Battle Hymn of the Republic". Frank and me and Janet really started crying then because it was the song we all had taught her to sing in a big booming voice.

Everyone started back to their cars then. None of us were going to stay around and watch them actually bury the casket. Janet and me and Frank were walking back to the limousine when I looked back and saw my daddy and momma taking a rose from someone's wreath and putting it on the casket. My mom started 1300 → crying then and I felt a lot better—I didn't want her to get ulcers.

On the way home Janet told me that when you die you no longer feel sick, feel pain, or even feel sad. I hope that's true because it if is, Judy has nothing to 1350 → worry about.

______ STOP__ASK FOR YOUR TIME ______

Record time immediately and answer questions on content.

Time __________ Sec.	RATE (from table on page 315):	R. __________
No. Correct __________ (key on page 330)	COMPREHENSION (10% for each correct answer):	C. __________
VI-2	EFFICIENCY (R × C):	E. __________

Record on Progress Chart on page 299

ANSWER THESE QUESTIONS IMMEDIATELY

1. (T—F) This story is written by Judy's brother.
2. (C.) When she died, Judy was only ________________ years old.
3. (T—F) The father was last to cry after Judy's death.
4. (C.) Janet said crying keeps you from getting ________________ .
5. (M.C.) In school, Judy was especially good at:

   ______(1) math.

   ______(2) English.

   ______(3) history.

   ______(4) science.
6. (T—F) Judy's mother was a chemist and her father was a lawyer.
7. (T—F) Of all the children, Janet seemed most upset by Judy's death.
8. (M.C.) Judy was killed:

   ______(1) in an automobile wreck.

   ______(2) in a plane crash.

   ______(3) when hit by a truck.

   ______(4) falling out of a tree.
9. (T—F) Everyone sang the "Battle Hymn of the Republic" at the funeral.
10. (T—F) This article shares with the reader the confusion a nine year old child has about death.

Length: 1350 words

Exercise VI-3

Readability Score: 70

Being On Your Own

By Stephanie T. Rispin

(Reprinted from an original article of the Uniwyo Reading Reasearch Center by permission of the Director.)

WAIT FOR SIGNAL TO BEGIN READING

Challenge

Learning to stand on one's own feet is probably the most difficult hurdle that people have to overcome during their lifetimes. In fact, many never take the leap. Hard work and perseverance are required. Many frustrations occur. Backslides and failures are not uncommon.

Before you can stand on your own feet you need knowledge about the world around you. You need to know that the chances of retaining some stability are greatly in your favor. Today's society has attempted these chances through certain institutions, such as the numerous elementary and secondary schools, universities, and churches. By exposure to these institutions, individuals should become more successful in their independence. They should learn to govern themselves with intelligence and awareness. Obedience to certain laws of life and customs of humanity are needed to achieve your goals.

Knowledge is the basis for a satisfying, productive life. While going through school you may feel that nothing is penetrating your mind, and that all your efforts at studying are futile. Someday, however, that knowledge you have stored away will surface. Perhaps it will be a specific historical or mathematical answer, or perhaps only a simple broadening of your outlook on life. Somehow, someday all of your studies will serve to enrich your life.

Make a Decision

Before you can get started, you have to decide what you want to do. You need a plan of action. If you are to get any satisfaction out of your life, you will have to make it yourself. You will have to stand on your own feet.

You must review your abilities and single out the one which seems most worthy of development. You must plan around it. You must decide how to go after what you want. You must assess your strengths and ambitions honestly to know just how far you can take yourself. When you have done all this, you must set out to develop yourself and your own lifestyle.

You should be prepared, but not establish rigid rules. You should always expect the unexpected. Always roll with the punches. The world is constantly changing. Knowledge and confidence will make the uncertainties easier to handle.

Ambition

To distinguish between ambition and selfishness may be difficult at some times. One simple objective for everyone is to become all that you can become, to progress from what is passable to what is excellent. Always move from what youth yearned for to what maturity can fulfill. Live up to your own expectations. In your heart you must always have the confidence that you possess the capabilities to do better. One word of caution, however: you can not feel the exultation of recognition and achievement if you have stepped on some other people along the way.

You must approach your goal step by step. Constantly evaluate where you are as well as where you are headed. A constructive thought process concerns which steps to take, when, and the best course of action. Such constructive thinking must flow endlessly through your mind and control all your actions. If you are not ambitious to succeed, you should not attempt to force yourself. Instead you should remain in a chosen position, making full use of your capacities to do that job well.

Failure

Everyone will, at some time, face some failures. To work for something and have it slide out from under your feet is discouraging, to say the least. You must retain your perspective, however. If something was worth working for once, it always will be. Just pick yourself up and begin again, learning from your mistakes. Use an even greater amount of energy, drive, and perseverance. It has been said that ninety percent of the world's failures are quitters.

Courage is necessary to begin again. Risks must be taken. If risks were avoided, you would never know how far you could go. It is better to have tried and failed than to have the ignominy of never having attempted great things.

Many failures could be avoided if one were to view the obstacles in one's way with calm intelligence. Risks must be calculated and weighed. When reasoned out, perhaps a better path will reveal itself.

Confidence

To achieve anything without reasonable confidence in your own ability is vitually impossible. When taking risks, self confidence is needed for that extra edge. If you believe in yourself, others will believe in you, too.

Self confidence, as with anything else, must be kept in check. Loud mouths who voice their abilities night and day often find themselves passed over with a disdainful glance. A happy medium is desirable. Accept opportunities with grace and confidence. One who quietly gets the job done well is more dependable than one who only talks about doing it. Talking about your abilities to others doesn't instill confidence.

Your personality can be either a great help or a hindrance to your success. If you continually abuse the trust of your fellow workers or belittle them, you will develop a bad name. The word will soon spread. The people you work with have the power of making life easy or miserable. If you demonstrate a rebellious personality, your superiors will probably choose another for the job.

Some people build a terrific facade. They are only attempting to hide their many insecurities. More often than not, a true personality is much more likable and conducive to success, than is one which is perceived as a mask. Look at the way people react to you. If you show yourself to be a hard worker, they will recognize you as such and respect you. If you show your honest liking for them, the chances are that they will return that liking.

Interest and Originality

Interest and originality are two big essentials. You may often face what you might consider to be dull, tedious task. Perhaps the reason it may seem so dull is because you are not considering it in any other way. The way to get around this is to believe that it is interesting, and make it interesting. Use some originality and give it a new twist.

Both of these qualities, interest and originality, are looked upon with favor by those in higher positions. Nothing can please one's superiors more than seeing enthusiasm for their work. They are always on the look-out for bright young people who enter into their work with zeal, and develop new ideas.

Being Accepted

Many people labor under the delusion that if they stand on their own feet they will not be accepted by others. This is not so. The very association with other people is the spice of life.

Independence is good, but not to the point that the self becomes all important and all others are needless. You can find great joy in knowing that you have helped someone else. They probably would help you if you should ever need it. One who attempts to understand and serve others is a much bigger person than one who carries personal independence to extremes. Gentleness, kindliness, and goodwill contribute to a peaceful, decent society.

If the time arises when you need to stand up for your rights, you should, by all means, base that stand on what you believe in. If good manners and consideration are employed, an understanding can easily be reached.

When you take a stand on personal values, you must be prepared to take on the responsibilities of an adult. Problems can't be solved in old, childish manners. You need an intelligent stability. You must always accept responsibility for yourself, your family, your community, and your nation. All obstacles must be met, and meeting them must still leave you standing up.

Standing on your own feet may not always be very easy. Nothing worth having comes without some effort. If you have the desire to do well at your chosen profession and to make some contribution, you can then achieve success. The opportunity to shine with brilliance comes to those who make the utmost of their talents and skills; you need the courage, desire, and energy to stand on your own feet.

_______ STOP __ ASK FOR YOUR TIME _______

Record time immediately and answer questions on content.

Time ______ Sec.	RATE (from table on page 315):	R. ______
No. Correct ______	COMPREHENSION (100 – 10% for each correct answer):	C. ______
VI-3	EFFICIENCY (R × C):	E. ______

Record on Progress Chart on page 299

ANSWER THESE QUESTIONS IMMEDIATELY

1. (T—F) Learning to stand on your own feet is probably the most difficult hurdle that you have to overcome.
2. (C.) You must review your ______________ and single out the one you feel is most worthy of development.
3. (T—F) You should establish rigid rules in support of your value system.
4. (C.) At times it is difficult to distinguish between selfishness and ______________ .
5. (T—F) The author suggests that you try to live up to your own expectations.
6. (M.C.) The author warns that the exaltation of recognition and achievement should never be based on:
   ______(1) setting up unachievable standards for himself.
   ______(2) stepping on other people along the way.
   ______(3) using his abilities excessively.
   ______(4) exploiting one's personal resources.
7. (T—F) If you are not ambitious to succeed you should attempt to force yourself enough to at least obtain a better position.
8. (T—F) This author claims that if something was worth working for once, it always will be.
9. (M.C.) The author suggests that dull work:
   ______(1) is the primary contributor to unemployment.
   ______(2) is not necessary with society's advanced mechanization.
   ______(3) is usually dull only to the highly educated worker.
   ______(4) can be made interesting if you try to make it so.
10. (T—F) Self-respect makes standing on one's own feet easy.

Length: 1350 words

Exercise VI-4

Readability Score: 68

Mystery People of Ponil Canyon

By William B. McMorris

(Reprinted by permission from *Boys' Life*
March, 1955.)

WAIT FOR SIGNAL TO BEGIN READING

The Lost Tribe

This yarn about the lost Indian Tribe of Philmont Scout Ranch out in New Mexico deals with a true Southwestern mystery. In fact, the mystery is so deep that even today nobody knows exactly what happened to the strange people who once made their home in Ponil Canyon or Philmont.

Consider that a warning. This tale does not guarantee to furnish a tidy explanation for whatever skullduggery did or did not take place in Ponil Canyon. If you like your mysteries solved in the last paragraph, read no further. This is a story for detectives.

This missing-persons case concerns a gang of ancient Indians. They were short, sturdy people, tough, but very primitive. They had no pack animals to carry their baggage. They did not work with metal, and for a long time they didn't have pottery. All their belongings were carried on their backs in baskets. They did not even know how to use wheels.

At first they probably had little law or custom within their tribe, and they certainly didn't give a hoot for international regulations, because they skipped across the Mexico-United States boundary without so much as a travel permit in the whole outfit. Of course, we have to forgive them for that, because they crossed the line about 1,400 years ago, and the border wasn't very well patrolled at that time.

Settlers

Once over the line, they settled in the canyons and on the mesas of Arizona, Utah, Colorado and New Mexico with basket making people similar to themselves. The particular bunch this story is about unpacked their baskets in North Ponil Canyon.

Now comes the tough part. Our Indians lived and prospered in the canyon for perhaps several hundred years. Then they vanished. We don't know where they went, and we can only guess why.

By piecing together evidence found in North Ponil Canyon and comparing it with material found in other ancient Indian dwellings in the Southwest, we can make a pretty good guess that the Ponil outfit left their homes for the same reason that their brothers all over the Southwest disappeared.

We Can Only Guess

There again we're stumped. We don't know for sure why any of them vanished.

Anyway, here's the evidence: Exhibit A is the caves in Ponil Canyon. Like some of the other confusing things about these ancient Indians, these are not true caves but shallow pockets weathered into the sandstone walls of the canyon. They are little more than dark narrow dens, but they furnished places for the Ponil people to sleep and keep dry and warm when it rained.

The men, besides being farmers, must have been excellent hunters, for they brought down game as large as deer with very crude weapons.

While the hunters might have had the bow and arrow later on, at first they had only a spear throwing device called an atlatl. The atlatl was simply a stick about eighteen inches long with a notch at one end. The butt of a light spear was placed against this notch and the hunter made his cast just as you would hurl a javelin, except that he gripped the notched stick instead of the spear shaft. The atlatl acted like an extension of the hunter's arm against the back of the spear and gave the toss added power.

It wasn't much of a weapon, so it must have taken a pretty clever stalker to creep within range of game as wary as deer, not to mention elk and antelope, which were fairly plentiful in the Philmont region.

They Had a Small Arsenal

Other weapons in the ancient man's arsenal included boomerang-shaped throwing sticks, axes and the usual armament of rocks, sticks, and clubs that could be used to kill small game. So far no axeheads or throwing sticks have been discovered in Ponil Canyon, but we do know that the brothers of these Philmont Indians used them.

We've said a lot about the "brothers" of these Ponil people. How do we know they were related to the other ancient inhabitants of the Southwest?

The answer is: We don't for sure, because not enough digging has been done and not enough evidence has been accumulated in Ponil Canyon as yet. However, all the signs point that way. The fact that pottery, living quarters, farming, hunting, and other things are the same among the Ponil people as among other groups in the Southwest indicates that the Ponil Indians were related to the others. That's what a detective would call circumstantial evidence. It doesn't make an airtight case, but it looks promising.

For instance, pottery in Ponil Canyon bears a design very similar to that found in large dwellings in Chaco Canyon, New Mexico, and Mesa Verde National Park, Colorado. Circumstantial evidence again, but it shows that the two peoples were related or at least carried on a friendly trade of goods and ideas.

At any rate we know that the Ponil group and other tribes in the Southwest lived pretty much alike.

They must have wanted to brag a little about their hunting exploits, because the sandstone slabs near their homes are covered with picture writing. Outlines of deer, birds, human hands and a strange-looking circular device that might have been a symbol for the sun are chiseled into the rock. Here again we see that the "writing" is similar to that found in Utah and Arizona. The Ponil people had no written language, but they got together often enough to use the same kind of pictures for various objects.

Even so, the story portrayed on the walls of Ponil Canyon is known only to the people who lived there. Perhaps there's no story at all.

At any rate, if the Pueblo Indians, who live very much like the ancient Indians did, are any help to us in this business, there must have been many superstitions and sayings, usually involving something in nature. These sayings may explain something in nature that the Indians did not understand. Scientists were scarce in those days, so the mysteries of nature must have seemed quite supernatural to the primitive men.

Superstitions

For instance, even today a Pueblo Indian may fear a whirlwind, believing it contains evil spirits which can enter a man's body and cripple him. It is also a belief that a dog's howl at night in a Pueblo village means death is near at hand. An owl's cry warns of disease in the air. Young animals at play bring rain, the Pueblos say. They also believe that spiders have the power to bewitch. When they kill a spider, it is customary to step on it hard and quickly and say at the same time, "A bluebird killed you." If the spider is only crippled, it may put a curse on the man who injures it. It is quite possible that the Ponil people had similar superstitions.

Twenty-three Year Drought

Agitation and raids by fierce attackers were teamed with a drought that experts in such matters tell us lasted twenty-three years. With the corn crops dying of thirst and the raiders lying in ambush outside the cliff houses, it's very likely the ancient Indians thought the spirits had turned against them. Perhaps that's why they fled. Flee they did, that we know.

But where?

You were warned that there is no tidy solution to that mystery. The question just hasn't been answered for sure. Some archaeologists think that the tribes of ancient Indians might have moved in with the Pueblo Indians of the Southwest. Still others believe that the ancient people spread east and south to escape the water shortage and were massacred by fierce plains and mountain tribes.

You can take your choice of any of these ideas or a dozen others, but one thing is sure: The mystery people of Ponil Canyon and their relatives in the Southwest went somewhere, and somewhere they left a trace of their passing. Someday the secret may be known and who knows, maybe the answer to the puzzle lies buried somewhere in a canyon at Philmont Scout Ranch.

______ STOP__ASK FOR YOUR TIME ______

Record time immediately and answer questions on content.

Time ______ Sec.	RATE (from table on page 315):	R. ______
No. Correct ______ (key on page 330)	COMPREHENSION (10% for each correct answer):	C. ______
VI-4	EFFICIENCY (R × C):	E. ______

Record on Progress Chart on page 299

ANSWER THESE QUESTIONS IMMEDIATELY

1. (T–F) The mystery of Ponil Canyon has not yet been solved.

2. (T–F) The mystery people were a primitive race that entered what is now the United States about 1,400 years ago.

3. (T–F) Although we know *where* the mystery people went, we have no idea *why*.

4. (C.) One of the first of the devices of these people in the line of weapons was the atlatl that enabled the hunters to throw their ______________ farther.

5. (M. C.) These Ponil hunters were:

   ______(1) well-skilled in designing of superior weapons.

   ______(2) clumsy, unsuccessful at bringing down any big game.

   ______(3) very good shots at long distances.

   ______(4) clever stalkers who got very close to their game for the kill.

6. (T–F) We have conclusive proof that the Ponil people were related to other Indians in the Southwest area.

7. (C.) Even today a Pueblo Indian may believe that ______________ have the power to bewitch.

8. (T–F) These Ponil people probably tried to explain nature through sayings and superstitions much like the Pueblo Indians did.

9. (T–F) The Ponil people were plagued for fifty years by raids and droughts.

10. (M. C.) The secret of the Ponil people:

   ______(1) has been solved recently.

   ______(2) will be solved in the near future.

   ______(3) may lie buried somewhere in a canyon at Philmont Scout Ranch.

   ______(4) will be solved by further study of their writings and pictures.

Length: 1350 words

Exercise VI-5

Readability Score: 65

Going, Going, Gone

By Joseph Stocker

(Reprinted by permission from *The Lion,* November, 1957.)

WAIT FOR SIGNAL TO BEGIN READING

Auctions are as ancient as the Parthenon and yet as modern as the guided missile. Since Biblical days, when fishermen auctioned off their catch on the shores of the Sea of Galilee, it has been a traditional and widely-practiced mode of commercial intercourse. And today, in the era of supermarkets, massive department stores and discount houses, auctions go on unabated.

In the small towns of the farm belt, there's the farm and cattle auction. In the South there's the tobacco auction. And in the medium-sized and larger cities, there's a Duke's mixture of auctions going on constantly.

If you live in the city, or the next time you visit one, why not take a few hours out for auction-going? You'll find it a different kind of diversion—and something more besides. The "something more" is the everpresent possibility that, if you're in a bidding mood and in the market for what's being sold, you're liable to pick up a bargain of a lifetime. Or if you're just a wayward tourist, craving some fun, you can find that at an auction, too.

Questionable Past

Time was when auctions in the U.S. had a distinctly unsavory quality about them. A familiar figure out through the grassroots was the nomadic auctioneer. He drifted from town to town, jollied the local innocents into bidding high prices for junk merchandise and then skipped out before they realized they'd been skinned.

In the big cities his counterpart was the "grind" auctioneer who usually dealt in cheap jewelry and stationed his "shill" or "caper" in the crowd to spark the bidding when it lagged. He was a pitchman, nothing less, and he wasn't averse to substituting a piece of worthless glass when a successful bidder came forth to claim the diamond he'd bid on.

Auctions still have their illicit practitioners, like any other field of endeavor. But, for the most part, it's an honest business. States and cities have seen to that by enacting laws and ordinances regulating auctions. And the auctioneers themselves have organized associations to police their ranks and elevate their standards. Many a modern-day auctioneer counts himself no less a professional man than the doctor or lawyer. His profession is auctioneering, and he takes pride in the skill with which he does it as well as the money he makes at it.

Big Business

It can be a very big business, too. Recently at Port Hueneme, California, two professional auctioneers conducted a sale of surplus Seabee equipment that brought in $3,245,000. So far as anybody knows, it was the largest auction in history.

In the bigger cities, like New York, Chicago and Los Angeles, you'll find extremely classy auction galleries, dealing in antiques, *objects d'art,* paintings and fine furnishings. Their clients are social *creme de la creme,* and so are many of their bidders.

An auction of these galleries may be the outgrowth of an estate liquidation. Or perhaps it's the case of an heiress deciding to change the decor of her Park Avenue apartment. Out goes the old, right down to and including the ash trays, and off to an auction gallery, to be sold to the highest bidders. And in comes an interior decorator to furnish the place anew from the floor up.

Souvenirs from Stars

Los Angeles contributes its own—and typically Los Angeles—fillip to the auction business. Out along Wilshire Boulevard there's a string of plush auction galleries specializing in box office names. A Hedy Lamarr couch or a Joan Crawford bed is as big a draw at the auction gallery as the Lamarr and Crawford names are at the movie houses.

These auctioneers do business both with movie stars on the way up and those on the way down. A star in ascendance may be getting rid of his belongings to move into a bigger and fancier home. A celebrity on the skids is selling out under compulsion (and can only hope the auction is held before the public realizes he's a has-been).

One of the largest and gaudiest auctions ever held in Los Angeles was that which attended Mickey

Cohen's sudden descent from grace. Mickey desperately needed money to get square with the tax collectors and put up almost all that he owned with auctioneer Marvin Newman.

Newman sold him out in one evening for $70,000 (and had to bring the cops in to hold back the crowds). There were buyers for everything including Mickey's bullet-proof door, which the Los Angeles sheriff's bid on for $65 (and for reasons unexplained).

Surprisingly enough, perhaps, the bidding at these "box office auctions" is pretty sensible and measured. It doesn't often happen, say the auctioneers, that people will bid vastly more than an item is worth just for the privilege of sitting in Clark Gable's chair or eating at Susan Hayward's dining room table.

There are exceptions, though. One such was the case of a woman who came all the way from an Eastern city to buy Alan Ladd's piano and then shipped it all the way home again. She could have bought the same piano at home, and new, for half the cost. But apparently the thrill of playing on the very keys that had been touched by the fingers of Alan Ladd was worth more than the money to her.

No Gimmicks

The modern and pridefully professional auctioneer doesn't often use gimmicks to stimulate his crowds and their bidding. He depends mainly on his warmth, sincerity, reputation—and a few well-timed jokes. He's not even particularly happy when, on occasion, the bidding soars far above the worth of some item or other. He knows that the successful bidder, carried away by the heat of competition or his own covetousness, is going to wish, on the morning after, that he'd kept his mouth shut. And he'll probably never allow himself to be lured into an auction again.

One auctioneer, for instance, recalls the time when two men fell to bidding against each other on a $300 clock. Bids went up and up until it finally sold for $1,750.

Respectable and responsible auctioneers have been known to stop the bidding, when it gets out of hand, and warn the bidders that they're trying to spend far more than they ought to. They want their future auctions to be attended.

The Cold Crowd

At the other extreme is the cold crowd. It's the auctioneer's nemesis and a challenge to his art. Not long ago one auctioneer, selling off some restaurant equipment, found himself confronting such a crowd and racked his brain for a way of warming it up. He looked over his items and saw 36 water pitchers. That gave him an idea.

"Who'll take these 36 pitchers for nothing?" he said.

There was heavy silence. Then, from the back of the room, came a lackadaisical voice: "I'll take half!"

Some Solid Sense

For the prospective auction-goer, there are some pointers to keep in mind, if you want to get what you're going for, and get it for the right price:

1. Know your merchandise. It's usually on exhibit in advance so the public can examine it. If you see an item you want, and you're not sure what it's worth, check the prices of similar items in retail stores ahead of time.

2. If you're going in for antiques, and you're not familiar with antiques, study up on them first. You can get books on the subject at public libraries, and museum curators will be glad to discuss values with you.

3. Be sure to deal only with reputable auctioneers and auction galleries. You can check with banks or with auction devotees of your acquaintance.

4. Keep your head while you're bidding. Fix a price you're willing to pay and stick to it. Don't be swept off your feet by hot competition. Unless, of course, you're a millionaire and you don't care what you buy or how much you pay for it. In that case, you don't have to pay attention to the first three pointers either.

STOP __ ASK FOR YOUR TIME

Record time immediately and answer questions on content.

Time ________ Sec. RATE (from table on page 315): R. ________

No. Correct ________ COMPREHENSION (10% for each correct answer): C. ________
(key on page 322)

VI-5 EFFICIENCY (R × C): E. ________

Record on Progress Chart on page 299

ANSWER THESE QUESTIONS IMMEDIATELY

1. (T—F) Auctions are of a very recent origin.
2. (T—F) At one time an auctioneer was considered a very unsavory character for good reason.
3. (C.) Although auctioneering still has its illicit practitioners, it is an ________________ business for the most part.
4. (T—F) Auctions never have anything of real value up for bidding.
5. (M. C.) In Hollywood auctioneers do business:
   ______(1) with movie stars on the way up and down.
   ______(2) for profits out of this world.
   ______(3) with the studios.
   ______(4) with charitable institutions.
6. (T—F) People almost always bid outrageously high prices for furniture that previously belonged to stars.
7. (M. C.) The modern auctioneer:
   ______(1) usually uses gimmicks to stimulate bidding.
   ______(2) usually depends on his own reputation and well-timed jokes to stimulate bidding.
   ______(3) is pleased when bidding soars above actual worth of an item.
   ______(4) uses reverse psychology and tries to discourage the bidders.
8. (T—F) The cold crowd is a challenge to the auctioneer's art.
9. (T—F) The prospective auction-goer is wise to check merchandise to be auctioned in advance.
10. (C.) The important thing at an auction is to keep your head while ________________.

Length: 1350 words

Exercise VI-6

Readability Score: 65

The School That Builds Guts

By Robert Bahr

(Reprinted by permission from *Fitness for Living,* May 6, 1970.)

WAIT FOR SIGNAL TO BEGIN READING

"I can't do that, I'll die."

The 17-year-old boy from Manhattan stood trembling at the edge of the pier. The air was frosty in the early morning, and he wore only a bathing suit. But it was fear, not the cold, which caused him to tremble.

Twenty-five feet below him, 11 boys 16 to 23 years old, splashed in sea water cold enough to kill a man in 45 minutes. He was the last of the team—the Watch, as it is called. So the others laughed at him, egged him on, and two boys shouted in anger, "What are you waiting for? If you don't jump, we all go without breakfast!"

100 ←

But the boy from Manhattan couldn't move. Although he knew how to swim, all his life he had been terrified of water. And the 25-foot plunge compounded his fears.

"I can't do it, I'll die," he muttered again.

"So what?" one of the boys yelled. "At least we'll get to eat breakfast." And suddenly the boy at the top of the pier took two steps forward and lunged desperately into the air. Sixty seconds later he was a hero, an honest-to-God hero. But more than that, he was on his way to becoming a different man because, call it social pressure or temporary insanity or whatever, he had tried where he knew he could not possibly succeed,—and he succeeded.

200 ←

The New York boy was one of over 8,000 who attended an Outward Bound School in the United States last year. Another 1,000,000 attended one of the 24 schools in Europe and other parts of the world. There are six schools in this country, located in the most spectacular, remote and ruggedly beautiful areas of Colorado, Oregon, Minnesota, North Carolina and Maine. At each there is boating, swimming, hiking—so it is easy to understand why once in a while a youngster makes the sad mistake of thinking that an Outward Bound School is a great place to spend a relaxing, fun-filled summer vacation.

300 ←

A Demand for Exertion

The Outward Bound program demands physical exertion on a level most men in their late teens and early 20's are unfamiliar with unless they have gone through a Marine training program. The first day's pre-breakfast morning run is a mile, but will be increased to two, then three. Sometimes there are surprise marathons in which, as one observer put it, "Boys who had rarely walked home from school learned they could run six miles and suffer nothing worse than the occasional loss of last night's supper."

400 →

At each of the six schools, the emphasis is on physical stress. Says Lee Maynard, Administrative Officer of Outward Bound, Inc., "The body is capable of quite a few things that most people think it isn't capable of. A guy who knows he can run around the block once thinks he might be able to do it three times. But he darn well is positive he can't run around the block five times. But his body is perfectly capable of doing that. It's just his mind which limits him.

500 →

"In Outward Bound we start out working on the body, and wind up working on the mind. The guy is able to determine more clearly what his physical and mental limits are through physical activities. The coupling of the two is the real secret of Outward Bound. Neither would be successful alone."

Physical activity is important because, through it, a boy gets a chance to prove something—not to others, but to himself. As Peter Willauer, an instructor at Hurricane Island, puts it, "This isn't a contest against others, or against any set standard. We are interested only in the progress each student makes relative to where he stood when he got here."

600 →

A Different Route to Fitness

Says Lee Maynard, "In our school we use calisthenics only during the first week, and I think we do it then only because it's recognizable by the students. But we get our fitness by going on expeditions and paddling canoes, sailing 30-foot open whale boats across the North Atlantic. That sort of thing. This leads to a kind of physical or fitness development that is brought about by taking part in educational, adventuresome circumstances. And it's a lot more rewarding we found than just having a guy doing push-ups all day long."

700 →

"A push-up is a very valid calisthenic," says Maynard. "But it's kind of boring, you know, to be bobbing up and down off that floor—especially when we can get the same kind of physical development by having a guy pulling an oar, helping to drive a whale boat across the bay."

Stress for All

From the moment the young men arrive at an Outward Bound School, physical activity begins. And it is the same for all, whether they come from an Ivy League college or are high school drop outs, whether they've paid the $400 tuition or have been granted one of the many scholarships. Before dinner that first night, they run breathlessly through woods, streams and swamps, stressing their bodies perhaps more than they ever have before. Every day after that the pace increases, and the guys with big mouths and bulging muscles don't always finish first.

The guys who finish do so not because of brawn but because of pure raw guts. And it is guts—or will power, courage, character if you prefer—that the Outward Bound Schools specialize in teaching. Stephen Nagie and the others in his Watch accepted the challenge to climb the 14,100-foot Capitol Peak. Every step they took brought them closer to the characteristics we call guts.

"The first night," says Nagie, "We pitched our ponchos over the few flat and partially protected places we could find.

"But the wind rose, and early in the evening a freak snow and lightning blizzard broke over us. It came from nowhere—suddenly it seemed as if the mountain were crumbling in the storm. The hiss of the lightning was indistinguishable from the boom and roar of the thunder which seemed to follow it immediately. I huddled in the dark as snow sprayed in on me, sneaking through the cracks in the boulders and under the edge of the poncho."

This was on the jagged side of a mountain 13,000 feet in the air!

The Final Project

The final project for every young man attending an Outward Bound School is a three or four day "solo" in which he stays all alone on an island in the Atlantic, a mountain top in North Carolina, Colorado, Oregon, or in the woods at the edge of a lake in Minnesota. The experience is always physically strenuous and emotionally trying. As one boy, John Huisman of Portland put it, "The hardest part for me was the solo. The most wonderful thing in the world is for someone to know what 'to suffer' means. Then he can see what the world really is when he has nothing. I spent the three days up 8,000 feet. I never got my fire going. It was windy and rainy and miserable, and all I ate was the ground cover."

Says Timothy Speyer, a student at Penn State University, "I learned what it felt like to be hungry, cold, miserable and exhausted. I found that no matter how tired I got, I was capable of pushing myself further. Outward Bound has not been all enjoyable. It has been hard for me. But I went through it, and I'm a better man because of it."

Britain's Prince Phillip, a strong supporter of Outward Bound Schools, says, "It is hard to believe that such a complete and lasting transformation can be achieved in such a short span of time. But in nearly every case the cocoon of youth drops away and the true fiber of the man emerges."

It is a matter of overcoming what appear to be enormous physical obstacles through a crash program in physical fitness—then, in the solo, applying those lessons in confidence to psychological obstacles as well. It's Outward Bound's proven method for building guts.

______ STOP__ASK FOR YOUR TIME ______

Record time immediately and answer questions on content.

Time ________ Sec.	RATE (from table on page 315):	R. ________
No. Correct ________ (key on page 330)	COMPREHENSION (10% for each correct answer):	C. ________
VI-6	EFFICIENCY (R × C):	E. ________

Record on Progress Chart on page 299

ANSWER THESE QUESTIONS IMMEDIATELY

1. (C.) A grouping of boys in an Outward Bound school is called a ________________ .

2. (T–F) In these groups if one boy does not accomplish the task, the whole group is denied some benefit.

3. (M. C.) The original primary focus of the Outward Bound school is:

   ______(1) physical development.

   ______(2) intellectual development.

   ______(3) spiritual development.

   ______(4) learning cooperation and interdependence.

4. (T–F) In the Outward Bound schools there is a great emphasis on interpersonal competition.

5. (T–F) Calisthenics are emphasized each morning during the entire course.

6. (T–F) Students who finish the long runs usually do so because of their raw guts.

7. (M. C.) The "final project" is done:

   ______(1) alone.

   ______(2) with one other person.

   ______(3) with three other persons.

   ______(4) by the whole group together.

8. (T–F) The "final project" is usually not too difficult.

9. (C.) Britain's Prince Phillip says in Outward Bound schools the cocoon of ________________ drops away and the true man emerges.

10. (T–F) According to Timothy Speyer the Outward Bound school was not particularly enjoyable.

Length: 1350 words

Exercise VI-7

Readability Score: 64

Remarkable Lady Moon

By Olga Curtis

(Reprinted by permission from *The Denver Post,* March 20, 1977.)

WAIT FOR SIGNAL TO BEGIN READING

Our Gal Sunday

Catherine Grattan Lawder Gartman Moon insisted on being called a Lady. She was a real one, although circumstances soured her title. It was as Lady Moon, the Colorado washerwoman who married an English peer, that she became famous—or maybe notorious—at the turn of the century.

In one sense, Lady Moon died before she could enjoy real fame. She was the inspiration for one of the longest-running radio soap operas in history, *Our Gal Sunday*.

From 1937 until 1959, when CBS finally ended the saga, thousands of people listened to the show every weekday. The mournful strains of *Red River Valley* would introduce each installment in the "thrilling adventures of Sunday, the orphan girl from Silver Creek, Colo., who married England's richest, most handsome lord."

In his book about early radio, *Tune in Yesterday,* John Dunning of Denver says *Our Gal Sunday* was based on a 1904 melodrama called *Sunday,* which starred Ethel and John Barrymore. (The play is best-remembered for its curtain line, "That's all there is, there isn't any more.")

But Dunning and other historians note that playwright Thomas Racemond probably got the idea for his plot from the real-life adventures of Katie Lawder Moon, which were reported in detail by the newspapers from 1900 on.

Certainly Sunday's marriage to Lord Henry Brinthorpe was just as rocky as Katie's marriage to Lord Cecil Ernest Moon.

The only major difference is that when the soap opera ended, Sunday apparently lived happily ever after. Katie Moon did not.

Fact and fancy have become tangled over the years in the story of Lady Moon, who was the subject of a novel and an opera as well as a radio show. But most accounts agree she was born May 17, 1865, on a ship off the coast of France, to parents from County Wicklow, Ireland.

Two Marriages

She came to the United States as a teenager, and worked as a maid. In 1883, at the age of 18, she turned up in Larimer County, Colo. One account says she stepped off the stage at Livermore and was immediately hired as a maid by the local hotel and health resort.

Sometime in the next few years, she married Frank Gartman, a miner. Gartman earned about $1 a day in the mines at Manhattan, a short-lived mining camp above the Cache La Poudre River south of Red Feather Lakes. His bride took in washing to earn extra money.

She also occasionally worked as a practical nurse, which is how she met Moon. He was a "remittance man"—a younger son sent abroad because of lack of prospects or indiscretions, but his family was famous. The Moons were reputed to be the owners of the Ceylon mines which first produced a gem that still carries their name, the moonstone.

At the time Cecil Moon was working in Colorado as a laborer, his grandfather, Sir Richard Moon, was chairman of a railway company in London. But several heirs stood between Cecil and the title.

Katie successfully nursed Moon over an attack of "mountain fever."

It is anyone's guess what attraction an Irish immigrant known to the miners as "Cussing Kate" and "Hotheaded Kate" had for an English aristocrat, but she was "a pretty woman with large blue eyes."

Some say Moon paid Gartman to get a divorce; others say Gartman took off in disgust.

But it is a matter of record that Katie and Cecil were married in Denver, July 19, 1888. Apparently, Moon was still getting his "remittance," because the newlyweds bought a ranch on Elkhorn Creek, near Manhattan.

Either in 1889 or in 1899, Moon inherited the family title. (Most accounts speak of the new Lady Moon as "a bride of less than a year"; others give the date as 1899.) His grandfather and father died. Two older brothers were killed serving in the army; a third succumbed to illness.

A fortune came with the title. When the Moons went to England to claim the inheritance, Lady Moon took along trunks full of velvet gowns, plumed hats and jewels; she also took along her favorite horse.

But Lady moon never achieved the social position she sought. An article in the *Denver Times,* Sept. 20, 1901 explains why:

"Lady Moon was not accustomed to distinction of any kind . . . she had not the proper estimation of what it means to be a 'lady.'

"So the ancestral halls were decked in festal splendor and a brilliant assembly of rank and fortune were invited to welcome Lord Cecil and his American bride.

"Into all this splendor burst poor little Lady Moon, quite as unexpectedly as she had found herself a lady.

"Ain't it grand?" was all she could say.

"The distinguished family only raised its distinguished eyebrows. Clearly, Lady Moon would never do. She was quite impossible."

Gabbling Kitty

Lady Moon told friends, who repeated the story with relish, that the Moons often tried to keep her from accompanying Lord Cecil, and that they blamed her for "his excesses, as they called his drinking and gambling."

One night, she said, the Moons gave a ball without telling her. She saw the carriages arriving, put on her best Paris gown and most glittering tiara, and joined the party.

"Dearie, I did look lovely," she was quoted.

"When the crowd saw me they stopped their dancing to stare at me. Lord Moon gave a start and then smiled. I went and laid my gloved hand on his arm, and we started to dance. That night I kept my damn mouth shut, and Dearie, he was proud of me!"

But Lady Moon, who was nicknamed "Gabbling Kitty" in her youth, had trouble remaining silent. People who knew her described her as kind, gentle and generous—and also as horse-loving, hearty and rough-spoken. Wesley Swan of Livermore, in his *Memoirs of an Old Timer,* says Lady Moon used "language colorful enough to cause even the most hardboiled pioneer to wince and envy her facility of expression."

Lord Cecil, however, was no angel either. He not only drank and gambled (he kept a losing $10,000 card hand framed in his ranch house) but as Lady Moon once complained to a reporter, he also had "lady friends."

Divorce

The marriage held long enough for the Moons to make their home on Elkhorn Creek a showplace, with fancy furniture, carpets, even a billiard table. They also brought back from England an English carriage, plus a genuine English butler.

Lady Moon ran the ranch; by her account, Lord Cecil "sat in the library all day and read and amused himself."

The marriage began to deteriorate. It came apart for good on Oct. 19, 1909, when Lord Moon filed suit in Denver District Court against Lady Moon to recover $61,000 in securities.

He admitted he had entrusted the money to her while they were in England because he was spending too much. But he claimed that his wife had taken possession of his entire estate, leaving him penniless.

Lady Moon countersued for divorce in Larimer County Court. There were dramatic stories of how Lord Moon took the witness stand, held up a dime, and exclaimed, "This is my entire fortune!" There were also dramatic stories about Lady Moon being forced to pay alimony.

Unfortunately, there is no record of either the testimony or the alimony. The whole affair was over in five minutes, with Lady Moon winning her divorce on grounds of desertion and nonsupport.

Soon afterward, Lord Moon went to New Zealand. He never returned to Colorado.

But Lady Moon, still insisting on the title she no longer had legally, remained a well-known character in the Fort Collins area until her death in 1926.

She is buried in Mt. Olivet Cemetery in Denver. A seven-foot-tall pyramid-shaped granite stone marks her grave. On the top it says "Catherine" in small letters, then "May 17, 1865" and Sept. 4, 1926." On the base, in big capital letters is carved "MOON."

The friends who put up the stone could at least have given the remarkable Katie the title she loved so well—Lady Moon.

______ STOP __ ASK FOR YOUR TIME ______

Record time immediately and answer questions on content.

Time ________ Sec.	RATE (from table on page 315):		R. ________
No. Correct ________ (key on page 322)	COMPREHENSION (10% for each correct answer):		C. ________
VI-7	EFFICIENCY (R × C):		E. ________

Record on Progress Chart on page 299

ANSWER THESE QUESTIONS IMMEDIATELY

1. (C.) Catherine Grattan Lawder Gartman Moon was an immigrant from ________________ .
2. (M.C.) Catherine was the inspiration for one of the longest-running radio shows in history:
   _____(1) "Little Orphan Katie".
   _____(2) "Moon Mullens".
   _____(3) "Our Gal Sunday".
   _____(4) "The Moonstones".
3. (T—F) When Katie married Frank Gartman, he was a newspaper reporter.
4. (C.) Katie met Cecil Moon when he was ill with mountain fever and she was a ________________ .
5. (T—F) Katie was often rough-spoken and used very colorful language.
6. (M.C.) When Katie Moon first met the elegantly dressed English friends and relatives of Cecil Moon, she was reported to say, "________________ ."
   _____(1) "Look at all them foreigners."
   _____(2) "Ain't it grand."
   _____(3) "That's all there is; there isn't any more."
   _____(4) "Dearie, I did look lovely."
7. (T—F) Katie Moon was nicknamed "Galloping Kitty" because of her love for horses.
8. (T—F) Lady Moon won her second divorce on grounds of desertion and nonsupport.
9. (T—F) After the divorce, Lord Moon left Colorado and never returned.
10. (T—F) Her massive granite tombstone carries the title she loved so well "LADY MOON."

Length: 1350 words

Exercise VI-8

Readability Score: 63

Grown-Ups Can't Cry

By Diane Mizialko

(Reprinted by permission from *Health*, September-October, 1976.)

WAIT FOR SIGNAL TO BEGIN READING

Scared Enough to Cry

Becoming a hospital patient may be a frightening and threatening experience whenever you have no adequate preparation for the actual registration and admission procedure.

The little girl waited quietly while her mother talked to the lady behind the desk. There were lots of papers to fill out. It seemed to take so long.

Nobody talked to her. Mother was busy with the papers. The lady behind the desk was busy typing something. The hospital looked very big. And scary.

Then a tall lady with big dark eyes came. She said "hello" in a soft friendly voice and called the little girl by name. The lady said she was going to take the little girl up to her hospital room.

100 ←

When she heard her own name spoken in such a nice voice, the little girl couldn't hold back any longer. She began to weep.

Starting to Feel Better

So the lady with the friendly voice took the little girl to the cafeteria and bought her some cold juice. Then the lady and the little girl—who was still scared but no longer crying—rode up on the elevator together. The lady put her arm around the little girl's shoulder. She was starting to feel better.

200 ←

Grown-Up Patients May Withdraw

"Many of our adults are like that." Erastine Davis smiled, after telling the story of that little girl's first hour in Chicago Osteopathic Hospital.

"But they can't cry." Instead, grown-up patients may withdraw, or complain about the food, or refuse medication, or act out their distress in any number of ways. These patient difficulties can and do collide with hospital staff or service problems, resulting in situations which everyone would prefer to avoid.

That's what Erastine Davis's job is all about.

She is Chicago Osteopathic Hospital's first patient representative. With the help of two assistants, Mrs. Davis runs the new patient services program.

300 ←

Minor Patient Care Problems

Instituted in May 1976, the program is designed to prevent minor patient care problems from escalating to a more drastic stage.

Thus, Mrs. Davis steps in right at the beginning of a patient's stay. After a nonacute patient has been admitted and is settled in his or her room, Mrs. Davis drops in for an introductory visit.

After the Get-Acquainted Visit

Usually any initial complaints revolve around the patient's own medical problems. Still, Mrs. Davis asks him specific questions: whether he has read the patient handbook, whether his valuables have been stored properly for safekeeping, whether his food trays are satisfactory. After this get-acquainted visit, the patient knows whom to call for a quick response to any question or complaint.

400 →

Don't Want Any Enemies

The staff knows it too, and after a month on the job, Mrs. Davis felt—much to her relief—that the hospital's professional staff had been more than cooperative. "No one has considered us as interfering, and so far no one has attempted to restrain us. We've taken steps to show the staff we're part of the team effort to deliver health care. We certainly don't want any enemies," she smiled.

500 →

Staff members have begun to turn to Mrs. Davis for help and information. "Many nurses ask me, 'Are my patients complaining about anything?'" she reported. Recently, an intern called Mrs. Davis when a patient needed a better mattress. In turn, Mrs. Davis made her own calls and produced the needed item.

The Eve of Surgery

Each day the patient representative sees some 30 newly admitted patients. That's a lot of walking and talking. She also makes it a point to see patients on the eve of surgery and to visit again after surgery. Besides that, she has a list of "special" patients whom she tries to see at least once a day.

600 →

A Way to Get Home

Moira Fay, the assistant patient representative, guides patients through discharge, often helping them untangle their dealings with the business office and making sure they have a way to get home.

With this wide range of duties to supervise or perform, unless a problem is very involved, Mrs. Davis must limit the amount of time she can spend with each patient. But, she said, she has found the quality of her time makes up for any lack of quantity.

Directly Into the Eyes

Part of Mrs. Davis's unique style stems from her habit of looking directly into the eyes of anyone she encounters. She does this consciously with patients. "You know, just those few minutes of coming up close to them and asking 'How are you doing?' is just what it takes," she explained. Mrs. Davis is not of the poke-your-head-through-the-doorway-and-wave school.

A Little More Time

Of course, there are patients who must have a little more time. Mrs. Davis recalled a man with terminal cancer who knew he was dying but still was engaged in searching for the elusive "cure."

He called for the patient representative to discuss a relatively minor matter. "But then I realized he really wanted someone he could talk to. So I sat down with him for about an hour, and we got to know each other. I went back each day, morning and evening. And that's what we did every day—just talked."

A Tear or Two

On the day that he was discharged, Mrs. Davis admitted, she wiped away a tear or two. "I like him," she said simply. "I was even a little surprised with myself, that I didn't go under when he left."

Emotional Demands of Work

Mrs. Davis knows that the strong empathy which makes her an effective patient representative also could burn her out. She seems to struggle to create a synthesis between "professional" objectivity and ordinary human response. Still, she recalls a recent evening when, after dealing with two severe human crises almost simultaneously, she went home feeling "just drained." Because of the emotional demands of her work, Mrs. Davis is not sure how long a good patient representative can last. However, she feels sure she won't ever leave her job because of boredom.

The Tender Years

Mrs. Davis's insights into the needs of people in difficulty weren't learned in any school of social work. Her preparation goes back farther than that.

"The only training I've had that remotely relates to this probably started when I was a child. I wanted to be a foreign missionary. I went to a neighborhood Bible class and learned all about the hard times people in other places can have. Because of my tender years, I was susceptible to all those difficulties."

But instead of becoming a foreign missionary, she married a minister, "and that's just people-oriented-period. I was constantly called upon to function wherever a minister's wife should fit," she recalled.

Another part of her "training" occurred after her marriage. For a long time, Mrs. Davis suffered a very painful, undiagnosed illness which, she said, drove her nearly to the point of complete apathy toward her own survival. Finally, her diseased gallbladder was diagnosed and removed, but the length of her illness and the experience of surgery and recuperation taught her how it feels to be on the receiving end of health care.

About two years ago, Mrs. Davis came to the Chicago College of Osteopathic Medicine as secretary to the hospital administrator. To ease the load for her busy boss, she began dealing with patient-care problems. "I learned the institution, the personnel, and how to work through the system," she said. When it came time to appoint a patient representative, Mrs. Davis was the logical choice.

Prime Goal

As the patient representative, Mrs. Davis obviously strives to provide solutions to problems. But her prime goal, it seems, is to supply large doses of understanding. Even the wrath of a "difficult" patient, she says, is understandable:

"When they get to the point where they're irate, it's usually because they don't understand something that's been done to them. We try to explain the specific circumstance, and ask the nurse to help explain it too.

"They don't calm down right away, but by the next day when I go back, they're usually calm."

______ STOP __ ASK FOR YOUR TIME ______

Record time immediately and answer questions on content.

Time __________ Sec. | RATE (from table on page 315): | R. __________

No. Correct __________ (key on page 330) | COMPREHENSION (10% for each correct answer): | C. __________

VI-8 | EFFICIENCY (R × C): | E. __________

Record on Progress Chart on page 299

ANSWER THESE QUESTIONS IMMEDIATELY

1. (T—F) Adults and children usually react to their fears in the same way.
2. (T—F) Mrs. Davis is employed as the first patient representative on the staff of the Chicago Orthopedic Hospital.
3. (T—F) The program is designed to prevent minor patient care problems from escalating to a more drastic stage.
4. (T—F) Mrs. Davis had met with a considerable amount of resistance from the hospital staff, but has continued her service anyway.
5. (C.) Aside from welcoming new patients, Mrs. Davis makes a point of seeing patients on the eve of __________ .
6. (T—F) With the number of patients and the duties involved, Mrs. Davis must limit the amount of time she spends with each patient.
7. (M.C.) Mrs. Davis has a unique style of:

   ______(1) sensing the patient's thoughts and expressing them.

   ______(2) looking directly into the eyes of the patient.

   ______(3) accompanying the patient to surgery.

   ______(4) loving the patients for their weaknesses.
8. (C.) Mrs. Davis knows that the strong __________ which makes her an effective patient representative also could burn her out.
9. (T—F) Before assuming her present job, Mrs. Davis was a nurse.
10. (M.C.) Mrs. Davis believes that the primary goal of her job is to supply large doses of:

    ______(1) advice.

    ______(2) personal service.

    ______(3) medicine.

    ______(4) understanding.

Length: 1350 words

Exercise VI-9

Readability Score: 60

Mardi Gras

By Tom Cavanaugh

(Reprinted by permission from *United Mainliner,* February, 1970.)

WAIT FOR SIGNAL TO BEGIN READING

On Fat Tuesday in New Orleans, the narrow streets of the French Quarter are jammed with revelers peculiarly incognito: a tall man with green hair in a lamé gown, a lady Christmas tree in complete ornamentation, two tiny boxcars coupled between a father engine and a mother caboose, several six-foot liquor bottles with legs, three Negro lads in burnt-cork blackface. And they are only some of the spectators. The raiment of those in the parades is *really* outlandish.

By day, the parades push their way through seas of people who are sure there is no tomorrow. By night, the bands strut to a swinging New Orleans cadence. The papier-maché floats with their gaudy colors glow eerily under street lanterns and smoking flambeaux carried by white-robed youngsters. The lacy grillworks of French Quarter balconies strain to hold their cheering merry-makers, even with special supports erected for the occasion.

In Rio, or possibly Trinidad, there might be something roughly comparable, but nothing in the U.S. approaches New Orleans' Mardi Gras for sheer *bizarrerie.* This once-a-year madness begins to gather steam just prior to the Sugar Bowl game on New Year's Day, takes on the characteristics of a hell-bender sometime after Twelfth Night, and roars on to epic proportions by Shrove Tuesday.

Religious Holiday

While Mardi Gras is technically a religious holiday, it is somewhat difficult to discern that fact. To a good many, the Carnival is a great excuse for a bash, and the solemn aspects are only incidental. Along with the general wassailing in the streets, it is days and nights of wonderfully colorful parades, lavish formal balls and fanciful tableaux and masquerades. It isn't essential for the meek to become carried away in the spirit of the thing. Simple people watching is usually excitement enough.

Literally translated, Mardi Gras comes out as Fat Tuesday. That's the day they killed the fatted calf in France for one last bacchanal before the penitential days of Lent. And thus the name Carnival, which comes from the two words *carné,* meaning meat, and *vale,* which means farewell—or "farewell to flesh" during the 40 days of fasting. The Carnival started out as a one-day holiday on Shrove Tuesday, but it was so much fun that it became a whole season in New Orleans, running roughly from Christmas to the beginning of Lent on Ash Wednesday.

More Than 250 Years Old

Louisianians have been celebrating Mardi Gras more or less constantly ever since Iberville and his band of French colonizers sailed 30 miles up the Mississippi on Shrove Tuesday in 1699. Near present-day New Orleans, they camped at a spot they designated "Pointe du Mardi Gras." Presumably, after many days at sea, they were in a mood to live it up a bit—and did.

If so, they started something that has been gaining momentum for more than 250 years. There have been some gaps, such as the time the Spaniards tried to ban Mardi Gras because a few light-fingered footpads took advantage of the anonymity of their masks to relieve merrymakers of their valuables. And again when some mid-1800 spoilsports thought the general gaiety and individual excesses were a bit much. In 1837, the *Picayune* (living up to its name) observed rather sourly on its editorial pages: "A lot of masqueraders were parading through our streets yesterday, and excited considerable speculation as to who they were, what were their motives, and what on earth could induce them to turn out in such grotesque and outlandish habilments." Such priggery has regularly been met with loud jeers and catcalls, serving only to launch the celebrants to new heights of fervor.

Today's festivities bear little resemblance to those of early times. New Orleans is one of the more devout of our cities, and religious rites are still observed with dignity and solemnity. And certainly there are some sumptuous feasts in a city noted for its cuisine. But the 60-odd annual balls costing up to $25,000 each, and the 30 or more parades that go on night and day for two weeks, are the activities for which Mardi Gras is best known.

But this is not a gigantic civic show started for the purpose of luring the tourist dollar. Last year, the *Vieux Carré Courier* carried the far-from-encouraging headline, "Be brave—stay in town for Mardi Gras." If New Orleanians threw their party and nobody else came, they couldn't care less. Sure, room rates at hotels go up noticeably at Mardi Gras time (reservations are usually for a minimum of three days and must be made months in advance). There are souvenir stands and hawkers selling beer, drinks in hurricane glasses, hot dogs and corn on the cob. But New Orleans had its Mardi Gras long before it became a tourist attraction, and they're not going to stop now. If anyone else wants to join in, fine. The more the merrier!

Many Private Functions

But it isn't easy for an outsider to gain an invitation to any of the gala balls. These are strictly private social functions, and admission requires a formal invitation and usually a bit of blue blood. The balls are staged by Krewes—secret-membership organizations with mystic names which have no other function than to hold an annual dance and maybe a parade.

Nor is the *bal masque* essentially for dancing. While an orchestra of from 15 to 40 musicians is engaged, it plays for dancing only after much formality in ushering in the king and his court, presentation of debutantes and important guests, tableaux and divertissements. But the dress balls are a great place for showing off finery—both elaborate costumes and lavish formal wear.

Rex, who is considered the King of Mardi Gras and reigns over a ball and parade on Shrove Tuesday, is always an outstanding civic leader—and may be out of pocket $1,000 or more for the honor.

Other Krewes of long standing, with their own royalty and celebrations, include Oberon, Twelfth Night, Nereus, Mystery, Osiris, Athenians, Atlanteans, Comus, Momus, Proteus and many others.

Parades for Everyone

But if the Krewes reserve their balls for members and guests, they stage their parades for all the people. The parades are not just for watching. The spectators can and do participate—either on an impromptu urge to join the marchers, or by begging the masked Krewe members on the floats for a souvenir doubloon or a string of beads ("Throw me something, Mister!"). Gentlemen hoist their lady friends onto their shoulders, the better to catch a prize. Young New Orleans entrepreneurs, who make a business of peddling souvenirs to tourists, shinny up light posts and employ butterfly nets to catch their stock in trade. The trinkets tossed from the floats are considered an improvement by old-time aficionados. The Krewe men used to throw flour on the spectators, who returned the favor in kind.

At times, while mounted policemen choose to look the other way, the spectators and the paraders become co-mingled. The casual observer may have difficulty deciding which is which, or he may decide that the parade is over. Usually it isn't, and if he stands his ground long enough, another float or band will come along. Then again he may have difficulty keeping his cool and, swept along in a wave of humanity, perhaps will find he has become part of the parade.

Between the scheduled activities and the occasional happenings, there is time for sight-seeing, antique shopping and exquisite dining. At night, the insomniac can pub-crawl in such French Quarter bistros and jazz spots as Al Hirt's, Pat O'Brien's, Pete Fountain's, Playboy, Red Garter and Preservation Hall.

But eventually, and regrettably, the morning of Ash Wednesday arrives. A gentle waft of *eau de beer* pervades the crisp air. The wonderful days of ecstasy, make-believe and earthly pleasures are over. The gay bong of cathedral bells reverberates through beclouded heads. Street crews with scoop loaders and dump trucks begin to shovel out the debris and miscellaneous leftover frolickers. Last night's sport opens one reddened eye, cautiously, and ponders the sobering prospect of 40 days of meditation and quietude.

STOP—ASK FOR YOUR TIME

Record time immediately and answer the questions on content.

Time ________ Sec. RATE (from table on page 315): R. ________

No. Correct ________ COMPREHENSION (10% for each correct answer): C. ________
(key on page 322)

VI-9 EFFICIENCY (R × C): E. ________

Record on Progress Chart on page 299

ANSWER THESE QUESTIONS IMMEDIATELY

1. (C.) Mardi Gras is really a ________________ holiday.
2. (T—F) The Mardi Gras celebration begins gathering steam just prior to the Sugar Bowl Game on New Year's Day.
3. (M.C.) The Mardi Gras celebration began with:
   _____(1) French colonizers sailing up the Mississippi.
   _____(2) a religious colony located in New Orleans.
   _____(3) French citizens who celebrated their separation from the King of France annually.
   _____(4) Spanish explorers.
4. (C.) The celebration represents the last festival before ________________ .
5. (T—F) The celebation is more than 250 years old.
6. (T—F) The Mardi Gras has received great support from local businessmen who saw an opportunity for greatly expanded tourist trade.
7. (T—F) The Krewes are philanthropic organizations which donate the proceeds of the lavish balls for charitable purposes.
8. (T—F) The *bals masques* are strictly private affairs.
9. (M.C.) Rex, the King of the Mardi Gras, is always:
   _____(1) a member of the oldest family in new Orleans.
   _____(2) an outstanding civic leader.
   _____(3) the Mayor of New Orleans.
   _____(4) the governor of the state.
10. (T—F) The police of New Orleans work double shifts in an effort to keep spectators out of the way of the parades.

Length: 1350 words

Exercise VI-10

Readability Score: 59

You Can Control Pain

By Jane Wilkie

WAIT FOR SIGNAL TO BEGIN READING

A Miracle

Ed Stokes will tell anyone who'll listen that his back is better.

After suffering a crushed spinal disk in 1974, Stokes was in pain even after corrective surgery. For two years, the pain was merciless and unrelenting. Then a physician referred him for admission to the Pain Center at the City of Hope, a hospital in Duarte, Calif.

"I'm telling you, it's a miracle," he says. "They put me through a schedule you wouldn't believe, but it did the trick. Oh, the pain comes once in a while, but I can handle it now."

Until recently, pain has been accepted as inevitable for many, especially in their later years. Now it is being studied, earnestly and thoroughly, by medical scientists dedicated to the idea that pain can be controlled, possibly even eliminated.

Acute pain, often a blessing, serves as a warning that something is wrong and needs to be fixed. An appendix is diseased, a hand is cut. So the appendix is removed, the hand wound is sewn up, and pain ceases.

But there is also chronic pain, which lingers after a cause is removed, and which sometimes comes even without apparent cause.

In personal terms, chronic pain does a great deal more than simply hurt its victim. It affects his work, his family and friends, his daily functioning. He worries that it will continue for the rest of his life, wonders if he'll ever again be a useful member of society.

Pain is an elusive subject; it cannot be described nor measured. And so the questions:

What is it? Where and why does it start? Why doesn't it stop?

Answers?

In the search for answers pain clinics have sprung up throughout the world. Some focus their attention on special types of pain—back, headache, etc. Others specialize in type of treatment, working only with anesthetics, hypnosis, or acupuncture. From the clinics have grown the real giants of the research, the pain *centers.*

At the centers all types of pain are attacked with all types of treatment, but the hub is the unit where inpatients are taught multidisciplinary methods of controlling their pain.

The City of Hope hospital operates an eight-bed unit where patients suffering benign pain spend 6 to 10 weeks. They are diagnosed, tended and taught by a team of 16; every department of the hospital is involved—physicians, pharmacists, psychologists, nurses, lab personnel, surgeons, clinical researchers, psychiatrists, paramedics, social workers.

Complex? Yes, but so is the subject. Pain is not a substance, not a sensation, not a perception. Says Dr. Benjamin L. Crue, who heads the City of Hope Pain Center, "We feel pain in our brain. Chronic pain is a phenomenon of the central nervous system, when it fails to turn off the pain after the initial cause is corrected."

Medicine's adage, *it is more important to learn what kind of patient has the disease than what kind of disease the patient has,* is well heeded during diagnosis. Is the patient defensive? Is he under stress? Does he *want* his pain?

Some people actually do—as punishment for guilt, as a means of getting the drugs to which they've become addicted, as an excuse not to perform, in areas ranging from sexual functioning to financial responsibility. Victims don't know these things, of course.

Doctors have dropped the past attitude of looking the other way when a patient continued to suffer without apparent reason. Now they are beginning to face the fact that pain is an entity to be challenged.

Treatment

At the City of Hope's inpatient unit, the days are filled with individual psychotherapy as well as group psychotherapy, necessary not only for diagnosis but for resulting self-awareness. There is training in muscle relaxation, even instruction regarding diet, which is sometimes part of a cause.

There is group marital therapy; it has been found that the great majority of patients with intractable chronic pain have unsatisfactory marriages.

Biofeedback training provides instruction in regulating bodily functions. The control of blood flow, even of the brain's electrical activity, are possible through biofeedback, and can reduce pain.

A future with less pain is anticipated by occupational therapy that helps develop skills allowing for rehabilitation.

No possible aid is omitted. The reassurance of a human voice, the mere laying on of hands are wondrously effective. The underlying principle is the relief experienced by a child when a mother might say, "Tell me where it hurts" and then touches the spot with her lips.

Harder to comprehend but often dynamically productive is the use of imagery. Bordering on the mystic is the experience of deep breathing and concentration on "white light" that comes with inhaling and leaves with exhalation, taking the pain with it.

An even more abstruse approach is the mental search for an "adviser." UCLA's David Bresler, Ph.D., has found this method successful with those mentally able to generate a trance wherein they meet an imagined friend and the patient then entreats this imaginary friend to be his adviser, to give him counsel.

Teaching

At City of Hope's intractable pain unit, patients have pain that is benign, yet even this is sometimes untouched by the work of the hospital's pain team. After all, it is not a treatment per se; it is teaching a sufferer to help himself.

"It's often hard for us to convince the patient we can't fix his pain," says Dr. Crue. "We can only educate him that his pain is a symptom of something within his psyche, and then teach him to control it himself."

Patients ask doctors, "Why me?" and the doctors can only answer, "Some part of you has begun this, and if that's true, then some part of you can overcome it."

How?

The doctors ask themselves endless questions:

Why can one patient "transfer" back pain to his feet and then "walk the pain away" while another cannot?

Which treatment for which patient? Will implosion work for this woman? That's a process wherein she concentrates on her pain to a point where it disappears. If not, don't try it; implosion can backfire.

Should I worry about theory or just use the techniques and trust that theory will come later?

How can we measure pain?

The latter is the question most frequently asked, and so far the answer can come only from the patient—"I feel worse," or "I think I feel better." Says Dr. John Bonica, who directs the pain center at Seattle's University hospital, "We need a definition of pain, need a way to record it, to determine its magnitude."

The answers are slow in coming, but there is considerable, although cautious, optimism. Says Dr. Bernard Millman, "Maybe we're deceiving ourselves, but so far we think it's working." Says Dr. Crue, "At least our patients are no longer dependent on drugs, no longer seeking relief by running frantically from one doctor to another."

Patients are required to report for follow-up care and reassessment over a period of three to five years after discharge. So far, records of pain centers at the University of Washington, City of Hope, Scripps in La Jolla, Calif., Emmanuel Hospital in Portland, Ore., and Duke University prove the centers are still few in number and each is booked heavily for the future—a backlog of 14 months at the City of Hope alone.

Warnings

For those who think themselves potential patients in such centers, the advice from physicians is to first consult the family doctor and make certain the pain is not acute, a warning symptom of something wrong. When aspirin and the family doctor aren't enough, consult him about where to go for a second opinion. If pain is benign and unremitting for six months or more, a referral to a pain center is possible.

In the interim, find comfort in the assurance that more and more doctors are studying pain, and that more clinics and centers will be created. Recognize that those already involved are dedicated; they feel deeply sympathetic toward your problem. They are concerned about what your pain has done to your life.

STOP — ASK FOR YOUR TIME

Record time immediately and answer questions on content.

Time ________ Sec.	RATE (from table on page 315):	R. ________
No. Correct ________ (key on page 330)	COMPREHENSION (10% for each correct answer):	C. ________
VI-10	EFFICIENCY (R × C):	E. ________

Record on Progress Chart on page 299

ANSWER THESE QUESTIONS IMMEDIATELY

1. (T—F) Acute pain serves as a warning that something is wrong and needs to be fixed.
2. (C.) ________________ pain lingers on after a cause is removed.
3. (M.C.) Pain is best defined as a:
   ____(1) perception.
   ____(2) phenomenon.
   ____(3) sensation.
   ____(4) substance.
4. (T—F) All pain clinics specialize in the classification and measurement of pain.
5. (T—F) One of the major purposes of pain centers is teaching people to control their pain.
6. (M.C.) The therapist asks several questions in diagnosing a patient's chronic pain. Which one of these questions was not asked?
   ____(1) Is the pain psychosomatic?
   ____(2) Is the patient defensive?
   ____(3) Is he under stress?
   ____(4) Does he want his pain?
7. (T—F) It is more important to learn what kind of pain the patient has than what kind of patient has the pain.
8. (T—F) At the City of Hope hospital treatments are limited to group therapy and biofeedback.
9. (C.) Dr. Crue is pleased that patients in the centers are no longer dependent on ________________ .
10. (T—F) Patients in the pain clinic are required to report for follow-up care over a period of three to five years.

Length: 1350 words

Exercise VI-11

Readability Score: 58

Beware the Flimflam Man

By Donna St. John

(Reprinted by permission from *Dynamic Maturity,* May, 1977.)

WAIT FOR SIGNAL TO BEGIN READING

The Oldest Con

When P.T. Barnum—one of America's shrewdest entrepreneurs—said, "There's a sucker born every minute," he probably didn't realize it at the time but he was including himself. Three times, Barnum was hornswoggled out of several fortunes. (One scheme involved a machine said to make artificial snow.)

Most people think you have to be naive or stupid to be taken in by a con artist, and that "it can't happen to me." But it can and it does—to the tune of billions of dollars a year.

Why?

Because—as con artists themselves say—"There's a little bit of larceny in all of us," as well as that eternal hope of getting something for nothing.

The oldest con, in fact, originated in China 1,000 years ago. This scheme—called the "pigeon drop"—is so outlandish that it's hard to believe anyone could fall for it. But in California alone, half a million dollars was "dropped" in just one year. There are several variations of this "all-time favorite" con, but basically here's how it works.

A young woman approaches an elderly person—usually a woman. The younger woman will engage her in conversation, in an attempt to win her confidence. A third party, usually another woman, will interrupt, holding an envelope or brown bag, and ask if it belongs to anyone. The three of them will open the envelope. Inside will be a wad of money and some kind of evidence indicating the money was gained through illicit means (a gambling note, for example).

One of the swindlers will say that, since she works nearby, she'll check with her employer about what they should do with the money. When she returns, she tells them her "employer" said that since they all "found" the money together, they can divide it three ways. But—now here comes the clincher—each must show financial responsibility and "good faith" by matching her share of the "find" with her own money. The befuddled victim will withdraw money from her savings account and hand it over to one of the young women to take to the employer for safekeeping. Of course, she'll never see her savings, or the swindlers, again.

Trap-A-Teller

Another old trick is the bank-examiner scheme. Names of women, usually, elderly and living alone, are taken from the phone book. A con artist telephones a selected victim, posing as an officer of her bank. He asks her to help him trap a teller who is suspected of embezzling funds.

The "Bank officer" will give directions that the victim is to withdraw a sum from her savings account and hand the money over to an FBI agent—or other official—who will go to her house to pick it up. When the "agent" arrives, he'll say that he will list the serial numbers and then return the money so she can redeposit it. Only the money and the agent vanish into thin air.

This con plays on the "being a good citizen" angle. The victim actually thinks she is assisting in the apprehension of a criminal, which helps to make the bank-examiner scheme a very easy game.

Mail Orders

Of all types of fraud, the mail-order variety is the most pervasive and the most lucrative. You've no doubt seen those beguiling magazine ads that invite the reader to enter a simple "identify the movie actor in this picture" contest and "win enough money to last you the rest of your life." The unsuspecting contestant, who would like to believe he or she can get something for nothing, replies and soon receives a letter that goes something like this: "You are a winner! Please send us $5 as an entry fee so you will be eligible to win our top prize of $5,000." Little does the recipient know that the same letter has been sent to thousands of "winners." But in this case, the only *real* winners are the promoters of the contest, who will skip town after collecting the entry fees.

Within the past ten years, several developers, particularly in the Southwest and Florida, bilked 30,000 people—mostly residents of cold, Northeastern states—out of $350 million. Some buyers never even saw the land they were buying. When retirement day finally rolled around, many purchasers found that "the land of their deams" was, in reality, a swamp in Florida or a Southwestern desert.

One New Jersey man fell for an ad that urged him to "buy now—before it's too late," a tract of land "near Las Vegas, where the movie stars live!" When he eventually saw the site, his plot of arid ground turned out to be 400 miles "near" Las Vegas, and his only neighbors were rattlesnakes.

Developers may offer a free vacation to the development site, where a prospective purchaser is wined and dined and pressured by a smooth-talking salesman.

One such prospective buyer, not about to be pressured into signing up for what seemed to be worthless property in a New Mexican desert, was stranded by an angry salesman who jumped into his car and drove off. As soon as the customer managed to get back to town, he reported the incident to the authorities.

Some advertising just borders on the illegal, making criminal prosecution difficult, if not impossible. This ad for instance: "Send $2 for a foolproof way *not* to lose money on the horses." Those who answered the ad received a sheet of paper for their $2, on which was printed: "Don't bet 'em."

A little closer to your doorstep are home-improvement frauds. Criminal experts think that your chances for being duped by this type of con are excellent.

A couple of men will drive up to your house with the name of a phony company painted on their truck. They'll tell you that they've just finished a repair job in the neighborhood, have some materials left over (paint, roofing, siding, whatever) and will do a job for you at a cheaper-than-usual rate. What these roving swindlers do, in fact, is use paint that will wash off in the first rain or aluminum siding that soon falls off. By the time you've discovered the shoddy material they've used, they're a hundred miles away—with your money.

Related to this con is the fake-inspector scheme. They'll make claims that repairs or adjustments are needed, or that you have termites in your basement, and contract with you to have the work done. The repairs are unnecessary, and the termite they show you is probably an ant.

Quite a lot of money is finagled in this scheme—some of it through fear. One man was told his furnace was a fire hazard, and he shelled out $1,700 for an unneccessary repair job. In another case, a woman paid, in advance, for a year's contract with a phony pest-control service, when the two representatives had emerged from the basement holding two snakes. They had, of course, brought the snakes into the basement with them.

Mouse Trap

Con artists try to keep up with the times. Consequently, new variations of old cons are constantly coming into play. During last winter's fuel shortage, when citizens were asked to lower thermostats, several thieves in New Jersey posed as state inspectors and began making house-to-house thermostat checks. One man would look over the house—to grab a few items then or return later for a bigger take.

You might never be asked if you'd like to buy a deed to the Brooklyn Bridge, or if you'll invest in a worthless artifical-snow-producing machine. But it's possible that you'll be visited by a home repairman who wants to paint your house for "practically nothing," or be taken in by an ad for a "free" Hawaiian vacation. If so, you can save yourself some money by keeping in mind this old Chinese proverb: "You can always get free cheese—in a mousetrap."

______ STOP__ASK FOR YOUR TIME ______

Record time immediately and answer questions on content.

Time __________ Sec. RATE (from table on page 315): R. __________

No. Correct __________ COMPREHENSION (10% for each correct answer): C. __________
(key on page 322)

VI-11 EFFICIENCY (R × C): E. __________

Record on Progress Chart on page 299

ANSWER THESE QUESTIONS IMMEDIATELY

1. (T—F) Con artists are successful because, as they say, "There's a little larceny in all of us."
2. (M.C.) The comment, "There's a sucker born every minute," is credited to:
   ______(1) P. T. Barnum.
   ______(2) Donna St. John.
   ______(3) Walt Disney.
   ______(4) an old Chinese proverb.
3. (T—F) Most people think you have to be naive or stupid to be taken in by a con artist.
4. (C.) The oldest con, called the "pigeon drop", originated 1,000 years ago in ______________ .
5. (T—F) The bank-examiner con usually is operated by a bank teller.
6. (T—F) Mail order frauds are now being eliminated because of increased mail service costs.
7. (T—F) Many real estate developers take advantage of buyers in cold northern states.
8. (T—F) Chances for being duped on home improvement schemes are limited if you have the work completed before you pay.
9. (C.) In the fake-inspector scheme, a person may pay out unnecessary cash because he is told his furnace is a ______________ .
10. (M.C.) Most flimflam men operate on the principle that people believe:
    ______(1) in any so-called public official.
    ______(2) they can save taxes.
    ______(3) they might get "something for nothing."
    ______(4) that prosperity is just around the next corner.

Length: 1350 words

Exercise VI-12

Readability Score: 57

Coffee—It's Not So Hot

(Reprinted by permission from *Executive Fitness Newsletter,* December 4, 1976.)

WAIT FOR SIGNAL TO BEGIN READING

Addiction

The brew that promised to make you more alert has you shuffling zombie-like to the coffee pot each morning for another "fix." And should you not get that all-important first cup one morning, your habit will soon let you know it doesn't like to be ignored: i.e., you will be zapped into a depressed and irritable incompetent with a splitting headache that responds to one thing—caffeine.

Stress

A cup or two of strong coffee contains enough caffeine to produce a rapid and irregular pulse, flushing, a slight increase in blood pressure, and increased acuteness of the senses. Caffeine stimulates the adrenal glands to secrete stress hormones such as adrenalin. The skeletal muscles become tense and less susceptible to fatigue. In general the body prepares for an emergency—which never comes.

100 ←

Studies show that caffeine given to a person not habituated to coffee has no mood-elevating effect, suggesting that the coffee drinker's mood lift is often actually only a lifting of the first symptoms of caffeine withdrawal. But it's undeniable that the added stimulation of caffeine can make a dull job seem more exciting. Hence performance of menial tasks, such as typing, may be improved somewhat. But a skill recently mastered may suffer from the added tension that caffeine can create. Similarly, if you are a nervous person, extra stimulation will probably be counter-productive for you. As far as intellectual performance goes, it seems highly unlikely that any drug can improve on the intelligence of a healthy, well-rested person.

200 ←

Coffee may not give you the competitive edge, but it can make you edgy. Sensitivity to caffeine varies tremendously from one person to another. A half cup of coffee makes some people tremble; others can drink several cups in succession and not seem the worse for it. But, whatever your individual sensitivity to caffeine, sooner or later, if you abuse your tolerance, chances are you will experience coffee nerves.

300 ←

The Executive

Probably the most likely candidate for coffee nerves is the executive who is running full throttle 16 hours a day under the influence. Suddenly he turns into a trembling, twitching, irritable, headachy little mouse with rapid breathing, acutely sensitive senses and reflexes, and a propensity for scurrying around the house in the middle of the night. He blames his plight on external pressures. (You rarely suspect the one you love.) He turns to Librium or Valium to anesthetize his raw nerves. A zombie now without his coffeepot, the vicious stimulant-tranquilizer circle is complete. The shrink diagnoses an anxiety neurosis, and initiates useless psychoanalysis.

400 →

Thyroid

The story doesn't always end like that. Sometimes the family physician misdiagnoses coffee nerves as thyroid trouble, and removes the thyroid gland.

The trouble is that coffee has long enjoyed an unimpeachable position in America life, high above other drugs of its kind. As coffee's dark secrets begir to surface, it's time we took notice.

Further evidence of coffee's insidious nature has been given recently by two Swiss researchers, who found that after drinking a quart of coffee in a three-hour period much of the body's thiamine had been destroyed. Thiamine happens to be a B vitamin which is important for preserving tranquility. A mild thiamine deficiency causes nervousness, irritability, fatigue, loss of appetite, loss of memory, depression, constipation, inability to concentrate, and feelings of inadequacy. A more severe deficiency causes tingling in the toes and nocturnal leg cramping. If you're a heavy coffee drinker, chances are you have a thiamine deficiency. It can lead to the same self-defeating type of drug treatment as coffee nerves can.

500 →

Blood Sugar

600 →

There is still another way coffee can get to your nervous system. The stimulant effect of caffeine (and nicotine as well) often prompts the body to mobilize its stores of energy. The blood sugar rises quickly, and you get a lift. But before the caffeine itself wears off, the pancreas has taken prompt action to stabilize the blood sugar level by injecting insulin into the blood stream. In some people the blood sugar level may drop precipitously. Shaking, dizziness, nausea, migraine headaches, depression, insomnia, and anxiety can result, as well as an intense need for food, or more coffee. Obviously, then, black coffee is not the ideal "diet" beverage. If you find yourself back at the coffee pot every hour or two, it is probably these exaggerated ups and downs of your blood sugar curve that you are responding to. Chronic abuse of the pancreas' ability to stabilize blood sugar levels can lead to hypoglcemia (chronic low blood sugar) and even diabetes. And a misdiagnosis of low blood sugar often means, again, tranquilizers and psychotherapy.

Protein

Alcohol, sugar, and other refined carbohydrates have the same effect on your blood sugar curve. It is wise to avoid any such food in more-than-moderate amounts. When you feel you *must* drink coffee, consider using artificial sweetner (or, better still, none at all) and real milk or cream. The protein and fat in milk can help stabilize your energy curve.

The long-range effects of constantly prodding your heart to work faster and harder are just beginning to be appreciated. Three years ago Drs. Jick and Slone of Boston University reported a statistical link between coffee drinking and heart attack. They claimed that a person drinking five to six cups of coffee per day was doubling his risk of a heart attack. Underlying factors in this scary statistic might be caffeine's ability to increase the blood's readiness to clot.

Withdrawal

As they say, the way to a man's heart is through his stomach, and coffee's irritating tar-like components can burn a trail through your gut a mile wide. Besides acid indigestion, nausea and diarrhea, there is a suspicion that coffee causes peptic ulcers. Certainly if you have an ulcer you should avoid drinking coffee on an empty stomach.

If you still won't give up coffee, at least try to cut down. Take a B complex tablet supplying 10 mg. of thiamine every day. And try to take it easy. Excessive use of caffeine is like using a whip on a tired horse: sooner or later he will drop from exhaustion.

Getting unhooked from caffeine will be a challenge; but if you face the fact that it is a bona fide addiction, you should be able to muster the strength to master it. A slow withdrawal from caffeine may avert the unpleasant withdrawal symptoms. Tea, cola and even cocoa contain lesser amounts of caffeine. Eventually you should be able to settle for a light-colored herb tea, a cereal drink like Postum, or a carob drink—all nice, warm, caffeine-free beverages. (Carob is a chocolate substitute.) If you smoke, watch out for an increased compensatory nicotine craving.

Meanwhile, try to avoid the *need* for a stimulant. When chronic fatigue is the problem, the intelligent thing to do is to offer your body more sleep. If that doesn't help, the fatigue may be stress related. Generous amounts of B vitamins may help, or yoga, exercise or meditation. A sluggish period in midday may be perfectly normal, and a snooze after lunch is not a bad idea. In fact, a short nap at midday is actually equivalent to several hours of nighttime sleep.

If you are one of the many who have to stifle their yawns and carry on, try getting some fresh air and exercise at lunchtime. Eat your best high-protein meal before your sleepy period. Save some minor indulgence specifically for this time of the day: write a personal letter, take a walk, or phone a friend.

Most important of all is to find something that is meaningful *to you* to liven up your days. You may have searched far and near, night and day, eyelids propped open by caffeine, but what you're looking for is intimately connected with your true self. A caffeine trip may take you farther and farther from that self. Unless you are strong enough to stand up to any concoction of man or nature and say, "No thank you," you may throw your potential out with the coffee grounds.

______ STOP __ ASK FOR YOUR TIME ______

Record time immediately and answer questions on content.

Time ______ Sec.	RATE (from table on page 315):	R. ______
No. Correct ______ (key on page 330)	COMPREHENSION (10% for each correct answer):	C. ______
VI-12	EFFICIENCY (R × C):	E. ______

Record on Progress Chart on page 299

ANSWER THESE QUESTIONS IMMEDIATELY

1. (T—F) Coffee is one of the few things that you can give up easily without encountering withdrawal symptoms.
2. (T—F) The added stimulation of caffeine may make a dull job more exciting.
3. (T—F) The author obviously considers caffeine as a drug.
4. (C.) Coffee nerves are really a form of psychological ______________ .
5. (M.C.) Heavy coffee drinkers often experience nervousness, fatigue, depression, and related symptoms because of a mild deficiency of:
   ______(1) oxygen.
   ______(2) thiamine.
   ______(3) nitrogen.
   ______(4) calcium.
6. (C.) Caffeine causes the blood ______________ to raise quickly which causes the pancreas to react and stabilize this action by releasing insulin.
7. (T—F) Heavy coffee drinking does not seem to develop hypoglycemia conditions or stomach ulcers.
8. (T—F) When removing caffeine from your diet, other liquids to avoid are herb teas, carob drinks, and Postum.
9. (M.C.) If withdrawal from coffee makes you sluggish at midday, the writer suggests all but one of the following actions. Which one was not suggested?
   ______(1) A snooze after lunch.
   ______(2) Take a walk.
   ______(3) Drink a cocktail before lunch.
   ______(4) Take generous amounts of Vitamin B.
10. (T—F) Most important to replacing the need for caffeine is to find some interest or activity that is meaningful to you to liven up your days.

Length: 1350 words

Exercise VI-13

Readability Score: 56

The Emperor of the Badlands

By Patricia Calvert

(Reprinted by permission from *Wyoming Rural Electric News,* August, 1977)

WAIT FOR SIGNAL TO BEGIN READING

New Eden

If Antoine de Vallombrosa, the Marquis de Mores had not existed, some enterprising historical novelist would probably have invented him—although it is unlikely that the literary creation could have been more flamboyant than the real article. The Marquis de Mores might have been known in his native France for his skill with a dueling sword and his dark, brooding handsomeness—but he was best known to North Dakota cattlemen in the 1880s as the "Emperor of the Badlands."

The Marquis' American adventures had a storybook beginning in Paris in 1881. At that time the dashing Frenchman met and married Medora von Hoffman, the beautiful, 19-year old redhaired daughter of a wealthy New York banking family. After a honeymoon tour of Europe the young couple settled in New York. A pleased and proud Papa von Hoffman invited his new son-in-law to join the family's banking firm but the young man politely demurred. Such a staid occupation held little fascination for the 26-year old French adventurer.

But if banking *per se* did not appeal to de Mores, money certainly did. The Frenchman was aware of America's reputation as the "new Eden," the place for a man of imagination and daring to make his fortune.

Opportunity called, oddly enough, in the person of the Frenchman's own cousin, Count Fitz-James. Fitz-James had recently returned from a hunting trip to the wilds of Dakota Territory and stopped off to visit the newly-married Marquis in New York City. He described the land of the Dakotas in the most glowing terms and emphasized its vastness, its abundance of wildlife, the richness of its soil and grass.

In the spring of 1882 de Mores left his bride in New York and set out for Dakota Territory to see for himself if what Fitz-James had reported was true—for the Marquis had devised a plan he hoped would make him a millionaire. He planned to locate a suitable cattle range, build slaughterhouses and packing plants at the same site, and ship beef in refrigerated railway cars to markets all over the U.S.

Prestige?

The Badlands of North Dakota were everything the Marquis hoped they would be. Immense grasslands stretched before his eyes. There was plenty of water from prairie rivers and streams. There was shelter for cattle afforded by the bizarre broken clay buttes that had made the Badlands famous.

The Marquis hastily returned to New York. He was wealthy in his own right and now he borrowed as well on the prestige and fortune of his father-in-law to create the National Consumer's Union. Men such as W. R. Grace, Mayor of New York City, and Eugene Kelly, the banker, joined de Mores in the incorporation of this union to the tune of 10 million dollars.

Next de Mores negotiated with the Northern Pacific Railroad and the federal government for the purchase of 45,000 acres of grazing land. He arranged his holdings so that they encompassed both sides of the Little Missouri River, the principal source of water in the Badlands. He succeeded in obtaining the whole package for a mere $32,000—or about 72 cents an acre!

Medora

In the following weeks the Marquis was a busy man as cold storage plants were erected. The Northern Pacific agreed to design and manufacture a refrigerated railway car, the first of its kind. When he returned to the Badlands, the Marquis selected a site on the east side of the Little Missouri River, broke a bottle of champagne over a metal tent stake, and christened the town soon to be built. He named it Medora, in honor of his young American bride.

In the town below he built a church, a school, a theatre, and a bowling alley for the use of the men soon to be employed there. A $250,000 yellow brick slaughterhouse was completed and by the autumn of 1883, de Mores was butchering 300 animals a day; by 1884 he was shearing 14,000 sheep.

Shooting

Storm clouds of resentment gathered and then the Frenchman committed a breach of rangeland etiquette that permanently hardened the hearts of his neighbors against him: he began to fence his lands. Since he owned all the water rights, his action was particularly threatening. Ranchers cut the wires, chopped down fence posts, ran off livestock. A shooting incident finally occured and when the smoke cleared away, a rancher lay dead and the Marquis found himself charged with murder.

The first murder charge was dismissed; the killing was judged to have been a justifiable homicide. But the Marquis was arrested again, tried before a second judge, who once again dismissed the charges. Yet a third time was he arrested and on this occasion was put on trial in Bismarck. He finally was acquitted but the dashing Marquis knew that irreparable damage had been done to his reputation—and worse yet, to his ← 800 business interests.

As if this had not been misfortune enough, other meat packers throughout the U.S., having felt the pinch of competition from the Marquis, began to circulate stories that frozen meat was unhealthy, that it had been doctored with chemicals that were poisonous. Unable to combat these rumors, the Marquis watched as business declined.

At last, in 1886, after only three tempestuous years as a prince of the prairie, the Marquis closed his packing plant at Medora at a loss of over 2 million dollars. ← 900 Disillusioned, he abandoned his chateau on the banks of the Little Missouri and fled back to France with his wife and two children.

Fatal Web

Now de Mores' career entered a truly ominous phase. The Marquis had hoped to make a fortune in America, a fortune that would enable him to overthrow the French Republic and establish himself as a new monarch. He had not forsaken this dream, despite his failures in Dakota Territory, and he became embroiled in a scheme to unify all of North Africa under French rule. This was to be the power base from which he planned to destroy the French ← 1000 Republic itself.

De Mores pursued this mad notion as fervently as he had pursued his dreams in the Badlands, oblivious to the fact that he was being ensnared in a fatal web of political intrigue. In 1893, at the age of 37, only 10 years after he had first set a boot in Dakota Territory, the Frenchman was murdered by wild Tuareg tribesmen on the lonely sands of an African desert. Later, facts emerged which indicated the Marquis' death had been plotted by some of his own jealous countrymen.

Life in the Badlands was everything the Marquis 1100 → had dreamed it would be. Money flowed like a river from his cattle operation. He had become the father of a son, Louis, who would carry on the de Mores name. The Frenchman's redhaired wife was described in an article in the *Bismarck Tribune* in 1885 as "one of New York's most popular belles . . . and now queen of the Rocky Mountains and champion huntress of the great northwest."

In the summer of 1903, the redhaired widow returned to the chateau with her two oldest children (another son, Paul, had been born in France). It was 1200 → her final, melancholy journey to the Badlands where she had shared three dazzling years with her colorful husband. Medora de Mores died in France in 1921 from injuries she suffered while acting as a nurse in World War I.

Emperor

Although they never again visited the Badlands, the de Mores family maintained a caretaker at the abandoned chateau. In 1936 Louis de Mores deeded it to the North Dakota Historical Society and it is now open for public tours. The imported furniture, the supplies of silver and damask, the wine cellar, the garments left behind by the de Mores family all remain 1300 → as they were left, waiting silently for those who will not return. The chateau, standing in solemn isolation amid the wild prairie grasses on a bluff overlooking the Little Missouri River, is the last testimonial to the broken dreams of a man who wanted too much too 1350 → soon—the unlucky "Emperor of the Badlands."

_____ STOP __ ASK FOR YOUR TIME _____

Record time immediately and answer questions on content.

Time __________ Sec. RATE (from table on page 315): R. __________

No. Correct __________ COMPREHENSION (10% for each correct answer): C. __________
(key on page 322)

VI-13 EFFICIENCY (R × C): E. __________

Record on Progress Chart on page 299

ANSWER THESE QUESTIONS IMMEDIATELY

1. (C.) Before settling in the Badlands, the Marquis de Mores and his wife had lived in __________

2. (T—F) The Marquis was offered a job as a cattle buyer by his father-in-law.

3. (M.C.) The refrigerated railway car needed for his plan was designed and manufactured by:
 ______(1) National Consumer Union.
 ______(2) Medora Packing Plant.
 ______(3) the Northern Pacific.
 ______(4) Antoine de Vallombrosa.

4. (T—F) The Marquis named the city Medora in honor of his wife.

5. (M.C.) He incurred resentment and negative reaction from the North Dakota ranchers because:
 ______(1) he was too rich and powerful.
 ______(2) he was a foreigner and did not belong.
 ______(3) he purchased his land at an unfair price.
 ______(4) he fenced his lands.

6. (T—F) The Marquis was put on trial for three murders, but was acquitted each time.

7. (C.) Stories that frozen meat was doctored with poisonous chemicals were circulated by some __________ .

8. (T—F) In 1886 the packing plant was closed at a loss of two million dollars because of the death of the Marquis.

9. (T—F) The fortune he had hoped to make in America was to be used to help him overthrow the French Republic and establish himself as monarch.

10. (T—F) Medora de Mores and her children continued to live in France and only returned once to the chateau in North Dakota.

Length: 1350 words

Exercise VI-14

Readability Score: 54

Sherlock Holmes Is Alive and Well!

By Paul Ditzel

WAIT FOR SIGNAL TO BEGIN READING

In the minds and hearts of countless numbers of mystery buffs and movie fans, Sherlock Holmes remains what every detective or would-be amateur sleuth should, in fact, be.

Holmes, who is a true folk hero, was the fictional creation of Sir Arthur Conan Doyle who never once tried to make him out to be anything else. Doyle went to his grave still hoping that readers would remember him for his historical novels and forget about his brainchild, Holmes.

The historical novels are all but forgotten, but to readers the world over, Sherlock Holmes lives on as the master hawkshaw. Although nearly half a century has passed since Holmes' final adventure, Scotland Yard still gets letters addressed to him. To his host of fans, Sherlock Holmes will, one of these days, astound all of us and return from the dead as he did before.

The sixty adventures of Sherlock Holmes have been translated into 45 languages and have sold in excess of 100-million copies. From these tales by Sir Arthur Conan Doyle have come more than 100 television shows, 500 radio scripts, 20 plays (including a Broadway musical) and 120 movies. Somewhere in the world today, at least one of the 17 versions of that most famous of all Holmes' adventures, "The Hound of the Baskervilles," is being shown in some theater.

A Sherlock Society

Exactly why the Sherlock Holmes mystique continues to grow is a question which intrigues, baffles, frustrates and defies anyone seeking a pat answer. Part of the explanation lies among the loyal legion of Holmes admirers who are dedicated to keeping the legends alive and concocting still more. They have formed "learned societies" to study "The Sacred Writings" of Doyle and to exchange tidbits of Sherlockian scholarship. When one buff, through sleuthing which would have made Holmes proud, produced a photo of the 221B Baker Street lodgings purportedly used by the detective, the reaction of fellow enthusiasts could only be compared to that of the rest of us the day that someone discovers a cure for the common cold. In reality, 221B never existed. Today in London, a tobacconist is at 218, next door to a valet service at 222.

Best known among the societies are The Baker Street Irregulars of New York City and the Sherlock Holmes Society of London. The pre-eminent Irregulars, named after the street urchins who helped Holmes, was formed in 1934 by Christopher Morley, an editor of the *Saturday Review of Literature.* Only those aficionados who can complete a crossword puzzle of Sherlockiana are eligible.

The constitution of the Irregulars says: "An annual meeting shall be held on January 6, to observe the birthday of Sherlock Holmes." Morley somehow managed to figure out that Holmes' birthday was identical to his own. During the meeting, "canonical toasts shall be drunk; after which members shall drink at will. The current round shall be bought by any member who fails to identify by title of story and context, any quotation from the Sacred Writings submitted by any other member. . . . All other business shall be left for the monthly meeting. There shall be no monthly meeting."

There is abundant material from which to draw questions. Holmesians are devoted to minutia matches. A two-volume "Annotated Sherlock Holmes" reprints the four novelettes and fifty-six stories, and contains maps, illustrations, thousands of footnotes and analyses ad infinitum.

All buffs know that Holmes was Doyle's alter ego, although he based the character upon a fellow physician, Dr. Joseph Bell, an Edinburgh surgeon, diagnostician and a master at deduction. Watson was patterned after a former major in the British Army who was Doyle's private secretary.

If the basics of the legend are elementary, my dear Watson, the buff is turned on by the profundities of the ramifications suggested by the Sherlock Holmes saga: Was Holmes really a Stuart Pretender? Was he a defrocked priest? Or was he the head of an anarchist conspiracy? Was Dr. Watson really Jack the Ripper, or a woman in man's clothing? Through Holmesian deduction, devotees can offer convincing proof, pro and con, to keep the mystique boiling endlessly.

Commemorating "The Final Problem"

Recently, forty members of the London society made a pilgrimage to Reichenbach Falls in Switzerland, where Holmes and his arch-enemy, Professor Moriarty, fought a death struggle in "The Final Problem," before plunging 300 feet over the falls.

Doyle, so the story goes, in 1891 disposed of Holmes in this story to rid himself of demands for more adventures. Despite public dismay, he insisted that, "Holmes lies dead at the foot of Reichenbach Falls and there he shall remain." Ten years later, Doyle breathed new life into Holmes, but only after upping his word rate to the point he thought no editor could afford him. He was astonished by those who lined up at his door.

How had Holmes survived the plunge? Easy, said Doyle. He'd merely clung to a ledge on the way down. What Holmes did during that ten-year hiatus from his fans has provided grist to this day for countless Sherlockian research papers and debates.

Commemorating the event, members of the London Society costumed themselves in Victorian plumage, including feathered bonnets for the ladies, deerstalker caps and capes for the men. The battle was reenacted with Sir Paul Gore-Booth, head of Britain's diplomatic service, playing Holmes. The *denouement* came with the pitching of two dummies dressed as Holmes and Moriarty, over the precipice.

Why Sherlock Lives

Editor Shelly Lowenkopf of Sherbourne Press lays much of Holmes' popularity to the happenstance of Basil Rathbone playing the role in the series of Sherlock Holmes movies, with Nigel Bruce as Dr. Watson. "In the minds of those millions of people who saw the movies, Basil Rathbone *is* Sherlock Holmes. Rathbone was perfect for the role. Strangely enough, his physical features were identical to those of Holmes as described by Doyle."

Doyle's official biographer, John Dickson Carr, believes that part of the reason why Holmes stands out among literature's best-known private eyes lies in Holmes' compassionate nature and Doyle's superb characterization. Doyle used "clever tricks," he writes. "Other writers have given us more ingenious plots. But we never know their heroes as we knew Sherlock Holmes. Let any man approach him in a civil fashion and he becomes at once an understanding friend.... He is chivalry itself toward femininity in distress.... On behalf of a client who has excited his sympathy, he will upset the law, he will bamboozle the police, he will take risks a cash-conscious private investigator would not dream of incurring for $1,000 a day."

Critic Kenneth Rexroth, writing in the *Saturday Review*, adds, "The secret to the fascination of the world of Sherlock Holmes is its terrifying normality .... Holmes is Justice—neurotic, capricious, but humane. The erring escape the vengeance of their own misdeeds, while the evil go to dooms they have prepared for themselves."

Only James Bond rivals Holmes in popularity. In many ways, Ian Fleming's creation parallels Doyle's. Both were English. Both had a flair for living. Bond falls short, according to books and arts critic George Grella of *The New Republic*, "because he was stupid." Bond "disobeys orders and blunders into situations he should have anticipated chapters in advance." Too, Bond was "entrusted with the mammoth task of safeguarding an entire civilization; the free world depends on his actions."

If there are a host of opinions explaining the Holmes phenomenon, perhaps I may be excused for having my own. Maybe we do not identify with Holmes at all, but with the affable Dr. Watson. Except, perhaps, for Sherlockian buffs, few of us really fantasize ourselves grappling with a Moriarty at the brink of Reichenbach Falls in remote Switzerland. With Dr. Watson, we are privileged to share a front-row seat and with him try to spot the clues that are so obvious to Holmes, but not to Dr. Watson or us. Perhaps we see in ourselves the bumbling, conscientious Watson, outraged by crime but unable to do very much about it, except to revere and support the unflawed champion who always does, that crime fighter par excellence named Sherlock Holmes.

STOP—ASK FOR YOUR TIME

Record time immediately and answer the questions on content.

Time ________ Sec.	RATE (from table on page 315):	R. ________
No. Correct ________ (key on page 330)	COMPREHENSION (10% for each correct answer):	C. ________
VI-14	EFFICIENCY (R × C):	E. ________

Record on Progress Chart on page 299

ANSWER THESE QUESTIONS IMMEDIATELY

1. (M.C.) Sherlock Holmes was the fictional creation of:
   _____(1) Earl Stanley Gardner.
   _____(2) Arthur Conan Doyle.
   _____(3) John Dickson Carr.
   _____(4) Mickey MacGonigal Spillane.
2. (T—F) The author of Sherlock Holmes wanted to be remembered for his historical novels rather than for his mysteries.
3. (T—F) Holmes' lodgings at 221 B Baker Street is a shrine for Holmes fans today.
4. (C.) Eligibility for membership in the Baker Street Irregulars is limited to those who can complete a ________ ________ of Sherlockiana.
5. (T—F) It has been suggested that Sherlock Holmes was really a defrocked priest.
6. (C.) Holmes' arch enemy was named ________________ .
7. (M.C.) At Reichenbach Falls, members of the London Society celebrated a battle which had ended with:
   _____(1) the villain killing Dr. Watson before Holmes could save him.
   _____(2) the villain being unsuccessful in an attempt to kill Holmes.
   _____(3) both Holmes and the villain being killed in a fall.
   _____(4) Holmes dispatching his arch enemy.
8. (T—F) It is believed by some critics that one reason for Holmes' popularity is his toughness, unmarred by weakness or compassion.
9. (T—F) Only Mike Hammer rivals Holmes in popularity.
10. (T—F) The author feels that perhaps readers identify with Dr. Watson rather than with Holmes.

Length: 1350 words

Exercise VI-15

Readability Score: 51

Legalize Marijuana?

By Arthur W. E. Eriksson

(Reprinted by permission from *Listen,* August, 1970.)

WAIT FOR SIGNAL TO BEGIN READING

Drugs Are Chemicals

Every drug has some effect on the user. Drugs do not usually cure illness, nor are they necessarily beneficial for the body. The right drug for any particular illness sets up conditions favorable for natural recovery. They permit the body to heal itself.

Drugs may act on several systems of the body, thus causing problems. A drug may help one part of the body and harm another. The wrong drug, or the right drug taken in wrong quantities or at the wrong time, can cause harm.

Prescription drugs are drugs that can be secured only on the order of a doctor who has carefully considered the patient's age, weight, sex, physical condition, and illness at the time. If the drug is taken at another time, it may be of no value or be harmful.

Over-the-counter drugs are considered safe without a doctor's supervision, if the instructions on the label are followed carefully and good judgment is used. Taking larger or smaller quantities than indicated may give no results or harmful ones.

Drugs of abuse may be secured from doctors or from drugstores through deceit, or purchased from "pushers." Since there is no guarantee of quality, or even that the product is the one that is claimed to be sold, the purchaser risks his money and often his life.

Any chemical can be harmful to anyone. A person may even find himself allergic to a drug carefully prescribed by a doctor. Persons taking drugs of abuse on their own whim, without specific directions, increase their chance of being hurt.

Harmless?

Some people say that marijuana is harmless. Let's compare it with tobacco. Smoking a joint produces the same irritation to the throat, due to heat and irritating smoke, as does smoking a tobacco cigarette. Long-continued exposure induces chronic respiratory disorders. Tar is a product of burning pot as well as of tobacco. The use of marijuana should also result in an increase in lung cancer in pot smokers after use over a number of years. Tobacco produces these results—why introduce another substance to do the same thing?

In Canada it is a criminal offense for any person to grow, import, sell, or possess marijuana. Marijuana has no known use in medical practice in most countries of the world. More research needs to be done to probe scientifically its effects, but many things are already known.

Unpredictable

With marijuana no one can predict what will happen each time it is taken. Effects vary from person to person, mood to mood, time to time, and place to place. A person may smoke five joints and feel good, but the sixth may cause him to walk out an upstairs window or step out into traffic. Experiments were tried on dogs, and the results were so unpredictable that they were given up in frustration.

Dr. Louis S. Harris of the University of North Carolina found that if a marijuana smoker also took barbiturates, the drugs could build up in the bloodstream and kill.

There is proof that THC, the actual drug in marijuana, easily crosses the placenta and enters the fetus, which leads to the question: "Will a pregnant woman who smokes marijuana damage her unborn child?"

Chronic marijuana users often are lethargic and neglect their personal appearance. For many students, the change from conforming achievement-orientated behavior to a state of relaxed and careless drifting has followed their use of significant amounts of marijuana. Should marijuana be legalized so as to increase its use and give these symptoms to more people?

K. A. Yonge, M.D., president of the Canadian Psychiatric Association, writes; "The psychedelic drugs, including marijuana, act by altering from the normal the processes of perception, emotion, and thinking. These mental distortions, however pleasant, are of the same order, though not necessarily the same magnitude, as mental illness. They are mini-psychoses—temporary, maybe, non-recurrent, maybe, without organic brain damage, maybe—but, by these criteria, unhealthy."

Panic Reactions

Cases of marijuana-induced, temporary panic reactions are not uncommon among inexperienced users. Marijuana is claimed to be mind-enhancing. This is a temporary distortion of the sense mechanisms. It is also claimed to enhance creative activity but experiments have shown this not to be fact. Any task or decision requiring good reflexes or clear thinking is affected by the drug. For this reason driving is dangerous while under its influence.

Protection

It is important that those too young to make mature and informed decisions be protected. If a personal problem is faced, it will likely be faced also the next time it arises. If one goes to drugs to help solve the problem, he will likely go to drugs to try to solve it the next time. This is not an effective method of attempting to solve a problem.

Good judgment is an essential part of our behavior and of our thinking processes and is the result of learning, education, and experience. Judgment is the ability to reach conclusions from learned facts by comparing and analyzing. Marijuana can seriously disturb judgment.

If a person is used to having eggs for breakfast regularly and he doesn't get them, he is slightly aggrieved. This may be thought of as a dependency. Life is built up of many dependencies, some of which are trivial, some benign and pleasurable, and some are harmful. Dependence on friends, family, and work help make us what we are.

Each time a drug is used increases the chances that it will be taken again. Persons who use marijuana continually can be said to become psychologically dependent on the substance if they use it to escape painful experiences of anxiety or depression, or as a means of gaining social acceptance.

Dependency Scale

Many chemicals can be put on a dependency scale. Heroin is 100 percent dependency-producing. Marijuana isn't that high, but it sometimes makes one want to be alone, or more often want to be with a group, feel good, have vivid visions, and feel somewhat exhilarated.

The Addiction Research Foundation of Ontario did a study on drug use in Toronto, Montreal, and Halifax. They found that marijuana smokers are sixty-two times more likely to use LSD than students who do not smoke marijuana. Marijuana smokers are twenty-nine times more likely to use opiates and twenty-four times more likely to use hallucinogenic drugs. Use of tranquilizers, glue, stimulants, barbiturates, tobacco, and alcohol was also found to be higher among marijuana smokers.

To the extent that marijuana use contributes to a general disregard for the realistic consequences of behavior in young persons, its use increases the probability of the use of more dangerous drugs. Weak marijuana use may give the student the belief that he can "handle" any drug.

Marijuana is illegal in practically every developed country in the world. Prohibition of sale of marijuana in some of these countries clearly indicates their social disapproval, in contrast to open sale permitted in other countries.

Compared to Alcohol

Some users say that marijuana is no worse than alcohol. The cost of absenteeism due to use of alcohol is about $2 billion per year in the United States. The use of marijuana makes a person more and more irresponsible, so a similar effect might be expected after a period of use. There are skid rows due to alcoholism in North American cities. It would not be desirable to add another type of degenerate area here in North America. Avoiding this type of problem is another reason for not legalizing marijuana.

Effects of Legalizing

The legalizing of alcohol in the United States did not do away with moonshining and bootlegging. Although barbiturates are dependency-producing, a short time after they were legalized in the United States, half the supply of this legal drug was in control of the black market. Legalizing heroin in England did not solve this problem for the British.

It seems evident that the legalizing of marijuana would not solve any of the problems connected with the drug. It would seem only to increase these problems as well as to make the use of the drug more widespread.

———STOP—ASK FOR YOUR TIME———

Record time immediately and answer the questions on content.

Time ________ Sec.	RATE (from table on page 315):	R. ________
No. Correct ________ (key on page 322)	COMPREHENSION (10% for each correct answer):	C. ________
VI-15	EFFICIENCY (R × C):	E. ________

Record on Progress Chart on page 299

ANSWER THESE QUESTIONS IMMEDIATELY

1. (T—F) Every drug has some effect on the user.

2. (C.) Drugs of abuse may be secured through deceit from doctors or drugstores, or purchased from ________________.

3. (C.) The purchaser of drugs of abuse risks his money and often his ________________.

4. (T—F) No comparison is made between the smoking of tobacco, cigarettes and the smoking of marijuana.

5. (T—F) No one can predict what will happen each time marijuana is taken.

6. (M. C.) Dr. Louis S. Harris of the University of North Carolina found that if a marijuana smoker also took barbiturates:
   ______(1) one would offset the other and therefore would be harmless.
   ______(2) he would tend to become sleepy.
   ______(3) he would become energetic and therefore get more work done.
   ______(4) the drugs could build up in the bloodstream and kill him.

7. (T—F) Mental distortions caused by smoking marijuana were compared with mental illness or mini-psychoses.

8. (T—F) Because drugs sharpen the wits of the user, driving while under the influence of marijuana is no real risk.

9. (T—F) The writer implies a possible dependency scale, but does not present any to compare to the one quoted for heroin.

10. (M. C.) The author believes that:
   ______(1) marijuana should be legalized.
   ______(2) by legalizing the sale and use of drugs, there would be fewer cases of drug abuse.
   ______(3) the use of marijuana would lead to the use of more harmful drugs.
   ______(4) the legal use of marijuana would be acceptable under careful supervision.

Length: 1350 words

Exercise VI-16

Readability Score: 49

Bottled Status

By Joseph Poindexter

WAIT FOR SIGNAL TO BEGIN READING

To Your Health

If you think back to five or ten years ago, you'll recall that people used to drink water to slake their thirst. It's one of those little things that is easy to forget as we become an ever more sophisticated species. Nevertheless, back in the days when drinking water came only from a tap, thirst was pretty much all there was to it.

Today, a lot of drinking water comes in bottles and does some things no one considered asking tap water to do. For one thing, today's drinking water is very good for you. Depending on which bottle you pour from, it may strengthen your heart, purify your kidneys, revitalize your bones, or make you more energetic, younger looking, thinner. Today's water can also identify you a tastemaker or as the member of an inner circle. Best of all, certain drinking water can bestow upon you the unmistakable emblem of power.

No one is sure which one of these things is responsible for the spectacular growth of bottled water. Or if it is due instead to a growing awareness of what, in addition to hydrogen and oxygen, is contained in tap water. Or if it's simply that American tastebuds have become refined to the point that they no longer are happy with being drowned in chlorine.

The fact remains that bottled water consumption in the United States has gone from a burble of 120 million gallons in 1965 to a geyser of nearly 400 million in 1977. To put it another way, in 1977 Americans spent about $190 million for a commodity they could get virtually for nothing.

This is impressive growth. Measured by volume alone, though, the United States runs well behind many European nations. France, with less than a quarter of the population of the United States, consumes seven times that amount of bottled water. All of Europe consumes twenty times as much.

Then, too, Europeans determined long ago that certain of their favorite waters contained therapeutic value. It's no coincidence that we get the word "spa" from a town in Belguim, Spa, that is noted for its curative waters. The therapeutic powers of the waters at Vichy are said to have been discovered by the Caesars, and the water from Fiuggi has had a loyal Italian following ever since Michelangelo endorsed it.

Many European bottlers submit their waters to medical analysis by their nation's academy of medicine (roughly equivalent to the American Medical Association) and then advertise the results of the analysis. Others print an exhaustive mineral analysis on their labels. These therapeutic reputations frequently accompany the water on its journey to the U.S. market, even though the Food and Drug Administration prohibits the advertisement of specific health claims.

Consider the Competition

Perhaps more potent than the claims made on behalf of bottled waters are certain qualities impugned to the "competition." Tap water has come under a lot of criticism lately—some deserved, some not. New York City's much-maligned water has a scant 30 to 40 parts solids to 1 million parts water. By the same token, water in certain areas of Texas belts you with 1,000 to 2,000 parts of solids per million. In 1974, those who didn't like the taste were joined by a large number who didn't like the risk. That was the year that an Environmental Protection Agency reported finding possible carcinogens in nearly all of the eighty municipal water supplies it had analyzed.

Of the 400 million gallons of water that will be sold in the United States any year, about 350 million will be processed water—tap or well water that is distilled, deionized, or put through reverse osmosis and then sometimes refortified with minerals. Such processed waters are inexpensive and enjoy a loyal following in places where water seems better suited to swimming pools than drinking glasses. As a nation, only one of every fourteen hundred of us drinks bottled water, but in Los Angeles the frequency is one in every six.

In fact, half of all the bottled water sold in the United States is sold in Southern California. According to Larry Fried, Marketing-Promotion Director of Arrowhead Water, this is due only in part to the condition of the tap water, some of which is considered quite good. This was not always the case, and many Los Angelinos have developed the bottled water habit from days when virtually all tap water was sub par. Some of his customers not only drink the Arrowhead product, but also water their plants, and change their fish bowls with it.

The remaining sales are from waters that come unaltered from a spring. The label will help you distinguish between the two. If it says "spring water," that's what is inside the bottle. If it says "spring fresh" or "spring pure" or the like, you'll know its the processed variety. The former commands prices from $.40 to $.70 for 28 to 32 ounce bottles. The latter, benefiting from the efficiencies of bottling in the marketing region, costs from $2.50 to $4.50 for a five-gallon jug.

Imports

Both kinds of waters enjoy a price advantage over the imports that are appearing in ever increasing numbers on delicatessen—and supermarket—shelves. They run from $.70 to $1.20 for bottles ranging from 23 to 33 ounces. Still only 2 percent of the water business when measured by dollar volume and less than 1 percent by water volume, the imports are showing some effervescent growth this year.

The main reason for this growth comes in a green bottle shaped like a bowling pin: Perrier. The naturally carbonated water from Vergeze, France, is in the midst of an intense, American-style marketing campaign, orchestrated by former Levi Strauss & Co. executive Bruce Nevins. Impressed by his ability to persuade Frenchmen to buy Levi's—he headed international sales—Perrier hired Nevins to turn the same trick with their product in the United States.

With the aid of a brilliant ad campaign, featuring the voice of Orson Welles, Perrier is now selling at an annual rate of 12 million bottles, up from 2.5 million last year. In 1977, Perrier began to reach beyond its primary markets in New York City, Los Angeles, and San Francisco to Boston, Washington, Baltimore, Miami, and San Diego. In 1978, Nevins had plans to sell 36 million bottles of Perrier and broaden its markets to Chicago, Houston, Dallas, Atlanta, and Philadelphia.

For those who had been attracted to the exclusivity of Perrier, there are still about a dozen other imports available that are as yet far less visible. Evian Spring Water—No. 1 in the world—is the second most popular U.S. import. It's a still water with vast curative powers, according to the French, who like to feed it to newborn babies.

Apollinaris from Bad Neuenahr, West Germany, and Vichy, from France, are both so highly carbonated in their natural states that they are bottled directly from the spring. Most natural sparkling waters are produced by capturing the gas and recombining it with the spring water under pressure during bottling.

Finally, if for you the Holy Grail is a bottled water with the tiniest of bubbles, you might try Badoit, a naturally sparkling water from Saint-Galmier, France. That's the finding of John Scott, president of Mountain Valley Water, which imports about a dozen European waters, including Badoit.

Scott believes that Badoit's small bubbles are related to its low sodium content, and he tells this story about his own domestic product. The wine steward at the Waldorf fell in love with Mountain Valley. He asked whether we couldn't provide him with a sparkling version of the water to be used as a mixer. But the carbonated bottles went flat as soon as they were opened. Finally we called in a chemist. He shook some salt into a glass, poured in the carbonated Mountain Valley and it remained bubbly for half an hour.

Water is a lot more complicated than it used to be. Maybe you ought to just sample some of the offerings at your gourmet food shop and see what suits you.

______ STOP __ ASK FOR YOUR TIME ______

Record time immediately and answer questions on content.

Time __________ Sec. RATE (from table on page 315): R. __________

No. Correct __________ COMPREHENSION (10% for each correct answer): C. __________
(key on page 330)

VI-16 EFFICIENCY (R × C): E. __________

Record on Progress Chart on page 299

ANSWER THESE QUESTIONS IMMEDIATELY

1. (T—F) The special ingredients of hydrogen and oxygen are the reason for the increased sales of bottled water.
2. (T—F) Pollution of stream water is a significant reason for increased sales of bottled water.
3. (C.) Many Americans simply dislike tap water because of the taste of __________ .
4. (M.C.) European consumption of bottled water exceeds the United States' consumption by about:
   ______(1) twice.
   ______(2) five times.
   ______(3) twenty times.
   ______(4) fifty times.
5. (T—F) More residents of Los Angeles drink bottled water than of any other place in the United States.
6. (T—F) Natural spring water is much less expensive than processed water labeled as "spring pure".
7. (M.C.) The area which has the greatest sales volume in the United States is:
   ______(1) Mountain Valley.
   ______(2) New York City.
   ______(3) Texas.
   ______(4) Southern California.
8. (T—F) Perrier water is the best selling imported bottled water in the United States.
9. (C.) Most natural sparkling waters are produced by combining __________ with spring water under pressure.
10. (T—F) John Scott believes that Badoit's small bubbles are related to its low sodium content.

Length: 1350 words

Exercise VI-17

Readability Score: 47

Rocky Mountain High

By Keith Reekie

(Reprinted by permission from *Holiday Inn Companion*, October, 1976, by permission of the editor.)

WAIT FOR SIGNAL TO BEGIN READING

The Tourist Trade

Salt Lake City is more legend than news story to most Americans. It's not often in our thoughts. But in a quiet, unadvertised fashion, Utah's capital has become one of the fastest-growing Rocky Mountain cities, a major manufacturing and distributing point for the western states. On the energy front, further price increases for Middle Eastern oil could turn this city into the hub of a multi-billion-dollar energy extraction and processing complex.

Utah's population stood at 1,207,000 as of 1975, a jump of 20 percent since 1970. Salt Lake City's is up 40.5 percent from 1970, to 783,400. Eighty percent of all Utahans live in the four counties of the "Wasatch Front," named for the mountain range looming to the east and comprising the Salt Lake City-Ogden and Provo-Orem metropolitan areas.

Passenger deplanings at Salt Lake City International Airport have increased from 448,206 in 1964 to 1,401,428 in 1974. The state has also succeeded in establishing itself as a capital for winter tourism—skiers love the area's "powder" snow.

In fact, 1976 might well be considered the year of recognition for Utah skiing. For years Utah has remained in the shadow of the Colorado resorts and Sun Valley. Into February, snow conditions throughout the West were terrible, and some areas actually had to close. But in Utah, light, fluffy snow kept falling, and skiers disappointed elsewhere kept on coming. For the first time, skiers experienced significant lift lines at the state's resorts.

"We've seen Utah come to maturity this year as a ski capital for the country," says Jack Gallivan, publisher of the *Salt Lake Tribune,* the city's morning newspaper. "All of our resorts were packed last season since before Christmas, and our major resort areas have averaged gains of 60 percent."

Business and Industry

Even without development of the state's energy resources, Salt Lake City and Utah are expected to keep up their fast rate of growth. "We see the population of the Salt Lake metropolitan area doubling by 1990," says R. Thayne Robson, director of the Bureau of Business and Economic Research at the University of Utah's College of Business. Salt Lake City, he explains, has shared with Denver and Phoenix a steady growth in manufacturing employment, primarily by outside firms locating plants in Utah.

But most observers say leaving energy development out of the picture is unrealistic. "I think there's an inevitable boom for Utah coal," Robson predicts. He foresees such development beginning in earnest within two or three years, as part of a serious commitment to make the United States self-sufficient in energy.

Salt Lake City would be the natural center for such development in western Colorado and southwestern Wyoming, and Utah itself has reserves of oil (410 million barrels), natural gas (1.7 trillion cubic feet), coal (115 billion tons, much of it low in sulfur content), and oil shale (320 million barrels).

One reason Salt Lake City is popular with manufacturers is that it has a wage scale lower than California's with a differential of as much as $.70 per hour for jobs in the $3 to $5.50 range. Another is the ethic expressed in the slogan, "A day's work for a day's pay," so often heard in Utah it's almost an unofficial state motto. There's general agreement that Utah employees work hard, and the motive is generally credited to "pioneer" influence or the teachings of the Mormons (properly, Church of Jesus Christ of Latter-Day Saints) that work is a blessing.

Downtown Shopping Area

Despite the fast growth, Salt Lakers have not sacrificed a vital downtown area. The Salt Palace, the city's convention center, was built in 1969, and several hotel and motel chains have built large units nearby.

The Mormons' department store chain, Zion's Cooperative Mercantile Institution has occupied a new enclosed shopping mall in a block catercorner from the temple, and refurbishment of old buildings, like the Arrow Press Square project, makes the central city an interesting place to visit.

Trolley Square, an imaginative shopping center created out of an old street-railway-car barn east of the downtown area, was orginally seen by locals only as a tourist attraction, but the restaurants, movie theaters and shops have proved so popular that a food market and other appurtenances of a neighborhood center are planned. Wallace Wright, the developer, has been invited to work his magic at a similar site in St. Louis.

Culture and Entertainment

The magnificent old City and County building, completed in 1894, is having its gargoyles and turrets cleaned for its second eighty years.

A music and visual arts center will be built with state funds and bond money just north of the Salt Palace, and is due for completion in 1979. The Capitol, a 1912 vaudeville theater turned cinema, will be revamped as headquarters of Ballet West and the Repertory Dance Theater. With the Utah Symphony and several theater groups, this gives the city a cultural weight far out of proportion to its size.

The present liquor law situation causes small inconvenience to the drinking public. Simply bring along your liquor and purchase a setup from the bartender. Liquor can be bought either at state stores or a store associated with a restaurant or night spot. Some bars are in fact liquor stores, too, and will sell you a 1½ ounce minibottle and the setup for about $1.25 to $1.50. To get a simple, already poured glass of liquor, you must visit one of the many clubs in the Salt Lake City area. These aren't private in the sense your country club is, but offer memberships for $12 to $50 a year, depending on the club and whether you're a resident of Utah or a visitor. Most of Utah's nightclubbing takes place at these clubs, which resemble discos with a high door charge.

Environmentalists are concerned about energy development and expansion of ski areas, and have fought both with varying success. But most Utahans seem unconcerned that major growth could sharply change the comfortable way of life they've created. Proposed land-use controls have been voted down, and local residents have pushed hard for construction of coal-burning power plants at Kaiparowits and elsewhere in the southern part of the state.

Some Future Problems

Mayor Ted L. Wilson of Salt Lake City foresees problems in the kind of growth now facing all of Utah. "We're in danger of becoming a colony to other states around us, as Appalachia became a colony to the Eastern seaboard," he says. "We have to come up with an energy statement for this state, just as the nation needs to. I could see developing the energy quickly, if we were sure that the demand elsewhere were critical. But we're not sure of that."

He says Utah has "the potential . . . to become one of the most incredible messes in the country," but also believes Utahans are evolving toward the Oregonian ethic of planned growth.

"It's going to take a lot of restraint, but Utahans are very capable of that," Wilson says. "We've always shown restraint."

Robson, of the Bureau of Business and Economic Research, says part of the problem lies in planning the new communities that will house workers during the energy boom. Communities associated with mining and petroleum development often have been little more than shantytowns, quickly erected and lacking amenities.

Unless either government or energy-company money is used for front-end costs of municipal development, Robson says, the situation will be repeated in Utah. There's simply no local tax base to fund schools, parks and the rest of the urban infrastructure. "I have a certain amount of faith that, when the crunch really comes, both the federal and the state governments will respond and take appropriate action," he says. "I'm an optimist. I have to believe that men can learn from their mistakes of the past. I really think we know what to do, and it's just a problem of getting the job done."

The future of Salt Lake City and its environs is bright, and its residents are enthusiastic and confident that progress will continue to be made while preserving the area's quality of life.

______ STOP ___ ASK FOR YOUR TIME ______

Record time immediately and answer questions on content.

Time ________ Sec.	RATE (from table on page 315):	R. ________
No. Correct ________ (key on page 322)	COMPREHENSION (10% for each correct answer):	C. ________
VI-17	EFFICIENCY (R × C):	E. ________

Record on Progress Chart on page 299

ANSWER THESE QUESTIONS IMMEDIATELY

1. (C.) ________________ percent of Utah's residents live in the four counties of the Wasatch Front.

2. (T—F) 1976 was an all time high for Rocky Mountain skiing in Utah.

3. (M.C.) R. Thayne Robson predicts that by 1990, the population of metropolitan Salt Lake City will:
   ______(1) decrease by one third.
   ______(2) remain relatively stable.
   ______(3) increase to about double the present size.
   ______(4) increase to about five times the present size.

4. (T—F) One problem facing Utah will be the limited energy resources to meet the needs of a growing population.

5. (M.C.) Utah now claims energy resources in all of the following areas except:
   ______(1) oil shale.
   ______(2) hydroelectric power.
   ______(3) natural gas.
   ______(4) coal.

6. (C.) Salt Lake City is attractive to a number of manufacturers because it has a relative low level of ________________ .

7. (T—F) Followers of the Church of Jesus Christ of Latter-Day Saints are taught that work is a blessing.

8. (T—F) With the fast growth rate, the downtown area of Salt Lake City has been redeveloped with many high-rise apartments and office buildings.

9. (T—F) Most Utah residents seem very concerned about the rate of expansion in their state and the danger that it may change their current comfortable way of life.

10. (T—F) One of the greatest concerns for the future, according to some authorities, seems to be the arrangements for planning and funding public schools, parks and community services in rapidly developing population areas.

Length: 1350 words

Exercise VI-18

Readability Score: 47

Communication and Propaganda

(Reprinted by permission from
Guidebook for Prospective Teachers, 1948.)

WAIT FOR SIGNAL TO BEGIN READING

Communicating with Others

Can you imagine yourself living under conditions such that it would be impossible to communicate with other people? You could not get in touch with anyone by using the telephone, telegraph, or letter; you could not turn on a radio and hear other people; you could not attend a motion picture or look at a television screen; you could not get in touch with anyone by writing, talking, painting, reading, or playing any musical instrument. Without some means of communication you would be living in complete isolation. You would be unable to transmit your ideas to other people and unable to receive any ideas from anyone else.

Methods of Evaluating Communications

In this modern world we are constantly subjected to a barrage of information and misinformation, persuasion, deception, and variations of opinion. In our democracy we prize freedom of speech and freedom of the press. This means that we place on the individual a tremendous responsibility for evaluating the ideas which are relayed to him through the radio, press, movies, newspapers, magazines, and personal contacts. Americans are readers of many kinds of material.

As a citizen you have a responsibility for deciding what to believe and what not to believe; what to read and what not to read; what sources are representing special interests and what sources are striving to be fair. This is a process of evaluation which you will have to continue for life. Teachers have a more important task of helping young people to develop some standards for evaluating the material which they receive from the various media of communication.

One of the purposes of education is to develop individuals who will maintain suspended judgments until all available evidence is collected, act intelligently in terms of available information, and evaluate their activity in terms of other evidence that becomes available. Schools should help to give students a range of knowledge that will enlarge the outlook of their minds. But schools must recognize that there are groups which do not wish to encourage the development of that kind of a thinking citizen. Many groups use methods of mass communication to get individuals to make conclusions on partial, cross-sectional, or distorted information. They are desirous of leading people into attitudes which will make them jump to conclusions without paying much attention to available evidence. These attempts to lead people to emotional thinking are usually called *propaganda.* This threat to clear thinking is used on a large scale in the world today. It may not always be "anti-something," but it may be used to lead you to the support of some cause by painting a rosy picture of all the nice aspects of it. A thinking person should beware of communication channels that appeal to his emotions and that encourage him to act quickly without giving careful consideration to the matter at hand. Propaganda can often be detected by some general techniques which are commonly used to mislead your thinking.

Name calling—Bad names are given to those the propagandist would have us condemn; good names to those he would have us favor. Examples are "progressive teacher," "Communist," "bureaucrat," "Conservative," "Jew," "Fraternity Man," "Socialist," "regular fellow," etc.

Glittering generalities—We are told that "the American system is threatened" and are lured with such attractive phrases as "social justice," "the more abundant life," "economic freedom," "the welfare of the common man," etc. These vague terms may have different meanings to everyone, and we frequently put our own meanings into the mouth of the speaker rather than try to decide what he really means by seeing how his actions define his terms.

Flag waving—The propagandist associates his cause with the American flag, the Christian religion, or with some person of great prestige. He attempts to make you feel that loyalty to your God and your country dictates that you agree with him.

Slogans—The propagandist finds some catchy phrase which may stick in one's mind. Then he tries to get it generally accepted without an analysis of its meaning. Examples are "democratic way of life," "it's Luckies 2 to 1," "The skin you love to touch," "For men of distinction," "good to the last drop," etc. Applying the question, ***why, what,*** or ***how*** to some of these slogans may help you see how superficial many of them are.

Repetition and fabrication—The propagandist loves to take an incident and magnify its importance. He is similar to the old gossip who likes to make the story just a little better before she passes it on. By repeating it over and over he attempts to make you accept its validity. You may protect yourself from this to some extent by trying to get at the source of some of your information which you question.

Band-wagon technique—You are led to believe you should do something because "everybody's doing it," "it's smart to be seen at the Cliff Cafe," etc. Campaign managers and advertisers know the human tendency to follow the crowd and will invariably predict victory for their candidate or widespread use of their product. Here again you need to question, "Who is everybody?" "Why is it smart?"

Suppression and distortion of facts—Many of the socioeconomic cartoons lead to considerable distortion of the facts. Many of our labor journal cartoonists would have everyone believe that employers and capitalists are all bloated bigots with tall silk hats. Each political party has cartoonists who try to make the other party look ridiculous. Pictures showing only a limited view of a situation are often used to distort reality. The things that are omitted in a news report may be just the things that you need to know to reach a wise decision. By withholding the whole truth from you, you may be led to reach a decision which the propagandist favors.

Ambush and showmanship—Wealthy interests and pressure groups sometimes use the ambush method of winning public opinion. They may use pressures to get their employees or their debtors to promote their ideas. They may organize "front" organizations which take on an attractive name and carry on the publicity. They may give large sums to philanthropic institutions and then make the institution fight their battles. Oratory many times appeals to the emotions and does not present any facts. In case of doubt, you might try to discover who is financing the group of speakers in question.

These and many other methods may be used to lure the gullible thinker into false and sometimes dangerous conclusions. The tenseness of our international situation and the war of ideologies now going on make it important for you to consider carefully the ideas to which you are exposed.

One of the most important factors influencing the communication of ideas is the reader's understanding. Dr. Edgar Dale has suggested several questions which might be asked in an effort to evaluate your own ability as a reader. Although these questions apply to reading of newspapers primarily, you can frame some parallel questions to apply to magazines, radio programs, movies, speakers, etc.

1. Am I familiar with a number of newspapers, not only the good ones but the poor ones as well?
2. Do I plan my reading in terms of (a) time spent, (b) material read, and (c) the order and speed in which the material is read?
3. Have I examined all parts of the material to find out what's in it?
4. Can I find desired information quickly by using the index, summary, etc.?
5. Am I familiar with the way a typical news story is constructed?
6. Do I get the most out of the big news stories by following them day by day as they develop?
7. Am I able to read, understand, and criticize the editorials in daily newspapers?
8. Do I have an efficient speed and comprehension in reading?
9. Am I familiar with some important factors which influence the nature and accuracy of news: (a) the reader, (b) ownership of the paper, (c) political affiliations, (d) the reporter, (e) the editor, (f) the make-up editor, (g) space restrictions, and (h) advertising?

_______STOP—ASK FOR YOUR TIME_______

Record time immediately and answer the questions on content.

Time ________ Sec.	RATE (from table on page 315):	R. ________
No. Correct ________ (key on page 330)	COMPREHENSION (10% for each correct answer):	C. ________
VI-18	EFFICIENCY (R × C):	E. ________

Record on Progress Chart on page 299

ANSWER THESE QUESTIONS IMMEDIATELY

1. (T—F) Teachers should evaluate all materials presented to students to protect them from misunderstanding the ideas.
2. (C.) In a democracy the evaluation of ideas presented to the public is the responsibility of the ________________.
3. (T—F) Some people do not believe that students should be taught to analyze and evaluate the material they read.
4. (C.) Attempts to lead people to emotional thinking are called ________________.
5. (M.C.) The technique which appeals to one's own definition of terms such as "economic freedom" and "American way of life" is called the technique of:
   ______(1) repetition.
   ______(2) suppression of facts.
   ______(3) flag waving.
   ______(4) glittering generalities.
6. (T—F) The author suggests that you apply the questions "why," "what," and "how" to any slogan approach.
7. (T—F) The "Band-wagon" technique is described as that which uses a popular "name band" to gain attention.
8. (T—F) Socioeconomic cartoons usually present an accurate view of a situation.
9. (T—F) The "Ambush" technique implies the use of some "front" organization to expound the ideas.
10. (M.C.) According to the author one of the most important factors influencing the written communication of ideas is the:
    ______(1) reader's understanding.
    ______(2) political affiliation of the writer.
    ______(3) size and style of type used by the publisher.
    ______(4) newspaper which carries the story.

Length: 1350 words

Exercise VI-19

Readability Score: 42

Hypertension

By George T. Caleel, D.O. and Karen June Prupes

(Reprinted by permission from *Health*, July-August, 1975.)

WAIT FOR SIGNAL TO BEGIN READING

Diagnosing Hypertension

Hypertension, or high blood pressure, is one of the most serious medical problems in the United States today.

Hypertension is a silent disease—most people have few or no early warning signs. One can live with hypertension for years, not realizing that the disease is present, while its damaging effects on the body accumulate. This is why it is so important for everyone to have his blood pressure checked at least once a year.

If a patient has demonstrated elevated blood pressure on at least three successive visits, the physician usually will want to begin a diagnostic evaluation, which includes a detailed family and personal medical history and a thorough physical examination with pertinent laboratory tests. The goals of this evaluation are (1) to determine the severity of hypertension by the absence or the presence and extent of damage to the heart, brain, kidneys, and eyes; (2) to detect any coexisting disease which might affect the patient's outcome or alter the type of treatment to be used; (3) to identify other factors that increase the risk of heart disease and stroke, such as smoking and imprudent eating habits; and (4) to search for a curable cause of the hypertension, which, if corrected, would eliminate the need for life-long medical therapy.

The probability of a patient's becoming hypertensive is increased if he has parents, brothers, or sisters who are hypertensive or who have suffered from or died at a relatively early age of a stroke, kidney failure, or heart failure. In the patient's own history, the following factors increase the risk of developing hypertension and affect its outcome.

Race. Hypertension is more prevalent among blacks than whites.

Sex. Hypertensive women live longer than hypertensive men.

Age. The younger the patient is at the onset of hypertension, the greater is the reduction of his life expectancy.

Variability of blood pressure. A patient whose blood pressure fluctuates widely between high and normal levels will probably have less vital organ damage than a patient with more constant hypertension.

Cholesterol and diabetes. One-third to one-half of all diabetic patients develop high blood pressure. Hypertensive patients with high serum cholesterol or sugar levels have an increased risk of atherosclerosis (hardening of the arteries) and of coronary artery disease.

Cigarette smoking, obesity, and lack of physical exercise. These factors, combined with hypertension, greatly increase the risk of coronary artery disease.

Use of birth control pills and other estrogen therapy. This is a common cause of hypertension in women.

Use of salt. Excessive salt in the diet has been associated with an increased risk of hypertension.

After the physician has taken his patient's history, he will begin to look for physical signs of essential hypertension (the most common type, with no known cause) and for clues to the possibility of secondary or curable hypertension. The patient's height and weight will be measured to detect overweight. Blood pressure will be measured several times, in both arms and perhaps in the thighs, and with the patient standing, sitting, and lying down.

The physician may have to dilate the patient's pupils in order to examine the tiny arteries at the back of the eyes with an instrument called a funduscope. He will look for signs of atherosclerosis, hemorrhages, cotton-wool spots, and swelling of the optic nerve disk. These are often associated with moderate to severe hypertension and reflect the status of the arteries elsewhere in the body.

Examination with the stethoscope, along with a chest x-ray and an electrocardiogram, will reveal damage to the heart. The physician will also listen to the flow of blood through the major arteries to detect any signs of blockage.

Other important signs to be checked for are edema (swelling of the arms and legs due to water retention) and evidence of damage to the brain and nervous system, such as impaired memory and loss of coordination. Palpation of both kidneys will reveal signs of tumor, cysts, and hydronephrosis (retention of urine in the kidney).

Laboratory tests will be performed on samples of the patient's blood and urine to measure cholesterol and sugar levels and to evaluate kidney function.

A small number of hypertensives are ultimately found to have secondary hypertension caused by a curable disease or abnormality. If his patient does not respond satisfactorily to standard treatment for essential hypertension, the physician will begin to search for one of these curable causes. They include kidney diseases, overactivity of the adrenal gland due to tumor or other disease, and severe narrowing of the aorta (the main artery coming from the heart). These problems produce characteristic symptoms and can be diagnosed with sophisticated x-ray techniques and laboratory tests. They usually can be corrected with drugs or surgery.

Treating Hypertension

After the physician has evaluated his hypertensive patient, he will most likely begin a standard two-part therapy program: First, he will ask the patient to adopt living habits that will minimize as many hypertension risk factors as possible. Then he will try to discover the drug or combination of drugs that most effectively lowers the patient's blood pressure with the fewest and mildest side effects.

Hypertensive patients who are overweight must attempt to reduce, using as guidelines the tables of ideal weights published by life insurance companies. These tables are not based on considerations of fashion and personal appearance. They show which height and weight combinations are most frequently associated with good health and long life.

Patients without heart or kidney damage do not have to restrict their salt intake. With the proper drug therapy, even patients with these complications can tolerate about two grams of salt daily.

If laboratory tests show that there is a high level of fats in the blood, the intake of foods rich in saturated fats, cholesterol, and carbohydrates (starches and sugars) must be restricted. Some patients with kidney complications may have to restrict their consumption of protein.

Cigarette smoking is prohibited because it constricts the arteries and thereby raises blood pressure. The physician may allow cigar and pipe smoking if the patient "can't do without it."

Patients with severe heart and kidney damage may need extra rest during the day and may have to avoid strenuous exercise. The physician can perform exercise tests to check the patient's tolerance. Most hypertensive patients will benefit from moderate exercise, like walking, bowling, and calistenics, as long as these are done regularly, not in infrequent bursts of activity.

Anxiety can aggravate high blood pressure. According to one study, the events that most often affect health adversely include the death of a loved one, marital stress, trouble with the law, personal injury or illness, and job difficulties. If tension is a factor, the physician will probably urge his hypertensive patient to talk out his problems and to develop a healthier approach to coping with them.

Antihypertensive drugs fall into three main categories: oral diuretics, sympathetic inhibitors, and vasodilators.

Oral diuretics reduce blood pressure by decreasing the volume of both the blood plasma (the liquid portion in which the blood cells are suspended) and the volume of other fluids in the tissues. This is done by causing the kidneys to excrete excess salt and water in the urine instead of reabsorbing these substances from the blood.

Sympathetic inhibitors are drugs that block the action of what is called the sympathetic nervous system. Certain of these nerves are responsible for narrowing the arteries. When sympathetic inhibitors are taken, the muscles in the walls of the arteries relax, the arteries are widened, and blood flows through them more easily, thus lowering blood pressure.

Vasodilators lower the blood pressure by acting directly on the arteries to relax and widen them.

A patient with mild or moderate hypertension often responds to treatment with an oral diuretic alone. If the diuretic is not completely effective, a sympathetic inhibitor is added. If still more effect is needed, a vasodilator is introduced. The patient must return frequently to his physician for evaluation until the right combination of medications is achieved. And, once his blood pressure is normalized, the patient must adhere strictly to his treatment program in order to maintain that control.

______ STOP __ ASK FOR YOUR TIME ______

Record time immediately and answer questions on content.

Time ________ Sec.	RATE (from table on page 315):	R. ________
No. Correct ________ (key on page 322)	COMPREHENSION (10% for each correct answer):	C. ________
VI-19	EFFICIENCY (R × C):	E. ________

Record on Progress Chart on page 299

ANSWER THESE QUESTIONS IMMEDIATELY

1. (T—F) Hypertension and high blood pressure are different and require different medication and control.
2. (C.) A doctor probably will want to begin a thorough diagnostic evaluation if he discovers high blood pressure in at least ________ successive visits from a patient.
3. (M.C.) Which of the following personal factors was not listed as contributing to an increased risk of an individual's developing hypertension?
   ____ (1) Death of an immediate family member from a stroke.
   ____ (2) Variability of blood pressure.
   ____ (3) Use of birth control pills.
   ____ (4) Excessive physical exercise.
4. (T—F) A large number of hypertension cases seem to have been traced to tumerous cancer as a cause, according to this article.
5. (C.) The most frequent diagnosis for many people is ________ hypertension.
6. (T—F) Secondary hypertension is caused by a curable disease or an abnormality.
7. (T—F) Hypertensive patients with heart or kidney damage have to increase their salt intake.
8. (T—F) Cigarette smoking is prohibited with hypertensive patients because it will constrict the arteries.
9. (T—F) Most hypertensive patients will benefit from moderate exercise.
10. (M.C.) Which of the following was not listed as one of the types of drugs used to control hypertension?
   ____ (1) Anticoagulents.
   ____ (2) Oral diuretics.
   ____ (3) Sympathetic inhibitors.
   ____ (4) Vasodilators.

Length: 1350 words

Exercise VI-20

Readability Score: 36

Oh, Calcutta!

WAIT FOR SIGNAL TO BEGIN READING

It is Sunday afternoon, and scores of parents and their children gather beneath two giant cacti in the center of the city for the cheapest show in town—the "rat zoo." They buy a little grain from the bustling vendors and toss it to the rodents, hordes of which scamper about the area with the impunity of Central Park squirrels. A man dangles a peanut on a string, slowly lifting it above a swarm of stubby forepaws. The peanut descends again as the watching children laugh and clap. Nearby, an old man says that the rat colonies have been here for at least twenty years, eating from people's hands, breeding and dying. The old man says he knows because his family has been living on an adjacent sidewalk—begging, breeding and dying for the same twenty years.

It sounds like a scene from John Gay's "Beggars' Opera," but this is not eighteenth-century London. It is Calcutta, 1970s, an urban hole so black with deprivation and despair that each day at least one of its 8 million inhabitants flings himself off the bridge over the Hooghly River. To be sure, India's principal port—and the world's sixth-largest city—has been teetering on the brink of dissolution ever since the British granted independence and pulled up stakes in 1947. But today nearly every knowledgeable observer predicts that the end—or at least the end of Calcutta as it is now known—may be only a few gasps away. Even its political structure is crumbling.

Psychosis

Despite this, most Calcuttans believe that the city's ultimate demise will be the product of more powerful and pervasive forces than political turmoil. Calcutta's businessmen speak of the city's impending economic collapse as if it had already happened. Its psychiatrists talk of its citizens in terms of mass psychosis. Its sociologists warn that it has become a cultural sink, a place so stripped of human amenity that—as within the rat zoo—the predominant activity is ceaseless, clawing struggle for survival. To experts on cities, it is the last, unspeakable word in urban crisis.

Each day protest marchers block the streets that cows or cars haven't already clogged, driving off the police with Molotov cocktails, guns and even spears. Homemade bombs, which sell for the equivalent of 14 cents apiece, are a thriving business in Calcutta. In the "suburbs," which are no more than vast extensions of the central-city ghetto, mobs frequently surround and imprison any auto carrying a well-dressed driver. Public anger toward the daily transit trauma has reached the point where it is now standard procedure for passengers to overturn and burn stalled buses.

Such events may seem inconceivable to Westerners—even riders of the Long Island Railroad—but then few Westerners could conceive the horrors endured by the typical Calcuttan.

Shelter

Estimates of the number of permanent street-dwellers, whole families that never budge from the steps and gutters, range from 50,000 to as high as one million. At night, the rows of sleeping bodies resemble corpses lined up after a flood or epidemic. The more fortunate reside in slums or *bustees,* where the average roof rests four feet off the ground and the living space rarely exceeds 40 square feet per person.

Services

In the *bustees,* hundreds of thousands wash with and drink the unspeakably polluted water of the Hooghly. A third of the city is serviced by 120 miles of open sewage drains that turn Calcutta into a sea of excrement after a morning's monsoon rain. There is only one bridge spanning the Hooghly River—and 300,000 people struggle to cross it each day, a nightmare that must be seen to be believed.

Medical Care

Except for the wealthy few, medical service is practically nonexistent; the city has fewer than four hospital beds per thousand residents. Lepers languish on the streets and cholera has remained endemic despite a ten-year campaign to contain it. When an ambulance crew recently rescued from the street an old man suffering from smallpox, they could find no doctor to treat him. He wound up being returned to a street corner.

Employment

Calcutta's uncertain future has scared off capital investment and brought on an industrial slowdown. Calcutta University graduates 150,000 students annually, but despite their degrees they must compete for as few as 8,000 new jobs each year. A single civil-service opening may attract as many as 4,000 applicants. By 1986, when some 12.5 million people are expected to be packed along the banks of the Hooghly, economists predict that one million will be without any work and three million will not have enough work.

Inertia

There are those who maintain that Calcutta was doomed the day the British went home, for what they left behind was a wholly unworkable system of administration. Perhaps more so than anywhere else on earth, the local government—in its inertia and unresponsiveness—is the enemy of the people. The publicly held Calcutta Corporation, begun by the British as an experiment in Indian self-government, has degenerated into a politicians' stepping stone to a fat bank account and early retirement. Stripped of its powers after a rash of scandals, the corporation is limited to superintending garbage collection, water and roads—which is to say it does nearly nothing. Independent authorities, highly susceptible to financial chicanery, deal with housing, education and administering the port.

As a result, *ennui* pervades every echelon of administration. There is an old Calcutta saw that goes: "It is hard to succeed here, but it is even harder to fail." This is true. In a government more malignantly bureaucratic than any imagined by Kafka, no one is rewarded for doing well, no one is punished for doing poorly. Nepotism is rife. One expert estimates that very nearly every one of Calcutta Corporation's 30,000 employees is a relative or a close friend of one of the corporation's commissioners.

A major, if aborted, attempt at reform was the formation in 1960 of the Calcutta Metropolitan Planning Organization.

Hope

Amid all this sound and fury, and despite his own increasingly frequent outbursts, the typical Calcuttan maintains a lively and indefatigable sense of hope. Although far removed from the street-dweller's experience, there is a cultural and intellectual side to the city that generates a remarkable measure of civic pride. A bookseller with every reason for depression admits: "I must say, I really do love Calcutta." A coed looks up from her book of Gregory Corso poems and says: "Allen Ginsberg was here. He liked it. For a hippie, he is a very wise man."

Such cheerful equanimity may help make life bearable but it does nothing to arrest Calcutta's snowballing slide. But there is at least one genuinely propitious development. As an inland port, Calcutta's economic lifeline has always been the Hooghly River, which links the city with the Bay of Bengal—a tortuous 120 miles downstream. While world shipping is getting larger, the Hooghly is getting shallower. Already, shifting sand bars and silting have limited Calcutta to handling ships of under 10,000 tons, pretty small potatoes compared with the 100,000 ton juggernauts that Japan is turning out.

Fifty-six miles downstream, however, an army of workers is building a brand-new port—and what may be the world's largest new city. When finished in the mid-1980s, the deep-water port of Haldia will not only revive Calcutta's commerce but ease the population strain on Calcutta by offering housing, schools, recreation centers, and—most important—jobs, mainly in petroleum refineries.

Yet some Calcutta officials privately doubt whether the city can wait for Haldia. And if it topples, they point out, the implications would be global. Hanging over Calcutta—and over the Western nations that may be confronted with Calcuttas to come—lies a prophecy by a 1967 seminar of planning experts: "If Calcutta's final breakdown is to take place, it would be a disaster for mankind of a far more sinister sort than any flood or famine. It would be the confession of failure, at the first major confrontation, of mankind's ability to organize the vast, rapidly growing urban concentrations into which humanity seems inevitably destined to move."

________STOP__ASK FOR YOUR TIME________

Record time immediately and answer the questions on content.

Time ________ Sec.	RATE (from table on page 315):	R. ________
No. Correct ________ (key on page 330)	COMPREHENSION (10% for each correct answer):	C. ________
VI-20	EFFICIENCY (R × C):	E. ________

Record on Progress Chart on page 299

ANSWER THESE QUESTIONS IMMEDIATELY

1. (C.) In Calcutta the cheapest show in town is the ________________.

2. (T—F) Most Calcuttans believe that the city's ultimate downfall will be the product of political turmoil.

3. (T—F) Violent protest is a daily activity in Calcutta.

4. (M. C.) *Bustees* in Calcutta are:

   ______(1) large police raids on dope rings.

   ______(2) slum housing.

   ______(3) ladies' garments.

   ______(4) special drinks made of a particularly potent Indian beverage mixed with water from the Hooghly River.

5. (T—F) Ambulance crews find it occasionally necessary to return sick persons to the streets rather than take them to the hospital because of the shortage of doctors and facilities.

6. (T—F) Because of the new economic program, it is anticipated that by 1986 Calcutta will reach full employment.

7. (C.) The experiment in Indian self-government begun by the British was the ________ Corporation.

8. (T—F) Most Calcuttans, viewing the multiple difficulties the city faces, have given up hope.

9. (T—F) The Hooghly River has always been Calcutta's lifeline.

10. (M. C.) Haldia may be the:

   ______(1) new ruling class in Calcutta.

   ______(2) disease which will wipe out much of Calcutta's excess population.

   ______(3) organization which will ultimately save the city from its own pollution.

   ______(4) largest new city in the world.

SERIES VII
Study Reading Exercises

Instructions

You know very well that some of your reading requires concentrated attention to details with emphasis on long-term retention for examinations or other later application.

These study exercises provide practice in a self-recitation type of reading. They are designed to help you understand some of the principles of self-recitation and spaced review. In a limited sense they provide a practical illustration of the fact that it is easier to remember soon after reading than it is after an interval of time occupied by other reading or other activities. In actual practice, however, you will need to make up your own questions for the periods of self-recitation.

Here the stress is still on increasing the reading speed and the reading level, but involved also is a stress on a study technique that will help improve long-range retention of material read. Here you expose yourself to ideas not only by reading about them, but by pausing frequently to think about them and to apply them to practical questions on the material. You should find that this technique helps to break the monotony of reading and to enable you to read with less tension and less fatigue because you bring into use more than one type of study approach.

These exercises are matched with those in Series VI for length, difficulty, and type of questions asked. Comparisons of your reading rate and reading efficiency scores on these drills with the comparable exercises in Series VI will give you some measure of your progress in mastering this technique of self-recitation as you read.

General directions on these exercises are the same as for those in Series VI except that you do not call for your time until you have finished the tenth question in the exercise. You then compute your *rate, comprehension, and efficiency* as before, using the rate table on page 315 and the keys on pages 322 and 330. Then record your scores on the progress charts for study reading on page 299.

Suggestions

Although standardized exercises measuring efficiency in higher level study skills have not yet been devised, this series of exercises on a study type of reading provides a unique type of reading activity designed to combine some of the best features of developmental reading skills and higher level study skills. Your use of them will expose you to a practical application of some of the study skills that were discussed in detail on pages 19 to 24 of this book. Perhaps a rereading of that material would help you to develop a better understanding of what is attempted here.

This system of reading provides an automatic break every few hundred words, so that you may stop and think about the material read and answer questions about it. This break gives your eyes a chance to rest and to come back to more effective reading on the next unit. The alternating pattern of thinking, reading, thinking, writing, thinking, reading, and so on, helps to keep you more alert and to avoid outside distractions and daydreaming.

The efficiency scores you attain on this series will be a good indication of your success in mastering some basic techniques of self-recitation and applying them to your reading activities.

Nothing in this series will keep you from going back to reread in order to answer questions. There is nothing to keep you from going ahead and reading the questions first, then coming back to read the material. Either of these approaches takes extra time, however, and will keep your rate and efficiency scores down. Hard work and deep concentration should enable you to read materials at a maximum short-term reading rate and to achieve enough short-term retention to handle the questions adequately.

Note that asking and answering questions at intervals do provide additional study skill application to reinforce those ideas that you picked up in rapid reading and to plant them more firmly in your mind. This process reduces the dependence on high levels of initial comprehension and frees you to function at a more rapid rate of initial study reading—in short periods interrupted by the self-recitation activity.

Efficient reading in study situations is not merely word-by-word reading at any rate. Good study habits require other thought processes to back up the reading process and reinforce it.

Good reading habits cannot be defined in terms of rate and comprehension alone. They are characterized by an open mind, a wide range of flexibility in reading rate, a judgment as to relative importance of material being read, and a deep understanding of oneself as related to the reading project at hand. Reading rate as a reading tool is only part of the repertoire of a good reader.

Length: 1350 words

Exercise VII-1

Readability Score: 76

Reading For Culture

By Stephanie T. Rispin

(An original article from the Uniwyo Reading Research Center included with permission of the director.)

WAIT FOR SIGNAL TO BEGIN READING

Reading For Convenience

Henry David Thoreau once said: "Most men have learned to read to serve a paltry convenience. But of reading as a noble intellectual exercise they know little or nothing." Thoreau meant that books should be read as they were written, carefully and with deep thought. Reading in this manner expands your horizons. It challenges your intelligence. It gives you that special quality referred to as culture.

Our society today has become too mechanized. Advancements in technology have rendered us almost unaware of much besides machines or computers. These mechanized objects that we encounter daily leave us thinking and behaving as robots. Real flesh (100) and blood, thinking, feeling people become either unimportant or threatening. We may become afraid of them. Thoreau suggests that there is more to life. This can be gained from reading books. Do not read to merely inform yourself where the next sale is or who is getting married next month. Read to gain new ideas and information. Seek new perspectives and insights.

1. (T—F) The advanced technology of today's society tends to lead us to view other persons as thinking, feeling, people.
2. (T—F) Henry David Thoreau said that books should be read very carefully (200) and with much thought.

What Culture Can Do For You

Culture is found by reading. Through books you can come in contact with the finest minds. You can find the richest ideas. In this spirit, culture has no class boundaries. It is for the working person and the person of leisure alike. And no matter how busy you are in earning a living, you can always take a few minutes each day to read. Thus you can enrich your mind and your life.

It is never too soon or too late to begin. Learning is for all ages. It is for all lifestyles. You are never too (300) old to gain new perspectives of yourself and of the world. Questions must always be asked. Many answers are to be discovered in books. C. S. Lewis said: "In reading great literature I become a thousand men and yet remain myself. I see with myriad eyes but it is still I who see. Here, as in worship, in love, in moral action, I transcend myself. I am never more myself than when I do." Attaining culture helps you (400) to discover who you are, as well as who others are. It opens up the world to a clearer view. You are better able to observe important issues from all aspects, rather than from only the two extremes.

3. (M.C.) Reading is related to culture because:
   ______(1) only the wealthy have the leisure time required for reading.
   ______(2) the poor are pure in heart and therefore appreciate reading.
   ______(3) culture is an inherent trait of the intellectual class.
   ______(4) people of any class can find the time to read.
4. (T—F) Culture must be obtained early in life.

The Meaning of Culture

(500) Culture means many things to many different people. As it is used here, it means the enlightenment and refinement acquired from the development of the mind as a result of learning. This learning, it is believed here, is to be taken from books. Culture will not be found in an accent or on a clothes rack. Culture does not lie in one's behavior. It provides all of one's thoughts and beliefs.

Reading provides the basis for culture. Reading expands one's vision. Reading stimulates creative thought. This may produce emotion and action. Culture will lead to a happy, balanced life. By culture, (600) and thus by reading, can one prevent the stagnation of the mind.

5. (C.) Enlightenment acquired from the development of the mind as a result of learning through reading is labeled by this writer as ________ .
6. (M.C.) This writer believes that the best source of culture is your:
   ______(1) environment.
   ______(2) parents.
   ______(3) reading.
   ______(4) school.

What Kind of Books

When you read for culture, much new knowledge fills you and broadens you. You can stand firmly on your own feet. You can be confident in decisions you make. You will be more secure in making plans. All knowledge is to be treasured. 700 ←

The books you read should be chosen with the same care with which you read them. Books should be thought of as sources of knowledge and culture. Selections should be made wisely. Books can be companions. They can teach you. They can make you laugh or cry. They can open up new worlds to you.

It is very helpful to keep up with literary periodicals. Familiarize yourself with critics' and friends' opinions of books. Find out whether the author's story is one sided, or whether it covers all aspects of the problem. Skim through the book itself to see if the author's style appeals to you. Most 800 ← importantly, do not accept all you read as absolute truth. Only permit books to introduce thought. Respond with your own personal opinion, made clearer by the author's.

Do not avoid fiction. Novels provide us with new situations and new methods of solving problems. Most often a novel is written with the wisdom that the author has gained from personal experience in a similar situation. This insight is presented to the reader for consideration and use. Of course, the author's personal philosophy should not be applied randomly to your own life. Rather it should be considered 900 ← carefully, widening your outlook on a problem. You should make your own decisions.

7. (T—F) Seeking out the opinions of critics and friends is absurd.

Judgments

Judging a book deserves the same fairness given to both choosing and reading a book. Learning about an author in advance provides insight. You may learn why the book was written. You may learn of conflicts in the writer's own life which provided ideas for plots or attitudes. This knowledge should not color your opinion of the book itself. You may disapprove of an 1000 ← author's mode of living or of courses he has chosen in his life. Try not to let these cloud your opinion of the book's philosophy or literary worth.

Similarly, disagreement with the philosophy presented in the book should not color your opinion. Every person is entitled to voice his ideas. Simply because you disagree does not make the book any less worthwhile. The style may be good. At least it may present new and different ideas to you.

8. (C.) Simply because you disagree with an author's lifestyle or actions does not mean that the book has no ________ ________.

Keep A Record

1100 → You should keep a record of books you read, complete with title and author. Include a general summary, your own comments, and some concepts you especially liked or respected. By doing this, your reading can be more extensive and more worthwhile. You can refresh your memory with your records. Review any ideas you may have especially liked or feel may be appropriate for use in future situations.

Also, you might want to plan a long range reading program. Make a list of books you have always wanted to read, or have been curious about. 1200 → Include some of those classics whose names are legendary. Your list will expand as you become more aware of literary columns in current periodicals.

Do not limit yourself to one period, one class, or one author. Read broadly, expanding knowledge and culture.

9. (T—F) The writer encourages you to keep lists of books.

Reading In True Spirit

Reading done in true spirit, consists of seeking an understanding of the author. You must think about the material. You should relate your past experiences and reading in comparison. You should use what wisdom and knowledge you have in comprehension. 1300 → Construction and style need to be appreciated, as well as the content itself.

Reading enables you not only to exist in society, but to enjoy that existence. It makes you complete by encouraging thought.

10. (T—F) Reading should involve an attempt to understand the perspective of the author and to relate to your own experience. 1350 →

______ STOP __ ASK FOR YOUR TIME ______

Record your time immediately, compute your scores and record on your progress chart.

Time __________ Sec.	RATE (from table on page 315):	R. __________
No. Correct __________ (key on page 322)	COMPREHENSION (10% for each correct answer):	C. __________
VII-1	EFFICIENCY (R×C):	E. __________

Record on Progress Chart on page 299

Length: 1350 words

Exercise VII-2

Readability Score: 74

Tiger of the Night

By William C. Shuster

(Reprinted by permission from *Colorado Outdoors,* May-June, 1977.)

WAIT FOR SIGNAL TO BEGIN READING

A 1974 graduate of Colorado State University, William C. Shuster has done research on birds of prey in New Mexico and Colorado. He now works for the U.S. Forest Service and is currently stationed in Fort Collins.

Skunk

The skunk ambled across the clearing, unaware of the coyote who was working his way along the same trail from the opposite direction. A face-to-face confrontation was inevitable. As soon as the skunk raised up his tail in warning, the coyote, wise to the warning, jammed on his brakes and made a wide detour. The skunk ambled on once more.

Unknown to the skunk, two hungry yellow eyes ← 100 were watching his every move. Shortly, the silence of the night was broken by a scream from the skunk, and the night air was saturated with his pungent odor.

What beast is this that will attack a skunk, ignoring the smell which stops all other would-be predators? What animal can kill a skunk so quickly that it cannot fight back? This night hunter is none other than the "Flying Tiger," the great horned owl, ← 200 *Bubo virginianus.* Because of its fierce appetite, it has been trapped and shot by farmers and hunters who blame scarcity of game or loss of poultry on the owl.

The great horned owl—Colorado's flying tiger—hunts at night and is an important predator in nature's scheme. Because of its nocturnal life-style, the owl is rarely seen and is difficult to study.

1. (T—F) The skunk was aware of the owl, but ignored it because he believed that his pungent smell would protect him as it had with the coyote.

Search

During the spring of 1973, I became interested in these owls, and decided to study a pair to find out what they were eating.

Since great horned owls are mostly active at dusk ← 300 and night, I found it difficult to see what they were feeding on. As a result, I studied their pellets which are often deposited under the owls' roosting trees. These pellets are composed of bones, fur, feathers and other indigestible material which are gathered in the owl's ventriculus, or gizzard, and compressed into a pellet which is then regurgitated or "thrown up." By dissecting the pellets and studying their contents, I was able to see what they had been eating.

I had seen owls in Spring Canyon near Fort 400 → Collins off and on, so I decided to check the area out in hopes of finding their nest. Since I did not know where the owls would be, I started at the mouth of the canyon and began checking every pine for the owls and their nest. This may seem like a painstaking task, and I can assure you it was. I had not checked more than 10 trees, however, before I found my first owl, a barn owl. Since I knew his nest was in a small cliff not far away, I was not concerned about him. After taking 500 → a few photos, I moved on.

Magpies had been nesting on the slopes, and their nests were scattered in the pines. Each of these pines had to be climbed and checked out as great horned owls often use them.

2. (C.) Pellets are composed of fur, feathers, bones and indigestible materials which are gathered in the owl's ventriculus or __________ .

3. (M.C.) The writer began his search for the roosts and nests of the great horned owls by looking in the:
   _____(1) holes in the cliffs.
   _____(2) low underbrush.
   _____(3) pine trees.
   _____(4) cottonwood trees.

Jackpot

600 → Two hours and about 200 trees later, I hit the jackpot. While checking the trees, I kept an eye out for pellets and whitewash—sure indications of roosting trees. This one tree had many pellets cast around its base. Looking up the tree, I found myself staring into the face of a very awake owl. I soon won the staring contest—the owl leaped off its perch and glided to a nearby pine.

Knowing the nest would be nearby, I eagerly searched the area. As I approached a pine with a magpie nest, the other owl flew out of the nest to 700 → another tree. I had read reports of owls attacking people too close to their nest, so I warily climbed a tree near the nest tree. I made sure I knew exactly where the owls were at all times while I checked out the nest.

During this time, they were flying from tree to tree, hooting and bill-snapping. The nest was about 30 feet above the ground, so I had to climb to the top of the neighboring pine, which left me in an exposed position. My neck began to feel like the pivot of an antiaircraft gun from turning my head so often.

I did get to look inside the nest however. There ← 800 were four pure white owlets, two half eaten rabbits and one vole. Obviously, the owlets were not lacking food! The adults never did come close to me, but I always was careful not to turn my back on them for very long.

Once I found their nest, it was a simple matter finding their other roosting trees. Every time I went to the study area, I was able to find the owls, now that I knew where to look. I collected the pellets only under the roost trees to be sure the pellets came from the two ← 900 owls and not from the barn owl or others in the area.

4. (T—F) The writer was concerned about a possible attack from his back by adult owls.

Pellets

By studying the pellets, I found that the voles, which look like fat mice with short tails, were the most common prey. The rabbits and hares were second, but because of their large size, they were the most important prey item. It took a lot of voles to equal one rabbit!

Other people have studied the diet of the great horned owl, and it seems that the owl will change its ← 1000 diet according to what prey is available. At one study area in Oregon, a pair of owls fed on large bark beetles almost exclusively. Apparently there was a population explosion of these beetles at the time of the study, and the owls took advantage of this abundance.

Skunks are a preferred food, as the owl will quickly attack and kill any skunk it sees. The owl usually ends up smelly for a month or two, but this does not seem to bother it at all. Other prey taken by the owls include deer mice, woodrats, Steller's jays, ← 1100 magpies and prairie dogs.

5. (C.) The most commonly eaten prey by the owls were ________________, which look like mice with short tails.

6. (T—F) In Oregon, one pair of owls fed almost exclusively on large bark beetles which are abundant in that region.

7. (M.C.) The writer studied the food intake and eating habits of the great horned owls primarily by:
______(1) looking in nests.
______(2) observing hunting habits.
______(3) counting the owlets.
______(4) analyzing the pellets.

8. (T—F) 1200 → The owl is the only predatory bird that feeds on rodents and such, but will not feed on birds.

The owl is an important predator, keeping the animals it feeds on from becoming too numerous. For instance, rodents, because of their high reproductive rate, can soon overrun an area and cause serious agricultural damage should predation fail to control their numbers.

So by keeping the rodents from being too abundant, the great horned owl does a service to any neighboring farmer. In this capacity, the owl helps maintain the delicate balance of nature. Thus, the great horned owl is an intricate part of the environ- 1300 → ment and deserves the protection state and federal laws now give it.

9. (T—F) The owl is an inefficient predator because the numerous rodent populations are not controlled by the smaller size of the owl population.

10. (T—F) The great horned owl is an intricate part of the environment and de- 1350 → serves protection.

______ STOP __ ASK FOR YOUR TIME ______

Record your time immediately, compute your scores and record on your progress chart.

Time __________ Sec.	RATE (from table on page 315):	R. __________
No. Correct __________ (key on page 330)	COMPREHENSION (10% for each correct answer):	C. __________
VII-2	EFFICIENCY (R × C):	E. __________

Record on Progress Chart on page 299

Length: 1350 words

Exercise VII-3

Readability Score: 71

Hubbell Trading Post

By O. F. Oldendorph

(Reprinted by permission from *National Parks & Conservation Magazine*, October, 1970.)

WAIT FOR SIGNAL TO BEGIN READING

Origin

The name of Hubbell has been well known in Navajo Country ever since Don Lorenzo Hubbell founded his trading post at Ganado, Arizona, in 1876. The post eventually became the hub of a system of trading establishments that served the Navajo people in many parts of their reservation.

In the Southwest, the trader filled an important need; he was a link between the white man's world and that of his bronze-skinned neighbors. He brought them food, cloth, tools, saddles, and harness for teams—items that made life a bit more comfortable or secure. He provided the Indians a market for wool (100) from their flocks, and he encouraged the weaving of artful rugs by paying the women higher prices for their better work. He brought silver to the smith and bought the beautifully made turquoise and silver jewelry that is so much a part of the red rock Indian country. Sometimes a trader filled a more intangible but no less important niche in the lives of the people. Hubbell became an advisor, an arbiter of differences, and a source of help during sickness or domestic or financial difficulty.

1. (C.) Hubbell Trading Post was founded in Ganado, Arizona in ____ (year). (200)
2. (T–F) Hubbell encouraged the Navajo women to weave artful rugs by offering them better tools with which to work.

Development

Eventually Don Lorenzo built his home adjacent to the trading post, using materials of the country and furnishing it in a gracious manner that combined the furniture of the East with the art of his neighbors. Navajo rugs covered the floors and were used as bed coverings. In the long living room, a collection of Indian baskets was attached to the beamed ceiling, and pottery and countless other artifacts stood on shelves or over the fireplace. Well- (300) filled bookcases lined some of the living room walls, and through the years, sketches and paintings by dozens of artists who visited Ganado were hung to cover most of the available wall space.

The home was self-sufficient with a reliable source of water available, and the fields produced corn, grain, and vegetables. Bread was baked in an outdoor oven, and cattle and sheep were abundant. It is not surprising that Hubbell's became a stopping place for writers, artists, scientists, and Presidents who were attracted to the wide spaces of the Navajo country and its people.

(400) In 1920 a young lady came to Ganado from the East to serve as a schoolteacher, and in time she married Don Lorenzo's son, Roman. In 1930 Don Lorenzo died and was buried near his trading post. Management of the post passed, in time, to Mrs. Roman Hubbell, and she continued to operate it for many years.

In the meantime the rutted dirt roads were replaced with paved highways, and the American tourist discovered Navajoland. Many visited Hubbell's seeking the colorful rugs or the silver and turquoise, or they stopped only for cold soft drinks or camping supplies.

(500) The Navajo is not an impulsive buyer. Even today, a trip to the trading post usually requires a walk of several miles or a trip of many more miles in the family horsedrawn wagon or pickup truck. The visit to the post is an opportunity to meet friends and exchange news, and combines sociability and business.

In 1966 Mrs. Hubbell reached the difficult but inevitable decision to retire from the trading business. Much to their credit, the National Park Service, as early as 1957, had recognized in Hubbell's an irreplaceable bit of Americana and had surveyed it as a possible national historic site. The preliminary (600) work had been completed at the time of Mrs. Hubbell's decision, and the trading post came under the administration of the Park Service on April 3, 1967.

Even more important was the realization that Hubbell's must not be relegated to the status of a "preserved site." It was a viable enterprise upon being delivered to the National Park Service, and it offered the possibility for a truly unique addition to the Service. Since operating a trading post is not part of the National Park Service Charter, an interesting and ingenious arrangement was worked out.

3. (M. C.) Hubbell's home was furnished with furniture from the:
   ______(1) Indians.
   ______(2) East.
   ______(3) Orient.
   ______(4) Mid-west.

4. (M. C.) Which of the following people does the article NOT mention as stopping at Hubbell's?
   ______(1) Presidents.
   ______(2) Writers.
   ______(3) Scientists.
   ______(4) Mechanics.

5. (T—F) Don Lorenzo Hubbell died in 1957.

6. (T—F) The trading post became a tourist attraction.

Current Operation

The federal government acquired the 150 acres of real estate and the 11 buildings and structures that comprised Hubbell's. Included were the trading post, the Hubbell home and its furnishings, and other outlying buildings.

Operation of the trading post was undertaken by the Southwest Parks and Monuments Association, an organization headquartered in Globe, Arizona, that works closely with the Park Service. Visitors to southwestern parks know the Association through its publications of trail guide pamphlets and for the books, reports, and color slides that usually are for sale at the information desk in the visitor center.

The Association hired Bill Young to manage the trading business at Hubbell's and a more qualified man would have been very difficult to find. He had been trading with the Navajo for 47 years, spoke their language fluently, and was widely respected as a man of integrity. Today he continues to trade with the Navajo. He buys their rugs, silver, wool, and lambs with the same critical eye that he exercised when he operated his own trading post. It is a "strictly business" operation, separate from the Park Service administration of the site, but one that obviously cooperates with that administration.

The Southwest Parks and Monuments Association is not a commercial enterprise. Profits resulting from publications or from the operation of Hubbell's are turned back as help to the parks and monuments of the Southwest. The Association tries to provide equipment and interpretative aids that make the parks of the area better able to present their story to the public.

Wes Wolfe, the ranger in charge at Hubbell's and a historian by training, moved to Ganado about a year before Mrs. Hubbell moved away. During that year he helped in the trading post and learned to know the Navajo people and the background of the historic site from Mrs. Hubbell. He heard stories of the family, the home, and its visitors that, repeated, now give the conducted tours warmth and a human quality.

Entrance to the home is via a wide-screened porch; the porch floor is covered with Navajo rugs that Mrs. Hubbell said were already in place when she first arrived many years ago. The door opens into the long-beam-ceilinged living room that has comfortable looking chairs, a large fireplace, bookcases, and many works of art. Navajo rugs cover the planked floor, and Hopi pottery graces tables and shelves.

The Park Service intends to maintain the live atmosphere of the home just as in the operation of the trading post. There are no cords across doorways to exclude visitors from any of the rooms, and there are no protective covers on the Navajo rugs—a type of textile that literally defies wear. Wisely, visitors are not admitted to the home except during tours conducted by Park Service personnel.

Because of the dual management—with the Southwest Parks and Monuments Association—Hubbell Trading Post National Historic Site is unique in the Park Service. It is real. It is alive. It operates still as it did through the years that made it famous. So long as the Navajo people live in their traditional manner, Hubbell's will give visitors a glimpse of the old Southwest.

7. (C.) Hubbell's is an alive and unique operation because of its ________ administration.

8. (T—F) Southwest Parks and Monuments Association is a non-profit organization.

9. (T—F) Entrance to the Hubbell home is through a wide-screened porch.

10. (T—F) Cords are placed across the doorways to keep visitors from entering the rooms of the home.

______STOP—ASK FOR YOUR TIME______
Record your time immediately.

Time __________ Sec. RATE (from table on page 315): R. __________

No. Correct __________ COMPREHENSION (10% for each correct answer): C. __________
(key on page 322)

VII-3 EFFICIENCY (R × C): E. __________

Record on Progress Chart on page 299

Length: 1350 words

Exercise VII-4

Readability Score: 70

Sage Country Showman

By George Padget

(Reprinted by permission from *Wyoming Wildlife,* September, 1957.)

WAIT FOR SIGNAL TO BEGIN READING

Appropriate Name

If you hunted sage grouse last month you hunted the biggest grouse on the North American continent. You hunted the only native upland game bird in Wyoming whose numbers are still great enough to warrant a hunting season. You hunted a bird that despite its size—sometimes as big as seven pounds—can cover several miles, at the rate of 45 to 50 miles an hour. You hunted the bird whose mating antics are believed to have influenced the dances of American Indian tribes.

The sage grouse is aptly named for its range is restricted pretty much to sagebrush country, and in winter it lives almost entirely on sagebrush leaves. It's often called the sage chicken or sage hen, but don't confuse it with the prairie chicken, because it's a different bird.

In the early days, sage grouse abounded wherever sagebrush was plentiful. Flocks of thousands gathered at water holes in the west. Their home stretched from southern Canada to northern New Mexico.

Then the land was settled and was overgrazed. Large areas were burned as cultivation pushed westward. The sage grouse suffered sharp declines, was entirely wiped out in parts of its original home, not so much because pioneers used it extensively for food, but because its own home—its cover and food supplies—were damaged to the point of being untenable for sage grouse.

1. (T—F) The sage grouse is slightly responsible for some of the dances of the American Indian tribes.
2. (M.C.) The sage grouse population declined because of:
   ____(1) extensive hunting.
   ____(2) cultivation and civilization.
   ____(3) migration.
   ____(4) drouth.

Less Hunting Now

Although he was only slightly responsible for the fading of the sage grouse, the hunter suffered because hunting, necessarily, was stopped.

The decline reached its peak in the late 1940's. Then came more favorable weather, range conditions improved, better land use methods had been effected. The sage grouse staged a comeback. And this year, Wyoming—one of the top sage grouse hunting states—had its most liberal season in many years. All or parts of ten counties were opened to hunting.

Today, sage grouse live in large areas of Wyoming, Montana, Idaho, Oregon, Nevada, Utah and Colorado. They live more or less throughout Wyoming, except in the northwest and southeast corners of the state. They're found, too, in smaller areas of Washington, California, New Mexico, Nebraska, the Dakotas and in Canada, just above the Montana border. Even so, its range isn't nearly as large as it used to be.

On its upper body, the male sage grouse is mostly black. Its wings are grayish brown above, white beneath, tail feathers are black and gray. Its breast is white. Cocks and hens look a lot alike, but the males are almost twice as big. The hen's coloring is duller, more mottled and she lacks the distinctive white marking on the front of the neck and breast.

3. (C.) The sage grouse reached the peak of its decline in the late ________.
4. (T—F) The sage grouse is found entirely in the Rocky Mountain States.
5. (T—F) The male cock is bigger than the female but the female has the prettiest coloring.

Mating Season

The mating season behavior of the male sage grouse is spectacular. In April, cocks that live in an area several miles square congregate at "strutting" grounds. These are usually in open areas and may range in size from less than an acre to several acres. Here, on clear, quiet mornings, the males perform their mating dances. Maybe three or four hundred cocks show up, maybe only a few. The hens are on hand, but their role is less active. They merely pick their favorite spots to receive the male and settle down to watch the show. The male goes into his dance.

He arches his tail in full spread. Then he erects his head feathers into an umbrella and holds his head high. He sucks air into the air sacs on his neck and holds his wing tips near the ground. Next he sucks air in gulps, filling the air sacs. Then he runs forward. As he runs, the edges of his wings scrape the cape feathers, making a swishing sound. He repeats all this three times. By then his air sacs are full, bouncing up and down on his great, white breast. The contracted neck muscles cause the bare membranes to vibrate, and a loud, resonant plopping sound can be heard for long distances.

These pompous movements and the quick, short runs forward, accompanied by the swaying of the body, are believed to have been copied by Indian dancers, or at least to have influenced their dances.

If you think the males aren't busy boys at this time of year, keep in mind that the mating season lasts at least a month, sometimes three, and that a cock might repeat his strenuous dance as many as 12 times a minute. Fortunately for him, he needn't perform all day, nor every day.

6. (T—F) During the mating dance, it is the male who does the dancing instead of the female.

7. (M. C.) During the mating season the cock may repeat his dance as many as:
   ______(1) five times during the evening.
   ______(2) twelve times during the evening.
   ______(3) twelve times a minute.
   ______(4) three times a minute.

Care of the Young

By the time the mating season ends, most of the hens have left their nesting sites. They often nest close to low sagebrush plants, in dry areas, near water. The hen lays seven or eight eggs and sets on them about 25 days, until they hatch. The chicks are mottled, a grayish black in color.

Care of the chicks is left entirely to the mother. The cocks have long since gathered in flocks restricted pretty much to males. The hen teaches her babes their feeding habits and how to escape danger. If danger threatens, she calls a warning. The chicks run to escape, while the mother feigns injury. If this fails, she attacks the enemy with loud cackling and hissing.

Still, her watch over her brood doesn't seem to be as good as some birds. Maybe it needn't be since other hens in the area will readily adopt stray chicks. It's not at all unusual to see a hen with more chicks than she hatched.

Generally speaking, sage grouse don't migrate, but in summer adult cocks often live in higher altitudes, if water is available. They sometimes winter at higher elevations than the hens and young cocks, too.

The grouse feed during the early morning, loaf in high sagebrush during the middle of the day and feed again before roosting.

Their daily travels may cover a few hundred yards or several miles, in search of food. In summer they eat a variety of plants and insects, but in winter their food consists almost entirely of sagebrush leaves. If necessary, they can live for days without water, longer with no moisture but dew. However, good water supplies are necessary to healthy sage grouse flocks. In the winter they can get along by eating snow.

Experts agree that sage grouse should be hunted in the fall since they are comparatively tame in the summer. They prefer to walk, rather than fly and they are not much of a sporting proposition until fall when families break up and birds become extremely wary. Seasons have been opened in August because some hunters say early snows keep them from the hunting field. Others say they can't tell young birds from old ones in the fall. Frankly, sage grouse would be better off if they couldn't. The birds don't reach full physical size until late November. The man who knows his birds can tell the difference in young and mature birds in October.

8. (T—F) Both parents help raise the chicks.

9. (T—F) The sage grouse are not as good as some other birds in taking care of their brood.

10. (C.) Experts agree that sage grouse should be hunted in the ______.

______STOP—ASK FOR YOUR TIME______

Record your time immediately.

Time ________ Sec.	RATE (from table on page 315):	R. ________
No. Correct ________ (key on page 330)	COMPREHENSION (10% for each correct answer):	C. ________
VII-4	EFFICIENCY (R×C):	E. ________

Record on Progress Chart on page 299

Length: 1350 words

Exercise VII-7

Readability Score: 63

Vicious Genius

By George Ott

(Reprinted by permission from *National Wildlife,* June-July, 1970.)

WAIT FOR SIGNAL TO BEGIN READING

He's one of the most savage and relentless battlers of the wild; for his size, the most ferocious animal in the world. Pound for pound, claw for claw, no living thing can match the wolverine.

Squat and bear-like, seldom weighing more than 40 pounds, largest of the weasel family, he is a terror to all other animals. A wolverine in California's Sierra Nevadas once came upon two bears devouring a fresh carcass. Every hair bristling, he hoisted his tail and charged. As the little marauder leaped between them, the bears fled.

Once in the north woods a wolverine forced a pack of hungry wolves from a meal. After nonchalantly consuming all he desired of the kill, the wolverine sprayed the remains with his evil-smelling scent in order that the wolves would not return to eat.

Utterly fearless, he neither asks nor gives quarter. He can and will fight anything, anywhere. As he rushes into combat he growls and grunts. No matter what the odds, he never gives ground; it is victory or death. His jaws and teeth are immensely strong, capable of crushing large bones and tearing the toughest flesh. The heavy-clawed paws also are devastating, death-dealing instruments.

1. (M. C.) The subject of this article is a member of what family?
   ______(1) Cat.
   ______(2) Bear.
   ______(3) Weasel.
   ______(4) Otter.
2. (C.) The animal discussed in this article is the ________________.

Huskies Are No Match

Even a full team of Alaskan huskies is no match for him. On one occasion, a wolverine encountered a pack of the big dogs and swept through them like a tornado, leaving behind a trail of torn flesh.

Another time, one was known to have killed a polar bear; quite a feat when the great bear may weigh more than 1,000 pounds, and is regarded as master of the polar world.

The wolverine is driven by a ravenous appetite, waging a never-ending campaign for food. He plods through the forest, feeding on anything edible. He is so skilled a hunter he rarely is found in a starved condition. However, his voracious appetite sometimes is the wolverine's undoing. When pressed for food, he will attack even a porcupine. Dead wolverines have been found, their insides loaded with quills.

Compared to some of the animals he preys upon, he is a slow traveler. So he kills caribou or mountain sheep by cunning and stealth. Climbing into a tree or onto a rock ledge, he springs onto his prey, ripping their throats with his fangs, or crushing their spines with his powerful jaws.

Most short-legged animals are handicapped by deep snow, but not the wolverine. Stiff hairs extending from his large paws provide him with built-in snowshoes, enabling him to cover great distances without tiring. In winter when snow lies deep upon the ground, the wolverine will run down and kill elk or moose which are bogged down in drifts.

Eskimos call him the Evil One; they believe that the soul of a great hunter dwells within his body, a soul that exists only to annoy other hunters. Indians say he houses the spirit of the devil.

To North Canadian trappers the wolverine is "The Devil of the Woods," with the "cunning of ten men." They hate him. Not only will he eat anything, but no animal can match his ability for devastation.

Should any woodsman encounter the wolverine in his territory, he prepares for the worst, knowing he will be followed as he makes the rounds of his trap lines and that the bait will be stolen from trap after trap. If a fur-bearing animal has been caught, it may be eaten or ripped to pieces. The traps may be carried away, buried, or put in a river.

As if this were not menace enough, a wolverine coming upon a trapper's cabin may break in, devour what he can, and strip the cabin bare, stealing things he can't possibly use.

One of the little raiders once spent night and day for almost a week working his way through a huge pile of logs to get at a food cache. An expert from Chicago's Field Museum reported the hungry animal chewed through logs a foot in diameter. Other logs which he pulled aside were ten times his weight. At another time one dug through several feet of hard frozen earth to get at a supply of food. His teeth and claws are not designed for this kind of work, so these achievements are all the more impressive.

3. (T – F) The only animal feared by the "vicious genius of the woods" is the husky dog.
4. (T – F) This animal climbs trees and attacks deer and caribou by dropping on them.
5. (T – F) This animal never kills or destroys wantonly.

Learn from Mother

These destructive activities give the wolverine a reputation as a relentless marauder. However, wild animals are neither good nor bad; they earn their living according to instincts bestowed by their Creator.

800

Antisocial and belligerent, the wolverine avoids even his own kind. Adults live alone except during the short mating period in the spring. A female will den in a dense growth of conifers, beneath the shelter of an overhanging rock, or at the base of a hollow tree. Sometime in May or June her two or three wooly cubs are born. Though the species may defile the possessions of man and animals, the mother keeps a tidy den.

900

During the short summer the cubs get a brief course in hunting. With the coming of fall, when they are two-thirds grown, the mother leaves them to kill their own food.

Following the general rule, the most dangerous wolverine is a mother with her young. She is pure ferocity, absolutely without fear, and so powerful and quick of movement that she endangers an armed man. It has been said that a mother bear may attack you; a she-wolverine with young is certain to.

This plunderer's only weakness is his eyesight—he is particularly susceptible to snow blindness. Sometimes on bright days he will sit erect on his haunches, shading his eyes with one paw. Though he prefers to forage by night, he often prowls the woods by day.

1000

6. (T – F) The mother with cubs seldom attacks unless cornered or threatened.
7. (C.) The animal's main weakness is his __________________.

Valuable Fur

The world's annual harvest of wolverine pelts is about 1,000. The fur has an unusual characteristic which makes it especially valuable in the Far North. It is the only fur that won't accumulate frost when the temperature drops to 60 or 70 below zero. Knowing this, the Eskimo uses it to trim the parts of his parka which contact his face and wrists for, unlike other furs, it will not mat and freeze to the skin in very cold weather.

1100

A lover of cold climates, the wolverine roams the northern parts of Eurasia and North America. On our continent he once ranged from the Arctic Ocean south into Pennsylvania, Colorado, and California. But long ago this fierce predator was exterminated in all states east of the Rocky Mountains. Michigan, the Wolverine State, has seen none for more than a century. A few still roam the Sierras and the Montana Rockies but, for the most part, they are found today only in Alaska and northern Canada.

1200

However, there is no immediate danger of the wolverine becoming extinct. Craftier than a fox, bolder than a grizzly, the shaggy little creature seems destined to forever prowl the Northland.

It is good that he will endure, for this wild, free rover of the woods is part of the unspoiled, primitive world, an animal which long has played a unique role in the never-ending drama of the American earth.

1300

8. (T – F) The fur is valuable because it accumulates no frost in extremely cold weather.
9. (M.C.) This animal is found mostly in:
   ______(1) Alaska and Northern Canada.
   ______(2) the Sierras and Montana Rockies.
   ______(3) the Tetons.
   ______(4) the Appalachians.
10. (T – F) There is little danger of this animal becoming extinct.

1350

______STOP__ASK FOR YOUR TIME______

Record your time immediately.

Time __________ Sec.	RATE (from table on page 315):	R. __________
No. Correct __________ (key on page 322)	COMPREHENSION (10% for each correct answer):	C. __________
VII-7	EFFICIENCY (R × C):	E. __________

Record on Progress Chart on page 299

Length: 1350 words

Exercise VII-8

Readability Score: 63

Burglar Safe

By Lorinda Redmond

(Reprinted from an original article of the Uniwyo Reading Research Center by permission of the director.)

WAIT FOR SIGNAL TO BEGIN READING

Burglary Rates Soaring

Burglary rates are going up everywhere. There is an increase in burglaries taking place during the day. We not only have to make sure everything is locked up when we go to bed, such precautions also need to be taken for the daytime when we go to work and the house is left unoccupied for the day. A skilled burglar can pick up key information without anyone knowing. All a burglar need do is keep track of such cues as when people go to work and when they come home.

The first precaution to be taken to protect your home and belongings is to lock your doors. This provides a barrier so that a burglar cannot just walk in. If the door is locked, the burglar will have to try other measures to get in, and he is risking getting caught, especially during the day.

Watch for peculiar or strange persons hanging around the neighborhood. Be aware of any peculiar person ringing the doorbell and asking for a fictitious person. This is a burglar's way of staking out the area, searching for a home where no one will answer.

If you suspect that something strange like this is occurring, call the police and report it. This will help prevent more suspicious behavior and, therefore, will help prevent more crimes.

1. (T—F) Burglary rates are increasing because more burglars are now operating during daytime hours.
2. (C.) Locked doors increase the possibility of the burglar getting ______ ______.

Advice for Homeowners

In addition to locking your doors day and night, there are other safety measures to remember. At night, and when gone on vacations, keep all entrances to your home illuminated. Make it look like someone's home. Besides being a cue that the house may be occupied, this helps neighbors to watch for strange activities. Always have a neighbor keep a watch on your home when you are on vacation. In addition, you can call your local police department and they will assign someone to check your property periodically.

A mailbox crammed with mail is another indication that a house is unoccupied. If you are going on vacation, have your mail stopped or else have neighbors pick it up every day. Other indications of an unoccupied home include uncollected milk, newspapers, an unanswered telephone, an empty garage, and notes indicating that the occupant will return at some time later. Leaving such cues is a serious risk to your belongings and your home. Protect your home by having neighbors pick up such items daily.

A strong lock on your doors is essential, but not very efficient without the backup of a strong door also. The best type of strong door for added protection is a metal door with no glass panes in the surrounding frame panels. A solid-core wooden door which is at least an inch and three-quarters thick is also beneficial for the purpose of added protection.

Besides the door itself, the door frame should be a well-reinforced one, preferably made of a strong metal. With a weak frame, the occupants are risking the possibility of the frame being spread. This can be done with an automobile jack or jimmy, which in turn by-passes the effectiveness and safety provided by the door and lock. Therefore the door should fit snugly within the strong, reinforced frame in order to provide greater protection.

3. (T—F) Always keep a neighbor informed when you are away on vacation.
4. (M.C.) The safest door to install is a:
   - ______(1) metal door without glass panes.
   - ______(2) metal door with glass panes.
   - ______(3) solid-core wooden door.
   - ______(4) combination storm door.
5. (T—F) All reinforced door frames are metal.

Locks

When it comes to locks there are a number of types to be chosen from. The main point is to install locks which increase protection. A good mortised-in lock with a dead bolt can help increase the security of a good door. A dead bolt is a straight bar which is usually rectangular, with a squared off, not beveled end.

Advantages of a dead bolt lock are that it is strong and it cannot be opened with a plastic card or a thin steel strip. The dead bolt of a lock or any slide bolt which is used to back up the lock should be long enough to extend three-quarters of an inch to one inch into the door jamb when the bolt is in the locked position. If it is any shorter than this, there is a possibility of spreading.

Locks which are not mortised and that are placed at the edge of the door inside are called rim locks. Rim locks are generally locked by a key on the outside and by a knob inside. Two types of rim locks commonly in use are the horizontal bolt and vertical bolt. The vertical bolt resists an attempt at forced entry by the spreading of a door frame. This is considered the more secure of these two types of rim locks.

Making Windows Burglar Proof

Providing a home with additional safety by window locks is advantageous toward keeping burglars away, but this also provides disadvantages. There is a problem of compromising fire safety when increasing burglar security. A dead bolt lock opened from the inside and outside with a key provides safety from intrusion but could cost a life if it interferes with quick escape in the event of a fire emergency.

6. (T—F) The best rim locks have horizontal bolts.
7. (T—F) Keyed locks on windows may increase security at the risk of personal safety.
8. (C.) A good mortised-in lock should have a ____________________.

Community Efforts for Crime Prevention

Community crime prevention programs are taking place across the country. The biggest program is "Neighborhood Watch", administered by the National Sheriff's Association. Essentially, the program is a block-by-block organization of citizens who are trained by the police to secure their own homes and to watch out for burglars. The overall effect of this program is the reduction of burglary rates. This reduction is made possible through placing "Neighborhood Watch" decals in windows of your home, which hinders criminal acts.

Operation Identification is another nationwide program in which valuables are engraved with the owner's social security number or driver's license number. Operation Identification decals are given to the participants of this program to be put on the windows or doors of their homes. If a burglar is caught with marked property, he's as good as convicted. Therefore this identification helps to keep burglars away. An additional advantage to the owners of marked stolen property is that the owner gets his marked property back if it is recovered. With the proof of identification on file with the local police department it is easy to prove who the stolen property belongs to rather quickly.

Alarms

Electronic alarm systems will deter burglars, but are quite expensive. Two kinds of electronic systems are a local alarm, designed to frighten burglars and a silent alarm which signals police headquarters or a security service. The silent alarm systems may cost up to $600 for installation, plus an additional monitoring charge.

The least costly alarms are "contact devices" which are mechanical switches attached to doors or locks. Contacts cause an electric circuit, sounding an alarm when broken. These devices are relatively cheap, costing as little as $2 each, but one needs to be installed at every point of entry for maximum security to be possible.

To provide your home and your family with the security needed, take the necessary precautions, such as installing strong locks and using them; support your windows and doors; and by all means, make it appear that someone is home by illuminating your home inside and also entrances.

9. (M.C.) Which of the following is a block-by-block organization administered by the National Sheriff's Association:
   ______(1) Operation Identification.
   ______(2) Nite Watçh.
   ______(3) N.S.A. Patrol.
   ______(4) Neighborhood Watch.
10. (T—F) Contact devices are one of the most expensive alarm systems available.

______ STOP___ASK FOR YOUR TIME ______

Record your time immediately, compute your scores and record on your progress chart.

Time __________ Sec. RATE (from table on page 315): R. __________

No. Correct __________ COMPREHENSION (10% for each correct answer): C. __________
(key on page 330)

VII-8 EFFICIENCY (R×C): E. __________

Record on Progress Chart on page 299

Length: 1350 words

Exercise VII-9

Readability Score: 61

Memories In Stone

By Dorothy Brant Warnick

(Reprinted by permission from *Travel Magazine,* January, 1970.)

WAIT FOR SIGNAL TO BEGIN READING

The Convict

As you wander about the United States, you will see many strange and unusual statues, memorials and monuments. Many of these have heart-warming stories or unusual tales of why they were erected.

For example, in Crestline, California, there is a statue of a man bending over with both hands holding an axe. But even more curious is the face of the man. The eyes are Oriental, the nose Negro, and the mouth and chin Caucasian. Yet no one in the little village seems to think the statue peculiar. You have only to ask to learn the story.

Crestline is a quiet hamlet, a place where tourists are made welcome, but also a place where the natives are glad when the visitors leave and they once again have the peaceful surroundings to themselves. Accustomed to their quiet retreat, the 4,800 citizens were concerned when, in 1956, ground near Pilot Rock, adjacent to the town, was being cleared for a new campsite. When they further learned that the camp was to be one for convicts and that these convicts would live in a park-like setting where they could roam freely, with no walls or fences to stop them, the citizens were horrified.

Yet, despite their violent objections, the camp was completed. In 1960, carefully screened convicts, who had been trained in conservation and fire fighting, began to stream into the little village by the truckloads. Crestliners turned their backs on the newcomers and installed double locks on their doors.

Despite the fact that the men worked on re-seeding burned-out forests and building firebreaks, which benefited the area, the people refused to relent. It took a tragic event to change things and that occurred when an enemy far worse than the threat of convicts struck the little town: fire! It raged and roared its way closer and closer to the lovely village—a fire that could not be controlled from the State Forest Service's borate bombers, and fire that had to be fought from the ground.

The well-trained convicts were called in. They were spread thinly through the fire area and put to work. Men had disappeared before when fighting fire. What was to stop them? They faced a difficult fight, possible death by burning, and had only a town that had repulsed them to the rear. But they did not run. They stayed and fought, and the fire was turned away from its path of destruction. The weary men, many with burned faces and blistered hands, went back to their prison. If some noted that the people had smiled and waved as they returned through the village, they were sure the Crestliners would soon forget and that everything would be the same as before. It did not happen that way, however.

The people remembered. They remembered with Pilot Rock Appreciation Day. It was the Governor of California who unveiled the statue. It is since then that the people hold meetings with the convicts in an attempt to make them a part of the community. Crestline is proud of its convicts and the statue, purposely designed as a composite of them all.

1. (T–F) The natives of Crestline were against construction of a camp for convicts near their town.
2. (T–F) The roaring fire which threatened Crestline could not be controlled by Forest Service bombers.
3. (C.) The people of Crestline are ______ of its convicts.

The Sea Gulls

It was a miracle that is commemorated in Salt Lake City, Utah. It is perhaps a familiar story to many, but bears retelling. The Monument shows two bronze sea gulls in flight, mounted atop a granite shaft. It was erected by the Church of Jesus Christ of Latterday Saints in 1913, to commemorate the unprecedented salvation of the Mormon pioneers during the early summer of 1848.

Some 5,000 acres of grain were planted during the winter and early spring that year by a vanguard group in preparation for the large number of colonists expected to arrive later in the summer. The grain flourished and prospects for the hoped-for crop looked bright. Then one day swarms of crickets appeared and began devouring the grain. The people rushed to the fields to try to fight the invaders. They used every method at their disposal.

The exhausted colonists had no other earthly weapons with which to fight. They turned to prayer. Suddenly, they heard the screech of sea gulls and looked skyward to see thousands of the birds flying in from the west. Thinking it was only another foe who had come to complete the devastation, many of them wept. But the tears turned to those of joy when the gulls descended and began to devour the crickets, disgorging only to continue eating and not stopping until the grain was cleaned of the predators. The gulls saved enough of the grain to enable the pioneers to survive the difficult winter.

4. (T—F) The sea gulls devoured crickets that were destroying crops.

5. (M.C.) The statue was erected by:
_____(1) the Mormon Church.
_____(2) the Bird Watcher's Club.
_____(3) the V.F.W.
_____(4) the Farmers Organization.

The Pioneer Woman

An exceptional statue of a bronze figure of a young woman, striding forward with a sure step, a Bible clasped in her right hand, a bundle hanging from her right arm, stands in Ponca City, Oklahoma. She is a woman of erect carriage and resolute, clear eyes looking out from under a sunbonnet. She is also a woman with chin up and firm mouth, a woman whose eager son treads at her side, his hand in hers. She is known as the Pioneer Woman.

It was in the latter 1920's that someone suggested to Ernest Whitworth Marland, tenth Governor of Oklahoma, that someone should erect a statue to the "Vanishing American"—the Indian. Deploring the flapper of that age, he is said to have retorted that it would be more fitting to create a memorial to America's vanishing womanhood. The above mentioned statue resulted and it is inscribed, "In appreciation of the heroic character of the women who braved the dangers and endured the hardships incident to the daily life of the pioneer and homesteader of this country."

6. (T—F) The statue is of an Indian woman.

7. (M. C.) The woman is accompanied by:
_____(1) a dog.
_____(2) a horse.
_____(3) a boy.
_____(4) her three sons.

The Monarch Butterflies

In Pacific Grove, California, not only is there an ordinance that imposes a $500 fine for their protection but there is a monument dedicated to the Monarch Butterflies which flock to the little town each year. No one knows why the beautiful creatures chose this particular area to spend the winter—from late September through March—nor how they find their way back year after year. It is almost certain that no Monarch ever makes the trip more than once.

The butterfly migration must also have been familiar to the Indians, for there is an Indian legend which says that the sight of the first Monarch scouts returning to Pacific Grove occasioned the chant: "They have come, they have come, bringing peace and bringing plenty."

8. (C.) Monarch Butterflies annually flock to Pacific Grove, California in late ________________.

9. (T—F) The Indians considered the Monarch Butterflies to be a bad omen.

Mother Goose

Even Mother Goose is remembered. Oh, there are those who say she is not the original Mother Goose. In fact, there are those who say there never was a Mother Goose. But there are others who believe Elizabeth Goose, who is buried in Boston's Old Granary Burying Ground, is the one who recited the little verses to her sixteen children.

Whether or not she is the real Mother Goose, there can be no doubt that a frequently visited spot in the cemetery is off the main path at her grave.

These are only a few of the exceptional and sometimes unconventional memorials that are to be found in America.

10. (T—F) It is a stated fact that Mother Goose is a legend.

________STOP__ASK FOR YOUR TIME________

Record your time immediately.

Time__________ Sec. RATE (from table on page 315): R.__________

No. Correct__________ COMPREHENSION (10% for each correct answer): C.__________
(key on page 322)

VII-9 EFFICIENCY (R × C): E.__________

Record on Progress Chart on page 299

Length: 1350 words

Exercise VII-10

Readability Score: 60

The Hummingbird

By Bennie Bengtson

(Reprinted by permission from *Conservation,* July-August, 1957.)

WAIT FOR SIGNAL TO BEGIN READING

Backwards

Some years ago a well known British scientist stated in a book that no bird could fly backwards. He was mistaken, of course. There are no hummingbirds in Britain, for they are found only in the Western Hemisphere, and so he had apparently never had the opportunity to watch a "hummer" back away from a flower after taking a snifter of nectar.

Not only fly backwards, but up, down, and sideways too, as well as forward, if the whim takes him, for he's about the most talented and versatile thing on wings. He might very well have been the model from which the helicopter was developed, for he can do anything a 'copter can and some things besides, like taking a drink from the throat of a lily, for instance.

There are nearly five hundred species of hummingbirds all told, but by far and away most of them prefer to remain in the South American tropics. Only one, the familiar ruby-throat, is to be found east of the Mississippi in these United States. He's pretty well known though, for he makes frequent visits to the flowers growing around the house searching for the honey to be had from the fragrant blossom depths. He likes the tiny insects, spiders, and gnats that congregate in the flower corollas too, and these make up a considerable portion of his diet.

1. (T—F) A British scientist accurately stated that there are no birds in the world that can fly backwards, even hummingbirds only *appear* to fly backwards.
2. (T—F) Of all the five hundred different species of hummingbird only one is found east of the Mississippi in the United States.

Meals in Flight

I have on occasion seen hummers bob here and there, up and down, through the air as if snapping at something. On closer investigation it was plain they were feeding on the tiny gnats that so often whirl through the air on still warm days, picking them out of the air one by one. This pastime might get them admitted into the union of the flycatchers, though it is conceivable that the kingbird might object that the capture of a gnat is too insignificant a feat to earn membership in the clan that specializes in picking its meals out of the air. There is a close relationship between the hummingbird and the swifts, nevertheless, since both have wonderful powers of flight, and feathers that lie compact against the body, offering little wind resistance in flight.

Hummingbirds are sometimes referred to as winged gems or jewels, and the term fits them very well indeed. The green of the head and the upperparts certainly suggest an emerald, and the deep ruby-red throat of the male ruby-throat provides still another gem. The rest of the underparts are gray, the sides being washed with green. The female is satisfied to let the male supply the name—she lacks the ruby patch, being entirely grayish below.

3. (C.) The manner in which the hummingbird flies around catching ________ and small insects would almost warrant giving it membership in the flycatchers union, along with the kingbird.
4. (M.C.) Ruby-throated hummingbirds:
   _____(1) are sometimes referred to as winged gems or jewels because of their coloring.
   _____(2) do not have exceptionally pretty coloring, especially the female.
   _____(3) are found in nearly every state except North and South Dakota.
   _____(4) have no real power of flight but hover around the flowers in a suspended fashion.

The Mighty Midget

The bill is long and pointed, the better to serve as a probe when investigating trumpet-shaped flowers like glads and tiger lilies. But, in spite of the assist from the long bill, the ruby-throated hummingbird attains a length of only three and a half inches. His lack of size doesn't at all handicap him, for it has no effect on his courage. He will dart with a bullet-like whiz at other and much larger birds, even hawks and crows, that trespass within the area around his home. They have a wholesome respect for him too; every hummingbird's nest that I have discovered came to my notice because of the actions of the parent birds. Repeated angry dartings at my head 700 as I passed close by convinced me the nest was in the vicinity, and a careful distance and watching the female through a pair of binoculars will do the trick, for she will return to the nest when the intruder retires.

5. (T–F) Because of his long bill the hummingbird attains a reasonably long length, sometimes as much as eight inches.

6. (T–F) The hummingbird has a daredevil personality and doesn't seem afraid of anything, and will even attack such birds as hawks or crows when 800 they trespass in the area around his home.

Works of Art

The nest is a work of art, one of the classics of avian architecture. Made of plant down, the outside is stuccoed with lichens, moss, and tiny bits of bark so that it blends completely with its surroundings. Fastened to the limb of a tree by cobwebs firmly matted down, it looks exactly like a thimble-like lump of growth on the branch. As a rule it is fairly high up in a tree. The two white eggs, almost always two, are but little larger than peas, and, early in the incubation period, so transparent that they resemble 900 pearls. The young are fed by regurgitation, the predigested food being pumped down the throats of the fledglings by the mother bird. Anyone observing the feeding performance would almost certainly arrive at the conclusion the young bird was being stabbed to death by the rapier bill of the parent.

During the late summer and early fall, when such flowers as the hollyhocks, glads, and tiger lilies are in bloom, the hummers are a never-ending source of amusement. Furiously they dart and chase each other about the garden, for they will not tolerate 1000 even other members of their own species. If two are seen feeding or perched close together, they are almost sure to be the mother and one of her offspring.

Some afternoons most of the time will be spent in aerial dogfights, with the combatants streaking through the air like a couple of feathered jets, changing position so rapidly it is at times impossible for the eye to follow them. The only sound I have heard from a hummer—aside from the whirring hum of their rapidly vibrating wings—is an angry mouse-like squeak heard when they are engaged in these encounters.

1100 7. (M.C.) In the nesting season, the hummingbird:

_____(1) has about six tiny eggs in the nest at once, sometimes more.

_____(2) makes his nest right at the foot of the tree where he conceals it with the use of moss and leaves.

_____(3) has eggs so thin they look like pearls.

_____(4) is very tame and friendly.

8. (C.) During the late summer when many of the larger flowers such as hollyhocks, glads, and tiger lilies are in bloom the hummingbird is a never-ending source of ____________.

9. (T–F) The humming sound the hummingbird makes is not really a song but 1200 only the sound of their wings beating so rapidly in the air.

Moths After Sunset

Years ago I read a poem in a magazine in which the poet painted a very lovely picture of the hummingbird feeding on the flowers of his garden in the twilight of a summer evening. He had probably confused his hummers with the hawk or sphinx moth, however, a large and somewhat hummingbird-like moth that comes out in the evenings. It is smaller, and less brightly colored, than the ruby-throat, though it hovers over flowers in much the same way. 1300 It is seldom that I see a hummingbird after sunset. They are birds of the open day, who love the sunshine and the warmth of the daylight hours.

10. (T–F) The hummingbirds are usually the 1350 most active during the sunset hours and just slightly after as the flowers are starting to close.

_______STOP—ASK FOR YOUR TIME______

Record your time immediately.

Time __________ Sec.	RATE (from table on page 315):	R. __________
No. Correct __________ (key on page 330)	COMPREHENSION (10% for each correct answer):	C. __________
VII-10	EFFICIENCY (R×C):	E. __________

Record on Progress Chart on page 299

Length: 1350 words

Exercise VII-11

Readability Score: 58

Writing a Resume

By Stephanie T. Rispin

(Reprinted from an original article of the Uniwyo Reading Research Center by permission of the director.)

WAIT FOR SIGNAL TO BEGIN READING

The main purpose of a resume is to enable you to obtain a job interview; it should promote the prospective employer's interest in you. Therefore you want to keep your resume concise, stating clearly your background abilities, accomplishments, and prospects, and not drag it out with lots of unncessary details.

Hints for Quality

First and foremost, you must deal with the positive elements. Don't be wishy-washy. Let your prospective employer see that you have the utmost confidence in your abilities and experience. Don't criticize a past employer or co-worker. The reader must, from your resume, be able to envision the ways that it is possible for you to be of use to his firm.

Leave out your personal opinions; state simply what you have done. It is essential to stick to the facts. Don't gush, or hint at half-truths. Lay your accomplishments on the line, leaving no room for ifs, ands, or buts.

Focus on those credentials directly pertaining to the job you are seeking. If you are simultaneously applying for several different types of jobs, write a separate resume for each, emphasizing background which demonstrates your qualifications for that specific work.

Rewrite your resume a few times, working it into a finer polish each time. Go over it repeatedly, making sure that each word has an essential meaning which lends credibility and interest, for it must be brief. Cut out all unnecessary words or phrases, and keep it at one page, or two at the most. You want the reader to be able to pick out easily the major points of your background without having to wade through several pages of detailed information. Remember: you simply need to promote enough interest to gain an interview. You can go into details at that future time.

1. (M.C.) The *main* purpose of a resume is:
   _______ (1) to give a sample of your work attitudes.
   _______ (2) to secure a chance for a job interview.
   _______ (3) to give a detailed account of your past work experience.
   _______ (4) to impress the employer with your writing style.

2. (T—F) It is a good idea to explain within your resume the reasons why each former job did not work out.

3. (T—F) When writing a resume you should be completely truthful, and give all the details you can to impress the employer of your sincerity.

First Impressions

Before your interview, the only impression which your prospective employer can get of you is through your resume. Therefore, the image it conveys must be one of a neat, organized individual who is able to relate important information quickly and with originality.

Use a conventional format, leaving space between sections of type, and for attractive margins. Use proper punctuation, grammar, and spelling, and underline and capitalize words when you wish to set things apart. Expert typing on good quality paper of standard size is a must. Make use of a Xerox machine, ensuring clean, legible copies.

4. (T—F) Neatness and organization are essential, for your resume is the first impression you make on a prospective employer.

Content

Before you can follow these guidelines for writing, you must first collect all of the information you wish to use. Plan on including these important elements: identification, objective, experience, education, and personal data.

Immediately state your name, your address, and both your home and office telephone numbers if possible. Be sure this information is right at the beginning of your resume, so that the employer doesn't have to search for it.

In relating your objective or job goal, don't go into specifics which could divorce you from possibilities you might like to consider. Instead of using a special job title, explain in a couple of lines your abilities for jobs, leaving the road open to the employer.

The most important aspect of your resume is the description of your career to date. Dive right into that, giving it the most space. Be sure to include (for each previous job) the name and location of the firm, the length of time you were employed (use dates), the title you held, responsibilities given, and your own specific accomplishments while there. 700 ←

List your high school or college, and your degree or major. Relate special skills (such as the knowledge of a foreign language), specialized certification, and any seminars you have completed, as well as post-graduate and special training courses. If you have limited work experience, note the areas of emphasis in your major, and activities you have participated in pertaining to your major. Also briefly state your age, marital status, health, honors and awards, military service, and business, professional, social and civic affilations.

Include all of the above, even if you feel that you don't have much to say about each. Omitting any 800 ← information could lead to rejections. Simply avoid dwelling on the negative without misrepresenting the facts.

5. (C.) In relating your objective, try not to be too __________________ .

6. (M.C.) The most important single aspect of your resume is your:
______(1) college major.
______(2) long-range objective.
______(3) career to date.
______(4) personal history.

A covering letter always should accompany your resume. Address it to the top official of the company or department in which you are seeking a job. Make it brief and to the point. Tell why you want a job there, 900 ← call attention to your enclosed resume, and request an interview. Don't tell the employer what you can do for his company, but refer to some aspect of your background relating to the company's interests, and showing that you would be an asset.

What Not to Include

Do not include references, but at the end of your resume say that references will be provided upon request.

The only time to include a photo with your resume is when applying for a modeling or acting position. If you are not looking for a job of this kind, let the employer wait until the interview to find out 1000 ← what you look like.

Do not explain your reasons for leaving previous jobs. This can be done in an interview, when you can present your side of the story.

Do not, in your resume, include any former salary figures, or indicate what salary you would like to receive in the future.

Do not emphasize the fact that you have been out of a job for a certain period of time.

7. (T—F) References should always be included in the resume.

8. (T—F) Salary information on previous jobs 1100 → should not be mentioned within the resume.

Formats

Two basic formats are available in writing a resume. Depending upon your personal preference and objective, both are effective techniques.

In a chronological format, you organize your previous jobs (the heart of the resume) in their order of occurrence, listing by dates and with an explanation of each.

The functional method is preferred if you wish to stress the positions you have held. This is also somewhat of a disguise if you have been out of work for any period of time. List the titles or positions held in 1200 → any order you wish. You may want to put the most important first, and give it the most space, so that it will catch the reader's eye.

9. (C.) The two basic formats used in writing resumes are chronological and __________________ .

Using a Professional Writer

On the whole, it is not a good idea to utilize a professional resume writer. If an employer recognizes that your resume was professionally prepared, he might doubt your ability to communicate. If you want to get advice, fine. But turn out the completed product yourself.

Ask friends for resumes which they have used 1300 → prior to landing good jobs. Study the techniques visible in theirs, and study also model resumes from books obtained at the library or from bookstores. Only use these models as guides, however, and make the final product your own personal presentation.

10. (T—F) If an employer recognizes a professionally written resume, he might 1350 → doubt your ability to communicate.

______ STOP__ASK FOR YOUR TIME ______

Record your time immediately, compute your scores and record on your progress chart.

Time __________ Sec.	RATE (from table on page 315):	R. __________
No. Correct __________ (key on page 322)	COMPREHENSION (10% for each correct answer):	C. __________
VII-11	EFFICIENCY (R × C):	E. __________

Record on Progress Chart on page 299

Length: 1350 words

Exercise VII-12

Readability Score: 56

The Koshares

By Stephanie T. Rispin

(Reprinted from an original article of the Uniwyo Reading Research Center by permission of the director)

WAIT FOR SIGNAL TO BEGIN READING

Feathered Fun-Makers

Koshar-e is the Pueblo word for fun-maker, and fun making is exactly what this group of 150 Boy Scouts of Explorer Post No. 2230 of the Rocky Mountain Council do. The famed Koshare Indian dancers expertly weave a spectacle to take the breath away. As the boys chant songs of long ago in their beautiful costumes while performing old Indian dances and ceremonies, viewers transcend their every day lives and are taken back to the time when buffalo abounded and the Indians were in possession of their undamaged country.

The group began in 1933 when 25 of J. F. (Buck) Bursheárs' scouts became intrigued with their Indian lore project, and decided to form their own group studying Indian lore. By October of that year, the Koshares performed for the first time, and developed and expanded their special knowledge and expertise until their interpretations of Indian ceremonies and dances were considered to be the finest known to the modern world.

Our Indian Heritage Is Kept Alive

Buck began researching Indian dances before he ever became a Scoutmaster. He has lived with the Indians, and written a book on their beadwork. His interest in Indian lore and dancing promoted his Boy Scout "tribe."

Buck feels that the Indians are an important part of our heritage and culture, and wants his group of all-white dancers to realize this. By organizing his Koshares, he felt he could instill the boys with knowledge of the American Indians, while keeping the older boys interested in scouting. He has accomplished both. Young boys can't wait to begin the hard work along the path to becoming a Koshare, and their enthusiasm for new dances and more knowledge of Indian lifestyles has no bounds. Buck has probably seen more boys attain Eagle rank than any other scoutmaster.

1. (T—F) Buck Burshears is attempting to relate Scouting to an understanding of the culture of the American Indian.
2. (T—F) Most of the boys who are active in the Koshare Indian Dancers are Indians.

Koshare Dances

The Koshares have built up a repertoire of approximately 100 dances which are constantly being added to and varied, so that no program ever becomes dull, either to the boys or to the audience. Their dances are authentic, and have been taken from studies of tribal life and authoritative books, but mostly from personal visits to the Indians.

Each year Buck and the boys attend the Indian ceremonial dances in New Mexico, where Buck makes films of the dances and tapes of the chants. These are later used to provide new material.

The great number of old dances were ceremonies for the worship of their gods, which included birds and animals, the sun and moon, wind and rain, and thunder and lightning. Other dances were celebrations for the harvest, marriage, and death.

The Winter Night Ceremonials take place during the week of Christmas each year, with old dancers often coming back to join in the performance. The audience is requested to hold their applause, and flash cameras are not permitted, thus nothing may interrupt the wonderful spell. Many shows are given during the months of July and August, and the summer shows are accentuated by the beautiful scenery the boys have made themselves.

One dance that is performed at almost every show, is the Koshare War Dance, in honor of the war-members killed in World War II, and those warriors who continue to serve in the armed forces.

3. (M.C.) Most of the dances are taken from:
   ________(1) the boys' creative imaginations.
   ________(2) Buck Burshears' rich experience.
   ________(3) personal living with Indian families.
   ________(4) studies of Indian tribal life.
4. (C.) Most of the old Indian dances were ceremonies dedicated to the ______ ______________.
5. (T—F) All the scenery used in their shows is specially made by Indians.

Koshare Headquarters

Most of these shows are presented in their own headquarters building, which is modeled after the sacred meeting place of the ancient pueblo, the kiva.

This famous meeting place of the Koshares, located in La Junta, Colorado, opened in 1949, and was a dream come true for Buck Burshears. The Koshares used $10,000 of their earnings towards the completion of the building, and the townspeople of La Junta also put up $10,000. As the building plans developed many people were highly skeptical when it became known that the building was to contain recreation rooms, a trading post, a little theater, an Indian art museum, and a ceremonial kiva seating 500. But Buck received great cooperation from the townspeople, as well as from the boys. Everyone donated whatever materials they could, as well as their labor for the actual erection of the building. And so with everyone hard at work, the kiva was finished. The Koshares' Art and Indian collections are found in the Kiva Museum and are among the best in the world.

6. (M.C.) The Koshares' headquarters is modeled after a kiva, which was a:
   ______(1) a sacred meeting place.
   ______(2) a secret hiding place used for protection during invasions.
   ______(3) residence of the Indian chiefs.
   ______(4) a series of underground tunnels.

Being a Koshare Is Hard Work

As the boys soon discover, being a Koshare is no idle play, for Indian dancing is very strenuous. The work of a Koshare is hard and relentless, involving infinite determination. When in junior high school, a boy becomes a Papoose, and must begin to assemble his Indian costume immediately. Items such as eagle feathers, owl claws, and horsetails must be collected, and his breechclout and vest must be beaded, often taking as long as six months. Learning the basic dance steps take hours of devoted effort, as does the reading of books on Indians, and the maintenance of a 75 per cent attendance at Scout meetings and a "C" average in school.

More costumes with intricate bead and feather work must be made, and to ensure the historic validity of their costumes, Koshares study Indian costume designs and colors. They also learn Indian music to accompany their dances. New dances are continually sought and learned. In addition, Koshares have tests of citizenship, character, and scholarship. Many have part time jobs, and time must always be found for practice and long-distance shows.

Any boy wishing to be a Koshare has his hands full. This seems to build strength of character, and they all seem to thrive on it.

7. (C.) One of the earliest responsibilities a boy has after joining the Koshares is the assembly of his ______________.

8. (T—F) The Koshares' activities are so demanding that they often create problems with school work or part time employment.

Many Miles Are Travelled

The Koshares are very much in demand, and so have done extensive travelling across the nation. Most trips are made during the boys' summer vacation, so that their schooling is not interrupted. The Koshares annual income from their shows is $30,000, which is divided between current expenses and the troop budget. The dancers receive no payment. They have their own bus, and fathers happily assist the scoutmaster on their many travels.

The trips are taxing, but exciting. After a rugged performance, all equipment is cleaned up and reloaded, and only then do the boys sleep. Up early the next morning, they drive for perhaps 400 miles. Upon reaching their destination, the show is set, and another performance given. Each year, the Koshares travel nearly 20,000 miles.

The Koshares are well known and joyously received wherever they go. They have enjoyed entertaining numerous distinguished groups, such as the Lions, Kiwanis, National Shriners, and the American Legion. Their biggest thrills have been visiting Presidents in the White House.

The education received as a Koshare is priceless. The travels around the country, skill-development, and endless work instill admirable qualities essential to the formation of fine, intelligent young men.

9. (T—F) Travelling is done primarily during the summer months in order to avoid interfering with school.

10. (T—F) The balance of income from the travelling shows after paying expenses is divided between the Troop and the individual dancers.

______ STOP__ASK FOR YOUR TIME ______

Record your time immediately, compute your scores and record on your progress chart.

Time __________ Sec. RATE (from table on page 315): R. __________

No. Correct __________ COMPREHENSION (10% for each correct answer): C. __________
(key on page 330)

VII-12 EFFICIENCY (R×C): E. __________

Record on Progress Chart on page 299

Length: 1350 words

Exercise VII-13

Readability Score: 55

In the Underground World

By Brother G. Nicholas, F.S.C.

(Reprinted by permission from *National Wildlife,* October-November, 1970.)

WAIT FOR SIGNAL TO BEGIN READING

There's total darkness as you walk into the inner cave. The silence is broken only by the drip of water. The environment is seemingly without life. But as your flashlight probes the walls, the roof and floor, you may discover a thriving community of unusual creatures.

Caves are not merely the hiding places of obscure, blind animals from the surface seeking shelter from predators. Instead, there exists a large and diversified fauna of the underground world with relationships as complex as those found in surface environments.

There are about 400 species of animals known to live out their life cycles within the caves of the United States. These permanent residents range from flatworms to salamanders. Many of these animals, blind and without coloring, rarely leave the dark zone of the cave.

1. (T–F) Many of the animals found in caves are surface-dwellers which have found a convenient escape from predators.

2. (C.) About ______________ species of animals live in the constant darkness of the caves.

Live in Darkness

Troglobites are the animals that live in the perpetual darkness of the cave. However, we know the complete life cycle for less than a half-dozen of the 400 species. Biologists are giving intensive study to the life habits of these mysterious creatures.

What do they eat in a habitat where there is no sun or green plants? How do they locate members of the opposite sex to mate and perpetuate the species?

The cave environment is seemingly hostile to survival. It is damp and muddy, frequently subject to flooding and isolated from light. Yet there are many advantages to cave living that make it a suitable habitat.

The constant dampness, or high relative humidity, enables aquatic forms and those terrestrial species that need constant moisture to thrive and never risk dryness. A film of water can be found even on rock surfaces. Small crustaceans, such as amphipods that normally remain in water, can migrate across large areas of cave floor and walls.

Most cave dwellers never experience the freezing temperatures or high winds that tend to disturb surface animals. Once beyond the twilight zone, an area where sunlight seldom filters in, the temperature remains relatively constant. Since all troglobites are cold-blooded, they assume this constant temperature. These animals have become adapted to this existence over thousands of generations and obviously find it essential to survival. Snakes, also cold-blooded, do not adapt well to these cave temperatures and are rarely found in caves.

Isolation from light is no handicap to troglobites, since they have the ability to detect stimuli by other means. Cave crickets have extremely long antennae that flick about, locating sources of food (and possible enemies) at distances three times the length of their bodies.

3. (M.C.) The discussed advantages of cave living include the constant dampness and the:
   - ______(1) relatively constant temperature.
   - ______(2) absence of predators.
   - ______(3) absence of people.
   - ______(4) quiet environment.

4. (T–F) Because they are cold-blooded, snakes adapt well and are found frequently in the caves.

5. (T–F) Cave crickets detect stimuli through use of their antennae.

Use of Lateral Line

Cave vertebrates, such as fish and salamanders, have the same highly developed lateral line system running the length of their bodies that is found in surface-dwelling fish and water-inhabiting salamanders. This sensitive line enables them to detect vibrations. Smaller animals moving about in the water are immediately detected, stalked and frequently caught by these specially equipped fish and salamanders, even though all the activity takes place in total darkness.

Troglobite salamanders are a good example of the way species adapt to cave life. Compared with their surface relatives, they display a complete lack of pigment, longer legs, reduced or nonexistent eyes, a slimmer body and a flattened snout. There is so little pigment in some cave salamanders that even the blood vessels are visible. The long legs help the salamander move carefully through the water while stalking food.

The bat is the best-known creature of the caves, and it is the primary source of food for much of the life that flourishes in the darkness.

Bats living in the northern and middle latitudes are primarily insect-eaters. Leaving the cave at dusk, 700 bats may travel up to 50 miles in the course of a night's foraging. During this flight, they eat food equal to half their weight.

Large caves may have colonies of bats with populations of a million or more. They produce prodigious quantities of droppings called "guano" as they hang from the ceiling of the cave all through the daylight hours. This guano is semiliquid when fresh but dries to form a powdery dark brown substance. In caves where bats have lived for thousands of years, guano may be 100 feet thick.

Guano provides food for large populations of 800 troglobites. Cave beetles, millipedes, snails, mites, cockroaches and moths thrive around guano deposits. Even the carcasses of bats are eaten.

6. (M.C.) Cave fish and salamanders can detect vibrations and stalk prey because of their highly developed:
_______(1) sense of smell.
_______(2) sense of hearing.
_______(3) antennae.
_______(4) lateral line system.

7. (T—F) Bats travel as far as 50 miles in their night's search for food.

Utilize All Food

At birth, many young fail to hold to either their mother's furry skin or the cave ceiling, and their fall to the floor of guano means death. During this period 900 the floor may seem to be alive with thousands of beetles, ticks, mites, various insect larvae and other invertebrates. Many cave spiders, crickets, harvestmen and scorpions also prey on the smaller insects.

Some guano is washed into streams and pools where it serves as a nutrient for aquatic forms.

The cricket is another important agent which supplies the cave with organic material from the surface—an integral part of the cave's food chain. American cave crickets perform the same role as bats. They forage outside the cave at night and return at dawn.

Daily observation of 4,000 cave crickets was 1000 made in Cathedral Cave, Kentucky, over a period of five years. The crickets were marked with paint so observers would know which section of the cave they came from.

When temperatures were above freezing, one-third of the population emerged each evening to feed amid leaf litter and grass on the surface. By dawn, 97 percent were back in the same section of the cave they had left. In some cases, this meant a round trip of 500 feet!

The following two evenings, the rest of the colony would emerge, one-third at a time. Then the 1100 cycle repeats.

Cricket guano in Cathedral Cave has accumulated to a one-inch depth. Beetles, spiders, millipedes, harvestmen, amphipods and other species exist there because the cricket guano provides them with a food source.

Some Precautions

Mexican free-tailed bats and other species can transmit rabies. The proportion of rabid bats may be small, but even this may consist of many rabid bats. And recent research in Texas and New Mexico caves shows that rabies can be transmitted without direct physical contact. Rabies is possibly spread through the light mist of bat urine in caves with large bat 1200 populations. If you enter such a cave, keep your body well covered for protection.

Even though this abundance of cave life is much greater than assumed only a decade ago, the conditions in most caves still make existence precarious. This is especially true where man disturbs the environment by polluting the water, dumping sewage and refuse and destroying natural formations that serve as shelter and dwelling places for animal life. Like many of their human counterparts, these animals want to be left alone. They will survive in their unique habitat only if they and their environment remain undisturbed.

8. (C.) In addition to the bat, the _______ 1300 is an important supplier of surface organic matter.

9. (T—F) Since rabies can be spread only by a direct bite, one has only to avoid touching any of the bats.

10. (T—F) Man's disturbance of their environment can seriously threaten the existence of the cave dwellers. 1350

_______STOP—ASK FOR YOUR TIME_______

Record your time immediately.

Time _______ Sec.	RATE (from table on page 315):	R. _______
No. Correct _______ (key on page 322)	COMPREHENSION (10% for each correct answer):	C. _______
VII-13	EFFICIENCY (R×C):	E. _______

Record on Progress Chart on page 299

Length: 1350 words

Exercise VII-14

Readability Score: 53

Forest Aflame

By Clyde Douglass

(Reprinted by permission from *Wyoming Wildlife,* June, 1970.)

WAIT FOR SIGNAL TO BEGIN READING

Nearly one-third of the United States is forest land, much of it ancient and rugged. Yet these stalwart primitive wilderness areas are so delicate that the flickering flame of a near-dead match can bring total destruction.

A forest fire fed by the right fuels and carried by strong winds is a terrifying sight. With explosive violence a fire can rage through giant trees and lay a path of destruction faster than a deer can run!

Most forest fires are caused by human ignorance, negligence or carelessness. Nearly nine-tenths of all forest fires in the United States are started by man, 100 and could be prevented. Statistics compiled by the U.S. Forest Service for the past decade reveal that 17 percent of the fires on protected forests and watershed lands in the United States were started by careless smoking habits of the public. At the same time 11 percent of the fires can be blamed on lightning and natural causes.

Campfires built in unsafe areas and abandoned before being completely extinguished, and smoking, are two big threats to forest lands in this part of the country. Fires are often started by hikers, fishermen, hunters and wood workers carelessly discarding burning matches and smoking materials. 200

1. (T – F) Nearly one-third of the United States is forest land.
2. (T – F) Man starts about ninety percent of all United States forest fires.
3. (M. C.) A relatively minor cause of fires is:
   _______ (1) smoking.
   _______ (2) incompletely extinguished campfires.
   _______ (3) discarded burning matches.
   _______ (4) lightning and natural causes.

Peak Periods of Danger

During the hot, dry summer months, fire danger is at its peak. These hazardous periods are often extended into the fall as warm autumn days accompanied by drying winds replace seasonal snow falls. During these dry summer and fall days when 300 hunters are present, the chance of human carelessness can, and often does, cause the complete destruction of forests and game populations from fire.

In the Western states, lightning shares a greater part of the blame for forest fires than it does in the Eastern states. From 1960-'63 more than half of the fires reported in the Rocky Mountain and Pacific Coast states were caused by lightning.

Fires started by lightning can be the hardest to reach and control for lightning often strikes in the rugged areas of the high country making accessibility 400 difficult. Fire fighting techniques must be changed as conditions are complicated in these rugged areas.

4. (T – F) Lightning fires are relatively easy to control because of their locations.
5. (C.) Fire danger peaks during the ________________.

Types of Fires

There are three distinct types of forest fires, known as ground, surface or crown fires. Each type is potentially dangerous and equally disastrous.

The slow-burning subsurface or "ground fire" is the name given to the type of fire fed by layers of decayed leaves and needles just below the surface of the forest floor. The ground fire can smolder 500 undiscovered for days or weeks because of small amounts of smoke emitted. Although the ground fire is slow burning, most of the trees in the path of such a fire are killed by the intense heat generated beneath the surface.

Many forest fires start as "surface" fires—the fuel being supplied by dry leaves, twigs and underbrush. Seedlings and smaller trees usually are consumed by surface fires while larger, established trees generally survive but bear permanent damages. These fire damaged trees are more susceptible to further damage from wood rot, insects, and wind.

Once the surface fire has a start, it can develop 600 rapidly with the right winds, into the most dangerous, destructive and costly type of forest fire—the "crown fire." Leaping from treetop to treetop, the crown fire can build enough momentum to jump fire lanes, open fields or large rivers. Winds carry sparks well in advance of the actual fire line starting new fires ahead. The crown fire destroys everything in its path—homes, farms, even entire communities.

If larger trees survive any type of fire, their growth is impeded. Generally some of the burned timber is salvageable if the larger trees are killed. The greatest losses resulting from fire, therefore, are not limited to the mature trees burned, but rather to the soil, seedlings and young trees. Should these smaller trees be burned, it can take years before seedlings are again able to get started in the area.

Following fires, in mountainous areas such as those found in Wyoming, watersheds are not able to fully absorb rainfall and retard subsequent runoffs. Fires in forest regions can be directly linked to the causes of flood damage, reservoir silting and stream and river pollution.

Game animals and birds, if not killed outright by the smoke and intense flames of a forest fire, are forced from their natural habitat by the lack of natural protection and food supplies. Ashes polluting the streams have been known to kill large numbers of game fish while the absence of natural foliage along stream banks can cause the temperature of the water to rise high enough to make the waterways unfit for trout.

6. (T—F) There are only two types of forest fires: surface and crown fires.

7. (M. C.) Greatest losses resulting from fire are in:
______(1) mature trees.
______(2) soil, seedlings, and young trees.
______(3) game animals.
______(4) fish, due to pollution.

Modern Fire Fighting

Fire fighting equipment has come a long way since the ax, shovel and the bucket brigade days. Accessible areas are now reached easily by all-wheel drive vehicles loaded with modern fire fighting equipment. Higher, rougher terrain can be reached quickly by smoke jumpers and helicopters. Chain saws have replaced fire fighting hand-tools. Electronic communications devices aid in coordinating fire fights and rescue missions. The water bucket has been replaced by airtankers capable of dropping tons of water and fire retardant in a single "bombing" mission.

Progress in fire control depends on many types of research—improved methods for measuring fire danger, fire detection, electronic surveillance equipment, what to do once a fire has started, and fire behavior.

These studies have revealed which type of trees are more often struck by lightning, the burning rates of various kinds of timber and fuels, and have led to the development of new methods for measuring fire danger. Fire danger meters recently developed to fit many types of forest conditions have been installed and are now being used on all national forests. These meters indicate when periods of extreme fire danger exist and when fire fighters should be standing by to meet suspected dangers.

Fire research also includes studies of atmospheric conditions which cause the whirlwind action that often allows a fire to escape control. It is hoped these studies will enable fire controllers to predict extreme hazardous conditions and help them employ the most effective fire fighting strategy.

Segments of the U.S. Forest Service, state forestry departments, industry and many conservation organizations have worked together to better educate the public and disseminate information about fire protection. During periods of high fire danger, portions of forest lands may be closed to public entry to help cut fire risks, and hunting and fishing seasons are sometimes temporarily suspended in danger areas during hazardous periods to minimize traffic.

Effective fire prevention programs have proved their worth in the reduction of fires. Campaigns such as those begun in 1945 featuring Smokey the Bear have played a significant role in fewer forest fires recorded in the past two decades. In the first half of the 1960s there were 60 percent fewer forest fires than in the five years before World War II.

But prevention programs are not the only answers to stopping the devastation in forest areas. There must be well-trained and equipped fighting forces ready to meet crises and a public aware of the need for forest fire prevention.

8. (T—F) Prevention programs have been effective in reducing fires.

9. (C.) Progress in fire control has depended on many types of ________.

10. (T—F) Prevention and fire control programs require intensive cooperation.

________STOP—ASK FOR YOUR TIME________

Record your time immediately.

Time __________ Sec. RATE (from table on page 315): R. __________

No. Correct __________ COMPREHENSION (10% for each correct answer): C. __________
(key on page 330)

VII-14 EFFICIENCY (R × C): E. __________

Record on Progress Chart on page 299

Length: 1350 words

Exercise VII-15

Readability Score: 52

Friend of the Lepers

By Henry F. Unger

(Reprinted by permission from *Listen* April, 1970.)

WAIT FOR SIGNAL TO BEGIN READING

There was no traditional Hawaiian lei of greeting as Ira Barnes Dutton came ashore at Kalaupapa on July 29, 1886. His only greeter was a smiling, stocky priest, whose face and hands were disfigured with the ravages of leprosy.

"Welcome to Molokai, Brother," the priest said, "and indeed how we welcome and need you."

Tall, well-knit, and blessed with a slim, muscular figure, Ira Dutton preferred this happy greeting to one from any celebrity in the world. He was finally ashore on the notorious leper colony of Molokai Island, and he could hardly believe it or believe the transformation that had occurred in his life. 100

Dutton, who was a heavy drinker for many years, was now face to face with the famous Father Damien de Veuster, SS. CC., who had sacrificed his life to work with outcast lepers. Until Dutton's appearance on the island, no one had offered to work full time and without pay as the Catholic priest's assistant and to minister to the scores of lepers who not only suffered the ignominy of disfigurement of face and body, but who agonized with pain and with the foul-smelling odors emanating from their dying bodies.

What seemed like a dream for Dutton—setting 200 foot on the leper colony—would stretch into forty-five years of self-sacrifice for the former Civil War veteran among the lepers. At that moment, Dutton did not realize that for nearly half a century he would never leave the leper colony.

1. (T—F) Ira Dutton came to Molokai Island to work without pay for the lepers.
2. (T—F) He was greeted gratefully by the lepers as the only person willing to work for them and help them.

Tried Solace in Whiskey

Born in the tiny town of Stowe, Vermont, Dutton later moved to Janesville, Wisconsin, where 300 he was reared as an Episcopalian. He volunteered his services with the Zouave Corps of the city, which in turn enrolled in a body as Company B of the 13th Wisconsin Volunteer Infantry during the Civil War.

Wiry and conscientious, Dutton served with gallantry in Kansas, Kentucky, Tennessee, Alabama, Louisiana, and Texas, and in 1865 was promoted to the rank of first lieutenant.

After he was mustered out of the service, Dutton foresaw a placid future as he married. But he soon discovered that his wife was a faithless type, and she 400 went to live with another man in New York. When she piled up bills for Dutton, he divorced her.

A great gloom descended upon the previously optimistic Dutton, and he sought solace in whiskey. For over a decade he staggered along with his menial job but always in a stupor, convinced that his whiskey habit was his balm.

3. (M. C.) Dutton served in:
   ______(1) the War of 1812.
   ______(2) the Civil War.
   ______(3) the Mexican-American War.
   ______(4) World War I.
4. (T—F) Dutton's wife died of leprosy.

Sought Rehabilitation

One day Dutton decided that alcoholism was 500 ruining his life and determined to cast off the habit. He saw a clergyman, asked for his help and for help from God. Knowing full well the struggle it would entail, he took the pledge and never returned again to alcohol.

Realizing that he had wasted much of his life with his whiskey habit, Dutton now determined to help others in their struggle against the habit.

The future friend of lepers contacted Catholic priest Father J. A. Kelley, O.P., and was received into the Catholic Church. "I thought that service within the walls of the Trappists would provide the 600 penance I was seeking," Dutton said, "but after two years with that strict religious group, I decided this was not the vocation for me."

Dutton left the monastery and went to Saint Louis. He met another priest there. Together they went on to New Orleans, where Dutton learned about the famous Father Damien on Molokai Island and his valiant struggles to help the outcast lepers.

Just as he had thrown off the drinking habit, Dutton now moved ahead swiftly, determined that this was the answer to his longing to do good for others. Dutton determined to make a visit to Molokai Island.

When he arrived in Honolulu, he sought out the Catholic bishop and received his and the Board of Health's permission to visit Molokai Island. Immediately he was offered money to work on the island with the lepers.

"I preferred to work without pay," Dutton said, "and so I was gladly accepted."

5. (T – F) Dutton became a Catholic monk.
6. (C.) In New Orleans, Dutton learned about Father ______________.

The Move to the Leper Colony

He had hardly come ashore that fateful day when he realized the immensity of his transformation from an alcoholic to a helper of his fellowman. He realized that he could also be infected with leprosy. As he rode alongside the priest in his buggy from the Kalaupapa landing, Dutton could see the twisted faces of the lepers he would live with. Never hesitating, Dutton listened to the many plans of Father Damien, who was to die three years later.

Dutton, now called Brother Joseph by Father Damien, expended every effort to make the lepers more comfortable. Always smiling, reserved, and thoughtful, Dutton preferred not to discuss his "wild years," but had words of caution for the lepers who were prone to depend on whiskey.

Given charge of the two churches and the orphanages, Dutton was constantly at work. He corresponded with persons all over the world, telling them about the plight of the lepers and about the urgent needs on the island. One of his letters reached President Theodore Roosevelt, who in 1908 ordered the Great White Fleet which was anchored at nearby Honolulu to divert its course and to pass in front of Molokai Island to honor the former Civil War veteran and his leper charges. Daily Dutton had raised and lowered the American flag on the high flagpole at the leper colony. He had told the leper children about the greatness of America and boasted about the immense United States Navy. He was startled when an entire fleet of battleships passed by the colony in a tribute to him. Again in 1925 the battle fleet passed in review before Dutton, an honor not ordinarily given to civilians.

Without his desiring it, Dutton's fame spread over the globe. After his death a notebook containing 4,000 addresses of correspondents was found.

7. (C.) On Molokai Island Dutton was called Brother ______________.
8. (M. C.) Some of Dutton's correspondence about the island colony reached President:
   ______ (1) Grover Cleveland.
   ______ (2) Chester Arthur.
   ______ (3) Theodore Roosevelt.
   ______ (4) James K. Polk.

Directed the Colony

Dutton became the director of the Baldwin Home on the colony and handled its affairs, supervising its physical setup and disciplinary problems. He also provided proper recreational facilities for the young leprous boys.

Dutton was so dedicated to the work among the lepers that during his forty-five years on the island he moved only from his lodging to the flagpole, to his work among the lepers, to the chapel, and then back to his lodging, writing letters until the early morning hours.

At the side of Father Damien when he died in 1889, Dutton continued the priest's efforts among the lepers. A school in Beloit, Wisconsin, was named after him. In 1929 the pope sent him his special blessing, and the Hawaiian parliament voted him a testimonial.

Called "the brother of all the world," Ira Dutton proved to the world, without wishing to do so, that alcoholism can not only be crushed but that it can become a stepping stone to a remarkable service for man.

Dutton, rarely ill during his long, remarkable stay on Molokai Island, finally died on March 26, 1931, and was interred there beside his friend, Father Damien. Later his work was widely recognized and a statue to his honor was erected in Statuary Hall in the United States Capitol.

9. (T – F) Dutton served on Molokai for nearly 25 years.
10. (T – F) For Dutton, alcoholism became a stepping stone to dedicated service.

________STOP—ASK FOR YOUR TIME________
Record your time immediately.

Time __________ Sec.	RATE (from table on page 315):	R. __________
No. Correct __________ (key on page 322)	COMPREHENSION (10% for each correct answer):	C. __________
VII-15	EFFICIENCY (R × C):	E. __________

Record on Progress Chart on page 299

Length: 1350 words

Exercise VII-16

Readability Score: 48

Changing at the Zoo

(Reprinted by permission from *Changing Times,* the Kiplinger Magazine [February 1970 issue].

WAIT FOR SIGNAL TO BEGIN READING

You're missing a rare delight if you haven't visited a good zoo lately. There, for a few enchanted moments, you may see a Caribbean rain forest where exotic creatures flutter through the air and scurry across the leaf-covered floor. You may stand beside a surf-washed beach, listen to the strident cries of gulls and watch an African plover strut along the strand.

It's fun, and it's only part of what zoos are doing today in the process of abandoning the Alcatraz look. William G. Conway, general director of the New York Zoological Society and director of the Bronx Zoo, notes that most people, city dwellers as they are, will never see a box turtle or a white-tailed deer. Yet those people will indirectly determine by their votes whether we have such things as national parks, zoos and conservation work aimed at protecting the birds, mammals, reptiles and amphibians who live with us and are threatened.

1. (C.) Zoos are gradually moving toward the abandonment of the ________ look.
2. (T—F) Whether zoos, national parks, and other conservation works will be maintained is indirectly determined by the votes of persons who often have never seen a wild animal.

From Cages to Natural Settings

Mr. Conway calls it the "lavatory look," and he scorns it. Zoologist and author Desmond Morris decries the "shame of the naked cage." It's what enlightened zoo people are trying to do away with—sterile tile enclosures that are easy to keep clean but are dull for the animals and the people alike.

Visitors to the Milwaukee Zoo can see tigers pad the plains while deer feed unconcerned nearby, protected in their outdoor enclosure by a hidden system of moats.

Desert life can be seen in natural settings at the Arizona-Sonora Desert Museum, which was a pioneer in this. Visitors to Washington, D.C.'s National Zoological Park can walk through a great flight cage where birds of many hues and sizes soar.

Chicago's Brookfield Zoo houses an exhibit of a swamp, where chattering monkeys, tropical birds, boa constrictors and iguanas live in harmony. The Bronx Zoo's aquatic bird house shows spectacular specimens in their natural settings—a jungle, a swamp, riverside treetops, even a sand beach with machine-induced waves and recorded cries of shore birds.

The most elaborate of all is the Bronx Zoo's new World of Darkness building, designed to display some of the many living things that sleep by day and stir at night. The lights are turned on at night so the animals can sleep when there are no visitors. By day the interior is dark, so dimly lit that your eyes must adjust to the gloom. And there, in a series of glass-fronted enclosures, you can see big-eyed galagos, tree snakes, and slow lorises, which are lower primates from Asia.

The World of Darkness also boasts a swamp, complete with fiber glass cypress trees, where alligators swish quietly through a stream; skunks and raccoons play on the shore, protected by an "invisible" glass separator.

A tropical cave and rain forest exhibit, copied from a location in Trinidad, contains bats and sloths, agoutis and other small animals. One of the most active and most watched exhibits shows South American fisherman bats, which swoop and flutter from one end of their enclosure to the other while their high-frequency cries are amplified outside for the public to hear. From time to time minnows are put into a stream so the bats can use their fishing skill.

You can see a small patch of desert and watch kit foxes and armadillos, pack rats and snakes.

"This, in a nutshell, is what zoos are trying to do," says Donald D. Bridgwater, general curator of the National Zoological Park. Instead of "postage stamp" collections of one or two of each of many animals, zoos are displaying fewer animals but putting them in settings that allow the public to understand them.

3. (T—F) People can enjoy visits to the Bronx Zoo's World of Darkness only at night, due to the fact that the animals sleep during the day.
4. (M.C.) People who visit the Milwaukee Zoo are kept separate from the animals by:
   - _____ (1) a series of thin electrified wire fences which the animals have learned to avoid.
   - _____ (2) bars on the cages of the animals.
   - _____ (3) an extensive and invisible series of moats.
   - _____ (4) extremely clear unbreakable glass enclosures.

5. (T—F) The World of Darkness has installed amplifiers so that the public can hear the night birds singing.

Saving the Threatened

"We would still have passenger pigeons and Carolina parakeets if zoo animal-management techniques had been up to their present level at the turn of the century," says Mr. Conway. Certainly, zoos have preserved some threatened species. Our North American bison is an example. Another is the Pere David deer, which was originally a resident of China. This odd creature survives only because a few of the species were held by European zoos when the only others were slaughtered in China during the Boxer Rebellion. The Mongolian or Przewalski horses which are the last of the true wild horses, are descended from 28 collected for Carl Hagenbeck, a German zoo enthusiast, in 1901. The great whooping crane is being bred and nurtured through a special government project at Patuxent, Maryland.

800 ←

But many other animals are threatened—the South American golden marmoset, the blackfooted ferret, the American alligator. So many species are endangered that the International Union for Conservation of Nature and Natural Resources publishes Red Data Books listing all of them. The books must be updated constantly.

900 ←

To counter the trend, some zoos are cooperating in special breeding programs and have agreed not to import certain animals. Orangutans, for example, are imported by zoos only under special arrangements. They are being bred in several places; at present time the Bronx Zoo has two expectant orangutans.

Specimens of the nene goose, the Hawaiian state bird, have been shipped from England to the 50th state, but some zoologists wonder whether the bird can survive there today with most of its natural habitat gone to civilization.

1000 ←

6. (M.C.) The International Union for Conservation of Nature and Natural Resources publishes listings of endangered animal species in:
   ________ (1) Red Data Books.
   ________ (2) Endangered Species Books.
   ________ (3) Animal Conservation Books.
   ________ (4) Zoological Case Books.

7. (T—F) Zoos have agreed to special breeding programs and import restrictions for the purpose of animal conservation.

8. (C.) Many modern zoos make a very important contribution to animal ________________.

Why Do Animals Do What They Do?

1100 →

How do birds find their way south in winter? No one knows. Scientists at zoos are among those trying to find the answer. Every night during the fall some researchers lug their radar sets out along the flyways, to watch bird migration. Others put birds in wind tunnels, as an aeronautical engineer might do with an airplane model.

The scientists would also like to know why whales descend to a depth of 3,500 feet and sing songs, which are described as surprisingly musical. They do know that other whales hundreds of miles away listen to the music.

1200 →

They would like to find out how chimpanzees communicate with one another. And they would like to know much more about the Komodo monitor, a giant Indonesian lizard.

Zoo people think that if they understand mammals, birds and reptiles better, perhaps they can save many of the endangered ones. As one zoo man asks: "When we no longer have any wild creatures except starlings and pigeons, will we still be human beings? Or, because we don't need these creatures any more, will we have evolved into something else, socially and psychologically?" It's something to think about while you're enjoying those marvelous creatures at the zoo.

1300 →

9. (T—F) Scientists employed by zoos are very interested in research to try to find explanations for many types of animal behavior.

10. (T—F) Most zoo people feel now that the only purpose served by the conservation of certain wild animals is strictly an aesthetic one.

1350 →

______ STOP __ ASK FOR YOUR TIME ______

Record your time immediately, compute your scores and record on your progress chart.

Time ________ Sec.	RATE (from table on page 315):	R. ________
No. Correct ________ (key on page 330)	COMPREHENSION (10% for each correct answer):	C. ________
VII-16	EFFICIENCY (R×C):	E. ________

Record on Progress Chart on page 299

Length: 1350 words

Exercise VII-17

Readability Score: 47

Mysteries of the Egg

WAIT FOR SIGNAL TO BEGIN READING

Oldest Collector

Consider the egg—plain white, slightly bumpy, dull, easy to crack, slimy inside. Illuminated by the harsh light of a bare bulb, it waits in its own plastic refrigerator cup to be deviled or scrambled or hard-boiled, upstaging the flashier foods only when it breaks prematurely or gets rotten—or both.

Yet there is a man in Colton, California, who has spent 90 of his 94 years collecting more than 200,000 eggs. And a museum in neighboring Redlands displays a hefty chunk of that collection.

The explanation for this mild mystery is not simply that Southern Californians are odd birds, it is, (100) rather, that eggs are a good deal more than just crackable, cookable protein units. They are as diverse and comely a group of cells as one is likely to encounter. They may well tie with legs as evolution's most significant contribution to life outside the primordial soup.

There aren't many official oologists (ooh-ah-logists—people who study eggs) in the world and, at 94, the man from Colton, Wilson Creal Hanna, has probably the longest tenure. His first memory, as a four-year-old in 1887, was of climbing a tree and retrieving a small nestful of eggs. Over the years he (200) went on to collect thousands of specimens, mostly in the southwestern United States, and, in the end, ammassed the world's largest private egg collection. Hanna's eggs are now housed in the San Bernardino County Museum, a building with an unmistakable brown metal dome that resembles a pineapple, nestled in a grove of orange trees between the freeway and the San Bernardino Mountains. In two large rooms filled with artful display cases, rest 4,000 eggs, the world's largest public display—and yet only a small percentage of the Hanna collection.

1. (C.) Wilson Creal Hanna has been collecting eggs for ________ years. (300)

2. (M.C.) A person who studies eggs is an:
   ________ (1) oologist.
   ________ (2) embryologist.
   ________ (3) ontologist.
   ________ (4) opthamologist.

3. (T—F) Hanna's entire collection is displayed in the San Bernardino County Museum.

4. (M.C.) Most of the eggs in Hanna's collection were found in:
   ________ (1) southern United States.
   ________ (2) southwestern United States.
   ________ (3) northwestern United States.
   ________ (4) South America.

Egg Shapes

The visitor is immediately struck by two simple facts: eggs aren't all "egg shaped," and most aren't white. Over millions of years, the shape of the hen's egg evolved for maximum strength, roominess, layability and hatchability; other shapes evolved to suit the (400) needs and promote the survival of other birds.

The eggs of slender, agile birds, swifts and albatrosses, for example, are almost cylindrical—a great relief, no doubt, to the slim mothers involved. Yet, this structural evolutionary logic didn't help the female kiwi, which lays a large grayish egg that equals nearly 30% of her body weight—the equivalent of an average-sized woman delivering a 38-pound baby.

While owls' eggs are nearly as round as ping-pong balls, the eggs of murres—small, diving sea birds—are almost as pointed as tops. But then murres lay (500) their eggs on wind-swept rock ledges, and pointed eggs simply blow in a circle rather than rolling off to an early rupture.

Egg coloration is probably even more startling than egg shape, however. Easter baskets haven't a thing on the bird world, where eggs can be cream-colored, gold, light green to olive to dark green cinnamon-brown to red, one of a dozen shades of blue and lilac, light gray, dark gray or nearly black. These colors help hide the unhatched generation among the open vegetation, rocks, sand or nests in which they are laid, and an unbelievable array of markings—drizzles, threads, dots, speckles, splatters, reticulations, (600) Rorschach blots—aid the camouflage. The dark olive eggs of loons, with their bold brown splotches, are virtually invisible as they lay bare and unprotected on the tundra mosses and lichens. The eggs of Burchell's courser, from Africa, are covered with a network of black lines, remarkably like the heaps of animal dung amid which they are laid.

5. (T—F) Various egg shapes have evolved to meet specific functional needs.
6. (C.) The female Kiwi lays an egg which is about ________________ % of her own body weight.
7. (T—F) Egg coloration is a camouflage survival system.

Chicken or the Egg?

One can hardly help wondering just exactly which did come first—the chicken or the egg? 700

The egg, quite incontrovertibly, came first. Several decades ago, a small, club-shaped fossil was discovered in Mongolia and identified as the egg of Protoceratops, a dinosaur with a high, stiff collar and a parrot-like beak. It was the most celebrated in a line of dinosaur-egg discoveries confirming that these creatures were laying eggs long before their odd-looking Archaeopteryx cousins stretched out reptilian wings and glided into an avian future.

Thus, the answer to that age-old riddle is easy. But it leads to a more interesting consideration. The history of eggs goes back far past the dinosaur. Life 800 began as clumps of molecules suspended in the primordial, organic soup; and there, too, began eggs. One modern descendant of that early life is volvox, the tiny, emerald-like algae colony that lives in freshwater pools and ponds. Although these collectives of individual cells are among the simplest life forms, even they occasionally produce minute, shell-less eggs and sperm in order to exchange germ cells.

Clearly, the egg was one of life's earliest organizations, providing an escape hatch from stressful environments and the guarantee of a new genetic mix to carry Self one generation further. So successful a 900 devise it was, in fact, that it now occurs throughout the plant and animal kingdoms, with elaborate support systems to maintain the biologic investment. Since the egg must be coddled and protected and stocked with resources; it is therefore huge compared to other cells. It must be primed and timed and readied to explode into embryonic development at the first sign of a victorious sperm, and the resulting embryo must float gently and be well-fed until it can hatch or be birthed.

The complex machinery used to package a fertilized bird egg with four separate membranes and a 1000 shell, then color and mark it to match its environment, is just one example of such a support system. Yet it's a particularly important one for the internal organs that made that packaging possible also ultimately made possible the conquest of land. The first strange amphibian that crawled from the water and laid a shelled, land egg, which contained its own internal pond, passed on that organic packaging machinery and thus unlocked the continents for the explosion of reptiles, birds and mammals that followed in its shaky footsteps.

1100 A rather disturbing thought occurred to me on my tour of the Hanna collection: what's so laudable about collecting 200,000 eggs, killing the unborn embryos and cataloging and displaying the empty shells?

The answer turns out to be comforting in one respect, but sadly ironic in another. Birds divested of their eggs will usually begin a new phase of nest-building and egg-laying within a few weeks, and spring storms down more nests than all egg collectors put together. Add to this the fact that researchers used the Hanna collection to study eggshells before and after DDT, as well as the less tangible but far greater 1200 contribution to public education, then the collection starts to look invaluable, indeed.

But there won't be any more collections like this one. It is now illegal to take an egg, even in one's own backyard, without state and federal permits, and it is totally prohibited in certain states. So many former bird habitats have been taken to house and feed humans that we just can't spare many eggs anymore, and that's where the irony comes in. The shelled, land egg that made human collectors possible in the first place has led to such a proliferation of those collectors 1300 and other bipeds that egg collections themselves are no longer possible, with the exception of that mundane variety illuminated by the harsh light inside refrigerator doors.

8. (T—F) Petrified dinosaur eggs prove that the chicken really came before the egg.
9. (T—F) The egg is a very complex life support system.
10. (T—F) Egg collecting is becoming more popular. 1350

______ STOP ___ ASK FOR YOUR TIME ______

Record your time immediately, compute your scores and record on your progress chart.

Time __________ Sec.	RATE (from table on page 315):	R. ________
No. Correct __________ (key on page 322)	COMPREHENSION (10% for each correct answer):	C. ________
VII-17	EFFICIENCY (R×C):	E. ________

Record on Progress Chart on page 299

Length: 1350 words

Exercise VII-18

Readability Score: 45

Express and Discover

By Lorinda Redmond

(Reprinted from an original article of the Uniwyo Reading Research Center by permission of the director.)

WAIT FOR SIGNAL TO BEGIN READING

Conformity or Individuality

The concept of individuality is being destroyed because of big government, big business, and a growing society. In place of individual creativity, conformity is taking over. Rather than following the devices and desires of our own hearts, we are being pushed into conformity, which is creating emotional problems.

Individuality should be regarded as having social value and is an inalienable right of each citizen. Through education, the child's hope is to find himself, and to be an individual. We have the right to be treated as a person rather than being classified in a group, performing in a particular way just because everyone else is. 100

To prevent emotional problems leading to a breakdown you must search for and find your true identity. Exercise your freedom of choice by determining the inner standards that rule your life. Once you can identify how your subconscious rules keep you locked into rigid ways of being, you can work at changing. In searching for your true identity, do not identify solely with the work you do. You must realize and remember that your identity is not defined only by your role as worker. Discover your individuality by opening yourself up to creativity as well. 200

Two fundamental concepts of creativity related to finding your true identity are available: (1) Continuity relies on the best achievements of the past in any important field of human endeavor. (2) Significant novelty involves going beyond the boundaries of the known into the perilous realm of the unknown in quest of knowledge that is really important. In either case, build your own superstructure on the foundations laid by geniuses of the past.

In seeking your true identity reflect on the nature of ideas. Ideas involve consciousness and always refer to an object which is in one's state of awareness. Ideas 300 transcend the immediate and merely subjective into a broader and deeper quest for objectivity.

1. (T—F) The writer suggests that we conform to the expectations of the mass society to maintain our sanity.
2. (C.) The concept of significant novelty involves going beyond the boundaries of the known in our quest for ____________________.

Expressing Your Creative Ideas

Creative ideas are important in human affairs. First, without the ability to see the relationship existing between large constellations of facts in terms of significant events, man could have no conception of 400 history or progress of ideas. Secondly, creative ideas lead to those magnificent accomplishments which constitute civilization at its highest and best. The last point to consider is that in the face of crisis, man has no other recourse than his creativity. Mere power without the direction of creative ideas, in the bitter end brings nothing but disaster.

Each of your various roles in society calls for a different pattern of behavior and each expresses a different aspect of your personality. Underlying each of these different aspects of personality is an assortment of traits and characteristics. By allowing 500 free reign of expression to each of your roles, you are expressing various behaviors and indicating individual creativity through achieving an integration of your assortment of traits and characteristics.

Recognize your needs and strive to meet them fully by expressing yourself more freely and seeking your true identity. Freedom to question and create is one way to become more individualistic. Variety of choice has been brought to us through technology. Technology also has broken established family patterns, loosened controls of once monolithic, isolated social units, and in Western Society has made promises that anyone may become anything he or she likes. This gives us choices and a responsibility for our 600 own destiny. Utilize the freedom of choice by being creative and expressing yourself. Involve yourself in expressing whatever goal or goals prove to be meaningful to you.

3. (T—F) Creative ideas are based on comprehensive understanding of large blocks of data.
4. (T—F) Different roles help to define consistency in one's behavior.
5. (M.C.) Personal variety of choice has been made possible by:
   ______(1) conformity.
   ______(2) identity.
   ______(3) responsibility.
   ______(4) technology.

Creation of Inner Conflicts

Inner conflicts are created by ignoring or subduing our various subpersonalities. To help eliminate or reduce inner conflict we must identify and give expression to all our subpersonalities. Society creates a problem, though. It seems that Society makes ever more complicated demands on us regarding individuality. Not only should we control some of our impulses much of the time, but we should act like individuals happy and fulfilled at the same moment. We don't know how much freedom we have to push ourselves or how much we really can develop ourselves.

To fulfill demands of individuality we must attend to our own personal growth in areas of interest or risk stagnation. We must do something, anything, that will allow free reign for our various traits and characteristics to be expressed.

Above all, we must remember not to define ourselves only by the work we do. No one role is able to encompass all the many superpersonalities that demand expression. However, many of those around us seem to expect us to follow the leader and conform to the expectations of big business society rather than one in which we express ourselves individually. Perhaps when one develops his individuality too far, the same kind of destructive imbalances occur within the personality that occur within nature when one resource is built up at the expense of another. Limits of our individuality seem to be related to needs of society.

6. (T—F) Our own personal growth must be considered to be something more than just work.

7. (M.C.) In fulfilling demands of individuality our primary concern must be:
   ______(1) our own innate selfishness.
   ______(2) our own personal growth needs.
   ______(3) our ability to understand others.
   ______(4) the needs of society.

8. (C.) The need for individual expression is complicated by demands of ______.

Importance of Individuality

Sameness carried to an extent could result in a dull life. If everyone is doing the same thing, it would be easy to become bored and tired. Seeing a little variety in our everyday lives is what helps us to exist in this ever-changing society. People performing the same types of tasks differently is what makes life interesting. Showing a little bit of individual creativity in our daily lives expresses that each person is different and he deserves a little praise for the things he has accomplished.

Conformity insures a simple life. It doesn't take much to watch the other guy and do the same things he does. But, on the other hand, individual creativity demands a little work. Many in our own society would rather sit back and then follow a good example rather than try out new ideas.

In all of us the individual creativity is there to be expressed, but often we don't even care. We should get a sense of pride from expressing individual creativity. We should attempt at least to try out some new ideas to see how they work out. Maybe no one will object. Maybe our ideas might be accepted and we might feel freer to try other ideas.

Individual creativity needs to be expressed in order to fulfill the concept of being an individual with separate desires and needs. You can express your creativity by exploring the wide range of choices technology has created in this modern world, and by trying out new ideas in your work and in your recreational activities. You can find many ways of expressing yourself without violating the freedom of others.

In summary, in order to escape the monotony of a conforming society, find new and different ways to meet your needs, and you may be surprised to discover creative abilities you never recognized before.

Show the world that you are an individual and bring your individual creativity out into the open. You may find that society does allow a great deal of freedom of choice and action.

9. (T—F) Conformity is a simple life with few demands.

10. (T—F) Society doesn't allow much freedom of individual choice.

______ STOP ___ ASK FOR YOUR TIME ______

Record your time immediately, compute your scores and record on your progress chart.

Time ________ Sec.	RATE (from table on page 315):	R. ________
No. Correct ________ (key on page 330)	COMPREHENSION (10% for each correct answer):	C. ________
VII-18	EFFICIENCY (R × C):	E. ________

Record on Progress Chart on page 299

Length: 1350 words

Exercise VII-19

Readability Score: 42

Killers in the Air

by Judith McPherson, R.N.

(Reprinted by permission from *Health*, May-June, 1970.)

WAIT FOR SIGNAL TO BEGIN READING

A plague, urban-centered and world-wide, threatens devastation and death. People, plants, and animals sicken and die. Masonry crumbles, metal corrodes, and rubber and leather become hard and brittle. The cause of the plague is no strange virus or unidentified germ. It is pollution. The air carries a startling mixture of harmful substances, reacting with each other and influenced by solar radiation, temperature, winds, and moisture. It has been estimated that 70 percent of pollutants are still unidentified, but here is a list of those we do know: sulfur oxides, arsenic, carbon (soot), excess carbon dioxide, carbon monoxide, cyanide, hydrocarbons, ozone, asbestos, nitrogen oxides and aldehydes. 100

Most widely publicized of the air pollutants is sulfur dioxide, an atmospheric poison that can be lethal to plants and people, as well as damaging to buildings and monuments. Sulfur dioxide is produced mainly by the burning of coal and certain fuel oils. When the level of sulfur dioxide in the air remains for three days at 0.52 parts per million, public health authorities have come to expect an increased human death rate. Even a level of 0.11 parts per million, maintained for three days, will have an adverse effect on the health of the people of the contaminated community. 200

Sulfur dioxide also attacks plant life. Both flowers and trees can be damaged and even killed by it. Thousands of acres of deciduous forest have been killed by pollution; specific examples have been identified in Montana, Tennessee, Ontario, and British Columbia. Citrus yields in the Los Angeles Basin have been cut in half by pollution; lettuce and spinach have been practically eliminated as healthy crops in that area. The lethal effects of the sulfur oxides do not stop with the gases. The prime means of atmospheric cleansing is through rain and snow. When sulfur oxides combine with water vapor, the 300 result is sulfuric acid. It is this that eats away at our buildings, our monuments, even our gravestones!

When sulfuric acid falls in rainwater, it is thought to be the cause of rapid and dramatic increases in acidity of lakes and rivers. This increase in acidity in the lakes and rivers of southern Sweden is thought to be the cause of the virtual extinction of the once-prosperous salmon industry.

1. (T—F) Seventy percent of air pollutants are still unidentified.

400 2. (M.C.) Sulfur dioxide is produced mainly by:
   _____(1) the burning of coal and certain oils.
   _____(2) the burning of gasoline.
   _____(3) the burning of sulphuric acid.
   _____(4) the burning of wood.

3. (C.) When sulfur oxides combine with water vapor the result is _________.

Carbon or Soot

Carbon, another common pollutant all too obvious in urban areas, is a product of fuel combustion. Soot soils our clothes, penetrates closed windows, defaces fresh-fallen snow, and gets in our eyes. In New York, Chicago, and Detroit more than 730 tons of suspended particles, including carbon, are deposited in each square mile every year.

More than a nuisance, however, soot is known 500 to carry cancer-causing hydrocarbons beyond the protective nucociliary lining of the lungs. Hydrocarbons are found specifically in petroleum, natural gas, and coal. One aromatic hydrocarbon, benzopyrene, has been proved in laboratory experiments to cause cancer in animals. Health hazards from jet exhaust are not to be ignored. Jets spew out large quantities of hydrocarbons. It has been estimated that one four-engine jet at full take-off throttle produces the per-minute equivalent in pollution of 6,000 automobiles. Consider how much of the exhaust from the first plane in a take-off line-up is sucked into the 600 ventilation system of the plane following—and so on through the line.

Odorless and colorless, carbon monoxide has long been known as a killer. It has recently been estimated that this gas reaches the highest relative concentration of any gaseous pollutant in the urban atmosphere.

4. (T—F) The main problem with soot is its unsightliness.
5. (T—F) Carbon monoxide is foul smelling and carries hydrocarbons which cause cancer.

More Health Hazards

Carbon monoxide is dangerous because of the body's normal arrangements for oxygen transport.

The red blood cells contain hemoglobin, with which oxygen combines freely for transport to the target tissues and which then freely releases the oxygen for local use. Like oxygen, carbon monoxide has a great affinity for hemoglobin; but unlike oxygen, carbon monoxide forms a tight bond with hemoglobin and is not freely released again. Even when air contains only small quantities of carbon monoxide, the situation is dangerous, because molecule after molecule of hemoglobin is rendered unavailable for carrying oxygen. Thus the body receives insufficient oxygen, and asphyxiation results.

Because carbon monoxide is among the pollutants released in automobile exhaust, it is quite possible for oxygen deprivation to affect persons who drive for prolonged periods on heavily-trafficked roads. Studies are presently under way to demonstrate the connection between highway accidents and blood levels of carbon monoxide in drivers.

Not only the exhaust of the automobile is dangerous, according to Dr. Rene Dubos, microbiologist and experimental pathologist. The auto braking system is also a pollution culprit, by virtue of discharging into the atmosphere particles of asbestos. Such particles have been found in significant amounts in the lungs of urban dwellers, Dr. Dubos has said, "... and there is no doubt that asbestos is a great health hazard."

6. (C.) Carbon ________ may possibly cause oxygen deprivation in drivers on heavily-trafficked roads.

7. (M.C.) The auto braking system is a pollutant because of its discharge of:
   ______(1) rubber.
   ______(2) steel.
   ______(3) aluminum particles.
   ______(4) asbestos.

What Shall We Do?

Although the way in which some air pollutants cause reactions in the lungs is only partially known, it is apparent that the gases, particles, and liquid droplets can cause the air passages to constrict. Also, pollutants can get through the protective lining of the bronchi and form deposits in the lungs, and thus cause excess production of mucous. Proper exchange of gases in the lungs can be impaired by mechanical or chemical blocking of the alveoli, the tiny sac-like cells in the lungs through which gaseous exchange between blood and air occurs.

Studies in Japan and in Great Britain have shown that school children living in highly polluted areas show more evidence of lung disease than those living in nonpolluted areas. A study in New York following the "killer smog," of 1966, during which there were 168 deaths reported as related to the smog, showed a relationship between the severe air pollution and the increase in obstructive respiratory symptoms in children under age 16.

In view of the fact that the new generations are now being exposed to extensive air pollutants, it is likely that the young will suffer the effects of pollution much more than those who are adults now. As the infant grows up, his clean pink lungs will turn more rapidly to gray and then to black.

Professor Dubos indicates that pollution will not have its maximum effect until the turn of the century. Harvey Wheeler, writing recently in *Saturday Review*, warns us of what that maximum might be:

> This is not merely a question of unsightliness nor even of the threat of a rise in lung cancer and emphysema. Even more serious hazards may develop if pollution particles are carried by superjets from the lower atmosphere into its upper, turbulence-free layers. Scientists warn that these jet contrails may not be dispersed and could act as an insulation layer between earth and sun, cooling the earth and leading to a new Ice Age. Of course, no one is certain what will really happen.... Today it does not seem inconceivable that pollution particles could quickly clog the upper atmosphere, and before we know it, utter havoc could be upon us.

8. (T—F) Following the 1966 New York "killer smog," many deaths were related to the smog.

9. (T—F) Children will suffer the effects of pollution much more than adults.

10. (T—F) Conceivably, according to Harvey Wheeler, jet contrails could so hold in heat from the sun as to melt the polar icecaps and inundate the world.

_______STOP—ASK FOR YOUR TIME_______

Record your time immediately.

Time __________ Sec. RATE (from table on page 315): R. __________

No. Correct __________ COMPREHENSION (10% for each correct answer): C. __________
(key on page 322)

VII-19 EFFICIENCY (R×C): E. __________

Record on Progress Chart on page 299

Length: 1350 words

Exercise VII-20

Readability Score: 38

The Pests' Pests

WAIT FOR SIGNAL TO BEGIN READING

For years Rudolf Lindemann and his son George had sprayed a chemical insecticide over the hundreds of acres of tomatoes on their farm to control the tomato fruitworms and yellow-striped armyworms that otherwise would have destroyed the crop. But this month, George Lindemann will scatter 750,000 eggs of green lacewing and chalcid flies among the tomato plants. The lacewings and chalcids are natural enemies of the worms and when the eggs hatch, the predator larvae will attack and kill the worms more thoroughly and more effectively than the insecticides ever did in the past.

The Lindemann family's new tactics reflect a ↲100 growing awareness by U.S. farmers that biological agents can control crop pests as effectively as the miracle chemicals that have flooded the market since the end of World War II. Interestingly enough, the new trend in agricultural pest-control techniques is prompted less by a concern about environmental pollution than by the simple economic law of diminishing returns.

"We're businessmen, like any others," says the younger Lindemann, now president of the family-owned farm. Five years ago, when confronted with a particularly severe infestation of tomato fruitworms, the Lindemanns sprayed their crops with carbaryl—a general purpose insecticide. "We killed the worms, ↲200 all right," he recalled, "along with every other damned bug in that field." But the worms returned later in the season, and it took repeated sprayings of the chemical to suppress them. The family spent up to $80 an acre just for pesticides on some badly infested fields. "At the end of the year," Lindemann said, "we were looking at a tremendous insecticide bill." It was then that Lindemann contracted with Louis Ruud, Jr., a graduate entomologist, for pest-control counseling.

Predator

Lindemann pays Ruud $7 per acre to inspect his tomato fields and $2 per acre to examine some of his ↲300 other crops (melons and cotton) and to prescribe pest-control methods. By using such biological controls as the lacewings, Lindemann currently is spending only about $5 per acre on pesticides where previously he was paying an average of $30 per acre—and saving almost $9,000 a year on chemicals. "We're getting results," Lindemann said. "We had to get our costs down without sacrificing yields, and this was the way to do it."

But bug-eating bugs are just one of the many different approaches that can be followed under the concept of "integrated pest control." Along with 400→ predatory insects, there are parasites, pathogens, sterilization, decoy plants, hormonal stimulants, sex lures—and even the judicious use of pesticides—to help growers in their never-ending war against pests. Ruud uses whatever combinations of these various techniques he feels would be most effective against the insects pestering Lindemann.

Predation, of course, was the first natural method used by U.S. farmers. In the late 1800s, the cottony-cushion scale, a louse-like insect, migrated from Australia to the U.S. and infested the orange groves of California. To counter the pest, the U.S. imported vedalia beetles, a type of ladybug. "They 500→ really went to town," said James E. Gilmore, an entomologist with the Agricultural Research Service, "and saved an industry worth millions of dollars."

1. (M. C.) New pest control techniques are prompted mostly by:
   - _____(1) concern for environmental pollution.
   - _____(2) economic laws of diminishing returns.
   - _____(3) consumer refusal to purchase chemically treated produce.
   - _____(4) inadequate pesticide supplies.

2. (M. C.) The first natural method of pest control used by U.S. farmers was:
   - _____(1) parasites.
   - _____(2) sterilization.
   - _____(3) decoy plants.
   - _____(4) predation.

Importation of Predators

Since then, more than 650 species of predatory 600→ insects have been imported into the U.S. for search-and-destroy missions against one or more of the 10,000 types of resident bugs classified as pests. Not all of these experiments have been successful, but the winners are impressive. During the 1950s, for example, a species of weevil began severely damaging alfalfa fields in the eastern U.S. The ARS then introduced five species of tiny wasps—one from Italy, one from Sweden and three from France—into the alfalfa, and the wasps did the job.

"New Jersey now has the weevil under good control," says Dr. Reece I. Sailer, an ARS entomologist. "In 1963, 94 per cent of the alfalfa farmers there used chemicals on their crops. Last year, only 8 per cent used insecticides, and this is a measure of how effective biological controls can be."

Sailer and other scientists believe that there is a role for chemical insecticides, although on a much more limited scale than farmers used up through the mid-1960s and the fact is that farmers are already using lesser amounts of chemicals than before. The pressures of increasing legal restrictions against the use of "shotgun" chemicals like DDT has produced research aimed at the development of insecticidal "bullets" effective against very specific pests.

3. (C.) Increasing legal restrictions governing use of chemicals like DDT encourages more ______________.
4. (T—F) Scientists believe there is a role for chemical insecticides.
5. (T—F) Predation experiments have been 100% successful.

Pathogens

The use of pathogens, such as viruses, to keep pests down on the farm is still in the development stages. Ruud, for instance, sometimes sprays a mixture of diseased cabbage loopers, a caterpillar species, and water on fields where the pest is prevalent; the cabbage loopers pick up the virus and die five to seven days later, while other species—and the plants themselves—remain unharmed.

At present there is only one safe, commercially available pathogen, *Bacillus thuringiensis*. Dr. Louis A. Falcon, California entomologist, describes this as a bacterial infection effective against 137 different species. Falcon is hopeful that an experimental "flu-bug" for bugs, known as nuclear polyhedrosis virus, will soon be approved for use against certain types of bollworms. "It is ideal in integrated control situations," he says. "It is harmless to other insects, doesn't pollute and doesn't get into the food chain."

One way of keeping pests like lygus bugs out of crops like cotton is to offer the insects another plant, such as alfalfa, which they prefer. Cotton farmers in California now cultivate strips of alfalfa as decoys among cotton fields, and the lygus bugs gravitate there instead of the bolls. Not only does this reduce the farmers' insecticide costs, but it also preserves many of the natural insect predators that feed on destructive bollworms and leaf perforators.

6. (T—F) Pathogen use is a highly developed technique.
7. (T—F) There are many safe pathogens commercially available.
8. (T—F) One way of keeping pests out of crops is to offer other plants.

Other Approaches

Other approaches include synthetic juvenile hormones that disrupt insects' growth patterns, preventing them from maturing and reproducing, and the synthesis of insect sex attractants. This technique uses prolonged exposure to a synthetic female attractant to try to satiate or dull the senses of male insects, disorient the bugs to hinder reproduction, or lure them into traps where they might be sterilized by irradiation.

Cobalt irradiation is the technique used in the most spectacular case of pest control so far. Starting in 1962, the ARS released in the southern U.S. millions of male screwworms that had been sterilized by gamma rays from cobalt-60 sources. Screwworms lay their eggs in open wounds of cattle and other livestock, and the larvae, when they emerge, eat the flesh; a heavy infestation can kill a full-grown cow.

By 1965, the sterile males had reduced the screwworm population in the U.S. by 99 percent, according to the Department of Agriculture, and livestock losses were cut to a tiny fraction of the estimated $100 million of past years.

But the real cost of freedom from pests is eternal vigilance—as the screwworm persists in proving. Thus last month, the Department of Agriculture reported that the parasitic insects are now showing up on animals in California and Texas, which means that another host of irradiated males will be needed there.

9. (C.) The most spectacular technique of pest sterilization is ______________ irradiation.
10. (T—F) The real cost of freedom from pests is eternal vigilance.

_______STOP__ASK FOR YOUR TIME_______

Record your time immediately.

Time __________ Sec.	RATE (from table on page 315):	R. __________
No. Correct __________ (key on page 330)	COMPREHENSION (10% for each correct answer):	C. __________
VII-20	EFFICIENCY (R × C):	E. __________

Record on Progress Chart on page 299

SERIES VIII
Critical Thinking Exercises

Purpose

Merely scanning for main ideas or more intensive reading for facts will not develop the critical reading skills demanded in so many situations in adult life today. In addition to the development of assimilation and retention skills, certain basic abilities of critical reading must be developed. You must be able to grasp literal and implied meanings and to relate to them by generalization. You must form evaluative reactions to what you read as you inquire about quality and accuracy of material. You must learn to judge rationally what you read. You must develop insight and understanding in applying the ideas you acquire from reading.

A whole book could be developed around the concept of critical reading skills. To some degree you began to apply them in your Study Reading Exercises. Although critical reading skills involve a different approach to reading that does not result in a measure of efficiency, you should recognize this type of reading as a part of your pattern of flexibility. Therefore, this book has been expanded to include some brief introductory exercises of this type.

Instructions

In this series, rate of reading is not considered as being of primary importance. You may read these little samples as fast or slow as you please, but you must take time to *think* about them carefully, either during or after the reading process—or both. The articles are all short excerpts presented with only a number and no identification of source. Each one is followed by a few questions to focus your thinking. Most readers should be able to read and react to each exercise in less than two minutes.

Try to draw from the content clues that will help you to make judgments. Consider also the rest of the critical reading questions presented here:

1. What is the author's purpose?
2. When was this written?
3. To whom is this appeal directed?
4. Who would have you believe this?
5. In what ways does the writer reveal a bias?
6. What do you question in this material?
7. What key words were used to influence your emotions?
8. To which of your basic needs does the writer appeal?
9. What would the writer like for you to do?

After you have answered as many questions as you can, turn to the "KEY" materials on pages 323 and 331. There you will find an identification of the source of the material and a few comments about the purpose of the presentation. Judge for yourself the accuracy of your responses.

Suggestions

The process of critical thinking in relation to reading is a never ending life process. One is deluged with communications of all kinds, many of which are loaded with emotional appeal and propaganda techniques. Series VI-18 in this workbook includes an analysis of several basic propaganda techniques and may be worth rereading in connection with these exercises.

The exercises in this book are only a token of the continuing work that you must do to be a critical reader. The ultimate dimension of effective reading is the skill of *reading critically.* Can you differentiate fact from opinion? Can you evaluate the validity of opinion? Can you detect unsound reasoning and propaganda techniques? Can you keep these points in mind, even when you are functioning at some of your higher levels of reading efficiency?

Are you sensitive to emotionally loaded adjectives and adverbs that frequently are inserted to influence your feelings about factual content being described? Can you sift these out of your thinking to get a less biased view of the facts? Are you alert to words which are used deliberately to try to appeal to your needs or values? Do you get too easily identified with the writers' point of view?

The twelve most persuasive words in the English language are said to be: you, money, save, new, results, health, easy, safety, love, discovery, proven, and guarantee. Perhaps you should be alert to excessive use of such terms in any type of reading material.

You need to develop the ability to comprehend ideas that authors do not state specifically, but that they expect you to infer. You need to develop skill in extending your thinking about ideas to such concepts as making generalizations, perceiving relationships, predicting outcomes, and anticipating authors' purposes. You need to make judgments about authors and their ideas. They can try to influence you, but *you* have the final word. You can choose to reject an author and his ideas, and he has no recourse. Good readers try to develop skill in identifying and understanding the ideas they encounter in reading, but ultimate acceptance and application of these ideas depend upon many personal factors that have nothing to do with the reading process itself.

You can be a good reader if you seek to make a personal application of the skills you have learned and if you maintain an alert inquiring mind. But you will not be reading in the deliberate concept of reading that sets 800 words per minute as a maximum. Neither will you be a good reader because you whiz through all materials at some fantastic rate of speed reading. You can develop a flexibility that enables you to judge and to adjust your reading skills to the needs and purposes of the moment.

You will discover that reading makes a great difference in your life. As you seek the ideas behind the words, you will find that flexible and polished reading skills are keys to a vast reservoir of knowledge and stimulation. Only you can determine your ultimate potential in using reading as a tool for personal development.

Even the "great books" are not gods: they are only tools for you to use. They may even be dull tools if you approach them with less than the sharpest of your wits. Authors are often dry and boring to some readers. They do not have the advantage of observing your reaction—responding to your enthusiasm—clarifying, when you look confused. They must go on monotonously with their one-sided monologue in total ignorance of *your* enthusiasm or boredom. If you remember this, you may be more tolerant and more effective in applying your skills to get the most from their work.

But what you need is not patience, but really an impatience with yourself that forces you to decide what you are reading *for* and then to read *for it!* You need to be impatient enough to center the energy for effective reading in your own head. True concentration in reading is not the effort to "keep other thoughts out"; it is a by-product of having a goal challenging enough to attract the whole mind to the task of seeking it.

If knowledge is your goal, then you can attain it only when you think for yourself, not when you have merely understood what someone else thought. Knowledge is not something you learn or absorb: it is something you think and use and bring to life in your own ideas.

In short, you will become a part of the reading you do. You will be able to read and to know what it is all about and how it bears on other things you have read or done. You will read in a way that makes you think, and finally produce some ideas with the look and mark of your own mind upon them.

Exercise VIII-1

Length: 247 words — Readability Score: 80

"They laughed when I wound up my shaver . . ." That's liable to happen to you when you first use it in front of anyone. A wind-up shaver may seem a plaything, or at best an emergency type of shaver (because it needs no cords or batteries). After all, how can a hand-cranked shaver rotate fast enough to do a clean and close job? And how many times do you have to wind the darn thing to finish one shave?

One answer at a time: The three-blade shaving head revolves at such a fast clip that it actually gives you seventy-two thousand cutting strokes a minute! Now, about the winding: the palm-shaped body is filled with a huge mainspring made of the same Swedish super steel used in the most expensive watch movements. You can crank the key just like a movie camera (about six turns) and the shaver shaves and shaves and shaves. From ear to ear, from nose to neck, without slowing down, it maintains its full shaving speed right to the end—and long enough to do the complete job. Hard to believe, but really true.

We have reason to believe that you will want to keep your shaver for the office, club, cabin or in a permanent place in your bathroom cabinet. Once you've tried it you won't let it go. The money that it leaves in your pocket; the dependability; the good, fast, clean shaves that you'll get—they'll give *you* the last laugh.

_____ _____ _____

1. What is the author's purpose? ____________________

2. To whom is this appeal directed? ____________________

3. Who would have you believe this? ____________________

4. What would the writer like for you to do? ____________________

See page 323 for source.

Exercise VIII-2

Length: 267 words — Readability Score: 74

So far, I had not opened my eyes. I felt that I lay upon my back, unbound. I reached out my hand, and it fell heavily upon something damp and hard. There I suffered it to remain for many minutes, while I strove to imagine where and *what* I could be. I longed, yet dared not to employ my vision. I dreaded the first glance at objects around me. It was not that I feared to look upon things horrible, but that I grew aghast lest there should be *nothing* to see. At length, with a wild desperation at heart, I quickly unclosed my eyes. My worst thoughts, then, were confirmed. The blackness of eternal night encompassed me. I struggled for breath. The intensity of the darkness seemed to oppress and stifle me. The atmosphere was intolerably close. I still lay quietly, and made effort to exercise my reason.

A fearful idea now suddenly drove the blood in torrents upon my heart, and for a brief period, I once more relapsed into insensibility. Upon recovering, I at once started to my feet, trembling convulsively in every fiber. I thrust my arms wildly above and around me in all directions. I felt nothing; yet dreaded to move a step, lest I should be impeded by the walls of a *tomb*. Perspiration burst from every pore, and stood in cold big beads upon my forehead. The agony of suspense grew at length intolerable, and I cautiously moved forward, with my arms extended, and my eyes straining from their sockets, in the hope of catching some faint ray of light.

_____ _____ _____

1. What is the author's purpose? ____________________

2. When was this written? ____________________

3. What key words were used to influence one's emotions? ____________________

4. Who would have you believe this? ____________________

See page 331 for source.

Exercise VIII-3

Length: 290 words — Readability Score: 69

I feel strongly compelled to relate the facts of my experience with marijuana. To start off, I'm a student at a suburban high school and live in an affluent neighborhood. By all standards I'm almost totally "straight."

Being a beer drinker, I've always been curious about "grass." Having heard so much about it and the plea to legalize it on the grounds of its being "a mild intoxicant," I got some and tried it out.

First time, nothing happened. Within an hour of smoking it the second time, I got vigorously stoned! Being stoned is being insane! I found out the hard way that there is no similarity between the effects of "grass" and beer.

On beer I've always been calm and even jovial, although with quite poor reflex actions. While stoned, I was in a panic, with suicidal thoughts. I was afraid I'd knife myself, jump out the window, or beat my head against the wall. My heart was beating a mile a minute, and I had incredible time and space distortions. I would have hour-long nightmares in the blink of my eyes, and I thought the room was hundreds of feet long.

While being in this terrified state, I couldn't call a doctor, because I was doing something illegal with heavy penalties. Fortunately, I had some straight-headed friends on hand, who put me in a blanket-covered bed and held me down for the next several hours. To me it was like several hundred years. I never imagined that marijuana had such a violent effect. No wonder it's illegal.

My message is this: Never believe any favorable propaganda about pot, and don't "find out" like I did. I'm glad I'm still alive to write this letter to warn others.

_____ _____ _____

1. What is the author's purpose? ________________

2. To whom is this appeal directed? ________________

3. What would the writer like for you to do? ________

4. What do you question in this material? __________

See page 323 for source.

Exercise VIII-4

Length: 279 words — Readability Score: 67

Some people find life ecstatic, exciting, or exhilarating. Others relate to life in a cool, calculated, or collected manner. Yet, for multitudes of human beings, life is merely lukewarm.

Why is life a lukewarm experience for so many people? Here are a few possible explanations:

Fear of involvement. Taking a stand, voicing an opinion, expressing an emotion, all mean getting involved. This is simply something the lukewarm cannot face up to.

Fear of facing oneself. If one is to run hot or cold, he must take the time to know himself. He must rid himself of those phony caricatures he displays to his friends and associates. For some, the task is too fearsome to tackle.

Fear of facing others. The shy, the timid, and the unsure fall into this category. Being lukewarm serves as a shield of armor.

Fear of failure. Active, aggressive, ambitious people succeed—and sometimes fail. Failure is too great a risk for a lukewarm human being. Apathy sets in when he realizes that although he won't be successful, he also won't blunder.

Seemingly, if life is lukewarm, it is at the same time neutral and negative. It is lived in shades of gray, breathed shallowly, and partaken of sparingly. It isn't marching: it's marking time Rather than challenging, life becomes a checkmate.

Is there an antidote for apathy? There are a number. One can become absorbed in a cause outside of and greater than himself. A person can treat it like any other bad habit—determine to break the habit. He can learn to be enthusiastic, a trait which is more often learned and practiced than inherited. Life can be full and dynamic and meaningful.

_____ _____ _____

1. What is the author's purpose? ________________

2. To whom is this appeal directed? ________________

3. What would the writer like for you to do? ________

4. To which of your basic needs does the writer appeal? ________________

See page 331 for source.

Exercise VIII-5

Length: 205 words Readability Score: 66

Do you or your loved ones ever have any trouble with the problem of worry, fear or anxiety? Do you get discouraged or depressed, and even lack faith in yourself? Does an inferiority complex ever plague you? Do you ever feel resentful or do bad relations ever develop between you and other people?

There is an answer to all such human problems, and it's an answer that works. It is to develop the process or right thinking and a faith that lifts you above defeat.

I believe we have something that can be of help to you and those whom you love. Right off, let me say we are not selling anything—just offering something that can bring new happiness to you.

And it is this: For many years I have talked every Sunday at my church on Fifth Avenue at 29th Street in New York City to large audiences on the above-mentioned matters and kindred subjects. There grew up a demand to have these talks, all of which dealt with practical, workable methods for happy and successful living, made available in printed form. One-half million people are receiving three of these practical guides to living each month and the total readership is several million.

_____ _____ _____

1. What is the author's purpose? ________________

2. To whom is this appeal directed? ________________

3. To which of your basic needs does the writer appeal? ________________

4. What key words were used to influence one's emotions? ________________

See page 323 for source.

Exercise VIII-6

Length: 249 words Readability Score: 63

Okay, so you've had your automobile checked and you figure you are ready for winter. Not quite, for there are several more minor items that you can check yourself which are bits of knowledge that every motorist should carry with him from November through March.

In checking equipment items yourself, make sure your heater is working properly. Do you have a car jack in your trunk and a fully inflated spare tire? A flat tire on an isolated road during severely cold weather can mean serious trouble, if you suddenly discover that you don't have a jack or fully inflated spare.

Police and professional drivers experienced in winter driving say snow tires are far better than ordinary tires for both starting and stopping on snow and ice. Although heavy-duty chains are best of all, some motorists have been known to carry bags of sand in their trunks to give them extra traction. They suppose that the added weight gives the tires more pulling power on ice. Fact is, it doesn't, and if it's of considerable weight, it may even cause the rear end to sway severely. The only value of sand in the trunk is that it can be sprinkled on the ice for short-distance traction.

Health officers summed up advice to winter motorists with a warning to those over forty, those who are overweight, and those who have a record of heart problems. Go to great lengths to avoid overexertion in your efforts to free a stranded car.

_____ _____ _____

1. What is the author's purpose? ________________

2. What do you question in this material? ________________

3. To which of your basic needs does the writer appeal? ________________

4. What would the writer like for you to do? ________________

See page 331 for source.

Exercise VIII-7

Length: 260 words — Readability Score: 63

About the only thing standing between a youngster and a car is one small word. That word is "no." It's the parents who must say it, and say it often, especially during the school year. A study covering 30 high schools and 20,000 students, explains why: 1. The more evenings a week the car is used the lower a youngster's grades fall. 2. Good students who go overboard on cars suffer the sharpest drop in grades. 3. If pleasure driving is permitted during the school week grades are certain to tumble. These days scholastic failure can ruin a youngster's future by closing the door to career opportunities that require a certain level of formal education. So failing to say "no" to your child may condemn him to a second-rate future. If you allow a teenager to wriggle free of parental "interference" by buying his own car you'll almost certainly be guaranteeing a drop in scholarship. It's often the poorest students who own their own cars, and the longer they own them the less chance they have of improving their grades. Whatever the scholastic ability of a youngster, ownership of a car tends to drop him down one grade. An "A" student becomes a "B" student, and so forth. And when he has a job the drop is quicker and farther, frequently to the failing level. Most teenage boys who hold jobs do so to earn money for car upkeep. They work even longer hours than do other job-holding youngsters, thus consuming any left-over time they ordinarily might have for study.

_____ _____ _____

1. What is the author's purpose? ________________

2. To whom is this appeal directed? ________________

3. To which of your basic needs does the writer appeal? ________________

4. What would the writer like for you to do? ________________

See page 323 for source.

Exercise VIII-8

Length: 203 words — Readability Score: 60

Unless enough Americans somehow unite, I must candidly say to you that freedom's days are numbered. Allow me to explain.

I have been asked to write to you because of your deep concern for your country. I am gravely disturbed, and I think you are too, about the very real possibility of a relative handful of union bosses seizing control of America's government.

Their thirst for power is not representative of either the American people or the hardworking members of labor unions, whose dues are used (often improperly and unlawfully) to finance the activities of these bosses.

Let me say at the outset that this letter should not be construed as an attack on labor unions. What I oppose—and I hope that you oppose it also—is the abuse of power by labor union bosses.

I know you are busy. I know also that you are constantly bombarded with solicitations, polls, and exhortations of every kind. Frankly, I was reluctant to add to your burdens—realizing that you may very well have the inclination to toss this letter and its enclosures into the trash can.

You may do precisely that anyhow. But before you do, I urge you to read the enclosures.

_____ _____ _____

1. What is the author's purpose? ________________

2. What key words were used to influence your emotions? ________________

3. To which of your basic needs does the writer appeal? ________________

4. In what ways does the writer reveal a bias? ________________

See page 331 for source.

Exercise VIII-9

Length: 318 words Readability Score: 58

"This is a push-button age." With a flick of your wrist you can watch a sports event, wash the dinner dishes, or adjust the heat. Sure, automated living is easy; but it eases your muscles out of needed exercise.

Regular exercise can do more than improve muscle tone. It erases fatigue and boredom better than a comfortable chair before the television set. It controls inches more effectively than does diet alone. It reduces nervous tension more constructively than a cigarette or a double martini. Exercise alone strengthens your heart and lungs and helps your digestion.

Exercise may be as vigorous as tennis and volleyball or as limited as daily calisthenics and gardening. Whether you are six or sixty, an amateur athlete or a handicapped individual, exercise will improve your health. When you begin an exercise program . . .

Check your health: Ask your physician's advice about types and amounts of exercise. He will suggest activities suited to your age, sex, and physical condition.

Train for action: Plunging a "soft" body into vigorous exercise can be harmful. If you are out of practice, begin with small doses of exercise and gradually increase them.

Stay in your league: Don't try to compete with persons who are younger than you, twice as strong, or more skillful. And remember: Being in condition for one sport does not mean that you are in condition for another.

Watch your reaction: The ability to recuperate after physical activity is a good guide to the amount of exercise you can take. If breathlessness and pounding heart persist more than ten minutes after exercise, you have probably overdone it. If weakness persists the next day or even two hours after strenuous activity, you should take your exercise more slowly until you build up stamina.

Check your gear: Check the equipment you use in exercising. For safety's sake, make sure that it is of top quality and in excellent repair.

1. What is the author's purpose? ______________

2. To whom is this appeal directed? ______________

3. What would the writer like for you do to? ______________

4. To which of your basic needs does the writer appeal? ______________

See page 323 for source.

Exercise VIII-10

Length: 259 words Readability Score: 57

Water and energy are intricately related. In the West, large amounts of our electrical power comes from hydro electric plants. In the future, more of our electric power will come from coal-fired steam generation, which requires water for cooling.

People here in the West learned early that water is one of their most valuable resources and they have worked hard to use it wisely. But today there is much more competition for water.

To the farmer, water means irrigation that can assure his ability to raise a crop. He sees it as an all important link in this nation's food supply. To industry, water creates jobs that are vital to the areas economy. To cities, water is a necessity for their growing populations. To people, water is a god given right to have, as much as, the air we breathe.

As the West grows and develops, there will be serious controversies over the uses of water. Tri-State and other electric utilities will be caught between competing forces. Agricultural needs for electric energy are growing rapidly. New businesses and industry will be built that require power. The population is increasing, and people demand power as a necessity of life.

This will mean that new generation plants must be built and they will consume water.

The decisions on how water will be used must come from state and federal governments.

These decisions will effect you. It's apparent that there is a limited supply of water available. Conservation and efficient electric energy use will also be the theme of the future.

1. What is the author's purpose? ______________

2. To whom is this appeal directed? ______________

3. Who would have you believe this? ______________

4. To which of your basic needs does the writer appeal? ______________

See page 331 for source.

Exercise VIII-11

Length: 221 words   Readability Score: 55

The original redwood forest covered almost two million acres. Today only ten percent or less of that original forest remains.

The depletion of the redwoods occurred mostly because the land was allowed to pass into private ownership before its value to the nation was fully recognized.

Nowhere is a major block of virgin forest presently preserved where the entire growing range of the species can be represented.

The National Park Service has pointed out that it takes a thousand years or more to grow mature trees; and once cut, much longer still to establish a climax forest, if indeed that is now possible at all.

In a matter of only two or three more years, if the past rate of cutting is resumed, no unprotected redwood area of sufficient ecological or recreational integrity will remain that is worth being preserved in a national park.

In the last 30 years, over half of the valley has been cut over. Logging roads have been pushed into every area. Logging, in fact, has gone so far that not a single streambed remains free from erosion, siltation, or choking debris.

So let us be very clear that the time for action is short. The time for leisurely discussion and further prolonged study is past. The opportunity, now ours, will not present itself to another generation.

_____ _____ _____

1. What is the author's purpose? _______________

2. What key words were used to influence one's emotions? _______________

3. In what ways does the writer reveal a bias? _______

4. To whom is this appeal directed? _______________

See page 324 for source.

Exercise VIII-12

Length: 247 words   Readability Score: 54

The collecting of unusual rocks and semi-precious stones—rockhounding—is gaining momentum as a family sport in this country. One big reason: In addition to providing fun for everyone in the family, it also can be a "fringe benefit" for many, providing bonus adventures to their travel vacations. That's because rockhounding can be so easily combined with other outdoor sports—say, doing a bit of rockhounding while camping or fishing. (Or, maybe it's really the other way around—saving the fishing for when the rockhounding slows down.)

If you're interested in adding new variety and fun to your travels by graduating from the ranks of the "looker" to that of a real rockhound, you'll find the move much easier than you may have thought. A small rock pick, knapsack, a book or two, notebook, prospector's pan, a couple of small screens, plus a desire for a little adventure and a lot of fun are all you need to join the rockhounding clan.

Even the objects of your search often are much easier to find than many think. Today's rockhounds are, for the most part, content to search for materials which though certainly far less valuable than gold or diamonds, are relatively abundant. Rocks like agate, jasper, petrified wood, chalcedony, onyx and sapphire are among the most popular and zealously sought after.

Join the mushrooming corps of rockhounds and you'll gain a hobby that promises rich bonuses in new adventures, some precious stones and a mother lode of fun.

_____ _____ _____

1. What is the author's purpose? _______________

2. To whom is this appeal directed? _______________

3. To which of your basic needs does the writer appeal? _______________

4. What would the writer like for you to do? _______

See page 332 for source.

Exercise VIII-13

Length: 349 words | Readability Score: 53

With stereo equipment, bigger isn't necessarily better than smaller and buying something at a big discount isn't necessarily better than buying at list price. It is important, however, to spend your money wisely. We try to make it as easy as possible for you to do just that. Rather than try and sell every brand on the market we select the ones we would buy ourselves. We then take what we feel are the best products in different price ranges and sell them as "best buy" systems. With hundreds of brands of stereo equipment on the market and the rapidly changing technology of today, we feel it's to our advantage and yours to constantly evaluate new and changing products. Every piece of home entertainment equipment we sell must meet all our extensive and demanding requirements.

What About Discounts?

Many, many of today's stereo stores would be better off if they were selling refrigerators and air conditioners. In fact many do. When you purchase stereo equipment you should know the advantages of buying from people who specialize in only sound equipment and a store with a long track record of selling only the best brands and providing service to back it up. When you go home with a system that sounds truly great, was within your budget, and fits precisely into your living room or den and that you selected from the finest components available at the time of purchase, you know that if you have any problems, they will be handled quickly and to your satisfaction. This is worth more than any phoney discount or BAIT AND SWITCH DEAL which only gives you the "illusion" of a discount when in fact you are not buying what you set out to buy and in many cases end up with an inferior system that is probably NOT BALANCED to your true needs.

You are much better off buying from a reputable local store which appreciates your business and treats you like a customer than from a discount appliance shop where you are just an addition to their huge gross sales volume.

——— ——— ———

1. Who would have you believe this? ____________
____

2. To whom is this appeal directed? ____________
____

3. To which of your basic needs does this writer appeal? ______________________

4. What would the writer like for you to do? ______
____

See page 324 for source.

Exercise VIII-14

Length: 221 words | Readability Score: 50

The drop-out problem truly is one of the most serious domestic problems facing America. We are told that approximately one million students are dropping out of school each year. This is not only a personal tragedy preventing full development of an individual's potential, but it also is costly to society. For the drop-out reappears in our spiraling crime statistics, in our juvenile delinquency rolls, in our penal and corrective institutions, and on our welfare rolls.

Dr. Conant in his book *Slums and Suburbs* warned that social dynamite was accumulating in our large cities. Much of this "social dynamite" results from those who have dropped out of school and are out of work.

This nation is faced with a drop-out rate of 23 per cent in 1970. This, at a time when technological change is occurring at an ever-increasing pace. This at a time when even educated Americans realize the truth of the Chinese proverb that "learning is like rowing upstream; not to advance is to drop back." With the knowledge explosion, the educated citizens find it a struggle to keep from dropping back. The drop-out, confronting both the education explosion and a shrinking job market, is likely to sink.

It has been estimated that the decade of the sixties, by its conclusion, will have produced some 7-1/2 million school drop-outs.

——— ——— ———

1. What is the author's purpose? ____________
____

2. To whom is this appeal directed? ____________
____

3. What key words were used to influence one's emotions? ______________________

4. In what ways does the writer reveal a bias? ______
____

See page 332 for source.

Exercise VIII-15

Length: 223words Readability Score: 48

Our contemporaries are constantly excited by two conflicting passions: they want to be led, and they wish to remain free. As they cannot destroy either the one or the other of these contrary propensities, they strive to satisfy them both at once. They devise a sole, tutelary, and all-powerful form of government, but elected by the people. They combine the principle of centralization and that of popular sovereignty; this gives them a respite: they console themselves for being in tutelage by the reflection that they have chosen their own guardians. Every man allows himself to be put in leading-strings, because he sees that it is not a person or a class of persons, but the people at large who hold the end of this chain.

By this system the people shake off their state of dependence just long enough to select their master and then relapse into it again. A great many persons at the present day are quite contented with this sort of compromise between administrative despotism and the sovereignty of the people; and they think they have done enough for the protection of individual freedom when they have surrendered it to the power of the nation at large. This does not satisfy me: the nature of him I am to obey signifies less to me than the fact of extorted obedience.

——— ——— ———

1. When was this written? ____________________

2. In what ways does the writer reveal a bias? ______

3. What is the author's purpose? ______________

4. What key words were used to influence one's emotions? ____________________

See page 324 for source.

Exercise VIII-16

Length: 300 words Readability Score: 47

How can a man be satisfied to entertain an opinion merely, and enjoy *it?* Is there any enjoyment in it, if his opinion is that he is aggrieved? If you are cheated out of a single dollar by your neighbor, you do not rest satisfied with knowing that you are cheated, or with saying that you are cheated, or even with petitioning him to pay you your due; but you take effectual steps at once to obtain the full amount, and see that you are never cheated again. Action from principle, the perception and the performance of right, changes things and relations; it is essentially revolutionary, and does not consist wholly with anything which was. It not only divides states and churches, it divides families; aye, it divides the *individual,* separating the diabolical in him from the divine.

Unjust laws exist: shall we be content to obey them, or shall we endeavor to amend them, and obey them until we have succeeded, or shall we transgress them at once. Men generally, under such a government as this, think that they ought to wait until they have persuaded the majority to alter them. They think that, if they should resist, the remedy would be worse than the evil. But it is the fault of the government itself that the remedy *is* worse than the evil. *It* makes it worse. Why is it not more apt to anticipate and provide for reform? Why does it not cherish its wise minority? Why does it cry and resist before it is hurt? Why does it not encourage its citizens to be on the alert to point out its faults, and *do* better than *it* would have them? Why does it always crucify Christ, and excommunicate Copernicus and Luther, and pronounce Washington and Franklin rebels?

——— ——— ———

1. When was this written? ____________________

2. What is the author's purpose? ______________

3. Who would have you believe this? ___________

4. In what ways does the writer reveal a bias? ______

See page 332 for source.

Exercise VIII-17

Length: 359 words Readability Score: 46

"In my letter of October 13 to Mr. Coolidge, I gave an account of the riot we had had at the University and of its termination. You will both, of course, be under anxiety till you know how it has gone off. With the best effects in the world, having let it be understood from the beginning that we wished to trust very much to the discretion of the students themselves for their own government. With about four-fifths of them this did well, but there were about fifteen or twenty bad subjects who were disposed to try whether our indulgence was without limit. Hence the licentious transaction of which I gave an account to Mr. Coolidge; but when the whole mass saw the serious way in which that experiment was met, the Faculty of Professors assembled, the Board of Visitors coming forward in support of that authority, a grand jury taking up the subject, four of the most guilty expelled, the rest reprimanded, severer laws enacted and a rigorous execution of them declared in the future,—it gave them a shock and struck a terror, the most severe as it was less expected. It determined the well-disposed among them to frown upon everything of the kind hereafter, and the ill-disposed returned to order from fear, if not from better motives. A perfect subordination has succeeded, entire respect towards the professors, and industry, order, and quiet the most exemplary, has prevailed ever since. Everyone is sensible of the strength which the institution has derived from what appeared at first to threaten its foundation. We have no further fear of anything of the kind from the present set, but as at the next term their numbers will be more than doubled by the accession of an additional band, as unbroken as these were, we mean to be prepared, and to ask of the legislature a power to call in the civil authority in the first instant of disorder, and to quell it on the spot by imprisonment and the same legal coercions provided against disorder generally committed by other citizens from whom, at their age, they have no right to distinction."

——— ——— ———

1. What is the author's purpose? ____________

2. When was this written? ____________

3. In what ways does the writer reveal a bias? ____________

4. What key words were used to influence one's emotions? ____________

See page 324 for source.

Exercise VIII-18

Length: 171 words Readability Score: 39

A. Corrupt the young, get them away from religion. Get them interested in sex. Make them superficial, destroy their ruggedness.

B. Get control of all means of publication and thereby,

1. Get people's minds off their government by focusing their attention on athletics, sexy books and plays and other trivialities.
2. Divide people into hostile groups by constantly harping on controversial matters of no importance.
3. Destroy the people's faith in their natural leaders by holding them up for ridicule and criticism.
4. Always preach true democracy, but seize power as fast and as ruthlessly as possible.
5. By encouraging government extravagance, destroy its credit, raise fears of inflation, and general discontent.
6. Foment unnecessary strikes in vital areas. Encourage civil disorders, and foster lenient and soft attitude on the part of government toward such disorders.
7. By specious argument cause the breakdown of the old moral virtues of honesty, sobriety, continence, faith in the pledge and word, and ruggedness.

C. Cause the registration of all firearms in some pretext with a view to confiscating them and leaving the populace helpless.

——— ——— ———

1. What is the author's purpose? ____________

2. When was this written? ____________

3. Who would have you believe this? ____________

4. What do you question in this material? ____________

See page 332 for source.

Exercise VIII-19

Length: 269 words — Readability Score: 35

The first extensive long-term study comparing the incidence of birth defects with parental use of LSD has concluded that the drug "must be seriously considered as a possible mutagen"—an agent that produces genetic changes in cells.

"Although we cannot rush in and say we have unequivocal evidence at this time that LSD use causes birth defects, we are on firmer ground, more suspicious, than ever before," says Dr. Cheston M. Berlin, of George Washington University School of Medicine, where the study was done.

Mutagens are agents, such as radioactive fallout or certain chemicals that cause biological mutations, or changes, in the genes or chromosomes of an organism. The mutagenic agent (the "changer") acts in some way to alter the normal configuration of the genetic material within the cells of an organism, often causing the organism to reproduce itself abnormally, to cause birth defects.

The researchers found that the rate of birth defects in children of LSD users, meaning either the mother or father or both, was 18 times as high as that of the general population.

Such abnormalities in the general population occur at a rate of 6 in 1,000, Dr. Berlin says. Among drug users it occurred in 6 in 62, about 18 times as high as might be expected.

Dr. Berlin reports that the mechanism by which LSD might interfere with reproduction is not known. But there is some suspicion that the structure of the LSD molecule, which is similar to the structure of nucleic acid found in all cells, may be binding to molecules of nucleic acid, thus interfering with the normal replication of cells.

——— ——— ———

1. What is the author's purpose? ________________

2. To whom is this appeal directed? ________________

3. Who would have you believe this? ________________

4. To which of your basic needs does the writer appeal? ________________

See page 324 for source.

Exercise VIII-20

Length: 203 words — Readability Score: 28

We hold these truths to be self-evident: that all men are created equal; that they are endowed by their Creator with certain unalienable rights; that among these are life, liberty, and the pursuit of happiness; that to secure these rights, governments are instituted among men, deriving their just powers from the consent of the governed; that, whenever any form of government becomes destructive of these ends, it is the right of the people to alter or to abolish it, and to institute a new government, laying its foundation on such principles, and organizing its powers in such form, as to them shall seem most likely to effect their safety and happiness. Prudence, indeed, will dictate that governments long established should not be changed for light and transient causes; and accordingly, all experience hath shewn, that mankind are more disposed to suffer, while evils are sufferable, than to right themselves by abolishing the forms to which they are accustomed. But, when a long train of abuses and usurpations, pursuing invariably the same object, evinces a design to reduce them under absolute despotism, it is their right, it is their duty, to throw off such government, and to provide new guards for their future security.

——— ——— ———

1. What is the author's purpose? ________________

2. When was this written? ________________

3. To whom is this appeal directed? ________________

4. To which of your basic needs does the writer appeal? ________________

See page 332 for source.

Vocabulary List

List all key words missed and all words underlined in error. *Look up* each word in the dictionary, *study* its meaning, see if it has different meanings in different contexts, *learn* some synonyms and *practice using* them in sentences. Many people find that "cue cards" are a valuable aid in vocabulary building. List the key word on the front of a small card and put definition and synonyms on the back. Carry a pack of these cards in your pocket to review at odd intervals. Try to use each new word consciously in your speaking and writing. If you use it a few times it will become yours.

Review this list periodically and check off those words you have added to your vocabulary.

1.	26.
2.	27.
3.	28.
4.	29.
5.	30.
6.	31.
7.	32.
8.	33.
9.	34.
10.	35.
11.	36.
12.	37.
13.	38.
14.	39.
15.	40.
16.	41.
17.	42.
18.	43.
19.	44.
20.	45.
21.	46.
22.	47.
23.	48.
24.	49.
25.	50.

Vocabulary List

List all key words missed and all words underlined in error. *Look up* each word in the dictionary, *study* its meaning, see if it has different meanings in different contexts, *learn* some synonyms and *practice using* them in sentences. Many people find that "cue cards" are a valuable aid in vocabulary building. List the key word on the front of a small card and put definition and synonyms on the back. Carry a pack of these cards in your pocket to review at odd intervals. Try to use each new word consciously in your speaking and writing. If you use it a few times it will become yours.

Review this list periodically and check off those words you have added to your vocabulary.

1.
2.
3.
4.
5.
6.
7.
8.
9.
10.
11.
12.
13.
14.
15.
16.
17.
18.
19.
20.
21.
22.
23.
24.
25.
26.
27.
28.
29.
30.
31.
32.
33.
34.
35.
36.
37.
38.
39.
40.
41.
42.
43.
44.
45.
46.
47.
48.
49.
50.

Vocabulary List

List all key words missed and all words underlined in error. *Look up* each word in the dictionary, *study* its meaning, see if it has different meanings in different contexts, *learn* some synonyms and *practice using* them in sentences. Many people find that "cue cards" are a valuable aid in vocabulary building. List the key word on the front of a small card and put definition and synonyms on the back. Carry a pack of these cards in your pocket to review at odd intervals. Try to use each new word consciously in your speaking and writing. If you use it a few times it will become yours.

Review this list periodically and check off those words you have added to your vocabulary.

1.	26.
2.	27.
3.	28.
4.	29.
5.	30.
6.	31.
7.	32.
8.	33.
9.	34.
10.	35.
11.	36.
12.	37.
13.	38.
14.	39.
15.	40.
16.	41.
17.	42.
18.	43.
19.	44.
20.	45.
21.	46.
22.	47.
23.	48.
24.	49.
25.	50.

Vocabulary List

List all key words missed and all words underlined in error. *Look up* each word in the dictionary, *study* its meaning, see if it has different meanings in different contexts, *learn* some synonyms and *practice using* them in sentences. Many people find that "cue cards" are a valuable aid in vocabulary building. List the key word on the front of a small card and put definition and synonyms on the back. Carry a pack of these cards in your pocket to review at odd intervals. Try to use each new word consciously in your speaking and writing. If you use it a few times it will become yours.

Review this list periodically and check off those words you have added to your vocabulary.

1.
2.
3.
4.
5.
6.
7.
8.
9.
10.
11.
12.
13.
14.
15.
16.
17.
18.
19.
20.
21.
22.
23.
24.
25.
26.
27.
28.
29.
30.
31.
32.
33.
34.
35.
36.
37.
38.
39.
40.
41.
42.
43.
44.
45.
46.
47.
48.
49.
50.

Reading Progress Chart

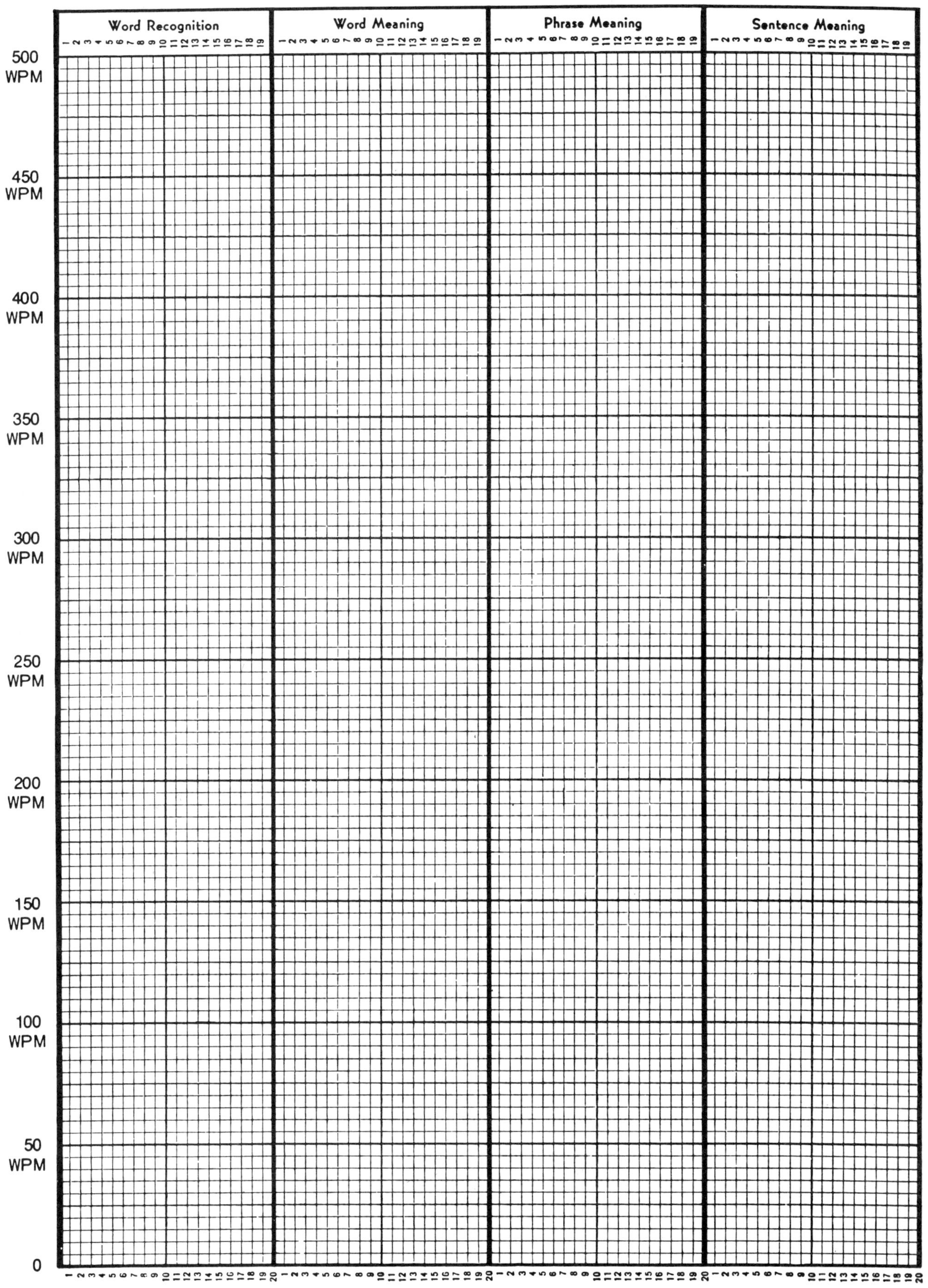

Plot RATE scores in pencil and EFFICIENCY scores in pen

Reading Progress Chart

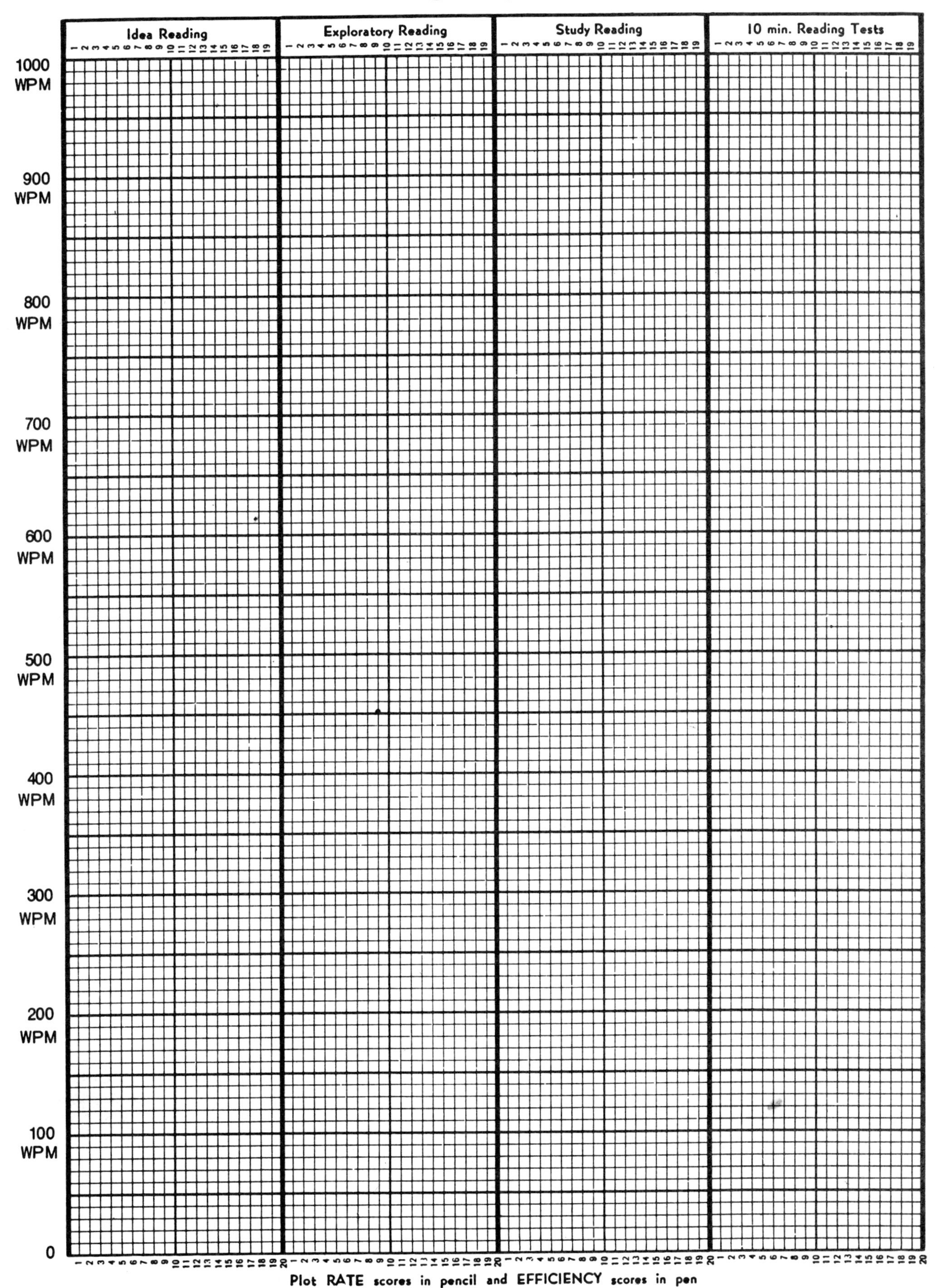

Extension of Reading Progress Chart

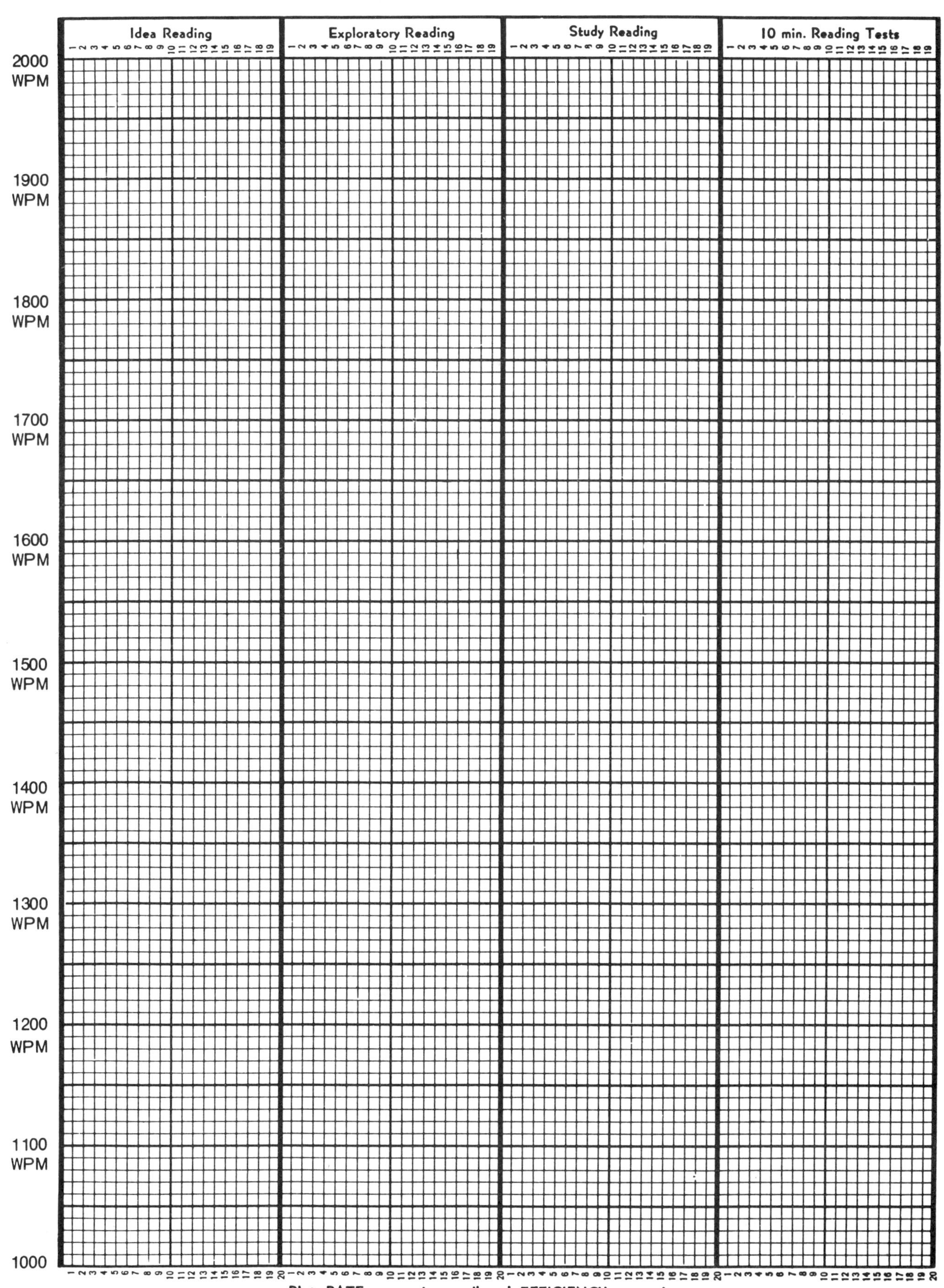

Extension of Reading Progress Chart

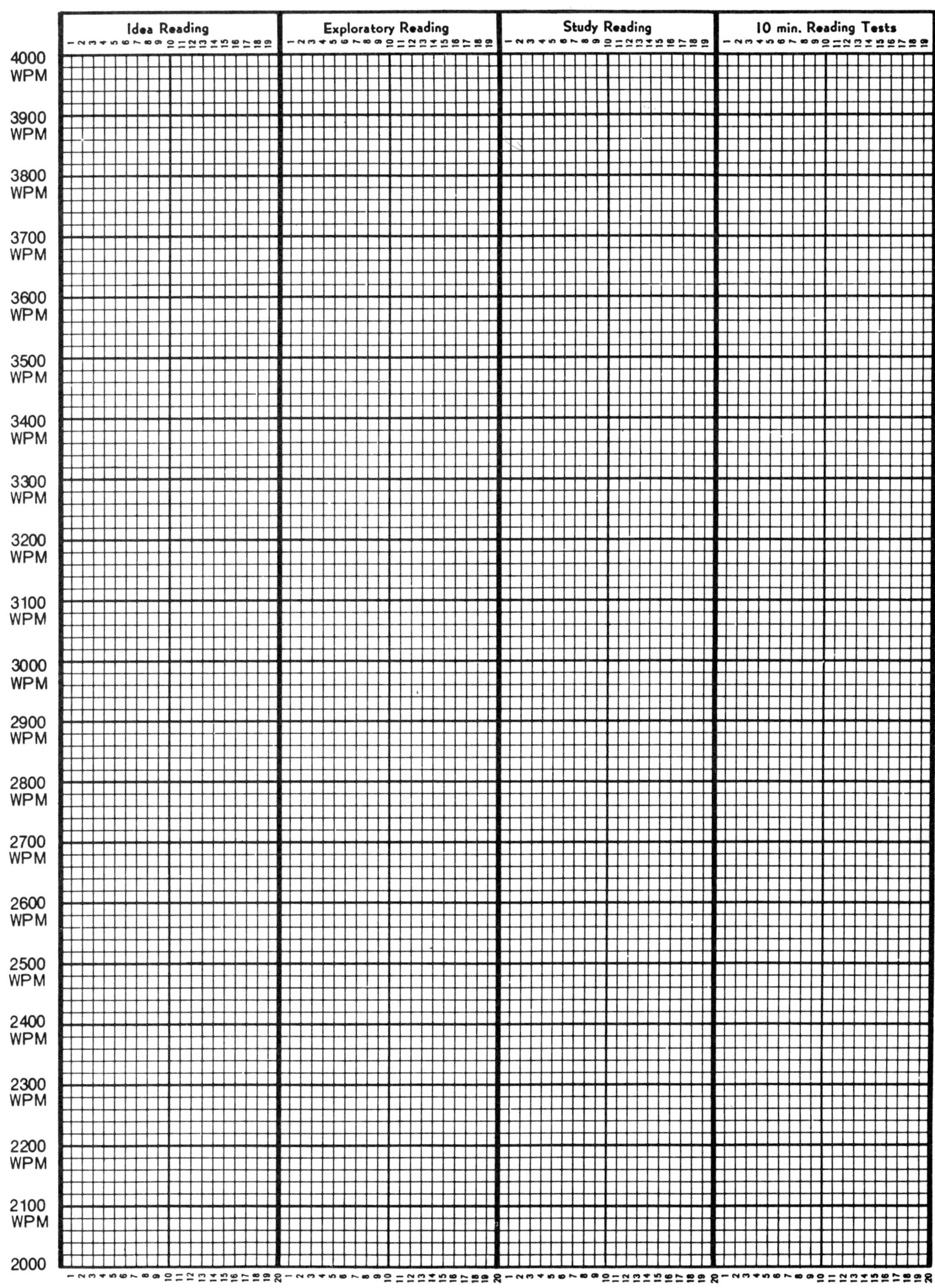

Extension of Reading Progress Chart

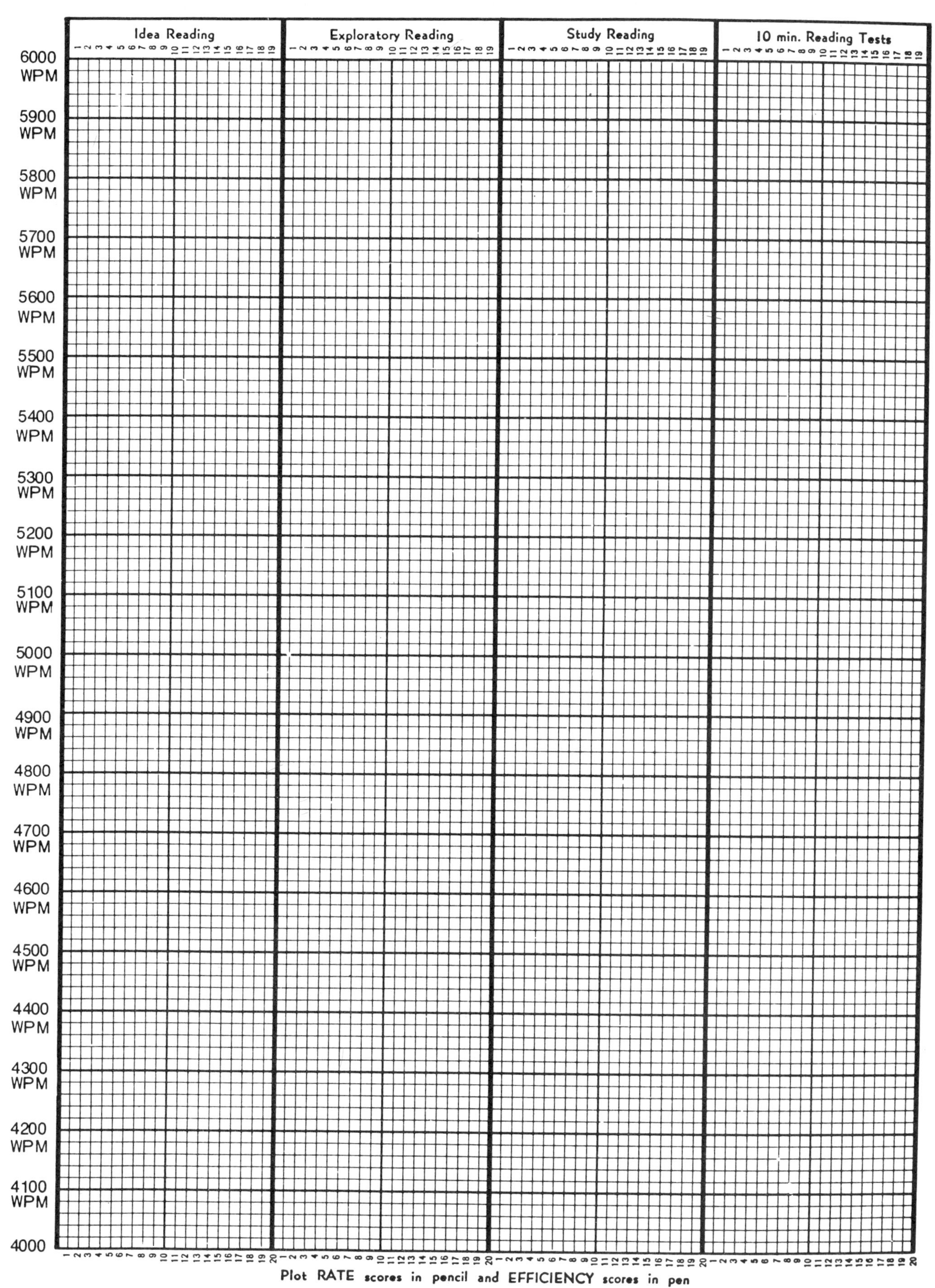

RATE TABLE FOR SERIES I AND II

Use for the word recognition drills and the word meaning drills.

Look up your time in Column I and read your rate in Column II.

I	II	I	II	I	II	I	II	I	II
				61	148	101	89	182-185	49
				62	145	102	88	186-189	48
				63	143	103-104	87	190-193	47
				64	141	105	86	194-197	46
				65	138	106	85	198-202	45
				66	136	107	84	203-206	44
				67	134	108-109	83	207-211	43
				68	132	110	82	212-216	42
				69	130	111	81	217-222	41
				70	129	112-113	80	223-227	40
1	9000	31	291	71	127	114	79	228-232	39
2	4500	32	281	72	125	115-116	78	234-240	38
3	3000	33	273	73	123	117	77	241-246	37
4	2250	34	265	74	122	118-119	76	247-253	36
5	1800	35	257	75	120	120	75	254-260	35
6	1500	36	250	76	118	121-122	74	261-268	34
7	1286	37	243	77	117	123-124	73	269-276	33
8	1125	38	237	78	115	125	72	277-285	32
9	1000	39	231	79	114	126-127	71	286-295	31
10	900	40	225	80	113	128-129	70	296-305	30
11	818	41	220	81	111	130-131	69	306-315	29
12	750	42	214	82	110	132-133	68	316-327	28
13	692	43	209	83	108	134-135	67	328-339	27
14	643	44	205	84	107	136-137	66	340-352	26
15	600	45	200	85	106	138-139	65	353-366	25
16	563	46	196	86	105	140-141	64	367-382	24
17	529	47	191	87	103	142-144	63	383-400	23
18	500	48	188	88	102	145-146	62	401-418	22
19	474	49	184	89	101	147-148	61	419-439	21
20	450	50	180	90	100	149-151	60	440-461	20
21	429	51	176	91	99	152-153	59	462-486	19
22	409	52	173	92	98	154-156	58	487-514	18
23	391	53	170	93	97	157-159	57	515-545	17
24	375	54	167	94	96	160-162	56	546-580	16
25	360	55	164	95	95	163-165	55	581-620	15
26	346	56	161	96	94	166-168	54	621-666	14
27	333	57	158	97	93	169-171	53	667-720	13
28	321	58	155	98	92	172-174	52	721-782	12
29	310	59	153	99	91	175-178	51	783-857	11
30	300	60	150	100	90	179-181	50	858-947	10

RATE TABLE FOR SERIES III – PHRASE MEANING

Look up your time (to the nearest 5 seconds) in Column I and read your rate in the Column under the appropriate exercise number. If your time is more or less than the limits of the table, or if you desire to compute your time more accurately to the exact second, divide the time (No. of seconds) into the "Division Constant" for that exercise.

Time	*Exercise #1-4*	*Exercise #5-8*	*Exercise #9-12*	*Exercise #13-16*	*Exercise #17-20*
# words	*300*	*350*	*400*	*500*	*600*
Division Constant	*18,000*	*21,000*	*24,000*	*30,000*	*36,000*
# seconds					
5	3600	4200	4800	6000	7200
10	1800	2100	2400	3000	3600
15	1200	1400	1600	2000	2400
20	900	1050	1200	1500	1800
25	720	840	960	1200	1440
30	600	700	800	1000	1200
35	514	600	686	875	1029
40	456	525	600	750	900
45	400	467	533	667	800
50	360	420	480	600	720
55	327	382	436	545	655
60	300	350	400	500	600
65	277	323	369	462	554
70	257	300	343	429	514
75	240	280	320	400	480
80	225	263	300	375	450
85	212	247	282	353	424
90	200	233	267	333	400
95	189	221	253	316	379
100	180	210	240	300	360
105	171	200	229	286	343
110	164	191	218	273	327
115	157	183	209	261	313
120	150	175	200	256	300
125	144	168	192	240	288
130	138	162	185	231	277
135	133	156	178	222	267
140	129	150	171	214	257
145	124	145	166	207	248
150	120	140	160	200	240
155	116	135	155	194	232
160	113	131	150	188	225
165	109	127	145	182	218
170	106	124	141	176	212
175	103	120	137	171	206
180	100	117	133	167	200
185	97	114	130	162	195
190	95	111	126	158	189
195	92	108	123	154	185
200	90	105	120	150	180

RATE TABLE FOR SERIES IV—SENTENCE MEANING

Look up your time (to the nearest 5 seconds) in Column I and read your rate in the Column under the appropriate exercise number. If your time is more or less than the limits of the table, or if you desire to compute your time more accurately to the exact second, divide the time (No. of seconds) into the "Division Constant" for that exercise.

Time	*Exercise #1–6*	*Exercise #7–14*	*Exercise #15–20*
# words	*120*	*160*	*200*
Division Constant	*7200*	*9600*	*12,000*
# seconds			
5	1440	1920	2400
10	720	960	1200
15	480	640	800
20	360	480	600
25	288	384	480
30	240	320	400
35	206	274	343
40	180	240	300
45	160	213	267
50	144	192	240
55	131	175	218
60	120	160	200
65	111	148	185
70	103	137	171
75	96	128	160
80	90	120	150
85	85	113	141
90	80	107	133
95	76	101	126
100	72	96	120
105	69	91	114
110	65	87	109
115	63	83	104
120	60	80	100
125	58	77	96
130	55	74	92
135	53	71	89
140	51	69	86
145	50	66	83
150	48	64	80
155	46	62	77
160	45	60	75
165	44	58	73
170	42	56	70
175	41	55	69

RATE TABLE FOR SERIES V—IDEA READING

Since all the exercises in this series have been standardized at 900 words, this table can be used for all 20 exercises. Look up your time (to the nearest second interval shown) in Column I and then read your rate from Column II. For an approximate rate, you may use the time figure nearest your actual time. For any time figures beyond the limits of this table, or between the intervals given, the actual rate may be computed by dividing 54,000 by the time *(in seconds)*.

I	*II*	*I*	*II*	*I*	*II*	*I*	*II*
5	10,800	45	1,200	205	263	405	133
6	9,000	46	1,173	210	257	410	131
7	7,710	47	1,149	215	251	415	130
8	6,750	48	1,125	220	245	420	129
9	6,000	49	1,102	225	240	425	127
10	5,400	50	1,080	230	235	430	125
11	4,909	51	1,059	235	230	435	124
12	4,500	52	1,038	240	225	440	123
13	4,153	53	1,019	245	220	445	121
14	3,857	54	1,000	250	216	450	120
15	3,600	55	982	255	212	455	119
16	3,375	60	900	260	208	460	118
17	3,176	65	831	265	204	465	116
18	3,000	70	771	270	200	470	115
19	2,842	75	720	275	196	475	114
20	2,700	80	675	280	192	480	113
21	2,571	85	635	285	189	485	111
22	2,454	90	600	290	186	490	110
23	2,348	95	568	295	183	495	109
24	2,250	100	540	300	180	500	108
25	2,160	105	514	305	177	505	107
26	2,077	110	491	310	174	510	106
27	2,000	115	469	315	171	515	105
28	1,929	120	450	320	169	520	104
29	1,862	125	432	325	166	525	103
30	1,800	130	415	330	163	530	102
31	1,742	135	400	335	161	535	101
32	1,688	140	386	340	159	540	100
33	1,636	145	372	345	156	545	99
34	1,588	150	360	350	154	550	98
35	1,543	155	349	355	152	555	97
36	1,500	160	338	360	150	560	96
37	1,460	165	327	365	148	565	96
38	1,421	170	318	370	146	570	95
39	1,385	175	309	375	144	575	94
40	1,350	180	300	380	142	580	93
41	1,317	185	292	385	140	585	92
42	1,286	190	284	390	138	590	91
43	1,256	195	277	395	136	595	91
44	1,227	200	270	400	135	600	90

RATE TABLE FOR EXPLORATORY READING AND STUDY TYPE READING
SERIES VI AND VII

Since all the exercises in Series VI and VII have been standardized to a length of 1350 words, rates for any of these exercises can be found by looking up the time in seconds in Column I of this table and reading the rate from Column II. Times are given at 5 second intervals. For an approximate time you may take the time figure nearest your actual time. (For example, by looking up a time of "200" seconds, a rate of "405" would be determined.)

For any time figures beyond the limits of this table or between the intervals, the rate may be computed by dividing 81,000 by the time *(in seconds)*.

I	*II*	*I*	*II*	*I*	*II*	*I*	*II*
5	16,200	105	771	305	266	505	160
6	13,500	110	736	310	261	510	159
7	11,571	115	704	315	257	515	157
8	10,125	120	675	320	253	520	156
9	9,000	125	648	325	249	525	154
10	8,100	130	623	330	245	530	153
11	7,333	135	600	335	242	535	151
12	6,750	140	579	340	238	540	150
13	6,231	145	559	345	235	545	149
14	5,786	150	540	350	231	550	147
15	5,400	155	523	355	228	555	146
16	5,063	160	506	360	225	560	145
17	4,765	165	491	365	222	565	143
18	4,500	170	476	370	219	570	142
19	4,263	175	463	375	216	575	141
20	4,050	180	450	380	213	580	140
21	3,857	185	438	385	210	585	138
22	3,667	190	426	390	208	590	137
23	3,522	195	415	395	205	595	136
24	3,375	200	405	400	203	600	135
25	3,240	205	395	405	200	605	134
26	3,116	210	386	410	198	610	133
27	3,000	215	377	415	195	615	132
28	2,893	220	368	420	193	620	131
29	2,793	225	360	425	191	625	130
30	2,700	230	352	430	188	630	129
35	2,314	235	345	435	186	635	128
40	2,025	240	338	440	184	640	127
45	1,800	245	331	445	182	645	126
50	1,620	250	324	450	180	650	125
55	1,473	255	318	455	178	655	124
60	1,350	260	312	460	176	660	123
65	1,246	265	306	465	174	665	122
70	1,157	270	300	470	172	670	121
75	1,080	275	295	475	171	675	120
80	1,012	280	289	480	169	680	119
85	953	285	284	485	167	685	118
90	900	290	279	490	165	690	117
95	853	295	275	495	164	695	117
100	810	300	270	500	162	700	116

SERIES II (ODD NUMBERS)

	NO. 1	NO. 3	NO. 5	NO. 7	NO. 9
1.	forehead	light	parched	trifle	crocodile
2.	tease	support	poor	stain	mark
3.	bed	smell	hood	mark	devote
4.	tranquility	wander	twist	port	salary
5.	ice	fowl	economical	servant	affection
6.	sound	furnish	overlook	bent	lift
7.	brisk	honor	prevent	rodents	speaker
8.	dent	bare	pageant	costume	need
9.	fine	cut	victim	remember	rule
10.	tatter	wealthy	smooth	leg	danger
11.	stick	ravage	song	cursed	vast
12.	use	slope	tinge	mist	sign
13.	tired	stay	author	relieve	hum
14.	grief	lower	stick	youthful	pretend
15.	father	signal	scorch	yield	law
16.	dash	postpone	bear	ball	hook
17.	trip	anxious	get	thigh	voice
18.	score	anger	dress	costume	adorn
19.	hotel	cage	chart	stately	power
20.	powder	crazy	threat	jewelry	form
21.	heathen	ancient	pageant	toil	spoken
22.	craft	liable	adventurous	mournful	bow
23.	rare	polish	clean	criminal	pastoral
24.	trap	dough	brace	tempt	chipmunk
25.	dictator	dazzling	impure	eruption	shake

	NO. 11	NO. 13	NO. 15	NO. 17	NO. 19
1.	listen	rip	stir	terrify	bitterly
2.	cow	estimate	flower	benevolent	concerned
3.	woman	cheat	vegetable	conclusion	convert
4.	style	pardon	distribute	forever	lasting
5.	gaze	serious	vicious	mournful	cyclone
6.	fever	drunk	massive	killer	yet
7.	limestone	intelligent	observe	recede	also
8.	excursion	bundle	hill	hurts	idea
9.	clear	estimate	spoil	railroad	chickens
10.	isolate	wise	oppose	servant	litter
11.	hidden	doubt	wipe	replace	splendor
12.	rude	escort	silent	rare	exchange
13.	nut	front	cascade	uneducated	feast
14.	box	lift	change	cutter	spine
15.	transparent	entrust	bud	university	waterfall
16.	mature	refuse	interrupt	scholar	formal
17.	starvation	haze	serious	abundant	trap
18.	shout	labored	liberty	sense	discard
19.	pitcher	cripple	throw	powerful	candy
20.	change	city	solitary	rural	diphtheria
21.	endure	melancholy	incubator	region	neglect
22.	ruin	taste	pretense	trellis	origin
23.	pretense	soft	bone	trust	satisfaction
24.	suspicion	ornament	ruler	fabric	stop
25.	helpful	strength	course	distant	wise

SERIES III (ODD NUMBERS)

	NO. 1	NO. 3
1.	a precious stone	physical vigor
2.	to say something	even surface
3.	an opening for	short of food
4.	divide evenly	exhibited envy
5.	quite happy	close at all times
6.	about medium	to reveal freely
7.	one fully grown	in great need
8.	a verbal wrong	a cheerful person
9.	to go ahead of	true to life
10.	distinct sound	a modest person
11.	view carefully	to hurry
12.	a rascal	rapid action
13.	rather meager	lighter than water
14.	to lean down	is incorrect
15.	to amuse	open to view
16.	a big tree	act of dominating
17.	for smelling	to prefer
18.	has mild temper	brought about by
19.	morning hymn	to frighten suddenly
20.	a search for game	to set free

	NO. 5	NO. 7
1.	some motive	a common junction
2.	to move ahead	to bid farewell
3.	man of decision	incessant existence
4.	not using care	to grant liberty
5.	a sudden disaster	keeping a secret
6.	act of forgetting	comes to an end
7.	the entrance	an exhibit of humor
8.	completely worthless	correct position
9.	gain full meaning	that which is beyond
10.	no set price	being very busy
11.	show satisfaction	to fascinate
12.	confirm the deed	likely a quarrel
13.	to take turns	considerable amount
14.	something odd	be punctual
15.	without a doubt	regular procedure
16.	on the offensive	a severe look
17.	make a thrust	join in a group
18.	a common matter	absence of sound
19.	have no boundary	honesty of mind
20.	serve as a guide	not completed

	NO. 9	NO. 11
1.	to mix up	a feeling of thirst
2.	to be outstanding	not certain to occur
3.	a critical moment	to be obedient
4.	more than is needed	that which is to come
5.	thought to be absurd	showing glee
6.	especially suitable	an acquired holiday
7.	covering all phases	one who is a criminal
8.	to understand	pass quickly from sight
9.	usual way of doing something	to be in right accord
10.	where one lives	of his own free will
11.	the last in the series	choosing from several
12.	boundary line	to come together
13.	a sound like a moan	simple in style
14.	a scenic painting	roughly sketched
15.	not public in nature	state of being strong
16.	to set back	a short hurried view
17.	a solitary existence	only one of a kind
18.	provide financial aid	changed in appearance
19.	a tidy person	to stand still
20.	an act of good will	to be thankful

	NO. 13	NO. 15
1.	associated with the press	considered to be brilliant
2.	usual course of events	a surface injury to flesh
3.	capacity of receiving impressions	that which is awarded
4.	one who displays warmth	something awkward or inconvenient
5.	one who is really concerned	in a contrary or reverse way
6.	overcome by amazement	an uncertain and disgusting experience
7.	a pleasing person	buildings which lodge soldiers
8.	an abundant amount of anything	not capable of producing vegetation
9.	set apart from others	a battle between two individuals
10.	agreeing to a set plan	be reduced to a state of want
11.	all over everywhere	rise and fall of the voice
12.	to anticipate the finish	cancel out the effects of
13.	becoming more complicated	the capital city of a state
14.	that which is spread	a state of being careful
15.	thought to be significant	the cause of an event
16.	related to the truth	taking a count of the population
17.	authorized by proclamation	that which is correct
18.	hold back a privilege	a summons to fight
19.	an act which is wrong	to assemble or mass together
20.	to be possibly secured	to meet in competition

NO. 17

1. the monarch of a region
2. that which is relatively low
3. to enlarge either in fact or appearance
4. a representation of the surface of the earth
5. one who will die for the sake of principle
6. using the faculty of remembering
7. reproduced on a miniature level
8. the sixtieth part of an hour
9. which is within reasonable limits
10. a system of teaching standards
11. a moderately feeble-minded person
12. a complicated situation or mystery
13. to have very narrow limits
14. quality or state of being neutral
15. a state of being nominated
16. does not vary from the average
17. that which stands in the way
18. counted as old-fashioned in style
19. to support or qualify an act
20. under the oppression of a tyrant

NO. 19

1. the earth upon which we live
2. to develop and cultivate the mental processes
3. practice of referring too much to oneself
4. to feel envy of the other person
5. to bé equal in quantity or degree
6. an error in the way a person thinks
7. that which becomes extinct
8. to be supported by evidence based on facts
9. to have a guided or set form
10. terror excited by sudden danger
11. to be full or complete in quantity
12. the gathering or increasing of profits
13. a gesture used to enforce an opinion
14. to give a gift to someone
15. the act or action of gliding
16. the goal to obtain in winning the race
17. a meeting face to face with an employer
18. to supply water to the land by canals
19. that which is regarded as an island
20. January, named after the Latin God, Janus

SERIES IV (ODD NUMBERS)

	NO. 1	NO. 3	NO. 5	NO. 7	NO. 9	NO. 11	NO. 13	NO. 15	NO. 17	NO. 19
1.	D	D	S	D	S	S	D	S	S	S
2.	S	D	D	S	D	D	S	D	D	D
3.	S	D	S	S	D	S	D	D	D	D
4.	D	S	D	D	S	D	D	D	D	S
5.	D	S	D	D	S	S	D	D	S	D
6.	S	D	D	S	D	S	S	D	D	S
7.	D	S	S	D	S	D	D	S	S	S
8.	D	D	D	D	D	S	D	D	S	S
9.	S	D	D	D	D	D	S	D	D	D
10.	S	D	S	S	S	D	S	S	S	D

SERIES V (ODD NUMBERS)

	NO. 1	NO. 3	NO. 5	NO. 7	NO. 9	NO. 11	NO. 13	No. 15	NO. 17	No. 19
1.	T	T	F	T	F	F	T	F	F	T
2.	2	1	4	1	4	2	2	4	1	3

SERIES VI (ODD NUMBERS)

	NO. 1	NO. 3	NO. 5	NO. 7	NO. 9	NO. 11	NO. 13	NO. 15	NO. 17	NO. 19.
1.	F	T	F	Ireland	religious	T	New York	T	80	F
2.	T	abilities	T	3	T	1	F	pushers	T	three
3.	crow	F	honest	F	1	T	3	life	3	4
4.	F	ambition	F	nurse	Lent	China	T	F	F	F
5.	1	T	1	T	T	F	4	T	2	essential
6.	F	2	F	2	F	F	F	4	wages	T
7.	T	F	2	F	F	T	meat packers	T	T	F
8.	Arctic	T	T	T	T	F	F	F	F	T
9.	4	4	T	T	2	fire hazard	T	F	F	T
10.	T	F	bidding	F	F	3	T	3	T	1

SERIES VII (ODD NUMBERS)

	NO. 1	NO. 3	NO. 5	NO. 7	NO. 9	NO. 11	NO. 13	NO. 15	NO. 17	NO. 19.
1.	F	1876	T	3	T	2	F	T	90	T
2.	T	F	inatten- tion	wolverine	T	F	400	F	1	1
3.	4	2	2	F	proud	F	1	2	F	sulfuric acid
4.	F	4	F	T	T	T	F	F	2	F
5.	culture	F	F	F	1	specific	T	T	T	F
6.	3	T	T	F	F	3	4	Damien	30	monoxide
7.	F	dual	T	eyesight	3	F	T	Joseph	T	4
8.	worth	T	sundown	T	September	T	cricket	3	F	T
9.	T	T	3	1	F	functional	F	F	T	T
10.	T	F	F	T	F	T	T	T	F	F

In this series there are no exact or "right" answers. You were asked to read critically in an effort to understand underlying purpose, emotional appeal, bias and propaganda techniques. You were asked to try to identify time and place of appeal.

As a key to checking on your own critical thinking, this key section consists of the identification of the source of the material and a few comments about the setting from which it was taken.

See how close you were to the identification of basic factors. Think about those which you missed and go back and read the material again to check out your own sensitivity to key words and ideas.

VIII-1

(an advertisement by the Haverhill's Company of San Francisco, California, in *Natural History* February 1968, p. 22)

The purpose of this article is to sell the Haverhill's new shaver, which the company claims will give the consumer dependable, fast, and economical service for some time. The advertiser appeals to the reader's need for quick, convenient shaves.

VIII-3

(taken from the article "I Have Been There" as it appeared in the June 1970 issue of *Listen.*)

Directed toward high school students, this writer attempts to dissuade them from experimenting with marijuana.

Written by a high school student who had two experiences with what he believed to be marijuana, this message is significant because of the rise in the use of "grass" by students. Although the author experienced bad effects after smoking marijuana, one might question whether these same types of effects would be experienced by others, whether he really had marijuana both times, and whether he could tell the difference from pure or adulterated materials.

The fright experienced by this student urged him to write this warning to any other person who feels compelled to experiment with "grass." It appears in a journal published especially for a teen-age audience by a national association concerned with the dangers of alcoholism and drug usage.

VIII-5

(An excerpt from an undated form letter from Norman Vincent Peale, Foundation for Christian Living, Pawling, New York, 12464)

In this letter distributed to a large public mailing list, Norman Vincent Peale is trying to promote the activities of the Foundation for Christian Living by appealing for the desire for happiness, and by promoting his general concept of the power of positive thinking.

With each letter was enclosed a card asking the reader to check a box to be put on the mailing list for "monthly inspirational literature" for a "trial subscription." Although the letter states: "No charge is made.", two paragraphs are devoted to explaining costs and suggesting a "free will contribution", and the card has a box to show the amount of the enclosed contribution.

VIII-7

(an excerpt from "When Boy Meets Car" as it appeared in the Autumn, 1962 issue of *Discovery*, published by Allstate Insurance Company.)

This article is directed mainly to parents and is designed to encourage them to limit the use of the automobile by their children.

This article summarizes findings of various studies relative to the effect of the use of the family car on grades of students. Although this article is directed mainly to parents, students could benefit from the stated results. Because of the ever-increasing need of academic success in order to meet individual goals, it is important that both parents and students view the use of the family car in its proper perspective. It is pointed out that overindulgence will not help students fully realize their academic potential.

VIII-9

(taken from "Pull a Switch to Exercise," *Timely Tips*, published by the American Medical Association, June 1970.)

This article, disseminated by the American Medical Association, appeals to the basic need of all persons to possess a healthy, vigorous body. The author's purpose is to persuade people to exercise rather than to engage in less healthful and muscle-tone-producing activities. The appeal is directed to all persons, especially those who do not exercise regularly.

VIII-11

(Representative Cohelan, [D], California; taken from the *Congressional Record*, Vol. 113, No. 6, January 18, 1967, p. H291.)

The Representative, in hopes of preserving the Redwood National Forest, speaks in favor of a bill calling for the establishment of a 90,000 acre park in northern California. The trees of the redwood forest are quickly diminishing and the speaker makes a patriotic appeal to save the redwoods which remain.

VII-13

(An excerpt from a special newspaper ad in a college newspaper, paid for by The Music Box, a local store)

This is the lead section from a special two page insert designed to get the reader to visit the store and see their line of stereo equipment. It has the intent of encouraging students to buy from a professional music store rather than from a discount house.

VIII-15

(taken from the classic, *Democracy in America*, written by Alexis de Tocqueville in 1835.)

The author wrote to stimulate the thinking of the individual about his government.

The conditions stated by the author over one hundred years ago are still with us today. Through the use of words such as "all-powerful," "tutelage," "leading-strings," and "despotism," de Tocqueville shows his negative attitude toward being pressured into a position of obedience. The author was very impressed with the democratic form of government he witnessed while visiting the United States. However, in order to insure the continuation of such a government, he did notice and was aware of certain fallacies as mentioned in this article.

VIII-17

(an excerpt from "Letter to Ellen W. Coolidge" written by her grandfather, Thomas Jefferson, November 14, 1825. Reprinted from the 1904 edition of *The Writings of Thomas Jefferson*, published by the Thomas Jefferson Memorial Association.)

The author's purpose is to relay the facts, at least from his point of view, of a riot at a university. It was written in 1825 by Thomas Jefferson, founder of the University of Virginia.

This is clearly written from an administrator's viewpoint as he describes the handling of the riot. One might question why, since the author seems so certain that the riot was well handled and was a learning experience for the students, he is, nonetheless, anticipating further trouble and expecting to call in civil authorities to handle future situations.

VIII-19

(taken from "LSD Cell Damage Confirmed," as reported in *Listen*, September 1970.)

The author's purpose is to report on the possible link between birth defects and the use of LSD. His appeal seems to be directed at young people, particularly those of marriageable age.

Admittedly the author states that not enough real, conclusive proof has been found to make the statement that LSD causes birth defects. There are other genetic factors entering into the causes of such defects. Yet, from the studies that have been undertaken, and from the statistics quoted by Dr. Berlin, the users of LSD are risking the chance of having abnormal offspring. The danger lies in the fact that users are exposing themselves to harm by experimenting with a substance that has not yet been proven to be harmless, especially when taken without the supervision of an authorized, competent individual present.

This publication is specifically designed to alert adolescents to the potential dangers of alcoholism and drug abuse.

SERIES II (EVEN NUMBERS)

	NO. 2	NO. 4	NO. 6	NO. 8	NO. 10
1.	cot	glimpse	cook	keen	mortified
2.	polite	pretender	house	ministers	form
3.	mount	settlement	fish	eat	boast
4.	legend	steps	gutter	empty	dominion
5.	total	confine	blaze	pork	deny
6.	predicament	cry	grass	tinkle	need
7.	memory	sharp	level	error	enrage
8.	dromedary	pout	attack	medicine	firm
9.	measure	condemn	braid	concerning	possessions
10.	conceal	stand	intended	cutlery	veil
11.	impaired	killer	weep	levy	stalks
12.	new	melt	saving	dirty	bag
13.	originate	salary	plant	gas	riches
14.	price	friendly	prayer	brush	see
15.	shell	child	chest	overcome	cheat
16.	doctrine	short	inlet	pigeon	venture
17.	dart	drop	revise	holder	hastily
18.	fortunate	struggled	scowl	wager	dealer
19.	contract	practice	announcement	smaller	opinion
20.	tidy	kindled	chance	trap	hash
21.	gait	trumpet	renters	harbor	echo
22.	dwell	choose	advance	fury	heal
23.	pat	answer	part	tricky	form
24.	happen	exhausted	relieve	dense	stop
25.	pocketbook	snug	ripped	excess	useless

	NO. 12	NO. 14	NO. 16	NO. 18	NO. 20
1.	embarrass	plentiful	wrong	uncertain	covet
2.	testimony	stake	bearer	assemble	rustic
3.	morn	teach	heal	consider	native
4.	burst	industrious	guide	servant	robin
5.	sore	plume	crepe	fine	cloth
6.	ask	listen	angry	nose	absorb
7.	heavy	hostess	spite	vegetable	elevation
8.	foreign	wet	path	immune	grateful
9.	adventure	torment	wisdom	tolerate	manufacture
10.	elder	depend	secure	loving	content
11.	element	site	attached	person	acknowledge
12.	sympathy	soft	below	admire	base
13.	receive	determined	foolish	ability	road
14.	injured	rub	confuse	watch	disaster
15.	staff	wife	perimeter	law	science
16.	thrust	official	relate	closet	producer
17.	crawl	bureau	get	cheat	trade
18.	tools	anticipate	separation	final	district
19.	house	useless	jewel	statement	consultation
20.	ray	probable	accident	teacher	fair
21.	state	torment	confined	mold	hunter
22.	director	bag	denial	buyer	mend
23.	revealed	quit	tray	unite	depresssion
24.	expanded	drench	shrewd	grand	exist
25.	conquer	flung	affected	confuse	disease

SERIES III (EVEN NUMBERS)

	NO. 2	NO. 4
1.	to recognize again	correct position
2.	precious metal	gentle animal
3.	a high polish	a gradual decline
4.	to empty out	decrease in size
5.	a belief held	abundant harvest
6.	prose fiction	be unclear
7.	of little width	upright position
8.	to belong to	to be stable
9.	endless in size	rather sleepy
10.	entertains another	lonely condition
11.	surface of earth	neglect of duty
12.	to thrust something	expression of pain
13.	made independent of	marked boundary
14.	to make peace	to destroy
15.	leave it out	this very instant
16.	possessing dignity	ramble along
17.	an enormous animal	most valuable part
18.	distribute justice	being clumsy
19.	omit essentials	to go to pieces
20.	one who knows	to complicate

	NO. 6	NO. 8
1.	hurrying for aid	rising in power
2.	nearly as easy	should be allowed
3.	more than needed	according to facts
4.	very small quantity	to dispose of
5.	one or the other	to reach the peak
6.	a great error	brought about by
7.	plain to see	prepared to go on
8.	not interested in	away from others
9.	disgraceful conduct	not very busy
10.	just the opposite	death by violence
11.	at the beginning	decent in character
12.	a minute part	free from blame
13.	evidently clear	keep from falling
14.	about dawn	a great din
15.	he who is a criminal	very necessary
16.	wishing something	completely exhausted
17.	offer your help	place for vacations
18.	to avoid something	one who is punctual
19.	being factually correct	one who is courageous
20.	dislike to work	shattered to pieces

SERIES III (EVEN NUMBERS—continued)

NO. 10

1. punishment for an offense
2. an act of entering
3. in complete contrast
4. to pronounce guilty
5. to complicate matters
6. free from blame
7. to throw with violence
8. from this time forward
9. a military foe
10. to come to an end
11. the art of carving
12. a large river barge
13. to have an objection to
14. to be part of an audience
15. anything very old
16. rough in countenance
17. pleasant hello
18. one mad dog
19. to rush some place
20. to be in a safe place

NO. 12

dedicated as sacred
betray a trust
not according to facts
bottom of the scale
training for an event
that which is immense
an act of teaching
prove to be right
an orderly arrangement
one of the seasons
table in a room
in a close-by vicinity
to answer yes
to be against
one noble in spirit
lack of attention
that which is interior
retain ownership of
to present for acceptance
to pause undecidedly

NO. 14

1. possessed with a severe handicap
2. soon to be needed
3. as often as necessary
4. an annual event or happening
5. appendix of a book
6. to engage with close attention
7. close to being correct
8. to submit to arbitration
9. military organization
10. something made without skill
11. to injure another person
12. acceptance of an established idea
13. quality of being bad
14. to make trials or experiments
15. sale of goods to highest offer
16. that which is real
17. to establish by authority
18. that written in his own hand
19. feeling of dislike toward something
20. a faith of some sort

NO. 16

to have and to keep
that which tortures
that which is done instantly
a confusing predicament
be on your guard
the part that is taken away
having gone astray
to arrange into chapters
idle chat in a conversation
the leader of the organization
to correct the issue or report
something grouped into classes
instrument such as a clock
any system of rules or principles
that which is beyond
that which lies next to
to receive with intention of returning
that which is the bottom
to apply a brake to
characterized by efficiency

NO. 18

1. to make plain by means of illustration
2. closely acquainted or familiar with
3. that which is in fashion
4. that which is without strength or hardness
5. a kind of a sealed tight structure
6. the foot of an animal or a person
7. to be everlasting or endless in length
8. that which happens or occurs
9. a person who gives evidence as to what happened
10. extremely good of its kind
11. that which exceeds what is usual
12. appropriate for the desired outcomes
13. something considered as exceptional
14. living under false pretenses
15. sequence with no interval or break
16. in the nature of an enchantment
17. dedicated to a noble purpose
18. the usual course of action
19. that which can deceive
20. that which happens early

NO. 20

1. an allowance to one retired from service
2. that which is confused
3. directly to the present condition
4. soft and yielding in nature such as clay or plastic
5. quality or state of being popular
6. the duties of a porter
7. within the powers of performance
8. a precaution taken in advance
9. an inquiry relative to a problem to be solved
10. safeguarded by divine care and direction
11. to puzzle out a mystery
12. a vessel holding one quart
13. to ramble or wander with no set goal
14. a place where anything is kept in store
15. a long loose outer garment
16. a part presented for inspection
17. to separate in different directions
18. coming first in correct order
19. to be slow or tardy in action
20. the guard going the rounds

SERIES IV (EVEN NUMBERS)

	NO. 2	NO. 4	NO. 6	NO. 8	NO. 10	NO. 12	NO. 14	NO. 16	NO. 18	NO. 20
1.	D	D	D	S	S	D	D	S	S	S
2.	D	S	S	D	S	D	D	D	D	D
3.	S	S	D	D	S	S	S	S	S	D
4.	S	S	S	D	S	S	S	D	D	D
5.	D	D	D	D	D	S	S	D	D	D
6.	D	D	D	S	D	S	D	D	D	D
7.	D	S	D	D	D	D	S	S	S	D
8.	D	D	D	D	S	S	D	D	D	S
9.	S	D	D	S	D	D	D	S	S	D
10.	D	D	S	D	D	D	D	D	D	S

SERIES V (EVEN NUMBERS)

	NO. 2	NO. 4	NO. 6	NO. 8	NO. 10	NO. 12	NO. 14	NO. 16	NO. 18	NO. 20
1.	F	T	T	F	F	T	T	F	T	F
2.	1	1	3	4	4	3	2	4	3	2

SERIES VI (EVEN NUMBERS)

	NO. 2	NO. 4	NO. 6	NO. 8	NO. 10	NO. 12	NO. 14	NO. 16	NO. 18	NO. 20
1.	F	T	watch	F	T	F	2	F	F	rat zoo
2.	six	T	T	T	chronic	T	T	F	individual	F
3.	F	F	1	T	2	T	F	chlorine	T	T
4.	ulcers	spears	F	F	F	stress	crossword puzzle	3	propa-ganda	2
5.	1	4	F	surgery	T	2	T	T	4	T
6.	T	F	T	T	1	sugar	Prof. Moriarty	F	T	F
7.	F	spiders	1	2	F	F	3	4	F	Calcutta
8.	3	T	F	empathy	F	F	F	T	F	F
9.	T	F	youth	F	drugs	3	F	gas	T	T
10.	T	3	T	4	T	T	T	T	1	4

SERIES VII (EVEN NUMBERS)

	NO. 2	NO. 4	NO. 6	NO. 8	NO. 10	NO. 12	NO. 14	NO. 16	NO. 18	NO. 20.
1.	F	T	T	T	F	T	T	Alcatraz	F	2
2.	gizzard	2	F	caught	T	F	T	T	know-ledge	4
3.	3	1940's	flight	T	gnats	4	4	F	T	research
4.	T	F	2	1	1	gods	F	3	F	T
5.	voles	F	manage	F	F	T	summer	F	4	F
6.	T	T	F	F	T	1	F	1	T	F
7.	4	3	T	T	3	costume	2	T	2	F
8.	F	F	T	dead bolt	amuse-ment	F	T	reserv-ation	society	T
9.	F	T	1	4	T	T	research	T	T	cobalt
10.	T	fall	F	F	F	F	F	F	F	T

In this series there are no exact or "right" answers. You were asked to read critically in an effort to understand underlying purpose, emotional appeal, bias and propaganda techniques. You were asked to try to identify time and place of appeal.

As a key to checking on your own critical thinking, this key section consists of the identification of the source of the material and a few comments about the setting from which it was taken.

See how close you were to the identification of basic factors. Think about those which you missed and go back and read the material again to check out your own sensitivity to key words and ideas.

VIII-2

(an excerpt from "The Pit and the Pendulum," Edgar Allan Poe, as it appears in *The Works of Edgar Allan Poe,* Volume II. New York: A. C. Armstrong and Son, 1902, pp. 465-466.)

Poe's story, "The Pit and the Pendulum," tells of the terror invoked upon men by the Spanish Inquisition. The character in this story has been arrested and thrown into the dungeon for heresy. The terror he feels upon awakening is a very real part of this story. Words which help portray the protagonist's feelings are: "horrible," "aghast," "desperation," "oppress," "stifle," "convulsively," "wildly," "tomb," "agony," "suspense."

VIII-4

(taken from the article "If Life is Lukewarm" as it appeared in the October 1970 issue of *Listen.*)

The author's purpose is to attempt a counter-attack against the vicarious experiences and monotonous lives that most people seem satisfied with. Therefore, she directs the appeal to the young reader.

In order to live a full, rewarding life, one must face the fact that he has to be himself and not turn away from difficult and challenging situations.

The author's use of such extreme terms as "lukewarm," "fear," "failure," and "apathy" reveal to the reader her strong feelings for becoming involved and for becoming a whole, stimulating person. Although her appeal is directed to a general reading audience, her message is especially significant to the young who will have to become active and involved if they are to be the leaders of tomorrow.

VIII-6

(taken from "Weathering the Winter," by A. R. Roalman, *Americana,* The American Motors Magazine, November/December 1967, p. 15, with permission of the editor.)

Appealing to the reader's need for knowledge of driving safety hints, the purpose of the article is to advise readers of some precautions for winter driving and car maintenance. The author of the article represents an automotive company which has an interest in making driving as pleasurable and safe as possible. He attempts to motivate people through words such as: "isolated," "severely," "trouble," "warning," and "stranded."

VIII-8

(an excerpt from an undated form letter from United States Senator, Jesse Helms, North Carolina)

Although this letter has a footnote in small print at the bottom: "not prepared or mailed at government expense," the stationery is "United States Senate" letterhead and emphasizes Senator Helms government position. The letter from him is one of a long series of letters mailed over a few years period to a large public mailing list on behalf of the organization "Americans Against Union Control of Government."

In his final paragraph, Senator Helms asks the reader to (1) "complete the poll" and return it, and (2) "send a contribution" to the organization to "help them prevent a takeover of America by labor union bosses."

VIII-10
(taken from a full page commercial advertisement for TRI-STATE)

This full page commercial ad appeared in several periodicals in 1977 and 1978, at a time when environmentalists were very concerned about new dams and power plants, and when costs of power were rising sharply.

The ad was paid for by the Tri-State Generation and Transmission Association, Inc. The general intent seems to appeal for a greater understanding of the needs and problems of the Electric Service Companies.

VIII-12
(taken from "Rockhounding," by Pete Czura in *Americana*, The American Motors Magazine, November/December, 1967, p. 17, with permission of the editor.)

The author, who represents a motoring magazine, appeals to the reader's sense of adventure and desire to make traveling more enjoyable and interesting by collecting rocks.

The author's bias in promoting travel might be prompted by the fact that increased travel could mean increased sales of the automobile which he represents. In order to entice the reader, he makes use of the words, "fun," "fringe benefit," "adventures," "variety," and "bonuses."

VIII-14
(Senator Murphy; [R]-California; taken from the *Congressional Record* Vol. 113, No. 198, December 5, 1967, p. S17914.)

Senator Murphy, a member of the Education subcommittee, and representing a state which he believes "has an education system unparalleled in the nation," speaks of the problem of "school drop-outs." The Senator speaks in favor of an amendment authorizing an additional $30 million for "projects designed for drop-out prevention." The adoption of such an amendment, the Senator believes, would be a step toward solving the special problems of the disadvantaged.

VIII-16
(taken from the classic essay, *Civil Disobedience*, by Henry David Thoreau, published in 1849.)

This appeal is directed to men who consider themselves free and moral, to behave as they think they should rather than as they are constrained to do.

The author, while basically a peace-loving man, is very concerned with fairness and equality in opinion. Thoreau was opposed to paying taxes to support a way which he considered immoral. However, herein lies the dichotomy. What is the individual's responsibility? Is it to the government and society as a whole? Or is an individual's responsibility first to himself and to society second?

VIII-18
(Representative Saylor, [R]-Pennsylvania; taken from the *Congressional Record*, July 19, 1968, p. H7114.)

Representative Saylor, having been given permission for extraneous remarks, brings to the attention of the House, the Communist Rules for Revolution, as he took them from the Scottish Rite Masons' publication entitled "Youth: Have We Failed Them?" These Rules were among the captured papers taken in Dusseldorf, Germany in May, 1919. The Florida State Attorney recently obtained a new copy of them from a known Communist Party member, who admitted that these Rules were a part of their unit plans.

VIII-20
(an excerpt from the *Declaration of Independence*, July 4, 1776.)

This statement written in 1776 to all people of the country, was drafted by a committee of representatives to justify extensive actions in breaking away from an oppressive government, and to lay the foundation of the government of the United States of America. Broadly written to cover extreme situations, it includes a warning that, if a change is desired, the changes themselves must be meaningful and not to the satisfaction of a few. If the people believe that a change in government would bring about a better life for the society as a whole, then it is the obligation of the people to pursue a logical course of action to initiate such change. This document extends to the dissenters of our present day, the right to initiate change. However, it does not extend the right to militant, anarchical overthrow of the present form of government.

SUGGESTED SEQUENCE FOR A TWENTY-HOUR READING PROGRAM

(Based on approximate schedule used in classes in the Uniwyo Reading Research Center)

All basic series and numbers refer to basic exercises in this book. Pretests, posttests, and the supplementary exercise book, *Maintaining Reading Efficiency,* may be ordered from Developmental Reading Distributors, 1944 Sheridan, Laramie, Wyoming 82070, (307) 745-9027.

(Schedule is designed for ten two-hour periods. For a 50-60 minute class, plan only about half the material scheduled. The "5-minute break" divides the material in two sections requiring approximately the same amount of time.)

FIRST PERIOD

Use a standardized, 10-minute reading test such as the *Maintaining Reading Efficiency Tests.*

(Score and collect.)

Discuss Materials and Personal Goals.

SERIES #	EXERCISE #
I	2, 4, 6

Explain Charts.

5-MINUTE BREAK

II	2
V	2
VI	2
VII	2

SECOND PERIOD

I	8, 10, 12, 14
II	4, 6, 8
III	2

Discuss Motivation.

5-MINUTE BREAK

V	4
VI	4
VII	4

THIRD PERIOD

I	16, 18, 20
II	10, 12, 14
III	4, 6

Discuss Materials.

5-MINUTE BREAK

V	6
VI	6
VII	6

Supplementary Reading Exercises from *M.R.E.*: 2

FOURTH PERIOD

II	16, 18, 20
III	8, 10, 12, 14
IV	2, 4

Discuss Progress.

5-MINUTE BREAK

V	8
VI	8
VII	8

Supplementary Reading Exercises from *M.R.E.*: 4, 6

FIFTH PERIOD

III	16, 18, 20
IV	6, 8
V	10

Discuss Personal Goals.

5-MINUTE BREAK

VI	10
VII	10
VIII	2, 4

Supplementary Reading Exercises from *M.R.E.*: 8, 10

SIXTH PERIOD

IV	10, 12, 14, 16
V	12

Discuss Progress.

5-MINUTE BREAK

VI	12
VII	12
VIII	6, 8

Supplementary Reading Exercises from *M.R.E.*: 12, 14

SEVENTH PERIOD

IV	18, 20
V	14
VI	14

Discuss Outside Application.

5-MINUTE BREAK

VII	14
VIII	10-12

Supplementary Reading Exercises from *M.R.E.*: 16, 18

EIGHTH PERIOD

V	16
VI	16
VII	16
VIII	14, 16

Discuss Progress.

5-MINUTE BREAK

Supplementary Reading Exercises from *M.R.E.*: 20, 22

NINTH PERIOD

V	18
VI	18
VII	18
VIII	18, 20

Discuss Progress.

5-MINUTE BREAK

Supplementary Reading Exercises from *M.R.E.*: 24, 26

TENTH PERIOD

V	20
VI	20
VII	20

Discuss Future Application.

5-MINUTE BREAK

Use a final, standardized, 10-minute reading test such as one of the *Maintaining Reading Efficiency Tests.*

SCORE IN CLASS

Discuss Comparisons with Beginning Test.

CROSS REFERENCE

	RATE TABLES	*KEY ODD*	*KEY EVEN*	*PROGRESS CHART*
SERIES I	**307**	**NONE NEEDED**		**297**
SERIES II	**307**	**317**	**325**	**297**
SERIES III	**309**	**318**	**326**	**297**
SERIES IV	**311**	**321**	**329**	**297**
SERIES V	**313**	**321**	**329**	**299**
SERIES VI	**315**	**322**	**330**	**299**
SERIES VII	**315**	**322**	**330**	**299**
SERIES VIII	**NONE NEEDED**	**323**	**331**	**NONE NEEDED**